Tradition

Edward Shils

Tradition

The University of Chicago Press

The University of Chicago Press, Chicago 60637

©1981 by Edward Shils
All rights reserved. Published 1981
Paperback edition 1983
Printed in the United States of America
90 89 88   4 5 6

Library of Congress Cataloging in Publication Data

Shils, Edward Albert, 1911–
   Tradition.

   Includes index.
   1. Tradition (Philosophy) 2. Progress.
3. History—Philosophy. 4. Civilization—
Philosophy. 5. Social change. I. Title.
B105.T7S5   306′.4   80-21643
ISNB 0-226-75325-5 (cloth)   AACR1
        0-226-75326-3 (paper)

80 - 21643

Contents

Preface

This book about tradition is evidence of the need for tradition. If there had been other comprehensive books about tradition and traditions, this book would have been a better one. It would have given me a point of departure easier to start from, it would have given me a standard, and it would have made me more aware of omissions and misapprehensions. But there is no such book. There are many books about particular traditions. There are books about tradition in Islamic theology and law; there are books about tradition in Judaism; books about tradition in Roman Catholic and Protestant Christianity. There are books about particular traditions in literature and art and law. There is however no book about tradition which tries to see the common ground and elements of tradition and which analyzes what difference tradition makes in human life.

This is what this book undertakes to do.

I began to write it nearly twenty-five years ago. It was the subject of many of my seminars at the University of Chicago, beginning in 1956. When I was invited by the University of Kent at Canterbury to deliver the T. S. Eliot Memorial Lectures at that university in the Michaelmas term of 1974, I welcomed the opportunity because I thought it would enable me to compose my mind about this bewildering subject and also to acknowledge my debt to T. S. Eliot, whose writings had done so much to arouse and nourish my mind on tradition.

The four lectures which I delivered have been revised many times since 1974. I am now submitting them for public inspection and criticism but not because I have satisfied myself that I have said all that is essential on the subject. I have come to believe that tradition, in addition to being a very important subject, is also an inexhaustible one.

There is a great need in the world for a better understanding of the nature of tradition and for a better appreciation of its value. I hope that, as a result of the existence of this book, thoughtful scholars will take up the matter in all good earnest and will clarify, correct, and deepen the notions which are contained in this book.

I wish to thank the directors of Faber and Faber and Professor

Molly Mahood and her colleagues at Canterbury for having decided to invite me to give the T. S. Eliot lectures for 1974 and for the sympathetic understanding which they showed when the lectures were delivered. I have also to thank the Committee on Social Thought of the University of Chicago and the Master and Fellows of Peterhouse for their patience and helpfulness and for the provision of conditions of work and friendship.

May the spirits of Max Weber and T. S. Eliot look with charity on this effort to work out some of the implications of their unfathomably deep thought on tradition.

Edward Shils

Introduction

Tradition in Disrepute

Very few persons argue for the revival of the beliefs and institutions of the remoter past which have been obliterated in the more recent past. Even if they desire their revival, they do not think that there is any reasonable chance that what they desire will be realized. The belief in the irretrievability of institutions and beliefs which have receded markedly is so widespread that it takes unusual intellectual courage, even a certain amount of foolhardiness, to be "reactionary" in intellectual circles. The contemplation of history and transience and the still prevailing certainty that progress is mandatory both discourage the belief that any pattern of belief or activity, once pushed into the background, should or can be brought again into the center of attention and attachment.

It even appears untoward to say that some things should be left as they are or have been in the recent past. Once a situation is brought to attention, the presumption is that it ought to be changed. Something better should be substituted for it. Complacency is the least of the charges brought against one who asserts that the received should be left as it has been or that it should not be deliberately reformed.

The present state of our relationship to the past is very heterogeneous. The acknowledged normative power of a past practice, arrangement, or belief has become very faint, indeed, it is almost extinguished as an intellectual argument. Correspondingly, the traditionality of a belief, practice, or arrangement offers little resistance to arguments which proceed on the presumption of the efficiency, rationality, expediency, "up-to-dateness," or progressiveness of their proffered alternatives. On the other side, the prestige of and fascination by aged objects and the eagerness to contemplate them have grown greatly in this period when the affirmation of earlier beliefs and the acceptance of the normative force of patterns recognized as coming from the past have diminished. The rhetorical adduction of standards embodied in past actions and persons has likewise diminished. All this in a time when the interest in the contemplation of past events, the interest in "history" is great, perhaps much greater than it has

1

been in epochs and societies in which things from the past endured more securely than they have in recent centuries. Perhaps most important is the fact that despite pervasive changefulness, a very great deal of the life of recent societies has been lived in long-enduring institutions in accordance with rules inherited from a long past; the beliefs in the light of which the world is judged are also parts of an inheritance which has been passed down through many generations.

These necessary and desired compromises with the past notwithstanding, the time through which we have just lived has been one in which what was inherited from the past was thought of as an irksome burden to be escaped from as soon as possible. This time is by no means over. Although the credit of the present and future is perhaps smaller than it was, there is no immediate likelihood of a restoration of the moral prestige of the past and of a firmer and more welcomed continuance of once-established practices, beliefs, or institutions. There are very few voices accredited among the educated which speak for "going back"; practically none for "standing still." Nonetheless, a slight turn in moral sentiment and in the intellectual credit of the past is perceptible. There is a little less unease in the presence of the idea of "tradition," but its long exile from the substance of intellectual discourse has left its meaning hidden in obscurity.

The Idea of Progress

In nearly every Western country, an increasing proportion of educated and enlightened persons has for a long time thought that a great many of the beliefs, practices, and institutions prevailing in their societies needed to be changed, replaced, or discarded in favor of new ones, which would invariably be better ones. The existent, and especially the inherited, suffered under a presumption of untenability; they had to be changed. Even with the slight recent turn in the fortunes of the inheritance and of the past from which it comes, the accent of intellectual and political discourse still remains on a movement forward from the recent and the remote past. The emphasis is on improvement.

It is not often that gratitude is expressed to those who have maintained institutions in the state in which they received them. Their founders are praised; innovators are praised, but not those who have maintained what the innovators created. (Abraham Lincoln is one of the very few, and even his reputation rests on more than his maintenance of the Union.) Western societies, and increasingly societies outside the West are saturated by the belief that things as they exist are very imperfect and very much in need of improvement. This is nothing new in human history. The prophets and sages who have established themselves in the pantheon of human greatness have for the most part been in agreement about the imperfection of human existence; some of them believed in the perfectibility of human life in a realm beyond the earthly kingdom. The novelty of the modern belief is its assertion that it lies within human powers to bring human existence closer to perfection on earth. In the present century, there have been many prominent intellectual figures who have thought that what we have inherited is as bad as can be but that a society without blemishes is at hand for the making. There has recently been some doubt cast on this belief but this doubt is not very popular in the educated classes. The doubt is flung back at the doubters; the proponents of progress accuse the skeptics of unwillingness to recognize that more strenuous exertions and more ample means would permit the achievement of the highest ends. But whatever the doubt about the attainability of the ideal, inherited institutions are deemed in need of thoroughgoing revision or discard, in favor of something much better.

This radical progressivism has never been complete. The artistic, literary, and philosophical works created in the past are much admired, although they are not regarded as models for future creations. Particular traditions of art and literature are often greatly appreciated by connoisseurs and by a wider public but artists and writers do not regard themselves as bound to work under the discipline of such traditions. The operation of traditions which influence the production of works of intellect, imagination, and expression is acknowledged and the results are appreciated, but traditions as normative models of action and belief are regarded as useless and burdensome. Those who are attached to institutions, practices, and beliefs which are designated as traditional are called "reactionaries" or rather "conservatives"; they are placed on the "right" on a line which runs from "left" to "right," and to be "on the right" is to be in the wrong.

It is not that the word "tradition" is proscribed. There are books called *The Socialist Tradition, The Tradition of Modernity, The Tradition of the New, The Symbolist Tradition,* and many others like these. The existence of traditions is acknowledged; they are traditions to which others have submitted. The validity of tradition is admitted occasionally in things one approves of.[1] It is rare to encounter persons who pride themselves on the espousal of a tradition, call it that, and regard it as a good thing. There are few persons among those who

1. See R. H. McNeal, "A Letter from Trotsky to Krupskaya, 17 May 1927," *International Review of Social History* 48, no. 1 (1973): 111–19. Trotsky, remonstrating with Krupskaya about her belittling of his criticism of Stalin as a "fuss," said in support of his way of proceeding, "And we never felt as deeply and unmistakably our ties with the entire tradition of Bolshevism as we do now in these difficult days" (p. 119) (in Russian, he says "традиции," literally "tradition"). Earlier in his letter he invoked 'the entire history of Bolshevism, starting with 1904'") (p. 118).

write on subjects which touch on tradition who argue on its behalf. Those who argue for tradition nowadays turn out moreover to be very progressivistic in the traditions they support; it is the "tradition of change" which they praise[2] and they do not think about what is involved in this paradox. More substantive traditions, traditions which maintain the received, receive less support. The "tradition of traditionality" has very few supporters.

There are, of course, practices which are supported on the grounds that "it is a tradition here that..." but the contents of these traditions are always matters of marginal importance; conformity with such traditional rules is desirable but not imperative. It is a much more serious breach to infringe on the imperative of change. Change must not be resisted; it must be accepted. Even better is to seek change; best of all is to initiate it.

These are among the achievements of the idea of progress. Change has become coterminous with progress; innovation has become coterminous with improvement. The notion of doing well what has been done before is not rejected; it is not thought of. In fact, a great deal of what has been is accepted but that falls outside the interest of intellectual discussion. It belongs to the routine of life and is too petty to be acknowledged.

Enlightenment

The progress of mankind has been the progress of empirical science and of rationality of judgment. These have been thought of as good in themselves and as the bringers of limitless benefits. Whenever science and reason have been praised as the proper sources for the rules which should regulate the lives of individuals and societies, tradition has come under criticism. Scientific knowledge has been declared to be antithetical to traditional knowledge; scientific procedure, resting ultimately on the experience of the senses and its rational criticism, has been contrasted with knowledge accepted on the authority of elders.[3] Rationality and scientific procedure, as their practice and prestige have waxed in modern times, have discredited particular traditional beliefs and tradition in general. Quite apart from its fundamental disqualification for failure to apply the test of conformity with rules of rationality and empirical observation to every belief which is

2. See, for one example among many others, Martin Marty, "Tradition, verb (rare)," *The University of Chicago Record,* 9, no. 4 (21 September 1975): 136–38.

3. See Ernst Cassirer, *Die Philosophie der Aufklärung* (Tübingen: J. C. B. Mohr [Paul Siebeck], 1932), chap. 1; Paul Hazard, *La Pensée européenne au XVIII siècle: de Montesquieu à Lessing* (Paris: Boivin, 1946), 1:34–57, and *La Crise de la conscience européenne (1680–1715)* (Paris: Boivin, 1935), 1:38–69 and 157–264.

offered or accepted, tradition has had to carry other burdens. The criticism of tradition as a ground for belief has coincided with an aversion to ignorance.

Ignorance of sacred things had always been regarded as an inferior condition. Ignorance of empirical events has acquired a similar status in modern times. Ignorance and traditionality became connected; both seemed to be ingredients of the abhorred *ancien régime* of Europe.

Rationality and scientific knowledge on the one side and traditionality and ignorance on the other were set against each other as antitheses. The party of progress, which believed that mankind must move forward towards emancipation from arbitrary and oppressive authority and towards the conduct of human affairs by scientifically illuminated reason, abominated the condition of superstition and ignorance in which most human beings lived. It associated that condition with ecclesiastically imposed dogma. It was in the nature of dogmas that they were to be accepted without rational reflection and empirical observation. The substance of most dogmas was often of long duration; it was part of tradition. Dogma and the coercion of belief were coupled with each other. Tradition acquired the bad name which had become attached to dogma.

A similar association was established between superstition and traditionality, although there is no necessary connection between them. Superstition is a vague term; it usually means belief in the existence and efficacy of empirically undemonstrable or nonexistent entities; it is a form of error. Superstitions have indeed often been transmitted traditionally although in principle new superstitions can and in fact do arise. Superstitions are certainly common among progressivists, secularists, and rationalists but traditionality has been made to bear the obloquy which superstition calls forth among progressivists; their own superstitions are spared. The same may be said of intolerance and dogmatism which were equally evils which enlightenment would eradicate. Traditionality no more requires intolerance and dogmatism than do scientism, rationalism, and secularism. In the twentieth century the most destructive acts of intolerance have been committed by revolutionary regimes, the progressivist revolutionaries being scarcely less intolerant than the reactionary ones. Dogmas are no less common among progressivists than they are among those who would give the benefit of the doubt to tradition.

The *ancien régime* in Europe which was at stake in the French Revolution of 1789 and in the wars which followed was an amalgam of many features. Traditionality was one of these. Many practices were traditionally legitimated; many practices and institutions were much like those which had been performed or had been in effect for some centuries. They had been performed with little reflection by those who benefited by them or who saw no alternative to them. This in itself would have been repugnant to minds which regarded it as necessary for every institution to be justified under the scrutiny of reason; every institution had to be justified by its consequences or by its consistency with an ostensibly rationally affirmed principle. This was clearly not the case with the institutions of the *ancien régime*. But in addition to this, there were many substantive features of the societies of the *ancien régime* which were repugnant to rationalists. The power and eminence of the Roman Catholic church, the intolerance towards Protestants and unbelievers, the steep and disjunctive hierarchy of deference, the prominence of lineage as a criterion of the allocation of rewards and opportunities were among the defects of the European societies which preceded the French Revolution. The traditionality which was pervasive in the *ancien régime,* but not to the exclusion of considerations of interest and power, helped to sustain these other features of the society which were abhorrent to rationalists, secularists, progressives, and egalitarians. Traditionality became associated with a particular kind of society and culture. Traditionality was regarded as the cause or the consequence of ignorance, superstition, clerical dominance, religious intolerance, social hierarchy, inequality in the distribution of wealth, preemption of the best positions in society on grounds of birth, and other states of mind and social institutions which were the objects of rationalistic and progressivistic censure. Traditionality became the ubiquitous enemy to every critic of the *ancien régime;* it was thought that when traditionality yielded place to reason and to scientific knowledge, all the vices which it sustained would fall away. The diffusion of rationality and scientific knowledge would destroy the power of the Roman Catholic church, it would restrain the power of the monarchy, it would abolish those privileges which were acquired through kinship and descent. The first entry on the agenda of the Enlightenment was therefore to do away with traditionality as such;[4] with its demise, all the particular substantive traditions would likewise go.

The party of progress which contended for *les lumières* against *les ombres* has had an illustrious history and it has accomplished much good for the human race. It has recently found itself in a blind alley; its program has been realized to a considerable extent. Its achievements have been accepted; they have fallen into the state of being taken for granted. Its failures stand out more and more clearly while its accomplishments are silently accepted and noisily disparaged. Nonetheless, despite the intermittent and inchoate discomfiture in the ranks of the party of progressive outlook, the rationalistic and scien-

4. Franco Venturi, "The European Enlightenment," *Italy and the Enlightenment: Studies in a Cosmopolitan Century* (London: Longmans, 1972), pp. 1–32.

tistic philistinism which it fostered will not hear the word "tradition" without bridling. To this outlook, tradition embodies all that is obstructive of the growth and application of science and reason to the affairs of human beings. The recent progressivistic critics of science have brought forward another item on the progressivistic agenda; when they turn away from science, they praise emancipation—not just emancipation from dogmatic and arbitrary authority but emancipation from all restraints. They too will hear nothing of tradition which is as repugnant to them as it is to their erstwhile confrères.

The Blindness of the Social Sciences to Tradition

The contemporary social sciences have a long tradition which reaches back into Graeco-Roman antiquity, but they owe most to the tradition of the Enlightenment. From the Enlightenment, they have received their skeptical attitude towards tradition and a conception of society which leaves little place for it.

If we read an analysis by a contemporary social scientist of what happened in a given situation, we see that the pecuniary "interests" of the participants are mentioned, their irrational fears are mentioned, their desire for power is also mentioned; internal solidarity of groups is accounted for by irrational identifications or by interests; the strategems of the leaders of the constituent groups are mentioned; tradition is seldom mentioned as having anything to do with important things. Realistic social scientists do not mention tradition.

Tradition is a dimension of social structure which is lost or hidden by the atemporal conceptions which now prevail in the social sciences. The recent embrace of history by sociology and the attention to the "longue durée" by historians of the équipe des Annales accord little place to tradition. Persistent identity of interests and persistent ecological conditions account for stability. Marxism speaks of "reproduction" but it has no place for tradition. Although there are undoubtedly other reasons, the "here and now" postulate of much of modern science, and, not least, of the more systematic and theoretical social sciences, has led to an oversight. The temporal dimension is obscured by the concept of equilibrium, stressing as it does the immediately present function of each of the variables in the system. Whatever history each of these variables possesses has been deposited in its present state; the mechanism of recurrent self-reproduction is not sought. Having no significant history, there is no need to refer to it in accounting for one's own or another's conduct. The ends and rules of action, the grounds and motives of the acceptance of those ends and rules and the recurrence to the "givenness" of those beliefs, practices, and institutions which we call "traditional" all tend to be viewed as unproblematic. The more theoretically sophisticated the branch of social science, the less attentive it is to the traditional element in society.

From the history of modern sociology, a few interesting instances of this suppression of pastness may be noted. In Pareto's "residue" of the "persistence of aggregates," there is a temporal reference which could open into a treatment of tradition but it is passed over by a descriptive physical metaphor. In the "four wishes" of W. I. Thomas and Florian Znaniecki, the "wish for security" is contrasted to the "wish for new experience," but it has been interpreted negatively to mean the desire to live in the same setting in the future as one is living in at the present. The persistence of past practices and arrangements is not taken up as something to be explained. Max Weber's fourfold classification of types of "meaningful" action does provide an uncertain place for the attachment to a norm of conduct which refers to the past; Weber himself seems to have dissolved the category of "traditional action" into reflexive habitual acts and action oriented towards ideals with the consequent erasure of the temporal dimension. The opportunity offered for a clarification of traditionality was missed by Professor Parsons and myself in our efforts at a more systematic reformulation of Weber's ideas.[5]

Social scientists avoid the confrontation with tradition and with their omission of it from explanatory schemes by having recourse to "historical factors." In this way, they treat tradition as a residual category, as an intellectual disturbance which is to be brushed away.

The prominence of tradition and its immense influence are too great to be disregarded entirely. Social scientists know very well that the biological organism does not generate the immense stock of knowledge and skill borne by an ordinary human being and they know too that the acquisition of that stock cannot be accounted for by the adduction of "interests" or "the desire for power" with which they explain the conduct of adults. Social psychologists and sociologists do study "the acquisition of language skills" and socialization, as they used to study "assimilation" and as anthropologists have studied "culture." They are committed by their traditions to study "socialization," "acculturation," and similar phenomena. While most of them are unsympathetic with the body of culture which is offered in their own societies, contemporary social scientists are also no less repelled by the possibility that human actions are biologically and genetically determined. For a long time sociologists justified their own existence as a discipline by the contention that "social forces" determine the actions of human beings, and they included the existing

5. See "Values, Motives, and Systems of Action," in Talcott Parsons and Edward Shils, eds., *Towards a General Theory of Action* (Cambridge, Mass., Harvard University Press, 1951), pp. 53–109.

stock of traditions as part of these "social forces." The stock of traditions was gradually dropped from sight as sociology and social psychology became more scientific and more systematically theoretical. But the ineluctable fact of the naked, ignorant infant and the no less ineluctable fact of the adult with skills, knowledge, and beliefs which are not learned entirely from experience, which are not contrived by reason alone, and which are not emergent properties of the growing biological organism, could not be disregarded. The acquisition of skills, knowledge, and beliefs had therefore to be acknowledged and studied. Thus the study of a part of tradition has been to some extent incorporated into contemporary social science; it is that part which appears in the process of acquisition, thinned down and reduced in content and narrowly confined to the relations of one generation to another. Those bits of tradition which pass from one generation to another in the process of "socialization" or of "assimilation" are not seen as part of a larger pattern of interconnected parts. (This does not apply to the studies of "language acquisition.")

The causes and reasons of the neglect of tradition by social scientists are diverse. Some derive from the general tastes of the culture in which the social sciences developed. Progressivistic in their outlook, social scientists disliked tradition, which they associated with backwardness and reactionary beliefs. They also subscribed, indeed oversubscribed to the naive view that modern society was on the road to traditionlessness, to the domination of action by "interests" and "power."

The greatest of all sociologists, Max Weber, who was certainly no unqualified enthusiast for progress, shared the common view that there were at bottom two types of societies: one which was in the toils of traditions and another in which the criterion of the choice of actions was rational calculation for the optimal satisfaction of "interests." Weber said that, "In earlier periods, the degree of economic rationalism varied. In the beginning there was traditionalism, a clinging to what has come out of long past times, which takes over inherited customs and imposes them on other epochs, despite the fact that they no longer have their original meaning. This condition was transcended only gradually."[6]

6. Max Weber, *Wirtschaftsgeschichte: Abriss der universalen Sozial- und Wirtschaftsgeschichte* (Munich and Leipzig: Duncker and Humblot, 1923), pp. 29–39. Ferdinand Tönnies, *Gemeinschaft und Gesellschaft: Grundbegriffe der reinen Soziologie* (1st ed. 1887; 8th rev. ed. Leipzig: Hans Buske, 1935), pp. 8–39, 95–97, 219–21, 241–42. See also Tönnies, *Die Sitte* (Frankfurt a. M.: Rütten and Loening, 1909).

A similar view was contained in much of sociological research and theory. Emile Durkheim, Robert Park, and William I. Thomas saw the situation very much in the same way. This fundamental theme of modern sociological analysis is well discussed in S. N. Eisenstadt, *Tradition, Change, and Modernity* (New York: John Wiley, 1973), pp. 1–11.

The corollary of this view is that modern society moves towards a state of traditionlessness in which interest pursued with the aid of reason is the predominant ground of action and tradition only a survival unfitting to the style of such a modern society. Max Weber certainly did not allow much of a place for tradition in his account of modern society. Although he expressed this view with a characteristically tragic eloquence, his views were not very different from those of his contemporaries.[7] It was implicit in his interpretation that traditions, carried by irrational fears and otherwise deviating from right conduct, would be obliterated by the invincible advance of rationalization.

The social scientists, especially in the period after the Second World War, were determined to make their subject scientific and to free it from sentimentality and from nebulous concepts which could not be "operationalized"; they were also the victims of an impoverished educational regimen. Since it was clear to them that culture was not of "biological" origin, they concluded that it must be "psychological" and the consequent studies of "national character" bore the mark of the psychoanalytical theory of personality. The structuralist approach to the study of culture is constrained by a similar inclination to reduce elaborate symbolic constructions to elementary patterns of the mind. Old-fashioned ethnologists and historians are more attentive to the weight of tradition, partly because they deal with societies remote from the present-day Western societies in which the discussion of tradition has been treated as if it were under a taboo. On the whole, however, historians and anthropologists have not been reflective about tradition. The more they come into the present, the less they are inclined to observe the influence of tradition and the more they fall into the idiom of contemporary social science. Traditionality as a property of beliefs, actions, and institutions is dissolved into other things.[8]

The Appreciation of Individuality and Present Experience

There is another, perhaps deeper, movement of the mind which, in the past century, has been inimical to the acceptance of what is offered by tradition. This is the metaphysical dread of being encumbered by

7. Max Weber, *Gesammelte Aufsätze zur Religions-soziologie* (Tübingen: J. C. B. Mohr [Paul Siebeck]: 1934), pp. 203–4.

8. Professor Colson in a recent work asserts that what has been called traditional law in East African societies was in fact the creation of colonial administrators who wished to circumscribe an area of social life in which indigenous judicial authorities could be given responsibility. See Elizabeth Colson, *Tradition and Contract: The Problem of Order* (Chicago: Aldine Publishing Co., 1974), pp. 77–87.

something alien to oneself. There is a belief, corresponding to a feeling, that within each human being there is an individuality, lying in potentiality, which seeks an occasion for realization but is held in the toils of the rules, beliefs, and roles which society imposes. In a more popular, or vulgar, recent form, the concern "to establish one's identity," "to discover oneself," or "to find out who one really is" has come to be regarded as a first obligation of the individual. Some writers on undergraduate education in the United States say that a college is a place where young persons can "find out who they really are." They suggest that the real state of the self is very different from the acquired baggage which institutions like families, schools, and universities impose. To be "true to oneself" means, they imply, discovering what is contained in the uncontaminated self, the self which has been freed from the encumbrance of accumulated knowledge, norms, and ideals handed down by previous generations.

The most recent refinements of the quest for the true self, to be attained not through contemplation but by allowing impulse to come to the surface and to be expressed in experience, may be traced back to the romanticism of the eighteenth and nineteenth centuries. The "affirmation of life" at the end of the latter century went together with the sense of the unsupportability of "artificial convention" and of the crippling restraints of Victorian morality. "The century of the child," announced by Ellen Key, the breaking of the hold of the super-ego offered by Freudian psychoanalysis, the release of the novelist's imagination from the discipline of the nineteenth-century novel, led by James Joyce, and the gratification of sexual impulses proposed by D. H. Lawrence were all phases of a great campaign of the *Zeitgeist* against the conventions and morals sustained by tradition. The muteness of tradition in the face of rational criticism weakened its position. The breaking of tradition opened the way for individuality to flourish.

There has been another, more recent change in the image of the world which has helped to reduce the weight of tradition. This is the increase in interest about the present. Of course, all human beings have always been concerned about the present state of affairs, their own affairs and conditions included. It could not have been otherwise. Yet the increase of interest in contemporaneity, proximate and remote in space, seems to be connected with a hedonistic concentration on the life-span of the individual and on the events which take place concurrently with it. This might be a consequence of the reduced confidence in personal survival; it might be a function of increased sensibility to sensual pleasures, increased intellectual alertness, and, in more recent decades, the much more profuse perception of contemporary events made possible through literacy and affluence and newspapers, radio, photography, and television.

The Meaning of Tradition

The Transmitted Thing

Tradition means many things. In its barest, most elementary sense, it means simply a *traditum;* it is anything which is transmitted or handed down from the past to the present. It makes no statement about what is handed down or in what particular combination or whether it is a physical object or a cultural construction; it says nothing about how long it has been handed down or in what manner, whether orally or in written form. The degree of rational deliberation which has entered into its creation, presentation, and reception likewise has nothing to do with whether it is a tradition. The conception of tradition as here understood is silent about whether there is acceptable evidence for the truth of the tradition or whether the tradition is accepted without its validity having been established; the anonymity of its authors or creators or its attribution to named and identified persons likewise makes no difference as to whether it is a tradition. The decisive criterion is that, having been created through human actions, through thought and imagination, it is handed down from one generation to the next.

Being handed down does not logically entail any normative, mandatory proposition. The presence of something from the past does not entail any explicit expectation that it should be accepted, appreciated, reenacted, or otherwise assimilated.

Tradition—that which is handed down—includes material objects, beliefs about all sorts of things, images of persons and events, practices and institutions. It includes buildings, monuments, landscapes, sculptures, paintings, books, tools, machines. It includes all that a society of a given time possesses and which already existed when its present possessors came upon it and which is not solely the product of physical processes in the external world or exclusively the result of ecological and physiological necessity. The *Iliad,* in a recently reprinted English translation, is a *traditum;* so is the Parthenon.

In the case of practices and institutions made up of human actions, it is not the particular concrete actions which are transmitted; that is impossible. An action ceases to exist once it is performed. Human actions are the most evanescent of things. They last no longer than the time required for their actual performance; once performed, they cease to exist. The transmissible parts of them are the patterns or images of actions which they imply or present and the beliefs requiring, recommending, regulating, permitting, or prohibiting the reenactment of those patterns. What particular actions and complexes and sequences of actions leave behind are the conditions for subsequent actions, images in memory and documents of what they were when they happened and, under certain conditions, normative precedents or prescriptions for future actions. The received image of a past epoch or of a historical figure is as much a tradition as an ancient custom, still practiced, or a long-used form of phrase. Those who accept a tradition need not call it a tradition; its acceptability might be self-evident to them. When a tradition is accepted, it is as vivid and as vital to those who accept it as any other part of their action or belief. It is the past in the present but it is as much part of the present as any very recent innovation.

When we speak of tradition, we speak of that which has exemplars or custodians. It is the *traditum,* that which has been and is being handed down or transmitted. It is something which was created, was performed or believed in the past, or which is believed to have existed or to have been performed or believed in the past. To be a *traditum* does not mean that the persons to whom it is made present and who accept it, do so on the grounds of its existence in the past. *Tradita* can become objects of fervent attachment to the quality of pastness which is seen in them; they may be accepted in a manner which takes them for granted as the only reasonable thing to do or believe.

The Identity of Transmitted Things

A particular painting remains the same over the course of its transmission, subject to the processes of deterioration and maintenance of physical substances and the modifications wrought by vandals and illicit improvers; a particular literary or religious text likewise having been definitively established—a very problematic conception—remains the same through numerous reprintings. The interpretation of the text does not remain the same equally among all the recipients at a given time or among the recipients who succeed each other in time. A rule of conduct, explicitly articulated or implied in a pattern of conduct, or a belief about the soul, or a philosophical idea about the common good does not remain identical through its career of transmissions over generations. An artistic style does not remain the same over its transmissions even though each of the particular paintings or statues in which it has been embodied does remain the same.

Constellations of symbols, clusters of images, are received and modified. They change in the process of transmission as interpretations are made of the tradition presented; they change also while they are in the possession of their recipients. This chain of transmitted variants of a tradition is also called a tradition, as in the "Platonic tradition" or the "Kantian tradition." As a temporal chain, a tradition is a sequence of variations on received and transmitted themes. The connectedness of the variations may consist in common themes, in the contiguity of presentation and departure, and in descent from a common origin.

Even in the course of a short chain of transmission over three generations, a tradition is very likely to undergo some changes. Its essential elements persist in combination with other elements which change, but what makes it a tradition is that what are thought to be the essential elements are recognizable by an external observer as being approximately identical at successive steps or acts of transmission and possession. The recipients of a tradition are seldom adequate judges of the length of their chain of tradition. Marxian socialists regarded themselves as separated from "utopian" socialists by a deep gulf; an external observer sees many points of identity, as well as filiation. The disregarded relationship between the tradition of scientific chemistry, as seen by its later adherents, and the tradition of alchemy is another such failure of adherents to perceive their point of origin.

Conversely, tradition might undergo very great changes but its recipients might regard it as significantly unchanged. What they are experiencing is rather a sense of filiation with a lineage of prior possessors of a tradition which, in any two successive generations, changes by variations so small as not to be perceived as significant changes.

A sense of identity and a sense of filiation with earlier recipients of a tradition are different things from the actual reception of a tradition. Sometimes the sense of identity and the sense of filiation coexist, sometimes they exist separately from each other. A sense of filiation or continuity is a sense of being "connected" with an unbroken chain of generations which have some significant quality in common. A sense of identity as experienced by members of the chain embraces "all" of the putatively successive members who might also be viewed as possessors of the tradition in times leading up to the present. The sense of identity and the sense of continuity do not require that there be an identity of the *traditum* recognizable by an external observer.

Over many generations of recipients, the *traditum* might have become altered from its earliest forms in many respects but not in those regarded as central by its custodians. There has been a persisting identity of central features of Roman Catholic belief, despite many changes in dogma. An institution may have a persisting identity of legal personality, of physical location, of name, of type and mode of activity as well as in the imagery of its prior existence in the minds of any generation of its members.[9] The use of the single name fosters the sense of identity. The existence of the sense of identity with an earlier state in the life of a collectivity renders the transmissions and receptions of a stable *traditum* more likely but it does not guarantee it and is not indispensable to it.

Traditions are not independently self-reproductive or self-elaborating. Only living, knowing, desiring human beings can enact

9. Karl Rothenbücher, *Über das Wesen des Geschichtlichen und der geschichtlichen Gebilde* (Tübingen: J. C. B. Mohr [Paul Siebeck]: 1926), p. 12.

them and reenact them and modify them. Traditions develop because the desire to create something truer and better or more convenient is alive in those who acquire and possess them. Traditions can deteriorate in the sense of losing their adherents because their possessors cease to present them or because those who once received and reenacted and extended them now prefer other lines of conduct or because new generations to which they were presented find other traditions of belief or some relatively new beliefs more acceptable, according to the standards which these generations accept.

The Duration of Tradition

How long must a pattern go on being transmitted and received for it to be regarded as a tradition in the sense of an enduring entity? This question cannot be answered satisfactorily. Obviously a belief which is forsaken immediately after its conception and which has no recipients when its inventor or exponent presents or embodies it, is not a tradition. If a belief or practice "catches on" but survives only for a short time, it fails to become a tradition, even though it contains, in nucleus, the patterns of transmission from exponent to recipient which is at the heart of traditionality. It has to last over at least three generations—however long or short these are—to be a tradition.

A way of expressing the duration of a tradition is to speak of it in terms of generations. This is not very precise because generations are themselves of different durations and their boundaries too are vague. In a school, for example, where children spend four years, a generation may be only four years long. A tradition, such as a way of referring to teachers or a style of playing a certain game might be of short duration in terms of years yet to its recipients it might be an "old tradition." Once it has undergone ten or fifteen transmissions over as many years, from second- to first-year pupils, it might appear to its recipients as having existed "from time immemorial." Where the generations are longer, a longer span of time will be needed for a *traditum* to form a chain of tradition. How long? is an academic question, difficult to answer in a wholly satisfactory way but also not necessary to answer except to say that, at a minimum, two transmissions over three generations are required for a pattern of belief or action to be considered a tradition.

A fashion existing within a short time-period might be the practice or belief of a single generation, let us say those between fifteen and twenty years of age. The same generation or age-cohort might persist in the particular belief or practice over many years but those who belong to the adjacently ensuing cohort might be unreceptive to it. A belief or practice might be accepted by a single generation for a year or even a single season; it might also be accepted by a number of different but concurrently existing generations but only for a short time. Brevity of duration is the mark of a fashion. Fashion and tradition have in common the presentation of a pattern and its reception by other persons; a fashion is not a tradition as long as its duration is confined to a single generation, even if it lasts through much of the life of that generation. Many fashions do not last that long. A fashion must find recipients relatively rapidly and over a larger proportion of the population in its short life; a tradition can grow more gradually since it has a greater longevity. What begins as a fashion might become a tradition. The boundary between tradition and fashion is indistinct; it cannot be specified except arbitrarily and in a way which cannot be applied. Nonetheless, despite the vagueness of the boundary, the difference is real.

In one form or another, a chain of tradition might last a very long time. The tradition of monotheism is now between two and a half and three millennia in duration. The tradition of citizenship is about two millennia in duration. The Christian tradition is nearly two millennia in duration. The liberal tradition is several centuries old, the Marxian tradition about a century and a third. The tradition of "modernism" in art and literature is of about the same duration as the Marxian tradition or a little longer. Institutions which have names, presumed dates of foundation, and known founders are frequently difficult to date precisely, and not just because of an insufficiency of records; their emergence may be a gradual process. It is more difficult to assert the point of origin of a traditional chain of beliefs or patterns of conduct.

The Substance of Tradition

Traditionality is compatible with almost any substantive content. All accomplished patterns of the human mind, all patterns of belief or modes of thinking, all achieved patterns of social relationships, all technical practices, and all physical artifacts or natural objects are susceptible to becoming objects in a process of transmission; each is capable of becoming a tradition.

Traditio was a mode of transferring the ownership of private property in Roman law. Tradition is whatever is persistent or recurrent through transmission, regardless of the substance and institutional setting. It includes orally transmitted beliefs as well as those transmitted in writing. It includes secular as well as sacred beliefs; it includes beliefs which were arrived at by ratiocination and by methodical, theoretically controlled intellectual procedures as well as beliefs which were accepted without intense reflection. It includes beliefs thought to have been divinely revealed as well as interpretations of those beliefs. It includes beliefs formed through experience and beliefs formed by logical deduction.

A distinction is sometimes made between sacred texts like the Pentateuch, the Gospels, and the Koran and the interpretations which have grown up around them such as the Talmud, the writings of the Church Fathers, and the commentaries on the Koran as well as the written record of sayings of the companions of the Prophet. The anonymous incrustations of tales about the central figures in the text—Jesus, Moses, Mohammed, and Buddha—are also *tradita*. The latter categories are sometimes referred to as "traditions," in order to distinguish them from the revealed or otherwise authoritative sacred texts around which they have been formed. Text and tradition here correspond to primary declaration and derivative interpretation. This was the standpoint taken by the Council of Trent when it pronounced both Scripture and the tradition of interpretative commentary on Scripture to be authoritative.

From the standpoint which I take here both declaration and interpretation are traditions. The physical artifacts—manuscripts—are traditions. The sacred text itself is a tradition. The "tradition" is accumulated understanding of the text; the text would be only a physical object without interpretation. The sacredness of the text sets it apart, but it would make no sense without an interpretation; yet the interpretation which makes it what it is, is regarded as different from the text. The works of literary figures like Homer, Virgil, Shakespeare, and Dante are placed in a somewhat similar situation; large bodies of interpretation form around them. The manuscripts and printed books in which the text is recorded, the text and the interpretations of it are all *tradita*. The writings of Homer, Virgil, Shakespeare, and Dante also lie at the roots of traditions of literary genres and of interpretations of life. Images, themes, phrases from the works of these authors enter into subsidiary traditions.

In many usages of the term "tradition" there are implicit delimitations of the substantive content of tradition. They imply that traditions are "genuine traditions" only if their substantive content is respectful of traditionality; if they are transmitted orally rather than in writing; if they are a matter of hearsay and not of established facts; if there is no evidence for their factual assertions and no ratiocination associated with their normative ones; and if their authors or originators are anonymous rather than individually identifiable by name.

The natural terrain of "genuine tradition" would appear from this modern standpoint to lie in rule by hereditary chiefs and elders and in monarchy or oligarchy in contrast with liberal republics or democracies; in paganism and polytheism rather than in monotheism; in customary law rather than in legislation and systematic legal codes; in religious interpretations of the world rather than in secularized ones; in families, especially extended patriarchal families, in contrast with voluntary associations; and more generally in hierarchical authority rather than in widely dispersed authority; in refined and differentiated etiquette rather than free-and-easy treatment of persons; in inequality in contrast with equality; in agriculture and fishing rather than in commerce and industry; in tools in contrast with mechanical technology; and in human, animal, wind, and water power rather than in power produced by more artificial means. A belief which is received by tradition seems by its nature to entail hierarchy, religious devotion, illiteracy. Tradition seems to belong to one kind of society and to be out of place in others.

As the idea of tradition took form in the eighteenth and nineteenth centuries, it tended to be confined by those who studied it to particular kinds of traditions: folklore, fairy tales, myths, and legends, oral literature, customary law, the *Sitte und Tracht* of peasant life, religious and secular ceremonies and rituals. It was connected with the transmission of expressive works which had not been reduced to written form. Tradition was sought in the culture possessed by strata which had little formal education and which were considered to be less articulate, less literate, and less ratiocinative. The founders of the modern discipline of folklore believed that in these strata there were at work some deeper mental processes which had been lost in the course of the progress of a rationalized civilization and that the results of the workings of these processes were passed "by tradition" i.e., orally, anonymously, and by example, from generation to generation, undergoing small increments of change but remaining substantially and visibly identical over long, unbroken stretches of time.[10]

The imaginative productions of the popular culture which fell under the heading of tradition were largely without nameable authors; they were said by some scholars to be the anonymous products of unconscious collective processes. According to the folkloristic interpretations of tradition, rational discourse played a very small part in the transmission and reception of "traditional" works, beliefs, patterns of conduct, institutional rules and arrangements. They were transmitted, allegedly, under the auspices of authority which commanded unquestioning acceptance; the dogmatic presentation of tradition was frequently cited as characteristic of tradition. Here the folkloristic conception of tradition came together with the rationalistic criticism of tradition in the century of the Enlightenment.[11] Unwittingness on the parts of transmitter and of recipient was also said to be characteristic of tradition.[12] Rote learning was another characteristic mode of acquiring this kind of tradition. The beliefs transmit-

10. See Peter Burke, *Popular Culture in Early Modern Europe* (London: Maurice Temple Smith, 1978), especially pp. 113–48.
11. See Hazard, *La Pensée européenne au XVIII siècle,* and Venturi, "The European Enlightenment."
12. H. B. Acton, "Tradition and Some Other Forms of Actions," in *Proceedings of the Aristotelian Society,* n.s., vol. 53, containing the papers read during the seventy-fourth session, 1952–53, pp. 1–28.

ted by tradition were asserted to have either no rational content or only the barest minimum; the mode of presentation and reception likewise. Most of the beliefs had no empirical validity. An unrational content had some affinity with dogmatic presentation and submissive reception with authoritative prescription and rote acquisition.

In the nineteenth century, in response to the threatened dissolution of Christian faith by the outlook of the Enlightenment, arguments were made for the acceptance on faith of the authoritativeness of Christian traditions contained in Scripture and in the interpretations of the Church Fathers, the councils, and the hierarchy of the Roman Catholic church. The doctrine of "traditionalism" was promulgated by a series of writers beginning with Bonald.

Traditional Societies

In the first half of the twentieth century animosity against modern civilization, which was a scientistic, rationalistic, individualistic, and hedonistic civilization, reached new heights; among the charges laid against bourgeois society was that it had "uprooted" human beings from an order which gave meaning to existence. Tradition was said to be an integral part of that order. Tradition was alleged to be a guarantor of order and of the quality of civilization.[13]

The rational construction of abstract principles and their use in explicitly defined techniques of action, observation, and analysis were regarded as the antitheses of tradition in substance, in mode of communication, and in the organization of belief and action. The image of a society living in accordance with a body of continuous common traditions was useful as a partial clarification of some real differences between traditional and untraditional cultures and institutions. Altogether, however, it was injurious to a better understanding of the scope and limits of tradition.

No society was ever as dominated by tradition as these writers made it appear most societies had been before the emergence of modern bourgeois societies. Nor was the acceptance of tradition on a scale wider than has been the case in more recent centuries in the West been a guarantee of social order, good conduct, and justice. Rulers were frequently rapacious, wars were cruel, priests were often not virtuous, outbursts of violence and fanaticism were recurrent. A "traditional society" is no more a reign of virtue than the societies which have been affected by the notion that traditions were hindrances to improvement and had to be set aside wherever possible.

13. This is a major theme of modern thought. Tönnies, Simmel, Spengler, Scheler, Barrès, Bergson, Weil, Gill, Chesterton, Tawney, Eliot, Henry Adams, Mumford, and many others, great and small, in a wide variety of ways, all implied that before the coming of the ruinous modern society, the human race had lived in a condition of unbroken traditionality.

It is probably true that the appreciation of past accomplishments and of beliefs inherited from the past as guides to conduct has been more widely observed in many societies of the past than it has been in Western societies in the last two centuries. In law, literature, politics, and religion there was—unevenly—more than there is at present a belief that past conduct, past practices, past beliefs had evidence on their side. Whether because of revelation or genius or experience or reverence for ancestors and for no reason other than the fact that such things already existed and "worked," human beings were often knowingly respectful towards the things which they had inherited from the past and they guided their behavior accordingly.

These societies were often engaged in passionate conflicts between families and tribes and between contenders for the positions of greatest power and eminence; poets tried to write poems which had not been written before and they were esteemed because of distinctive qualities which set them off from their contemporaries and which put them into the same high rank as esteemed poets of the past; philosophers and scientists tried to discover things which had not been known before and to discern truths with a precision and persuasiveness which had not been previously attained. Craftsmen invented and bettered ways of affecting the materials on which they worked. Merchants calculated the relative advantages of the alternatives before them. Peasants ran away to towns, became soldiers or thieves. Sometimes they engaged in *jacqueries,* burned, pillaged, and raped. Still in many respects the members of those societies adhered to and praised old ways and often, when something previously not done was done, they either denied its novelty or claimed that it had the benefit of conformity with a respected pattern previously observed. Not only were traditions often respected but it was often thought that they should be respected because they were traditions.

It is not that all actions were guided by traditional rules and practices or that all were justified by the invocation of tradition, i.e., by the assertion that they conformed with a traditional pattern. The view that societies other than modern Western societies were saturated by traditional patterns which pervaded and controlled all aspects of social and cultural life made it easier for the discoverers of traditional culture in the early nineteenth century to confine their observation of tradition in their own time to a restricted part of society and one which, moreover, was being pushed more and more into obscure and inconsequential corners. This view made traditionality appear to be synonymous with the archaic and the obsolete. This view also made it too easy to contrast this withdrawn, quaint, and "reactionary" body of beliefs and practices which was doomed to defeat in contest with its adversaries who were part of the forward movement of modern societies. The scientific, the rational, empirical, secular, progressive features of these societies, which seemed destined for certain victory in the battle with the archaic, were thus remitted from any trace of traditionality. The way in which the proponents of the forward movement understood themselves rendered them unwilling to acknowledge or tolerate any presence of traditionality in their own ranks.

The Traditionality of Reason

Substantive traditionality, i.e., the appreciation of the accomplishments and wisdom of the past and of the institutions especially impregnated with tradition, as well as the desirability of regarding patterns inherited from the past as valid guides, is one of the major patterns of human thought. In modern times, out of considerations of religious politics and the immanent impulsion of intellectual life, this pattern has been severely criticized.

The pure light of reason and scientific knowledge illuminated the path of the crusaders against substantive traditionality. Analytical reason and empirical science, believing in nothing which could not be proven by methodical observation and logic, stood in marked contrast with beliefs which were believed because they had been believed previously and which had never been rationally and scientifically tested. There was a vast thicket to clear but the great men of the Enlightenment and of nineteenth-century liberal scientism looked forward with confidence to a time when much of the area would be cleared. Then reason and scientific knowledge would reign and mankind would no longer be enslaved by tradition.

The outlook of the Enlightenment became more and more widely diffused within and among Western societies and in the twentieth century within societies outside the West. It has not triumphed wholly in any of them, even in the most scientific of them. The triumphs it has won have been achieved at a cost. The cost has not just been the laying waste of a quite large part of the territory once occupied by substantive traditionality, by Christian religious belief, and piety towards ancestors and respect for authority in the family and other institutions. This after all was their aim and it was paid by their adversaries. Part of the cost was paid by the victors themselves. That part of the cost has included becoming traditional. Another part of the cost was the troubling discovery of difficulties which they had not anticipated. The cost of becoming traditional is the one which concerns me here.

The patterns of reason and scientific method are not acquired by each possessor who works them out for himself. They are for the most part transmitted to him. They can be transmitted rationally, i.e., by the enunciation and demonstration of principles and the rules of their application. The fact that they can be rationally demonstrated does not make them any less traditional. Nonetheless, not everything about such principles and rules is transmitted by abstract exposition or even by particular logical and empirical demonstration. There are overtones, elements of "tacit knowledge," and insight where the principles and rules are inappropriate, which are not teachable by articulated assertions but which are acquired by intimate association and empathy with the acts of exemplification in the persons who perform them. Insofar as the transmission of tradition has an element of the "unconscious," it is also present in science and reason themselves. The subtleties of technique and the subtleties of understanding have arisen through experience and analysis. Each generation of scientists acquires what its predecessors have achieved through their successive experiences and analyses; the fruits of these experiences and analyses are passed onward. Many of these fruits are subjected to severe rational scrutiny and refined articulation. But not all that is presented and received is assimilated into this process. Some of it remains unarticulated, but that too is presented and received. The transmission of the articulated part of the rational, scientific tradition is made effective by the reception and mastery of its unarticulated part. The mind of the recipient is formed by this reception of both the articulated and the unarticulated. The presentation of the formed and reasoned gives shape to the intellectual possession of the unformed recipient; it arouses and shapes his own unshaped power of reason; he is then placed in a position to acquire the unformed and the unarticulated.

The program of reason and scientific knowledge could never have succeeded to the extent that it did without becoming overgrown by tradition. The confidence in the powers of reason and science became a tradition accepted with the same unquestioning confidence as the belief in the Judeo-Christian accounts of the origins and meaning of human existence had been earlier. Of course, new scientific discoveries in geology, archaeology, and astronomy were being made continually and fragments of evidence were being pieced together by the application of theories which would never have been constructed without the stringent exercise of reason. Nonetheless, for the great mass of those who did not make these discoveries, the results became traditions much like any substantive tradition. And the discoverers too proceeded from the traditions consisting of the results of previous discoveries and of the ethos of scientific discovery which were themselves traditions.

Around these primary traditions of the results of rational analysis and scientific observation and of the ethos of scientific discovery, passed down, elaborated, and built upon by subsequent investigators, there was a penumbral scientistic tradition regarding the redemptive powers of scientific knowledge and the scientific attitude. This ramified, pervasive outlook had nothing to support it in the minds of its recipients other than the technological achievements in agriculture and medicine and the prestige of science and scientists in general. Its espousal became as customary as any precedent in customary law.

The tradition of reason became a major contender against substantive traditionality for the suffrage of the human race. It became central to the progressivistic outlook. In the present century it has given legitimatory support to traditions which had relatively little to do with reason or science except that they too were hostile to substantive traditionality. These included among others the relaxation of restraints on sexual activity and the freedom of expressive impulse, the diminution of parental authority and the emancipation of the child, the equality of deference and power, a condoning attitude towards criminality, the praise of the scientific approach to the "treatment of social problems" and the "rational management of society." These were not new excogitations, newly arrived at by each recipient, by reason and scientific methods, but they shared with the latter the tradition of aversion from substantive traditionality.

Some of the proponents of this third strand of the tradition of reason insofar as they do not regard it as self-evident regard it as "natural." Such a view is obviously untenable; substantive traditionality is just as "natural" as hostility and indifference to substantive traditionality. The belief that every institution and practice must be constructed according to the principle of reason, that equality is good and inequality evil, that utility should be the criterion of goodness, that restraint of impulse is bad and gratification good might be supported by relatively rational arguments. These beliefs were not created by rational arguments and, even if they were, they have not been rationally invented by most of their adherents. Like the beliefs which make up the traditionalistic outlook, they were "there." "Being there" gave them an authoritative self-evidentness. They are sustained by that authoritative self-evidentness[14] which could not exist for their proponents if they had not already existed as a mass of accumulated specific ideas and general orientations.

The Normative Element in Tradition

There is an inherently normative element in any tradition of belief which is presented for acceptance; it is presented with the intention of producing affirmation and acceptance. Nonetheless, not all traditions are explicitly normative. Many traditions are explicitly factual or de-

---

14. M. Homais, the Voltairean pharmacist in *Madame Bovary* is prototypical of this traditionality of reason.

scriptive. A tradition which asserts that the founder of a religion disappeared into the wilderness for forty days—quite apart from whether there is documentary evidence for it—is such a factual tradition. A rumor accepted for a long time in a village to the effect that a long-dead master of the "big house" had to resign his commission in the eighteenth century because he cheated a brother officer in a game of cards is another such factual tradition without normative intimations other than that it is alleged to be true and commended for acceptance. It does have an overtone of a derogation of the rich and powerful.

Scientific and scholarly propositions, once they have been enunciated, have this "factually normative" character. Representing the state of correct belief in, let us say, mathematics or chemistry, their assertion both assumes their correctness and recommends their acceptance. This is the barest normative minimum of any tradition of belief. Beyond this, many ostensibly factual traditions such as the adage that "a stitch in time saves nine" or that "there is no fool like an old fool" are intended not only to command assent to their factual correctness but also to guide action. Most traditions of belief are normative in this sense, namely, that they are intended to influence the conduct of the audience to which they are addressed, beyond the limits of assent to their factual correctness.

Literary works from the traditional stock often contain normative intentions as well as literary form or style; they praise one set of arrangements and beliefs and attempt to show the wrongness of another. The moral judgments contained in literary works have often had extensive consequences for society. Think for example of *Childe Harold* or *Les Fleurs du mal*. There is another sense in which literary works have normative significance. What are called "classics" have normative consequences within literature and art; they provide models for the aspirations of subsequent authors and artists.

Tradition is thus far more than the statistically frequent recurrence over a succession of generations of similar beliefs, practices, institutions, and works. The recurrence is a consequence of the normative consequences—sometimes the normative intention—of presentation and of the acceptance of the tradition as normative. It is this normative transmission which links the generations of the dead with the generations of the living in the constitution of a society.

The cohesion of a society is ordinarily conceived of as a feature of a particular movement in time; it is the cohesion of its living members with each other. The older living members help to induct the younger living members into the beliefs and patterns which they have inherited from those who went before them. In this way, the dead are influential, exercising what critics of traditionality have called the "dead hand of the past." They are objects of attachment, but what is more significant is that their works and the norms contained in their practices influence the actions of subsequent generations to whom they are unknown. The normativeness of tradition is the inertial force which holds society in a given form over time.

Stocks and Possessions

Traditions are of varying duration. A tradition of conduct—the patterns which guide actions, the ends sought, the conceptions of appropriate and effective means to attain those ends, the structures which result from and are maintained by those actions—is more persistent than the actions themselves. Actions disappear with their performance; the patterns of belief which guide them and the images of the relationships and structures are transmissible. But they too do not last indefinitely, certainly not all of them. A pattern, an ideal, an ethical standard which has become established is a mortal creation. Roman religion no longer exists except insofar as some of its beliefs have been assimilated into Christianity. The etiquette of a medieval or Renaissance court no longer exists. The traditions of Greek military tactics embodied in the phalanx and of the use of elephants in warfare have disappeared from the conduct of military operations.

Many traditions which lasted for extended periods have undoubtedly ceased to exist in a recognizable form. In societies without writing such traditions could be retained in memory with the distortions which repeated transmission renders likely. The tradition itself having ceased to exist, its record becomes a tradition; as an oral tradition its chances of survival are diminished. In societies with writing the chances of survival of records of patterns of conduct which were once traditions are enhanced. Works themselves would appear to have a greater chance of survival but the mere fact of having been recorded in writing is no guarantee of the survival of the record. Much is lost by the decay or destruction of records and the failure to make new and additional copies to replace the older ones whose chances of life are smaller. Still, as the centuries have passed, the stock of written works that make up the physical precipitates and vehicles of intellectual and literary tradition for nearly every linguistic civilization, has become very large. In any major linguistic civilization such as the French, German, English, the number of books in the tradition is far too large for any person to read more than a small proportion of all that are known to have survived. Individuals can possess only a small part of the existing tradition of their own society and linguistic civilization. To possess the whole tradition is beyond their powers, given the brevity of life and the necessity of other activities. Selection is inevitable in the round of life of an individual.

The act of selection is not exclusively an individual choice. The parts of the tradition which a person encounters have already been subjected to many choices so that only a small part of what exists in the physical stock comes to his attention. The process of tradition is also a process of selection. Parts of the traditional stock drift downward into obscurity so that they are known only to a few persons or conceivably to none at all.

The possession of the stock of tradition is by no means wholly consensual in any society. There is much specialization in the possession of scientific and scholarly works within each domain of specialization in the sciences. Consensus of possession in science is quite high within a circle of specialization; it is high in scholarship too. In literature it is probably not as great. The amounts possessed and what is possessed are both extremely various so that the stratification of the stock is not disjunctive between a stratum which is nearly universally possessed within a society and a stratum to which the vast majority in the society is utterly oblivious. A very large part of the tradition in its physical form of a stock of works lies inert. It is not possessed and the patterns which it contains are likely to be neglected and left in a condition in which they are not likely to be developed. The patterns contained in this part of the tradition do not enter into the active imagination and the actively held beliefs or they enter only through other, sometimes better, works.

The same is true of works of art. Museum walls are smaller than the space which would be taken up by all the existing paintings not in private possession. The floor space is too small for all the surviving sculpture. Many pieces are therefore stored away unseen. The criterion of choice in art, as it is in literature, science, and scholarship, is a criterion of quality.

In art and literature, the criterion of quality is not closely related to the passage of time. There are variations in the criteria of choice but the passage of time is not one of them. In science and scholarship the passage of time is the backdrop of obsolescence so that scientific or scholarly works which were once of great value ceased to be so as their patterns were taken up and revised, extended, and differentiated. Thus works which made a mark on the subsequent character of the tradition cease to be of interest and fall into the dead part of the stock while their essential substance has been assimilated and lives on. Works of art and literature do not have this possibility. If they were not works of quality in their own time they sank to obscurity and in almost all cases remained there. There are exceptions. Some works have been misjudged at first, allowed to sink, and have subsequently been retrieved to become part of the more amply possessed stock.

At any given time within a particular society the traditions obtaining there regarding any object of attention or in any sphere of activity are multifarious. The possession of a tradition—its acceptance, observance, and espousal—can be very diverse. Some of its possessors usually have a much richer and more specific possession than do others; some possessors acquire only a very general disposition from the traditions. Within the "same" tradition there are not only levels of differentiation and specificity in possession but also substantively different interpretations and emphases.

The Intertwinement of Tradition and the Untraditional

The Limits of the Power of Tradition

In no society could life be lived entirely under the domination of tradition; no society could survive only from the stock of objects, beliefs, and patterns presented. Human beings have so much that is pressing to do in life; everyone faces some tasks to which there is no immediately available solution or where such solutions as there are leave a residue of dissatisfaction. Being respectful of their traditions is not the primary object of concern for most persons; there must be very few individuals in any society—perhaps the protocol officers of courts and foreign offices, and a few old fogies—who take as a primary task the strict adherence to what has been received as tradition. Most adult human beings must work under exigent conditions to gain their livelihood and to maintain the offspring they have brought into life.

In their leisure time, many persons in the nineteenth and twentieth centuries have been bored with routine and have tried restlessly to escape from it; they now listen to the "latest hits" and watch television programs which are produced by writers who are enthralled by the idol of "creativity" and deliberately seek to create something new. They read newspapers and watch or listen to broadcasts of "news" in order to know the most recent events to an extent unknown in poorer and less literate societies. The journalists wish to uncover and present what is "new"; they fear that their audience would be bored by reading or hearing the same accounts of the same events. Boredom with the usual and professional pride both demand journalistic novelty.

In religious life, which is thought to be the stronghold of traditionality, where ritual and holding fast to the old obtain, there has always been some pressure of innovation. New issues have always emerged within the churches themselves, new sects are founded, new attitudes towards ecclesiastical authority come forward, new doctrines are promulgated, new versions of sacred writings and new interpretations are made, new dogmas are enunciated, new variants of liturgy proposed, and new arrangements are agreed upon between spiritual and earthly powers. In recent decades there has been a strenuous and deliberate effort even in the most traditional of institutions—the Roman Catholic church—to find new forms of belief and liturgy which will be "appropriate to modern times" and which will be "consistent with modern scientific knowledge." Great changes have indeed been made.

In educational circles, even in the time of ascendancy of the classics, Greek displaced Latin as the primary subject; the classical authors most studied increased or diminished in their prominence in school syllabuses. Now there is much more emphasis placed on the encouragement of the creative potentialities of pupils. Spontaneity, being enabled to find "one's real self," establishing "one's identity," are now frequently put forward as the ends of education and these are deliberately intended to break away from traditional rules and beliefs. Yet even before these attacks began approximately on their present scale, educational practices underwent changes. New ideas of what should be drawn from the wide variety of cultural traditions appeared. Vicissitudes and exigencies never left the entire field of action and belief to tradition. Peasants had to struggle hard to produce crops under very unpropitious and unpredictable circumstances. They had to sow and harvest, to maintain themselves and to sell the surplus of what they had produced or to meet the demands of landowners or their feudal lords. Scarcity was always a strain on tradition. Craftsmen had to produce goods which they could sell in markets which were changing in the variety, price, and quality of goods available and in the tastes of customers. Merchants traveled widely trying to sell what they had purchased and to make a profit on their transactions; their markets too were changing and so they had to find new goods to sell and new customers to buy them. Moneylenders sought the largest possible returns on the money which they lent; their borrowers sometimes failed to repay. There were traditions for dealing with events which did not fit into expectations formed from traditions but they were not always efficacious.

Kings and princes exerted themselves to maintain their ascendancy over their subjects, to prevent the clergy and nobility from acting contrarily to the royal advantage. They had to struggle to protect themselves from the efforts of other rulers to gain dominion over them; they tried to extend their own power beyond its previous boundaries. They had to raise revenue from their grudging subjects in order to maintain a style of life appropriate to their power and to pay for some of the costs of warfare. Rulers, despite their insistence on the traditional legitimacy of their authority, were constantly being forced to depart from tradition. Philosophers and theologians engaged in disputes with other philosophers and theologians, each attempting to establish the superior correctness of his own views by arguments which had not been put forward previously and which dealt more effectively with some refractory observations or arguments. The emergence of modern society and culture have only strengthened the actions which pull against the moorings of traditional patterns of belief and action.

Politicians have continued to exert themselves to attain or remain in high office; they attempt to persuade their potential and actual supporters that it is right and advantageous to support them in their strivings for office. Literary men perhaps even more than in the past try deliberately to write books and poems which will express their own vision of the world and their judgment on it in a language which is shaped by aesthetic criteria and the sensibility which embodies these criteria. Businessmen no less than in the past and on a far greater scale seek to maximize their profits by a rational economic use of resources. They calculate more rationally and searchingly the costs and benefits of alternative ways of employing their resources. Scientists in far greater numbers and with far greater methodical rigor try to discover and resolve problems which have not previously been perceived or if perceived have not been solved, and they try more continuously to construct new hypotheses and to find new techniques to make new observations. They all deal with refractory realities, such as raw materials, machines, other human beings, laboratory specimens or natural events, the actions of which do not always conform with traditional expectations, regardless of whether these traditional expectations have been received from scientific textbooks or from the teaching of elders. To cope with them requires going beyond traditional rules and beliefs. The effort to achieve hitherto unrealized ends, the seeking of goals is always in some sense a departure from traditional standards; it entails entering upon or engendering new situations. The new situations require fresh observations and decisions.

In the effort to continue to achieve once more goals achieved previously, fresh observations and decisions are called for because the situations in which they have to be achieved are constantly in process of changing. Hence even to adhere to previously established patterns, it is necessary to contrive new ones because the situations of action, to which earlier patterns handed down by tradition were adequate, undergo changes of greater or lesser magnitudes.

It would have been contrary to the necessities imposed by contingency, the variations in nature's bountifulness and niggardliness, the restless striving of individuals to gain something not already possessed or to prevent the loss of what they already possess, for traditions to have been accepted as wholly adequate for the guidance of judgment and action in every situation. Traditions were probably more affirmatively presented and received in most societies than they are nowadays, and there was probably wider acceptance of the belief that they should be adhered to. The living human beings of those times were engaged in tasks which required overcoming the recalcitrance of external things and of other human beings and which were as demanding and as difficult for them as the tasks which are undertaken by the members of contemporary, self-avowedly "untraditional" societies. They, too, faced situations which were novel to them or which were disturbing and for which they had no wholly satisfactory explanations or guides to action. It is likely that they did not set out deliberately to invent new ways of doing things, which were better than those which had been transmitted to them; they accepted much in their intellectual inheritance which many would not accept today. Nonetheless, the pressures of unforeseen, threatening, or actually catastrophic events compelled actions which were neither counseled nor prescribed by the transmitters of traditions. The unsatisfactoriness of experience and the discovery of unresolved questions induced skepticism about the transmitted account and about the justification of particular traditional actions and institutions.

Even in the most "traditional societies," the traditional pattern could not have been the sole constituent of the actions taking place at any time. Human beings in all societies pursue certain ends because they anticipate advantages to flow from the realization of these ends. They think about these ends cognitively, i.e., they think about them in the light of the beliefs which they possess about the existent relations between particular causes and particular effects. They attempt to realize these ends by actions which they regard as causally most efficacious for the realization of the ends. They try, according to their lights, to make explanations of events consistent with experience and with each other.

Human beings do things because, as they see it, they want to do them, because they anticipate gratification from the actions leading to the intended state of affairs, and because they believe themselves compelled to do them. They often attempt to act rationally, adapting their scarce resources to the best and most economical attainment of their ends, considering the unchangeable conditions of their actions and the costs of attaining their ends. They act as rationally as they can, given the recalcitrance of external events, and of other human beings, their own ratiocinative capacities, and the limits of their knowledge of the ramification of consequences for themselves in the near and the remote future and for persons known and unknown in the near and remote future; they are also influenced in varying degrees by conceptions of rectitude or fairness or moral rights and obligations about what they and others are entitled to have.

Then, too, human beings are impulsive, compulsive, and passionate. They experience these impulses and passions in all their immediacy. They act under the immediate influence of powerful states of sentiment which are often irresistible. They not only overcome the restraints which rational decision would impose; they also break the bonds which traditional moral rules stipulate.

What Is Not Tradition

An experienced sentiment is not a tradition. It is a state of sensation at a given moment. A rational judgment is not a tradition; it is an assertion about the logical consistency of statements, about the consistency of a statement with an action. An action is not a tradition; it is a movement of the body which has an intention, although sometimes it is an enunciation, written or spoken, of words asserting or implying an intention. A visual perception is not a tradition; it is an image taken into the retina and transferred to the brain. A prayer is not a tradition: it is a set of words addressed to the deity imploring his favor. A scientific proposition is not a tradition; it is an idea external to its propounder which asserts a relationship between classes of events.

A process of industrial production is not a tradition. It is an organization of many individuals' actions, some almost wholly physical, some verbal, directed to the transformation of the form of natural, physical substances by the use of tools or machines. The product is not a tradition. An act of exercise of authority is not a tradition; it is a set of words spoken or written which is intended to elicit the performance of certain actions by other persons and which in fact often elicits such performances. The performance of a ritual action, whether it is an act of communion or the celebration of an anniversary or loyal toast to a monarch, is not a tradition; it is a set of words and physical movements expressive of a state of sentiment and belief.

None of these states of sentiment or mind is a tradition, none of these physical actions and social relationships is a tradition. None of these ideas is a tradition. None of them in itself is a tradition. But all of them can in various ways be transmitted as traditions; they can become traditions. They nearly always occur in forms affected or determined in varying degrees by tradition. They recur because they are carried as traditions which are reenacted. The reenactment is not the tradition; the tradition is the pattern which guides the reenactment.

There are also original beliefs, original intellectual works, original commands, and original social arrangements, structures, or relationships. There are also actions which are adaptations to changed circumstances, adaptations not previously made by the adapting person. They might be original as far as that person is concerned although they often are drawn from available traditions. If not already available as traditions, and if they do not in their turn become traditions, they die with the situations which called them forth or with the person who made them. But by their nature they do not remain original. They either fade away or they are transmitted as traditions when they are reenacted.

Tradition as the Guiding Pattern

Where does tradition come into the societies in which human beings are performing actions which they think are intrinsically right,[15] deliberately instrumental actions,[16] or which are explosively emotional actions?[17] These all seem incompatible with the observance of presented and received traditions of rules and beliefs. But the incompatibility is only apparent. To act, for example, as a "gentleman" or as a "hero" or as a "man," might all be intrinsically valuable patterns of actions; but each succeeding generation receives the model from an antecedent, transmitting generation. The affirmation of the intrinsic value of the pattern or model of the "gentleman" conforms with a tradition and has been received as a tradition. Indeed, most such ideals are usually put forward as both intrinsically right and as traditions worthy of reproduction and persistence. To be an enterprising businessman seems to be as untraditional as any role could be, yet there is much that is traditional about the practices in every field of business, and the very ideal of being a successful businessman is itself received and transmitted as a tradition; at least, it used to be that way in countries where the role and career of the independent entrepreneur was aspired to. The ideal of "success" is itself drawn from tradition; it is certainly not conceived and elaborated anew in each generation; the same is true of the ideas about what must be done to be successful. The ideal of "success" is a general ideal which does not give specific guidance to the person striving for success; he still must perceive the opportunities for rewarding action and he must make particular decisions about how to use the resources which he possesses in order to gain the advantages which are potential in the opportunities which he perceives in his own individual pursuit of the traditional ideal. He must moreover count on the equal strength of the tradition of success among his contemporaries, especially with his near associates from whom he hopes to gain the approbation and admiration accorded to the successful. In Max Weber's account of the strivings of the puritanical businessman—in his account of the Prot-

15. *Wertrationale* actions, as Max Weber called them; he also, in a different context, called them *gesinnungspolitische* actions. See *Wirtschaft und Gesellschaft* (Tübingen: J. C. B. Mohr [Paul Siebeck], 1924), vol. 1, pt. 1, chap. 1, pp. 12–13. See also his *Gesammelte Politische Schriften*, 2d ed. (Tübingen: J. C. B. Mohr [Paul Siebeck], 1958), pp. 534–48.
16. Weber, *Wirtschaft und Gesellschaft*, 1:12–14.
17. Ibid.

estant ethic—the ideal is an ideal given by tradition; in Max Weber's account, the idea of the relationship between success in rational business enterprise and the probability of eternal salvation was given as a tradition. It was certainly not acquired by the rational analyses of empirical observations by each of the generations of businessmen who accepted it.

The high estimation of an economically oriented action, the appreciation of the rational, economic mode of choice, and the evaluation of the successful outcome of such choices are patterns of judgment or evaluation which have been transmitted and received as traditions. These traditions do not prescribe the specific actions to be taken or the particular content of the choices to be made; they are simply prescriptions of the exercise of such modes of actions and judgment. The high estimation of wealth as the objective of rational, economizing action is to a considerable extent the result of the presentation and reception of a tradition. And in all the rational calculation and cognition, there is thus much that is traditional. This does not mean "wrong"; it does not mean "right"; it means only "traditional" in the sense that the end and the technique have been learned from others who taught or exemplified them. The rules for assessing logical coherence and for assessing the reliability of observations are acquired traditionally, in the form of the explicit learning of rational, abstractly formulated principles and in the form of "tacit knowledge," and subsequently fortified by experience. The "goodness" of the rational management of affairs is a tradition, although it is reinforced by considerations of advantage on the part of those who bear the burden of the cost or who receive the services provided.[18]

The efficacy of such action depends too on similar combinations of the rational or expediential and the traditional in the conduct of persons in actions other than the one in question. Tradition enters into the constitution of meaningful conduct by defining its ends and standards and even its means. It does so unevenly. Located at the boundaries of deliberate actions, setting the end or the rules and standards—the traditional stands around the boundaries of the field in which deliberate expediential actions and those which are filled with passion occur. Traditions here are often the "tacit component" of rational, moral, and cognitive actions, and of affect, too.

18. See John Stuart Mill, "Of Competition and Custom," *Principles of Political Economy, with Some of Their Applications to Social Philosophy*, ed. W. J. Ashley (London: Longmans Green, 1909), pp. 242–48.

1   In the Grip of the Past

The Past in the Present

If we could imagine a society in which each generation created all that
it used, contemplated, enjoyed, and suffered, we would be imagining
a society unlike any which has ever existed. It would be a society
formed from a state of nature. It would literally be a society without a
past to draw on to guide its actions in the present.

The human beings alive at any given time are very rarely more than
three generations away from any other members of their own lineage
alive at the same time. Their range of direct contact, physical and
symbolic, with things, with works, words, and modes of conduct,
created in the past, is far more extensive and it reaches much further
back in time. They live in the present of things from the past. Much
that they do and think and aspire to, leaving aside idiosyncratic variations, is an approximate reiteration of what has been done and thought
for a long time, long before anyone still alive was born. The adaptive
philistinism of the *juste milieu,* despised by antibourgeois aesthetes
and votaries of the cult of genius, is matched by the philistinism which
does not adapt itself but which sticks to what it has received. The two
philistinisms often reinforce each other. But even philistines change
and depart from the patterns which have been presented to them. The
philistines who incorporate the tradition and who reinforce the observance of tradition by other philistines among their contemporaries
resemble in an important respect the rebels and geniuses who deliberately break away from it. Both in fact espouse a motley combination of patterns inherited from the past and patterns of more recent
appearance, of identity with and divergence from the patterns presented from the past; their aspirations differ but they are like each
other in their containing much of the past in their beliefs and actions.

Those beliefs and patterns of action which are not identical with
past beliefs and patterns of action coexist with others which are closer
to those of the past. The coexistence is not mere juxtaposition; inter-
dependence is much more typical. Furthermore, those things which
are new owe a great deal of their form and substance to things which
once existed and from which they took their point of departure and
direction. What is new incorporates something of what preceded it

even though it is a step on a path which leads away from the past in the present.

The past does appear in the present and it does so against the obstacles of death and birth. Those who bore the things from the past within themselves die and the past things are left without anyone to possess them unless the newly born, who did not begin by possessing them, are induced to take them up. The succession of generations is the moving biological ground over which the past endures into the present or fades away as its possessors change and die.

Generations

Much has been made of the changes in culture and social organization which are made possible by the succession of generations.[1] Each generation comes to its task with a fresh mind, unencumbered by the beliefs and attachments settled in the minds of the generation antecedent to it. There is of course some truth in this, especially in modern times, when generations have been particularly associated with new departures; each new "idea" becomes diffused in society through its adoption and espousal by a correspondingly new generation. But no human being is born with anything from the past other than his genetic, biological past contained within him.

Each new generation seems to have the chance to begin again, to call a halt to the persistence of the past into the present and to make its society anew. It suffers from the handicap of weakness, isolation, and helplessness in the face of many others who have already fallen into the grip of the past.

The boundaries of any generation are vague; there are no natural boundaries. Where does one generation begin and another end? There is no satisfactory answer to this question. There are rhythms of births and deaths over years and decades, there are age-cohorts arbitrarily defined for purposes of statistical presentation. There are differences in susceptibility to, and reception of, beliefs and differences in conduct which are connected with differences in age. There is moreover a sense of affinity felt by persons falling roughly into given age-classes with other persons in those same classes. They have a sense of being different from persons in other, no less indeterminately bounded age-classes. They see the past more embodied, more present in their elders than they see it in themselves. They have less sense of affinity with the past prior to their own lifetime as they see it recalled or embodied in objects, images, and persons.

1. Karl Mannheim, "Das Problem der Generationen," *Kölner Vierteljahreshefte für Soziologie* 7, nos. 2 and 3 (1928): 156–85 and 309–30; translated in *Essays on the Sociology of Knowledge* (London: Routledge and Kegan Paul, 1952), pp. 276–322.

A "generation" which is conscious of itself defines itself but it does not by any means include all of its coevals, even those born in the same year. Many of these coevals are not so taken with the ideas of those who "speak for their generation"; some of them are "old-fashioned." The *Jahrgänge* run alongside of each other, overlap with each other chronologically, and, at any given time, those slightly older within a generation bear more of the culture of those older than themselves than do those who are younger than themselves by approximately the same number of years. It requires a polemical ideal to create a generation out of these parallel, overlapping *trottoirs roulants* of passage through time.[2]

All societies are aware of the different propensities and capacities corresponding to the different stages of life.[3] Many societies make arrangements which reckon with these differences with the intention or expectation that those who pass through those arrangements will then proceed to assimilate the inherited culture. Only the modern age has conferred on the "younger generation" the historical responsibility of seeking out and realizing the potentialities which the elders have neglected or suppressed.

Having taken into themselves less of the past, new generations offer the chance of getting free of the grip of the past and to make a great leap forward. They do not do so, although in the nineteenth and twentieth centuries some of the members of young generations have made resounding declarations about doing so. The modern age has taken to the idea of generation more eagerly than most because it has taken "youth" more seriously. "Youthfulness" has become a legitimation of demands for privileges and exemptions from the possession of past patterns. A "generation," especially the "young generation," has become a fighting formation for war against some of the beliefs and practices of the elders of the society who retain more of the past. The young generation does not succeed in reconstructing the world but it does make some difference. It does make some innovations and in this respect forces the inheritance from the past into a smaller space or renders the force of what it displaces more indirect. Yet there is so much to replace that it is not within the powers of any single active generation to replace most of what it has begun with.

The Enchainment of Generations

If we follow the old definition and estimate that there are roughly three or four active generations to a century,[4] there have been by this

2. See Robert Wohl, *The Generation of 1914* (Cambridge, Mass.: Harvard University Press, 1979).
3. S. N. Eisenstadt, *From Generation to Generation* (Glencoe, Ill.: The Free Press, 1956).
4. Francois Mentré, *Les générations sociales* (Paris: Editions Bossard,

problematical mode of calculation between three and four hundred generations in the course of the history of human societies which have had settled agriculture and domesticated animals. There have been about one hundred and twenty generations in the course of the history of Western societies and those of the Middle East from which certain important beliefs and patterns of action have grown.[5] These generations have probably been unequal in the number and the scope of the innovations which they have created. Some have lived and died in circumstances much like those they were born into; others have experienced many changes in beliefs, practices, institutions, and types of technological equipment. Yet it seems reasonable to say that many of the beliefs and patterns of action of any Western society a century ago still exist and are important. The contemporary societies of the West are linked to those of a century ago by approximations to identity in modes of political life, the organization of universities, types of religious institutions, beliefs, and ritual, and the legal system. It is sometimes said that our societies have been totally transformed in the past century, but this is hyperbole. They have certainly changed but they have also changed along lines laid down by their previous state, and certain features have not changed as much as others.

Modern Western societies exhibit unprecedented degrees of differentiation; they present to their members unprecedented tasks which demand reflection, adaptation, and adjustment. These societies, more than the societies a century or two centuries ago, have sustained institutions and professions which seek and actually achieve innovations in economic, social, and political organization and in technology and scientific knowledge. They have in their possession vast stocks of practical knowledge and rules, of relatively recent creation, some parts of which are contained in written works, others contained in memory; they possess an immense stock of works, technological and artistic, which have been created by still-living gen-

1920); Wilhelm Dilthey, *Gesammelte Schriften* (Leipzig: B. G. Teubner, 1914), 5:36–41.

5. Alexander von Rüstow said that no single generation makes a major contribution to the stock of patterns of conduct and belief which it possesses. In this striking assertion of a common argument, he assumed that each generation contributes to the existing stock only the fraction corresponding to its part of the total life-span of civilization. Rüstow's view rested on the further assumption that innovations and their scope can be quantitatively estimated, which is an open question. Still, once we grant this assumption up to a point, his view must be qualified by the observation that some generations are probably much more creative than others and that the generations in the last two centuries are far larger than generations one or two millennia ago. These factors alone would make for quite unequal contributions of generations to the total stock. Nonetheless, his arithmetic exercise expresses, in a perhaps metaphorical form, the important proposition that no generation creates most of what it uses, believes, and practices. See Alexander von Rüstow, "Kultur-tradition und Kulturkritik," *Studium Generale* 4 (1951): 37 ff.

erations. They have in their possession, from their own creation, an immense stock of intellectual works—philosophical, theological, ethical, scientific, and scholarly—and the beliefs about reality which they contain. Their societies are constituted by structures which are unique in their concrete particularity. They manifest a great deal which is certainly not identical with what the societies of their biological or territorial ancestors possessed. They possess works of painting and music and literature which are unique in style. Their governments do many particular things which governments did not do in preceding centuries. Their economic institutions and their technology produce things in kinds and quantities which were never produced before.

Nevertheless, despite unquestionable distinctiveness, no generation, even those living in this present time of unprecedented dissolution of tradition, creates its own beliefs, apparatus, patterns of conduct, and institutions. This is true of now living generations and of contemporary Western society as a whole. No matter how talented it is, how imaginative and inventive, how frivolous and antinomian on a large scale, it creates only a very small part of what it uses and of what constitutes it.

There is no reason to believe that the level and distribution of genetic endowment in any one generation are markedly different than they are in its predecessors; this should make for constancy in the capacity and disposition to displace things from the past. The size of the generation and the conjunctures of circumstances can make for change. Some generations do create more beautiful works and more new ideas than their predecessors; some make more scientific discoveries; some make more influential technological innovations. These generations which are more creative live in less dependence, happily and unhappily, on their inheritance from previous generations than do others. Yet there is not only continuity, there are many identities of great importance.

A larger number of geniuses and productive conjunctures of circumstances produce many novelties; catastrophes such as wars and famines destroy or change tangibly many once existent things and arrangements; carelessness, negligence, and deliberate destructiveness account for many failures of old things to survive long enough to reach the present. Nonetheless, the creative contributions, negligences, and depredations of any single generation still leave extant much that is recognizable, both of the good and the evil, in the inheritance which it has received from preceding generations.

Simultaneity of the Unsimultaneous

Karl Mannheim thought that the crisis of Western societies which he saw in the 1930s was a result of the fact that newly emergent ideas were incompatible with already established ones; the deeper conflict lay in the fact that "things of different ages" coexisted at the same time."[6] The coexistence of features of the past of Western society (the principle of laissez-faire in economic and social policy) and of its nascent future (social and economic planning) seemed to him to be the cause of the disorder. Mannheim implied that if a society were consistent in the application of a temporally homogeneous principle all would be well. William Ogburn's conception of "cultural lag" as the cause of the difficulties of modern Western societies was much like Mannheim's view that trouble is caused for a society when past and present things coexist. There is implied here the notion that ideas and patterns of simultaneous origin are consistent with each other; those which originated at different times are necessarily in conflict.

Apart from the curious view that an idea which was accepted in the past is bound to be wrong in contrast with an idea which has been promulgated more recently, and that the same relationship to goodness and badness obtains for institutions, Mannheim implied that there could be a society completely "up-to-date" in the sense that everything would be of equal age and of recent origin. Who would create that wholly contemporaneous culture and those wholly contemporaneous institutions? What kinds of human beings of great intelligence and imagination and without experience and without any contamination by past cultures would be required to create this pastless culture and to act in these pastless institutions? Mannheim would have been wiser had he not regarded the presence of the "uncontemporaneous in the midst of the contemporaneous" as an anomaly; he would have done better to have understood this as an inevitable feature of all societies. How could it be otherwise? Even if we accept that each generation modifies the beliefs and changes the patterns of action from those which have been presented to it by its predecessors, there is bound always to be a plurality of previously and still espoused beliefs and previously and still enacted patterns of action coexisting with and in particular patterns which are of more recent origin.

Even within the group of coevals which declares itself a "generation" and strikes out for its own ideals, those who espouse the "advanced" ideas are not uniformly advanced. They draw on and extend the beliefs which existed before them—perhaps the belief of earlier "young generations"—for their advanced ideas. But their "advanced" ideas are not applied equally over the whole range of their activities and beliefs. What looks, to those who have "joined" an avant-garde, like a wholly new program is never as comprehensively

6. "Die 'Ungleichzeitigkeit' des Gleichzeitigen." See *Mensch und Gesellschaft im Zeitalter des Umbaus* (Leiden: A. W. Sijthoff, 1935), pp. 14–16. He was applying an idea of Wilhelm Pinder, *Das Problem der Generation in der Kunstgeschichte Europas* (Berlin: Frankfurter Verlagsanstalt, 1928), pp. 1–16.

new as they imagine. Futurists who claimed to be revolutionaries in art and in everything else sometimes were or turned out to be patriots or radicals of a rather traditional sort.[7] Those who hate contemporary society and who declare that they wish to abolish it are often attached to the traditional society which they say they abhor[8] and their rebellion is often limited in range; it also does not last. Many who welcome revolutionary or other drastic innovation when they are young find virtues in the traditions of their societies when they become older.[9]

To espouse a relatively novel idea does not mean that all the ideas of the exponent of innovation break equally with the past. Newton's ideas as a physicist and mathematician did change the direction of thought about the cosmos but his biblical studies sustained older objects of attention and older attitudes towards them.

It might be argued that society might be better if all its ruling ideas were of equal age, although there is no reason whatsoever for accepting such an argument. It would in any case be a vain argument. Such a society could not exist even in the hands of a ruthless oligarchy which exterminated all who disagreed with its own ideas. It is simply not in the nature of societies to discard all parts of the past at a uniform rate.

Natural and Traditional Uniformities

Not all the identities which continue through generations are to be described as evidence of the presence of the past. Some of them are undoubtedly the results of the neurophysiological similarity of human beings over a very long period of time and of the fundamentally similar types of ecological situations in which human beings live. Sexual dispositions require activities which find enactment in families; the speechlessness and intellectual contentlessness of infancy result in the establishment of schools or their equivalents. The niggardliness of nature imposes economizing on the use of resources. But these biologically and ecologically imposed uniformities are very general; the uniformities imposed by tradition are more differentiated.

7. See Renato Poggioli, *The Theory of the Avant-Garde* (Cambridge: Harvard University Press, 1968), pp. 94–97.
8. See for example, Wyndham Lewis, *Blasting and Bombardiering*, new ed. (London: Calder and Boyars, 1967), pp. 46–49. The simultaneous attachment of Ferdinand Lassalle to revolution and to traditional high society is only one instance of many.
9. The history of the renegades from revolutionary and aesthetic radicalism is very populous. Between Wordsworth and John Dos Passos the space is very amply filled. Every European country in the age in which intellectuals have believed that their main obligation is to be scourges of their own societies has produced numerous instances of the movement from the passion for a new society to an affirmation of the old one, even in very extreme revivalist forms. I mention here at random Paul Ernst (cf. Robert Michels, "Eine syndikalistische-orientalische Strömung in der deutschen Arbeiterbewegung," in *Festschrift für Carl Grünberg* [Leipzig: C. L. Hirschfeld, 1932], pp. 343–64), Michels himself, N. Berdyaev, Sergius Bulgakov, and Georges Valois.

The traditions of belief and action arise from the fundamental necessities of human existence given the nature of the organism, the mind, and the cosmos. They are generated and maintained because human life in the cosmos raises problems to which the mind needs answers. All that human beings do is done within the limits imposed by their neurophysiological properties and ecological situations, but there is much room for variations within these limits. The variations are determinate; a particular variant, once established, becomes relatively uniform through time. The uniformities of conduct through time may be functions of constancy in authority, of constancy in the conditions to which individuals adapt themselves, of a constancy in their tastes and desires. Many of these constancies are direct results of tradition, others are the results of orientation to the gratification of interests. But the interests may be directed toward ends which are themselves traditional.

The Determinant Function of the Past

It has been common among historians to speak of given beliefs and patterns of action as a "populist tradition" or a "socialist tradition" or a "revolutionary tradition"; frequently they have not meant anything more than that over a stretch of time a number of individual writers have had similar beliefs about particular things such as the moral virtues of the poor or the iniquity of the institution of private property or the need for violent action in order to introduce significant improvement in societies. Sometimes the historians have spoken as if the ideas, once created and made visible, acquired devotees and proponents because the visible and available ideas imposed themselves by their persuasiveness; sometimes they deal with them as a series of solutions to problems which happened to be similar to each other because the situations to which they were oriented remained uniform over an extended period. Reference to a body of ideas as a tradition should mean more than the assertion that there has been a sequence of believers in approximately the same ideas and ideals.

This account of a tradition as a sequence of approximately uniform patterns of belief or action has its merits but it obscures the formative influence of the particular beliefs, as they existed at a given time, on whatever was thought subsequently about the objects to which the beliefs referred.

A person not hitherto a socialist becomes a socialist not primarily because he has thought it all out for himself but because, having certain inclinations of the mind, e.g., an aversion to poverty or a dislike of egoistic hedonism or of the power which is connected with the private ownership of property, his mind inclines or is disposed in the direction set by experience and sentiment, toward general beliefs acquired from tradition. If he had to think out entirely for himself his views about how to improve the economic order in Western societies, as they were in the last part of the nineteenth century, he might never have become a socialist or he might have become a very different sort of socialist from the one he actually became. But once launched in the direction of wishing to abolish or diminish poverty, private power and egoism, he was taken over by the ideas which others had thought before him and thus he came into their possession. Nothing melodramatic or mysterious is meant by this. All that is meant here is that when a disposition is formed and aroused—within the frame set by some preexisting and acquired perception and assessment of certain features of society or of nature—the person so disposed finds ready to hand a more differentiated picture and a more differentiated plan already in being. This picture and this plan are intellectual traditions. He becomes a possession as well as a possessor of the tradition. If he is very imaginative, curious, ratiocinative, and studious, he will modify the picture and plan to suit his own more idiosyncratic intellectual and moral powers. If he is weak intellectually, he will accept it as it stands, to the extent that he can assimilate it; he will add nothing to it, he might even simplify and impoverish the tradition of the idea or complex of ideas which he receives. As the situation to which the idea refers changes, the ideas might change too; the ideas change as their possessors attempt to improve them by making them more consistent, by taking into account ends other than, for example, the elimination of poverty, or by correcting the factual assumptions of the programmatic part of the idea.

At each of the successive points in time, the already existing, presented idea gives form—and substance—to the not yet formed inclinations of the new adherent; it gives form to the prior impulse which has potentialities for many forms. Some of these potentialities are foreclosed in the presence of the preexistent, presented idea; the precise road is laid out for those who are broadly inclined to move in a certain general direction.

At a moment in time, it would appear that the relationship between the available idea and the seeking, absorbent postulant is a brief process, which is no longer than the time taken to discover the already existent idea and to absorb it. This however is too simple; it hides the presence of the past in which the presented idea moved into the form in which it appears at the moment of presentation. The tradition—the thing presented—as it appears at the moment of presentation is a telescoped, foreshortened picture from which the history of its past career has been washed away. The naked eye can see it only as it is at the moment in the here and now; it does not see the layers of past experience and perception, and past reflection which shaped and reshaped it throughout its history. The picture at the moment is the precipitate or composite made up of many successive presentations and receptions and re-presentations over many points in time. The individual who acquires the idea takes his place in the sequence of those whose minds were taken into possession by what they saw before them.

The Restricted Autonomy of the Individual

The perception of other individuals is a confrontation with the past in the present. Sometimes we say that someone's views are "old-fashioned" or we say that so-and-so is a member of such and such a school of economics. In the former case, very explicitly, a time of origin is attached to the view of the "old-fashioned person"; his views are described as having been received from the past. In the latter, the views of the economist are subsumed under a tradition of economic thought which is not necessarily a recent creation. Even when the pastness of origin or the filiation to pastness is not so clearly designated, the attitudes and conduct which individuals exhibit can be temporally stratified. All the features of an individual exist, of course, in the here and now; but most of these features are the latest states of a tradition which has moved through various distances down from the past with varying degrees of modification.

Like a city which is made up of old and new buildings, so human beings perform patterns and hold beliefs some of which are old and some of which are newer. Just as it is reasonable to omit the age when describing the condition, size, and form of the buildings of a city, so it is reasonable to characterize an individual as he is at the moment. But the accounts in both cases are shallow if they omit the age of the buildings or the age of the constituent actions and beliefs of individuals.

Every human action and belief has a career behind it, it is the momentary end-state of a sequence of transmissions and modifications and their adaptation to current circumstances. Although everyone bears a great deal of past achievement in his belief and conduct, there are many persons who fail to see this.

It was a great achievement of moral and political philosophy to postulate the existence of a self-contained human being as a self-determining moral entity free from original sin and from the toils of a dark inheritance. The ideal was to expunge from human beings all that came from the past and hindered their complete self-regulation and expression. It was a great achievement of modern societies to try to assess human beings with regard to their own actions and dispositions and not as representatives of biological and social lineages. Much progress has been made in this regard. But it has its limits. There are undoubtedly many persons who regard their past as beginning only with their own birth. They believe that it lies within their powers to order entirely their own existence by their "own" decisions and those of their contemporaries. These are persons whose "organ" or sense of the past is wholly empty, and they are wrong as well.

Tradition as a Starting Point and Constituent of New Beliefs and Patterns of Action

The body of traditions prevailing in a differentiated society is a very heterogeneous thing. Responses to these traditions are selective. Even what appears to be a single coherent strand is subject to a selective response. The givenness of a tradition is more problematic than it looks. Every tradition, however broad or narrow, offers a possibility of a variety of responses. Every tradition, given though it is, opens potentialities for a diversity of responses.

The Selective Rejection of Tradition

Only traditions which have ceased to be possessions are viewed with indifference. Indifference to a confronted tradition is unlikely, if the presentation is widespread and if those who present it are in a position to compel attention to it, even if they cannot compel acceptance. Resistance through seeking out an antithetical or alternative tradition, is usually confined within the same family of traditions. The loosening of the grip of the Victorian moral tradition in the half-century after 1875 did not occur from the indifference of its audience or from a wholly fresh search for a gratifying way of life. The aesthetic and moral departure from the tradition of Victorian morality was aided by the easy availability of the tradition of romantic individualism. The tradition of Victorian morality as it grew in scope and adherence became too suffocating for a sensitive person to bear; it became insupportable. It appeared to be saturating life to such an extent that it would allow no room for sensitive, tender-spirited young persons— and older persons too—to give expression to what was stirring in them. Its breakdown was fostered by its own praise of ideals and its austere Protestantism, as well as by the alternative tradition of romanticism which came from the same family of tradition, the tradition of individualism.

A tradition usually is not at such a high point of saturation as Victorian morality seemed to be when it confronted its actual and prospective recipients. Nevertheless, coming as it does to the attention of the generation of expected recipients, a tradition has behind it a process of accumulation of refinements and authoritative arguments which do not exhaust its possibilities of diverse interpretation. At every point in time in the course of its growth, a tradition of belief or rules of conduct is an amalgam of persistent elements, and increments and innovations which have become part of it. It is that amalgam which is the given; the relative novelties in it are indistinguishable from those elements which have lasted longer. An external observer of sufficient discernment might retrospectively see it as unfinished and incomplete—and open therefore to extension and elaboration— but to the prospective or intended recipient it might look like a single thing. In fact, nothing called a tradition is a single thing; each of its elements is open to acceptance, modification, or rejection. The response to any tradition can be selective. Even those who believe that they are accepting or rejecting "the whole thing," do so selectively. Even when they are ostensibly rejecting it, they still hold on to a lot of it. The grip of the past is evident even in revolutions which claim to break away completely from the past of their own societies.

The Persistent in the Midst of Innovation

A tradition—a particular interpretation or a mode of interpreting a sacred text, a particular style of painting or a particular form of the novel—once established and authoritatively presented might become a fairly long-lasting possession. Nonetheless, in those categories of human activities which attract persons of strong intelligence and imagination, it is not likely to be held very long in the exact pattern in which it was received. Even a sacred text or a somewhat less sacred commentary, committed to memory and supported by a written version, cannot remain wholly intact. A ritual might remain wholly intact over generations, the tradition of an intellectual achievement is not likely to do so. It might be the intention of the recipient to adhere "strictly" to the stipulation of what he has received but "strictness" itself opens questions which are not already answered and which must be answered. If it is a moral or a legal code, or a philosophical system, the very attempt by a powerful mind to understand it better will entail the discernment of hitherto unseen problems which will require new formulations; these will entail varying degrees of modification. Attempts to make them applicable to particular cases will also enforce modifications. Such modifications of the received occur even when the tradition is regarded as sacrosanct and the innovator might in good conscience insist that he is adhering to the traditions as received. The traditions of literary works and forms are less sacrosanct, although there have been epochs when they approximated this status—the requirement of the three unities in the structure of a dramatic work—but there is an inherent rule in literary and artistic production which compels a minimal element of substantive novelty. A painting which reproduces another painting is "only a copy" and is a part of the history of commerce and manners but it is not part of the history of painting. It testifies to the power of tradition but it adds nothing to it. A novel which is an exact reproduction of another novel with the name of a different author is not even a copy; it is a plagiarism and as such belongs in the history of petty crime and madness and not in the history of literature. In literature, tradition to be fruitful and not fatal can only be a starting point for another work which, although similar in some respects in form and perhaps even in substance, must contain an element of significant novelty. (This should not however obscure the identical elements which are also significant.)

The desire to create something new, to discover something new, fostered by the conceptions of genuine, sound originality in the arts and literature and the obligation to discover something significantly new which is constitutive in scientific activity render it inevitable that tradition in these fields of activity must be treated as no more than a starting point. This statement leads only as far as a limited under-standing of the character of tradition but it must be reckoned with in dealing with the fortunes of tradition. Not all traditions are bedeviled by the imperative of originality, nor are all moral traditions so oppres-sive that they instigate rebellion. Even an agreeable tradition must be modified as a result of changes in the circumstances to which it refers or assumes. The conduct which a tradition imposes might become less feasible under changes in ecological conditions; what is feasible for a farmer might not be for an urban factory worker. A mode of conduct, in competition with other modes of conduct, might be forced to the wall by a change in the condition of the market. Individuals and in-stitutions have to act and believe differently from the ways in which they did previously. It is not always the free imagination which gener-ates a new pattern; it is often the "necessity" of adaptation. Certain traditions are bound to become something else from what they are even for those who persist in doing and believing in accordance with the patterns which were offered to them from among the possessions accumulated by those who went before them. For the former, tradi-tions are not only possessions but they are also points of departure for new actions and constituent elements in these new actions.

Differing Depths of Tradition within the Individual

The movement of a tradition through time might be like the endurance of a historical monument all of which was made at approximately the same time; or it might be like an old building, lived in and used and modified over the years, continuing to be similar to what it was and to be thought of as still being the same building. A sector of culture is more like the latter than it is like the former. Karl Mannheim, and before him, Wilhelm Pinder called attention to the important fact that, in any modern society, some persons (they thought of generations) accept beliefs and enact patterns which are older than the beliefs and patterns accepted by others. This heterogeneity in the ages of the beliefs and patterns of action characteristic of different sections of society is also characteristic of the beliefs and patterns of action of individuals as well.

Within any category of action or belief, an individual possesses a culture of which the constituent elements are of different ages. Some of his beliefs, especially those derived from scientific research, might be relatively new (a belief about how to reduce the probability of becoming arteriosclerotic) according to knowledge recently discovered. That same person might be a faithful member of the Church of England, praying according to the Prayer Book of 1662 and he might wear garments of a style which became widely adopted fifty years ago. He might be a painter in a style developed in the 1950s and wear garments of the bohemian style which began to be formed in the 1830s.

If we take a single sentence or paragraph written or spoken by a contemporary, the words have histories of durations of differing lengths and very few of them have been created in the writer's or speaker's own generation.[10] Practically none are created by the person who utters or writes the sentence or paragraph. The words came into their present meaning, sound, and spelling at various times in the past, and many of them are at least several centuries old. And beyond the specific form and meaning which they have at present, they usually have a long prior existence in an anterior language. Our political beliefs are little different; recently acquired beliefs might in fact have been long in existence before a particular individual was converted to them; others might have been thought of quite recently but before he came upon them. The policy of full employment combines humanitarian ideas of the eighteenth century about the horror of poverty, ideas about the right to paid employment developed by socialists in the nineteenth century, and Keynesian ideas developed in the 1920s and 1930s and monetarist ideas developed long before and since.

The Individual Constituted by Tradition

The Sense of the Past. At any moment, an individual human being is a given, not only to others but to himself as well. His character with all its contradictions has already been formed, his beliefs with all their ambiguities and uncertainties have been formed, his mental and physical capacities have been formed. His characteristics, beliefs, and capacities might be unsteady and they might undergo changes subsequently; they might furthermore be only dimly or erroneously perceived by the individual himself and by others. Nonetheless they

---

10. I cite a few examples of words taken from this sentence. The dates are those of the earliest usage given in the *Oxford English Dictionary*: sentence, 1447; paragraph, 1525; contemporary, 1631; duration, 1384; generation, 1340.

are what they are at the moment in question. They have been formed on the foundation of the individual's original genetic endowment and by a process of precipitation through experience and the reception of traditions in a given environment in which certain beliefs and practices prevailed. Whatever changes his character and beliefs might subsequently undergo in the future, his character and beliefs at any given moment are what he has acquired and formed previously. Some individuals are more labile than others, but, whether he is labile or rigid, any change is an annulment of some of the effects of the past. Stable, well-formed characters are not their own creation, however large the part of deliberate self-discipline in their conduct. Their stability is the unshaken dominion of the pattern acquired in the past.[11] Even unstable characters with ambivalent and obviously contradictory beliefs remain in the grip of some of the diverse traditions in which they have lived; it is not primarily the conflict of native impulses which disorders them. To disembarrass oneself of the precipitate of beliefs which one has acquired and developed is at least as difficult as to curb native impulses. For the most part, individuals accept in varying degrees what they have become, not always happily. If they succeed in changing themselves, escaping from what they have been and from the situation which helps to keep them that way, they acquire for themselves the results of pasts other than those previously present in them. They usually enter into an already charted territory with its own already established rules, demands, and exigencies. They acquire a past which was not theirs previously.

Individual human beings grow and change with biological and neural maturation and under the formative pressure of the conditions and traditions which are presented to them. Most of them float with little resistance in constantly shifting streams of events, and they change unwittingly in response to events which occur along the stream. The events are conditions which set tasks and offer opportunities; both of these are impregnated by tradition in different ways. The tasks are normative and cognitive expectations largely formed in tradition. The opportunities are in part resources, physical, social, and cultural, which are allocated by traditional criteria; they are also chances for exposure to traditions of particular kinds. In the course of their response to these demands and opportunities, individuals acquire tastes and skills which are new to them but which are not new to the culture which they have entered. Their religious beliefs and political attitudes change, which means that, in place of the traditions that provided their previous beliefs and attitudes, they submit to other traditions or retract the scope and content of their minds.

11. According to psychoanalysis, the "superego" is a pattern of rigid ideals, formed in the individual's early years.

The Past as a Component. Almost all human beings, although they change perceptibly, usually remain recognizable when seen over an interval of many years. Quite apart from physiognomic and bodily similarities, they are recognizable because their qualities of character and belief developed and acquired in the past are reiterated in the present in a pattern which closely resembles patterns of that past time. They might even change in character and temperament. For a person to change himself deliberately with the aid of psychoanalysis is extremely strenuous, indeed, very painful; and even where it is relatively successful in ridding the person of certain images of his own past and certain attachments to those images of it, he remains recognizable to himself and others, which means that he remains much as he was before. If he does succeed in getting rid of the patterns of conduct from his own past and the pasts from which they grew, he replaces them by a pattern of rational conduct in accordance with an ideal drawn usually from an ancient tradition.

Over long stretches of time, individuals exist in the substratum of their identifiable, continuously existing bodies, and they are aware of this. They do not see the changes in themselves except by an effort of memory, so that to themselves the essential identity of their present and their past is self-evident. They usually bear the same name. Many of their physiognomic features remain unrecognizably similar for other persons over long stretches of time; the other persons with whom they associate regard them as being the same as they were before and this renders it more difficult for each individual to escape from the sense of his identity with his own past states. Those who knew him in the past remember him as he was and they place what they see of him in the present into the pattern of his past actions and expressions. These remembrances telescope the individual known on diverse occasions in the past into a simultaneously existing entity in the present; they bring his pasts into his present.

The individual has a sense of himself as a continuously existing entity essentially more or less identical through time; fundamentally he sees himself as being what he was. He recalls particular events in which he was involved and he recalls these experiences as occurring in a sequence to himself. His self-image, his image of his own identity, which is variously visible to others in all his different manifestations, is not always in the forefront of the mind; the salience of the image fluctuates in his mind but the character, memories, and temperament of which it is a blurred record are operative more continuously. The sense and image of his own identity is not only a product of past events; it also contains within itself reference to the past. If a person thinks of himself—not just of his "interests," but of himself—he will frequently think of his sex, his age, his family, his ethnic, national, and religious connections, the places where he was brought up and educated, his profession or occupation. Most of these features are defined historically. If he thinks of his family, he thinks of his parents and perhaps of his grandparents, too; his ethnic connection is also ancestrally defined. If he is a Christian, certain historical events enter at once, above all the life of Jesus. If he thinks of a nationality, he thinks not only of its geographical location and shape but of its historical vicissitudes. If he is a "class conscious" worker, he thinks not only of present conflicts but of historically long-persisting conflicts of interest. If he is of an academic profession, he thinks of some of the great figures of those who established the field and who mark the hierarchy of merit by which he assesses himself.

What an individual regards as "the present time," as distinguished from the past, is, of course, not the immediately present time. That is only a moment which passes quickly. The "present time" always includes at least a little of the past; the boundary is extremely shadowy. As this century has advanced, the present seems to have been shortened so that it includes only a few years; at the end of the last century and earlier in this one, the individual's "present" seems to have included persons characterized in his mind by their involvement in events which occurred over a longer time in the course of his own life. Nevertheless, his past has not disappeared entirely from his image of himself.

Memory: The Record of the Past. Memory is the vessel which retains in the present the record of the experiences undergone in the past and of knowledge gained through the recorded and remembered experiences of others, living and dead. The individual's image of himself is constituted from what has been deposited in his memory from his own experiences of the conduct of others in relation to himself and the play of his imagination in the past. The stability of the individual's character, to an external observer and to himself, is possible only through the retention in memory of what he believed before, of what he experienced before. These things retained by memory are important parts of what he perceives himself to be. His sense of his own identity is partly a present perception of his past.

The individual as he perceives himself includes things which are not bounded by his own experiences; no more is his perception bounded by his own life-span. The image of the self reaches backwards beyond what is contained within the individual's own body at the moment of imagining, to incorporate, as part of its self-portrait and character, features of other persons in the past, of the same family, or the same sex, or the same age, or the same pigmentation or ethnic group, or the same locality, or the same religious belief or institutional connection.

Memory is furnished not only from the recollections of events which the individual has himself experienced but from the memories of others older than himself with whom he associates. From their accounts of their own experiences, which frequently antedate his own, and from written works at various removes, his image of his "larger self" is brought to include events which occurred both recently and earlier outside his own experiences. Thus, his knowledge of his past is furnished by the history of his family, of his neighborhood, of his city, of his religious community, of his ethnic group, of his nationality, of his country and of the wider culture into which he has been assimilated.

The view which treats the individual's past as only of genetic significance encounters, indeed, much resistance; the sense of the past will not suffer such restriction. Most human beings, even in modern society, have a craving which intermittently seeks to establish their prenatal past. It is a sensibility which is usually content with a very small measure of precision but it requires its objects in the past, however vague and fragmentary the perception of those objects is. Nor does the sense of the past rest content in larger societies with filling in the past by the construction of a biological lineage. It reaches more widely into the past—just as it reaches outward in the present—towards a definition of the self which includes occupation, class, religion, ethnicity, and nationality as terms in the construction of this past. The individual's image of his own occupation and that of his ancestors, of his class and religion and those of his ancestors, reaches him from his parents; even the image of his ethnicity and nationality comes to him first from his parents and from other persons to whom this was also conveyed as tradition. If he changes his occupation, there already is a tradition to govern his image of the new occupation.

A human being is self-conscious, sometimes even proud, of his larger past and not just his own individual past made up of his own activities within his own life-span. He is seldom indifferent in sentiment to all of his larger past; some of what appears as indifference might be the result of shame because of the status of his particular ancestors and his ancestral society.

The individual's experiences of his ancestors—his biological ancestors, and the ancestors who were earlier members of the collectivities and aggregates of which he has become a member—usually hold a less salient position in his memory than at least some of the immediate experiences of the individual's own lifetime. Nonetheless, a sensibility to past things and, more deeply, a category of pastness, is nurtured in the mind by all this unwritten and written history which is presented to the person growing into his society. The sense of the past is an organ of the mind. Knowledge of the past, deference to the past, attachment to the past, emulation of the past, hatred of the past, could not occur without such an organ of the mind which is open to receive them.

The organ in which the individual's sense of the past is formed, is, like sociability or rationality, an emergent category of human mental activity. Remembering and acquiring memories are the activities by which the sense of the past is gratified. The desire to know the past, to locate the present self in a setting of temporal depth, or to account for one's origin, is served by the memory of the individual, his elders, and by the historiographic discovery of what has been forgotten or never known. It is also served by imagination, which supplements or takes the place of memory when the latter fails. An individual can accept tradition although he has only a very feeble sense of the past.

Individuals vary in the force, clarity, and specificity of their sense of the past prior to their own births. The desire to know the past, to complement knowledge of the present by knowledge of the past is unequally distributed among human beings. In some individuals or parts or types of society it is very faint. Ancestors are very variously remembered especially in modern urban societies. Knowledge of the past heightens the sense of the past by evoking figures, objects, events, and beliefs of the past. Care to know the past is born of the sense of the past.

Living in the Past. Knowledge of and sensitivity to the past bring the image of the past into the present. They do not necessarily make it into a guide to action in the present. Images of the past are traditions but they are not the same as traditional ways of assessing present events or traditional ways of acting or traditional ends. They are traditions in two senses: they bring the past as an image into the present and they bring a past image of the past into the present. They make images of the past available as objects of present attachment, they increase the chance that the normative potentialities of past things will become effective. But they do not guarantee that they will aid the fulfillment of that normative potentiality. A society which is strewn with pieces of its own past does not necessarily love them. The scholarly study of the remote past may be assiduously cultivated in a society where most of the population knows little of that past and where even the scholars have no reverence or love for the past. Nonetheless, the past is not simply an object of factual knowledge or recollection, neither the individual's own past nor his ancestral past, nor the past of societies remote in time and place.

The possession of a sense of the past and the acquisition of knowledge about the past do not always arouse an appreciative attachment to those historically remoter elements of the self, no more than one's possession of an image of one's present self entails being happy about it. One might take one's Congregationalist or Jewish or Ukrainian past amiss and seek to undo it by changing one's religious affiliation and practice or by changing one's surname. Such a sense certainly does not often arouse the desire to revive that past as it was so that the present and future would be just like the past. An animated sense of the past does not require that. Sometimes these possessors of the image of their pasts vaunt them proudly and sometimes they have no strong feelings one way or the other; sometimes they reject them fiercely. The record of the past offers a potentiality for arousing attachment; it presents existent objects towards which attachments may be animated by particular events because those existent objects seem to be filiated to the past events recorded in that self-image. Thus a person who regards himself as a Jewish-American may be aroused by events in the Middle East, or an Irish-American by those in the Republic of Ireland, because they have a sense of their past in the Middle East and Ireland, although neither the Jew nor the Irishman might ever have been in the part of the region or country in which he believes his ancestors lived. Human beings can seldom wholly detach themselves in sentiment from present images of their past. If they become detached from their family or lineage, they become attached to their ethnic group or tribe or nationality or race or linguistic community and this entails regarding the past of these groups as their own. The image of the past is a reservoir of potential objects of attachment. The sense of the past finds its historically located object, it throws up boundaries defined by what a person believes his ancestors did, were, and believed. These boundaries formed by images of the past sometimes constrain his conduct.

This sensitivity to the past is very selective in its choice among past experiences and among the obligations to the present images of past individuals, actions, beliefs, and institutions, and it is very diverse in the forms which it takes. The obligations to be accepted are sometimes obligations of evocation, commemoration, and respect; sometimes they are obligations of imitation or emulation. There is probably a disposition very vague, very general and diffuse towards emulation which accompanies or arises from commemoration. The pattern of emulation which is conjured up is much more general than the particular past person, action, or event which is commemorated. It works osmotically and diffusely, if at all.

Attachment to the imagined past, to the past which has been installed in memory by books, buildings, statues and pictures entails a leap over the immediate past. Involving a break with the continuous tradition whch comes up to the threshold of the present, it establishes an attachment to a remoter past. Humanism in the Renaissance in Italy was such an effort to live in the past, neoclassicism in Germany was, medievalism in nineteenth-century France, pre-Raphaelitism, and the arts and crafts movement were such efforts. So was the play with the symbolism of the Roman Republic in France under the Jacobins. There were scattered traces of such desire to live in the past in Fascist Italy in which the symbolism of the Roman Empire was displayed.

This effort to reconstruct a past pattern of life and to "live in it," to use it as a model for a specific reconstruction of the immediate environment of present activities has very limited chances of success, if it has any at all. For one thing, very few persons ever love a past age so passionately that they wish to give up, even if they could, all that they might receive from their contemporary society. In addition to the difficulty of detachment from the pleasures and compulsions of the present world, they cannot completely divest themselves of the traditions which have imprinted themselves on their minds. They are what they are because they have been formed by the traditions they have received and by the contemporary circumstances to which they have responded. To live in an environment simulated from the past as a model and to do so as a person formed in the present is very different from living in a situation formed by the interaction of prevailing traditions and ineluctable exigencies and to do so as a person formed from those traditions and in those exigencies. "Living in the past" is at best a very selective and partial existence. For better or for worse, continuous traditions and contemporary exigencies leave a precipitate in the individual from which he can never wholly escape. This does not however gainsay that a past situation can be invoked as a criterion for passing judgment on the present. Nor does it gainsay that the image of the past can reach over the intervening time and draw from the remoter past a model in many spheres of life, as it has done a number of times in the history of art and recurrently in the history of philosophy and occasionally in the decorative arts. It certainly does not deny that the past can be loved and lovingly examined and yearned for.

The Sense of the Past and Historiography

The assimilation of beliefs and patterns of action and artifacts from the past is different from forming images of the past. Tradition offers to the present things created and set going in the past; these things include beliefs—scientific and scholarly knowledge, religious beliefs, conceptions of the right order of society, norms of conduct in private and public life. Images about the past of one's own society, of other societies, and of mankind as a whole are also traditions. At this point, tradition and historiography come very close to each other. The establishment and improvement of images of the past are the tasks of historiography. Thus historiography creates images for transmission as traditions. Critical or scientific historiography deals with received or traditional images of the past and attempts to criticize and improve them. Annalistic, moralistic, and scientific historiography have each had traditions which have been proper to them. The impulses of the human mind which have led to the creation and universal practice of historiography are at bottom akin to those which lead human beings to imagine their origins and prior development, to derive legitimacy from the pastness of things, to nurture the fame of past heroes and to "locate" models of conduct and of the organization of society in the past.

The sense of the past in itself has no content but it seeks a content in the recent and remote past. In Western antiquity the most esteemed historians dealt with the recent past. The sense of the past seeks that past in the history of lineage or ethnic group and nationality. It seeks that past beyond those boundaries in the records of a past civilization from which beliefs, patterns of institutions, and works have been inherited. Many *tradita* and the process of their transmission often have little temporal reference;[12] they only come from the past but they do not always speak about it. The *tradita* offered by historiography and the increments and corrections which it makes in them are explicitly temporal in their reference.

Scientific or Critical Historiography

Historiography is a way of establishing or revising an image of what happened in the past. Modern historiography has corrected the traditions which brought images of the past into the possession of present generations. It has done so by the development and use of techniques of studying sources contemporary with the events the sources describe or refer to. It has, through archaeology, epigraphy, numismatics, and written documents drawn on sources of information previously unused by historians.

Systematic or critical or scientific historiography critical of sources and searching out contradictions and imprecisions offers an account which purports to be true. It distinguishes itself from "tradition" in the sense of unverified historiography based on oral or written accounts which are not based on evidence which can be independently scrutinized by living historians. Modern critical historiography was not content with oral or written traditions, whether they were anonymous tales or the works of great historians like Thucydides and Herodotus which did not cite documents which other historians could

12. See Arnaldo Momigliano, "Time in Ancient Historiography," *Quarto Contributo alla Studi della Storia degli Studi classici e del antico* (Rome: Edizioni di Storia e Letteratura, 1969), pp. 13–41.

examine. It thought to establish the truth or falsity of the inherited historiographic accounts by the criticism of written texts and by juxtaposing them alongside other sources which bore on the same events.[13]

The study of Holy Scripture was for a long time only one extreme case of analysis of a tradition almost unsupported by independent evidence. The formulation of internal criteria sufficient to establish the authenticity of the text was the only way to answer the skeptic in the absence of independent documentary sources of any considerable amount of epigraphic and archaeological material.[14] The historical books of the Old Testament were paramount examples of such traditional historiography. They cite no documentary sources which were tested for their authenticity; dates and numbers are omitted or given in haphazard manner. Yet until the efflorescence of modern Middle Eastern and biblical archaeology, the historical books of the Old Testament were the only sources for the history of the Jews down to the Hellenistic age. Great feats of interpretation and correction were accomplished in disaggregating the various parts of the canonical historical books of the Old Testament. Similar problems were faced and dealt with in the construction and validation of the accounts of the beginnings of Christianity in the New Testament.

One outcome of these developments was a more accurate tradition, namely, the image of the patriarchal age, the sojourn in Egypt, the exodus from Egypt, the period of wandering, the conquest of Palestine and the time of the *gebirim,* charismatic warriors or judges, the unified kingdom, the two kingdoms, etc. Jews were presented with a new and more refined knowledge of their ancestors, ethnic and religious. Christians were provided with a more precise knowledge of one of the main traditions which has entered into the constitution of their religion and the civilization to which it contributed.

Closely related tasks were undertaken in the study of classical antiquity. Parallel to the historical texts of the Bible, there were great historians, Greek and Roman; there was also a rather large mass of literary works, orations, biographies, geographical works. A set of auxiliary disciplines became established to deal with the growing mass of inscriptions, coins, and archaeological disclosures. There was more freedom to reinterpret the traditional image than there was to reinterpret the Scriptures. Nonetheless, in both sacred and secular history the nineteenth century was a time of intense application of the techniques of critical historiography. The content of the tradition which represented the image of the world of biblical and classical

13. Arnaldo Momigliano, "Ancient History and the Antiquarian," *Contributo alla Storia degli Studi classici* (Rome: Edizioni di Storia e Letteratura, 1955), pp. 67–106.
    14. Ibid., p. 83.

antiquity changed as the methodological tradition of critical or scientific historiography became established.

The sixteenth and seventeenth centuries were the time of the great step forward of the methodological tradition of critical historiography. The collection and calendaring of manuscripts, the establishment of chronological tables, the critical analysis of the careers of the texts which had carried "the tradition," the work of the antiquarians in collecting, recording, and classifying coins, medals, and inscriptions and in describing monuments and other artifacts: these constituents of modern scholarly historiography became, for a long succession of generations of scholars, a supple, receptive tradition as authoritative as "the tradition" of the Hebrew and Greek Old Testament and the Gospels. The growth and differentiation of the new tradition took place in many branches of scholarship. It was propagated by interrelated initiatives, production of many works of classical studies, philology, the science of religion, ethnography, paleontology, legal history, and studies of the Middle Eastern empires; each new work was taken up in its own tradition, scrutinized, incorporated, or relegated so that tradition became enriched but also more specialized. As the traditions became more specialized, the less they had direct influence on the collective self-image. Intermittently, however, synthetic works reached beyond the circle of scholars, creating an image of the past which was much subtler and more differentiated. The newest advances have not had a shaking effect on the generally received image of the past. The transformation of the historiographic tradition in the course of the nineteenth century had changed the collective self-image of many educated individuals and then reached into the strata of the less educated. It changed the content of the sense of the past and insofar as fundamental normative and theological traditions were legitimated by traditions with temporal reference, they too were affected. For Christians, Jews, and former Christians and Jews, "the tradition" was supplanted by a more precise tradition, which acquired the authority of "the tradition" and which was acceptable in accordance with standards acknowledged to be "scientific."

The career of the biblical traditions, covering both the earlier "traditional" phase and its transformation into scientific historiography while retaining and refining much of the former, is one of the longest in history. There are chains of tradition which are as long or even longer.

The transformation of "the tradition" of the pre-Christian and early Christian ancestry of Western society was a result of the confluence of a number of historiographic traditions which originated in or flourished most in the West. One of these was the tradition of critical scientific historiography which, although most of its early work was on traditions fundamental and particular to Western civilizations, became a tradition in its own right, empowered to deal with all pasts.

Local historiography originated in the annals of the Greek city-states and in the work of Greek antiquarians. Adapted in Rome for writing national history and then receding after the fall of Rome, the tradition of national history began to awaken in modern times. Almost concurrently with some of the work on classical antiquity and on the Bible, modern scientific historiography—at least some parts of it—took the traditional beliefs about the national past as one of its major preoccupations. The study of monastic documents and charters of local governments was one section of the larger movement to put "antiquities" in order—to identify, classify, and record the materials necessary for the study of institutions.

Most of the world-cultures outside the West have been less ready to have their pasts subjected to the same critical scrutiny that has been allowed in the West as the precondition of interpretation. For example, India before the Moghul period did not produce historiographic works. The belief in the primacy of rational and empirical cognitive validity has not been accepted in these societies without historiography to the extent that they have been disposed to entrust the image of their past to professional scholars. In these other societies, the sense of the past has been allowed to be filled by sacred accounts edited into sacred texts, by hearsay, and by imagination uncontrolled by methodical scrutiny. Scientific historians in the West have succeeded in expunging images favored by political, religious, and other desires from their own accounts of the past.

The profusion of historiographic activity of the nineteenth century stimulated the promotion of historical teaching in lower and secondary schools. A considerable proportion of academic historical research was the work of professors who taught students who were in turn to become teachers of history, largely of their own national history and the history of their civilization; some of the students were to become archivists and paleographers who would look after the records of their own country and their own civilization. The study of history and the care of the records from which it was to be written seemed to some of its promoters in the nineteenth century to be required and justified by the belief that the national society would be legitimated and strengthened by the assimilation of knowledge of its own past by the oncoming generations.

National societies with increasingly popular sovereignty such as were being formed in Europe in the nineteenth century and the nationalities which had no sovereignty had an acute and urgent sense of the past. They believed that the legitimacy of their sovereignty or of their aspiration for sovereignty required the adduction of their collective past. Legislators, officials, teachers, and publicists believed that the national society could only be maintained or established as a society if its members looked upon each other as having come out of a common and meritorious past. National history was made into an important part of the syllabus in schools; legislators and civil servants were willing to spend public funds to train and employ teachers of national history and to support academic research in the field. It was accepted by parents as natural and reasonable that their children should learn "their own history." The promotion of a belief in continuity and identity with the national past, reverence for national heroes, the commemoration of great national events, above all, the commemoration of founding events such as revolutions and accessions to independence, were among the tasks laid on the teaching of national history.

Many of the great "national" historians of the nineteenth century in Europe and America were convinced that they were meeting the needs of their national societies to perceive and affirm the value of their own past while at the same time adhering strictly to the obligations imposed on them by the traditions of critical, scientific historiography which they desired to observe. They were not always successful in this dual undertaking.

The new techniques and methods which had been mainly applied to the study of the Bible and Western antiquity became detached from the particular subject matter in the study of which they had been formed. The techniques of critical historiography began to be used in the study of Asian, North African, and much later of Black African societies, by scholars outside those civilizations.

The historiographic construction of a picture of the past in order to confer on living generations a tradition of truthful accounts of their ancestry did not have the field to itself. The treatment of the Bible encountered many resistances from the proponents of "the tradition."[15] Nevertheless, critical scientific historiography won the day against the proponents of the traditional interpretation of the biblical tradition. The demands of critical scientific historiography on its practitioners were very severe and the sustenance received from the parallel and simultaneous devotion to science within the universities and in some parts of the lay public and government—as well as the faltering certainty of Protestant ecclesiasts in the governing bodies of certain churches—enabled the new scientific critical historiographic tradition to move forward. The Roman Catholic church was less easily persuaded; it was not amenable to the insistence that the traditions of critical scientific historiography required the modifications of its

15. See for example, John Sutherland Black and George Chrystal, *The Life of William Robertson Smith* (London: Adam and Charles Black, 1912), pp. 179–451; Geoffrey Faber, *Jowett: A Portrait with Background* (London: Faber and Faber, 1951), pp. 264–88.

tradition. The fate of Alfred Loisy was the result of just such a conflict between the proponents of "the tradition" and those who, while accepting much of it, wanted to correct and purify it by subjecting it to the techniques of scientific historiography.[16]

The stimulus which critical historiography received from the sense of nationality was not always unambiguous. The concern to establish nationality and the image of the national past came into conflict with the desire to make traditions truthful. Sometimes the desire to vindicate the tradition of nationality overpowered the concern for adherence to the tradition of critical historiography as a means of purifying tradition, of making it truthful. The tentacles of the tradition of nationality cannot always be pried loose by the discipline imposed by attachment to the tradition of critical historiography. The grip of the tradition of nationality is tightened by involvement in political conflict. Other kinds of political attachment have similar deformative effects, although sometimes they also help to focus attention on particular subject matters. To view history from the "standpoint" of a particular class is as damaging as viewing it from the "standpoint" of one's nationality or one's generation or one's village. The more elaborate the political belief and the more explicit its commitment to a particular view of history which has become traditional and indeed constitutive for its validity, the more resistant it has been to the tradition of critical historiography. There was a paradox in this. Scientific critical historiography owes some of its energy, support, and encouragement to the "historical state of mind" of modern political movements. Yet this "historical state of mind," a state of mind which regards the history of a collectivity as essential to its legitimacy, was not infrequently inimical to the practice of scientific critical historiography.

Despite these resistances to the work of critical historiography in the clearing of the thicket of tradition overgrown through hearsay, the historical view triumphed in the century which otherwise did so much to discredit the authority of so many other beliefs from the past. "The historian became king, all of culture heeded his decrees; history decided how the *Iliad* should be read; history decided what a nation was defining as its historical frontiers, its hereditary enemy, its traditional mission. . . . Under the joint influence of idealism and positivism, the idea of progress imposed itself as a fundamental category (Christianity was made 'out of date,' Christians were reduced to a timid minor-

16. See Alfred Loisy, *Mémoires pour servir a l'histoire réligieuse de notre temps* (Paris: Nourny, 1930–31); A. R. Vidler, *The Modernist Movement in the Roman Church* (London: Faber and Faber, 1934), and *A Variety of Catholic Modernists* (Cambridge: Cambridge University Press, 1970), pp. 69–139; and Michele Ranchetti, *The Catholic Modernists: A Study of the Religious Reform Movement, 1864–1907* (London: Oxford University Press, 1969), pp. 16–35.

ity . . . . Modern 'thought' became sovereign). At a stroke, the historian supplanted the philosopher as guide and counselor. Master of the secrets of the past, the historian, like a genealogist, provided for humanity the proof of its nobility and traced the triumphant march of its evolution. Only history was in a position to confer a foundation of plausibility for a utopia by showing it to be rooted in and, in a sense, already in process of growth in the past.''[17] Perhaps the authority of historiography was achieved at the expense of much else that was handed down from the past. Historiography became the arbiter of what was ''the permissible past.''

For this reason, the conflict between ''the tradition'' and the tradition being created through scientific historiography became generally less turbulent in the field of national history in Western countries. The chief custodians of the traditions of national history were historians; except in war time there was no dogmatic or restrictive promulgation of the national tradition as there had been of the ''old tradition'' in the Roman Catholic church. The historians did not arouse widespread apprehension when they set to work on the old traditions of national history. Their *bona fides* as patriots was generally accepted by the laity. The relationship was not quite so free of conflict in societies where nationalism was very intense. Even there, crises were relatively rare.[18]

In the newly sovereign states of Africa and in communist countries, critical scientific historiography has been under more severe pressure from the adherents of the political traditions dominant among many intellectuals and politicians. The African societies have no common tradition of works of culture or of a national history, but many of their founders and leaders have a sense of the past, and they wish that sense to be satisfied, to be filled with a tradition which bears witness to national culture worthy of respect in the eyes of the world. The historians of these societies, many of whom have been trained in the techniques of scientific historiography, are sometimes under strain when they think that they should supply to their fellow countrymen an image of a heroic and creative national past. The desire to confirm a tradition attesting to long national existence and to notable achievements, and the simultaneous desire to be faithful to the traditions of scientific historiography, sometimes contradict each other. The conflict is to some extent resolved by the

17. Henri-Irenée Marrou, *De la Connaissance historique,* 6th ed. (Paris: Éditions du Seuil, 1954), p. 11.
18. One of these cases of conflict was that in which Thomas Garrigue Masaryk became embroiled when he showed the spurious nature of manuscripts alleged to demonstrate that Czech was one of the first European languages to develop ballads like *Beowulf* and the *Chanson de Roland.* See R. W. Seton-Watson, *A History of Czechs and Slovaks* (London: Hutchinson, 1943), p. 246.

choice of particular topics which can be treated in a scholarly way and which at the same time present a gratifying image of events which occurred in the territory now falling within the national state.[19]

The conflict between critical scientific historiography and the eagerness to confirm a newly established tradition by making it appear old, and thereby legitimating the new national state, is resolved in favor of the latter through the allegation of a fictitious "golden age," a time of plentitude and glory before the coming of the foreign conqueror.[20]

In such situations, the sense of the past is successful in resisting the discipline of critical scientific history; it shapes its content so as to fortify the present order by showing it to be the inheritor and continuation of a legitimating past which had been buried by the misfortunes and corruptions of intervening time. This spurious historiographic recovery of the "golden age" enhances the self-respect of the bearers of this old "tradition" of indigenous achievement in the face of the tempting exogenous traditions. It generates a new "tradition" which, put forward as the "genuine" or the "old" tradition, is to be the vehicle to bring that "genuine" past into life in the present.

19. This is especially so in the treatment of anticolonial rebellions. See the discussion between Donald Denoon and Adam Kuper, "Nationalist Historians in Search of a Nation. The 'New Historiography' in Dar es Salaam," *African Affairs* 69, no. 22 (October 1970): 329–49. See also Vinayak Damodar Sarvarkar, *The Indian War of Independence, 1857* (Bombay: Phoenix Publications, 1947).

20. See Jawaharlal Nehru, *An Autobiography with Musings on Recent Events* (London: John Lane, Bodley Head, 1936), pp. 426–32, and Swami Vivekananda, *The Complete Works* (Calcutta: Advaita Ashrama, 1964–70), 3:105, 275, 285; 7:331, 356–58.

2   The Endurance of Past Objects

The Presence of the Past in Artifacts

Physical Survival

Material objects have a self-maintaining power which is inherent in their material nature. Once they have been created, they can exist as long as human beings leave them alone to move towards their own natural fate; they disintegrate from internal decay and the strain of usage, erosion, and catastrophe. Human beings affect the natural course of the life-span of objects by deliberately destroying them, by using them, and by deliberately protecting, reinforcing, preserving, and restoring them.

The inherent durability of material objects of stone, metal, and wood, and the durability of the physical landscape enables the past to live into the present. The costliness of the scarce skill and materials which have been invested in the making of material objects counsels generally against their deliberate destruction. It is often economically advantageous to maintain older buildings. However wealthy a society and however wasteful it is of its resources, it does not regard itself as able to afford, in every generation, to demolish buildings surviving from the past and to replace them by those of greater convenience and of greater conformity with contemporary taste. The most energetic policies in the modernization of the stock of buildings in a contemporary metropolis still leaves in being a large number which were built before the lifetime of the persons who live or work in them. Buildings have usually been built to last; intentionally "temporary" buildings are exceptional. Palaces, the seats of governments and parliaments, churches and temples, buildings for commerce and for public administration, academic buildings, museums, theaters and buildings for musical performances built long before the birth of those now living, mark the cities of the earth. The fame of a city depends on having such buildings.

Many residential buildings of more than one hundred years of age still exist although architectural tastes have changed, standards of amenity and convenience have changed, and the pressure for more concentrated use of space has increased. Nonetheless many older residential buildings survive, frequently with modifications, because their occupants are willing to pay the cost of maintaining and "modernizing" them. Others have survived because their occupants could not or would not pay the price demanded for more recent buildings. Sometimes the cost of "modernizing" buildings is so great that it is more economical to destroy them and to replace them by new buildings more suitable to contemporary taste and usage. Sometimes their maintenance is too costly to justify the expenditure. In countries in which the ownership of buildings is in private hands, the consideration of profit from neglect or demolition and then replacement makes old buildings vulnerable. In socialist countries, enthusiasm for novelty, hygienic social ideals and the desire to build visible monuments to the efficacy and benevolence of government lead to the destruction of old buildings. Considerations of familial piety and local and national pride in past achievements sometimes give motives for their maintenance and renewal. By and large, old buildings are always in danger from within themselves and from their users and proprietors.

Nevertheless, no urban community in the world has been rebuilt totally within a single lifetime with all its old buildings being deliberately demolished for replacement by a wholly new supply of buildings. There are instances of cities built from the beginning, such as Brasilia, Washington, D.C., New Delhi, Chandigarh, and the "new town" of Edinburgh, in places where there were previously no urban settlements of any significance, but they are rather rare. There are also some instances of cities being nearly entirely destroyed by a natural catastrophe or military action, and then being built anew where the ruins once stood. None of these is normal. As cities grow, new buildings are added where none stood before. Once built, they remain for a long time until the prospects of greater profitability from their demolition and replacement, or until inconvenience which is unacceptable and too costly to overcome, provide incentives to their destruction or allow their dilapidation by vandals or neglect.

Buildings do not take care of themselves. As they age, they become more fragile and their fabric and structure require increasingly expensive care. Sometimes they cannot be adapted to new uses and new standards of amenity except at a high cost. This sometimes encourages their deliberate destruction or negligent renovation. Nonetheless, many survive these dangers.

When buildings pass a century in age, they begin to attract protectors who attempt to defend them against demolition. This has become especially common in the middle of the twentieth century, after so many old buildings have been destroyed, having been allowed to deteriorate to the point of uninhabitability or having ceased to be as profitable to their owners as their replacement would be or having otherwise become obstacles to progress. Churches, academic buildings, seats of government, and the residences or birthplaces of famous persons are especially resistant to destruction not because they are made of harder stone or because they have been more skillfully built, but because they have become objects of piety and remain usable for their distinctive purpose.

The topography and spatial pattern of cities endure for even longer periods than most of the buildings in them. One reason is that certain old buildings, surviving because they are cared for, define the main topographic pattern. Some quarters change in the character of their occupants and in the tasks they perform in the division of functions in urban life. Features of the natural landscape like seashores and rivers are very difficult to change and the patterns of streets are likewise difficult to change because that involves the demolition of many buildings and the construction of new ones and all this is too costly. Hence despite the widening and straightening of certain main thoroughfares, the street pattern of a city, once set, remains as it was. Paris was profoundly affected by Baron Haussmann's reconstruction, but a great deal of the present network of the streets of Paris antedates his long boulevards.[1] Even the most easily visible parts of Paris are only in part the product of his visionary energy. The gardens of the Tuileries, the Place des Vosges, the Pont Neuf, the Pont Royal, are accomplishments of earlier centuries. The street patterns of those areas of London or New York which existed a century and a half ago, and even of the relatively recently obliterated and rebuilt Warsaw, are mainly what they were. The replacement of buildings seldom modifies markedly the pattern of settlement—particularly not the location of streets. New commercial buildings, monumental public buildings, and great boulevards are constantly under construction, but the back streets in which most of the inhabitants live retain an extraordinary resemblance to what they were many years earlier. Even in a city like Chicago, which had been to some extent cleared by a great fire and which has had a very large program of urban renewal since the Second World War, many changes in the character of the occupants of many areas, and a large amount of dilapidation by vandalism and neglect, is still mainly made up of buildings erected well before the First World War. Those areas of Manchester, Liverpool, Philadelphia, Boston, Baltimore, and Amsterdam which were settled before 1900 still retain many buildings erected before the beginning of the century. Six-lane motor highways and "flyovers" cut wide swaths through some of them; what they do not destroy remains as it was. The fabric of old streets and roads changes, being worn out through use and then re-

1. Henry Bidou, *Paris* (London: Jonathan Cape, 1939), pp. 395 ff.

newed; the width of the roadway might be extended and various meanderings straightened but the pattern remains largely as it was.

The old pattern persists in the face of new machinery for the removal of earth which produces innovations in the landscape. Striking, often horrible, innovations are often confined to the facade; behind it, much remains as it was. Behind the thin mask of national hamburger stands, "beauty parlors," and enterprises for the sale of used automobiles, the main streets of small towns in New England and the Middle West of the United States are often the same as they were; behind the main streets, the houses of a century ago stand intact and are still well cared for. Any great highway or flyover in Western Germany or Great Britain shows exactly the same juxtaposition of a promethean feat of drastically working the human will on nature alongside of the undramatic persistence of the accomplishments of earlier centuries. Patterns of land settlement and cultivation remain for very long periods.

Patterns of settlement are unlike buildings and roads. They have seldom been designed and they are generally not maintained in the sense of being intentionally maintained in their prior form. There are exceptions. The provision of opportunities for industrial employment, such as now practiced by governments in areas in which the supply of such opportunity has declined with the decline in the industry which previously gave employment, has as its by-product, if successful, the deliberate maintenance of a pattern of settlement. There are occasionally "settlement policies" which offer incentives to settlement in particular areas or which coercively transport whole populations to a hitherto unsettled area. There are also negative settlement policies which attempt to discourage or prohibit movement, particularly from countryside to large towns, or which forcibly deport populations from previously settled areas. These are, however, of marginal significance in the determination of the enduring pattern of settlement in most societies. The patterns of settlement continue to exist because they are given. In that sense they are traditions, in which interests are vested by those who live in these patterns and believe that they benefit from their continued existence.

Like other traditions, patterns of settlement are composites of many individual acts of tradition. Like other traditions they are subject to modification and drastic change. Sometimes within a few decades some areas become much more densely settled through immigration; other areas become relatively depopulated by emigration. The movements which break the old tradition of settlement themselves become traditional. Emigrants from Poland went to the United States and to France. The tradition was precipitated and sustained by the continuing possibility of remunerative employment but it acquired an independent determinative power.

The persistence of a pattern of settlement or migration is attributable to the convenience of those who have adapted themselves to it with some satisfaction or profit to themselves. The profitability of certain nodal points in the pattern, e.g., the availability of fertile soil, the availability of relatively well-paid employment, proximity to the sources of raw materials of manufacture, proximity to relatively inexpensive lines of transportation, proximity to a market for the goods which are locally produced, or military defensibility—all these confer advantages which, as long as the advantages flow from them, maintain the pattern as it was in the past.

Once a pattern of settlement has been laid down, additional traditions come to be formed around it. Towns and districts in towns acquire distinctive "characters" which are transmitted to ensuing generations and which set limits and ends for rational decisions. Many who live and work in a particular place want to go on doing so, because they are attached to the place, because they obtain benefits from it, and because departing from it is not an attractive path of action for them. One very important determinant of the persistence of a pattern is, in short, the fact that it is already in existence. It is a given to which each oncoming generation adapts itself; adaptations produce small changes in what was given. These in turn become the givens for ensuing generations. Although land previously uncultivated is brought under cultivation, new types of crops are grown, and old ones are discontinued because they cannot compete in price with similar crops grown elsewhere, some traces of the patterns of cultivation of the soil endure.

Buildings, insofar as they survive, do so only if they are maintained and protected. The same is true of roads, parks, and gardens and every other physical structure or arrangement deliberately made by man; they must all be maintained and repaired if they are to survive. Churches, public buildings, homes of famous men, must not only be maintained; they must also be protected from vandals who wish to desecrate sacred things, from scavengers who would use their materials for profit, and from "souvenir-hunters" who wish to have a fragment of a sacred object in their possession as a talisman. Constructions and landscapes persist only when they are deliberately maintained and protected.

The persistence of all of these stocks of settled spaces and buildings is partially the outcome of having been already in existence. Being there is an "argument"—unspoken—for not doing anything to change the already existent, unless considerations of convenience and profitability become very acute and the costs of retention and maintenance become too heavy. The lives of so many persons become organized around these inherited physical objects and arrangements that it is difficult in the extreme for large changes, even when the inheritors are able to imagine themselves making deliberate decisions which will prevail over the resistance of "vested interests." There are "interests" not just of profitability but of attachment, convenience, and desired opportunity as well. So many persons have adapted themselves to the given circumstances of the landscape and the stock of buildings and have somehow made for themselves a bearable and even satisfactory mode of life that newcomers or other persons who do not like the larger pattern can do little about it. They can withdraw together, or they can try to bring about a limited change, or they can reconcile themselves to the existent. Already settled persons whose tastes change pronouncedly have the same alternatives.

Rulers, proprietors or administrators who have the coercive powers of the law to enforce their decisions can, of course, break these traditional patterns of attachment, convenience, and profit. The "enclosures" in Great Britain showed the possibility of breaking traditional patterns of settlement and use; so, on a much more drastic scale and far more brutally, did the collectivization of agricultural production in the Soviet Union. Both of them also showed the consequences of the drastic disruption of traditional patterns—violence and demoralization in Great Britain, resentful inefficiency in the Soviet Union.

Thus, the actual physical environment and its patterns of use, insofar as they are creations of human effort, persist as traditions handed down in multitudinous acts of transmission; they are both accepted and modified by numerous accretions and replacements, like any other traditions. They change in response to new opportunities and new desires but they also shape and limit the opportunities and desires. They can be broken by coercion but at great cost, in the short and in the long run.

Veneration: Old Buildings

The persistence of certain features in patterns of settlement and of landscape, or of certain buildings, is enhanced if these things are objects of veneration. Veneration has nothing to do with utility; it is reverence towards age as such. Having come down to the present from a relatively remote past, these things are accorded special appreciation.

A large proportion of the buildings surviving for three or more centuries in most civilizations are buildings which were used for religious worship or for imperial and royal residence, or were otherwise connected with divine things or with earthly power and majesty. They are also very often objects of aesthetic appreciation, much art having been lavished on their construction. They were usually built with the intention that they should be beautiful and that they should last for a long time past the life-span of ordinary residential and industrial or agricultural buildings. They easily arouse attitudes of appreciation, which have also been inherited along with the buildings.

The protection of old buildings and historical monuments has become a significant private and governmental activity since the nineteenth century. Partly it appeared in connection with the heightened sense of nationality and from the legitimacy which the sense of nationality claims on grounds of antiquity; the demand for the preservation of old buildings is frequently justified by the assertion that they are part of the "national inheritance." The movement for the protection of the old buildings has also gone hand in hand with the demolition and despoilment of old buildings. The movement began in Western Europe and was extended by Western rulers to their imperial possessions in India and Indochina early in the twentieth century. It came to the United States much later; the government trailed considerably behind private individuals and associations which concerned themselves with "national shrines" and the "national heritage." The re-creation of old towns which were not famous for great events—Williamsburg in the United States, and the reclamation and refurbishing of old quarters of large cities which likewise were not famous for great events or persons—is another expression of this veneration for aged artifacts, for things inherited from the past.

The veneration of the old turns the reception of a physical thing into an appreciative tradition; the *traditum* is not just received, it is also appreciated for its association with the past. Association with past greatness is added to the appreciation of pastness as such. Pastness even generates greatness. The attribute of pastness makes the thing of the past worthy of preservation, of becoming a tradition to be maintained and passed on. Both the object itself and the belief about it become traditions.

Veneration: Ruins

Physical artifacts also survive in ruined form. Ruins of neglected and despoiled buildings survived in the Middle Ages and in early modern times primarily for a negative reason; they were simply neglected. They were sometimes used for purposes of shelter by persons of a social level much below those by whom the building was originally intended to be used; they were also used as sources of building stone. Both these uses ruined them even further. The admiration of ruins began in the seventeenth and flourished in the eighteenth and nineteenth centuries. They came to be objects of the tradition of appreciation of ancient things; they were valued because they were evocative of the past; they were late entrants into the traditional gallery of ancient things admired by humanists, books, manuscripts, and works of art having preceded them by several centuries. Antiquarians valued them because they were part of the national past which they were trying to discover and record. They were also the occasion for melancholy reflections on the transience of past happiness, on the superiority of the vanished past to the shoddy present.[2] They were a double challenge to the idea of progress; they showed the vanity of aspirations for permanence and the greatness of the accomplishments of the ancients, whose glory was eternal but whose physical works were transient.

Even ruins have to be maintained, if they are not to sink further into ruination and despoilment. As a result of the increased interest in the "national heritage" and the increased activity of thieves, they came increasingly in the course of the nineteenth century under the care of governmental departments of antiquities or of monuments and historic buildings. Previously they had been the concern of connoisseurs and dilettantes who, like Lord Thomas Bruce, seventh earl of Elgin, sometimes despoiled them for their own collections. The protection given to old buildings and monuments was also given to ruins. The theft of and commerce in fragments from ruins was quite different from the original despoilment which ruined old buildings in order to obtain already cut stones for new buildings. The sale of stolen fragments from ruins and archaeological excavations, like the solicitude to protect them, depended on the tradition of veneration towards ancient buildings. The undertaking to protect ruins as well as old buildings and monuments was an expression of the same attitude which had prompted the collection of old manuscripts and was one that even governments committed largely to the promotion of progress shared.

There is no practical use for ruins, except perhaps for the outlaws who hide in them, as did those sinister figures in some of the engravings of Piranesi. There are no economic arguments for retaining them as physical structures such as might be made for the retention of an old building which can be used for current residence. The tourists who come to see them do bring economic advantages to the country which possesses them but this is a consequence of the willingness of the tourists to spend their money for the experience of being in contact with old things. It is not only the beauty of the remains of Herculaneum and Pompei which draws visitors, it is also their antiquity. To be in contact with something old is in some ways like being in contact with sacred things like the Church of the Holy Sepulchre and the Stations of the Cross which are sacred in themselves; these also have the sacral character of ancient things. The ruins are maintained

---

2. See E. Panofsky, "Et in Arcadia Ego," in Raymond Klibansky and H. J. Paton, eds., *History and Philosophy: Essays Presented to Ernst Cassirer* (Oxford: Clarendon Press, 1936), pp. 223–54, esp. pp. 245 ff.

and protected only, and ravaged mainly, because they are survivals from a remote and ambiguously significant past.[3]

Veneration: Antiques

Old furniture and old table silver are like old buildings; they are used and they are appreciated for their utility, their beauty, and their age. Old furniture, like old buildings, deteriorates under the friction of use and decay. Those pieces which survive do so because they are carefully maintained. Wood and metal, like stone, yield to physical friction and moisture; they have inherent weaknesses. What survives is only a very small fraction of what was created. Some of it finds its way into museums where it ceases to be used at all; other pieces of antique furniture or of old silver lead a life half-way between domestic use and exhibition in a museum. Like privately owned works of painting and sculpture, they live in privately inhabited museums. Their utility provides part of the reason for their acquisition and maintenance, but since the same functions could be performed more economically and equally efficiently by recently made furniture and stainless steel cutlery, the veneration and aesthetic grounds for their acquisition are quite evident.

To be cared for and to be made into a *traditum* depends on becoming an object of a tradition of beliefs about the value of old and beautiful things, which partake in sacredness by virtue of their twofold extraordinariness.

The collection of old objects was apparently not a feature of artistic collections in Western antiquity or in the Middle Ages. It is an activity which became established in the Renaissance and amplified in the seventeenth, eighteenth, and nineteenth centuries in Europe and then in the United States. An interesting variant of this high evaluation of old things may be seen in the United States in recent years, where the appreciation of old things has spread from beautiful, old European and early American furniture, glass, and silver to hitherto disregarded, ugly, and crudely made old things. It is not that the farmhouse furniture and kitchen equipment of seventy-five years ago were previously unknown. They were known and had been discarded. Their entry into commerce was not directly into the "antique trade"; they first came in as "junk." Then, in a relatively short time, still ugly and in many cases still useless, they rose in status. An attitude of deference towards artifacts of the American past became more widely diffused among persons who had hitherto shared in a very anti-traditional tradition of chromium-plated furniture, and artificial fur upholstery. The artifacts of nineteenth-century Gothic America were reclaimed from the attic for the gratification of persons otherwise unsympathetic with tradition. Attachment to things which come from

3. See Rose Macaulay, *The Pleasure of Ruins* (New York: Walker, 1966),

the past becomes concentrated on small artifacts which have only their age to recommend them for appreciation.

Monuments

Monuments are like ruins in that their survival is wholly independent of utility and is fairly often independent of aesthetic value. Unlike palaces, great houses, temples, and cathedrals which are still used for administration, residence, and worship, or as museums, monuments were never intended for use. There is no use to which a triumphal arch, a column, an obelisk, or a statue can be put. Unlike all these other classes of artifacts, monuments were designed from the beginning to cause subsequent generations to remember the past. They were designed to commemorate; to make succeeding generations remember. They were intended to be traditions to future generations. Statuary and decorative constructions without practical utility, they almost always bear dates which are to make their audiences aware of their position in the past. The desire of those who erect them is in general respectfully complied with; they do become traditions in their own right, but the persons and events they were intended to celebrate lose their specificity for everyone except antiquarians and historians.

The survival of monuments is not an inherent property of their physical composition. Like buildings and furniture, they do not survive simply because they are made of durable material substances. They, too, require preservation and protection. They are, at least many of them are, in fact, preserved, and the landscape around them is adapted to acknowledge their monumental quality.

They are sometimes removed to other locations when the inconvenience which they cause to later generations becomes too great to be borne; this was the fate of Temple Bar, which separated the City of Westminster from the City of London and which was removed to ease the movement of traffic in the Strand. In formerly colonial countries such as India, eager to obliterate the memory of a past which has made Indians what they are but which they now wish to deny in favor of an indigenous past which they had neglected and which they now wish to establish for the collective self-esteem, statues of famous colonial soldiers, administrators, and sovereigns have been removed from the prominence which they formerly enjoyed and have been stored elsewhere.[4] (They are usually not deliberately destroyed except by zealots.)[5]

---

pp. 40 ff.; G. W. Bowersock, "The Rediscovery of Herculaneum and Pompeii," *The American Scholar* 47, no. 4 (Autumn 1978): 461–80.

4. See the charming story of R. K. Narayan, about the disposal of the statue of a servant of the Raj in Malgudi, "Lawley Road," in *Lawley Road: Thirty-Two Short Stories* (Mysore: Indian Thought Publications, 1956), pp. 1–7.

5. Such was the fate of "The Column" at the end of Sackville, now O'Con-

The construction of monuments to an actual or near contemporary is an effort to generate a tradition to the future. It is like the "perpetual" prayers for the soul of a dead person who left an endowment for them when he was alive. The desire for a posthumous reputation or glory is a variant of the desire for fame;[6] it is a desire which will continue to exist in the future. Much of fame is backward-looking. Not all monuments are successful in acquiring fame for their objects; they are nonetheless preserved because they come from the past.

Coins and Medals

Coins were once valued mainly for the wealth they embodied in the precious substance of which they were made. They have generally ceased to embody wealth and are intended nowadays merely as a convenience in the flow of commerce. They were intended to be of indefinite duration and they were often endowed therefore with the property of a monument. They bore the likeness of a sovereign or some other great personage who was thereby launched into the future so that his name would not be forgotten.

In their extraeconomic functions, coins have not been exclusively designed to give lasting commemoration only to living rulers. Coins—and now paper notes—frequently are impressed with the likeness of rulers, of great personages of the national past, or emblematic figures of the existence of the national state. In some states, they bear the likeness of a living ruler, perhaps as in Africa, because there is no commonly shared national hero who can be as effective as the living rulers in carrying into the future the traditions still to be formed which will, so the rulers hope, attach citizens to the state and society.

Medals had only commemorative intentions. They were intended to celebrate persons and events and to place them in the historical memory of future generations. Sometimes they celebrated the founding event and sought to give its symbolic representation a permanent place in the image of the past. They also celebrated anniversaries of great events, aiming to reanimate the memory of the past events in the minds of the small number of persons who came into contact with the medals.

Medals were like monuments hidden in private gardens; they gave evidence of tradition and of the desire to become part of tradition rather than of actual success in the attainment of the end. Ironically,

---

nell, Street in Dublin. British statues in India were often damaged or defaced. Nkrumah's statue in Accra and many of Stalin's monuments to himself were demolished or removed.

6. See Edgar Zilsel, *Die Entstehung des Geniebegriffes: Ein Beitrag zur Ideengeschichte der Antike und des Frühkapitalismus* (Tübingen: J. C. B. Mohr [Paul Siebeck], 1926), pp. 62–70, 159–211.

success was attained when the study of medals became an auxiliary discipline of historiography.

Medals were in a relatively favored position for survival. They had no practical use and did not therefore undergo the wear and tear to which coins were subjected. They were not clipped and deformed in the ways in which coins were and so they could tell their message to future generations with some precision. Medals also had the advantage of being in the possession of the upper classes, and were therefore better cared for and preserved for transmission to future generations. On the other side, there were very many more coins, and they carried a much greater variety of information about the past into subsequent ages. Coins, like medals, spoke to these subsequent generations through the mediation of historians.

Artistic Works

The modern world which has in many respects so resolutely set itself against traditional beliefs and traditional patterns of conduct has devoted relatively large resources to the assembly, protection, and exhibition of old works of art and old books in manuscript and printed form. What remains of the physical stock of ancient, medieval, and early modern artistic and intellectual achievement has been well looked-after in the past two centuries. From having been the property of individual rulers and wealthy private persons, great ecclesiastical dignitaries, churches and monasteries, these stocks have moved increasingly into public or quasi-public possession so that private foundations, municipalities, and central governments accept—where they do not arrogate—the legal responsibility for their possession and care. Where governments have not taken them as booty in wars (more characteristic of the conduct of rulers up to Napoleon)[7] or seized them in the course of revolutions, they have forced them out of private hands through taxation and death duties. Thus, short of natural catastrophes, war, theft, incompetent administration, and vandalism, the physical stock of the artistic and intellectual achievements of past ages has, after many grievous vicissitudes, found a secure resting place—as secure as anything can be in this vale of tears, vandals, and thieves.

This solicitous—sometimes capricious—custodianship has come late upon the scene. The sculptures and mosaics of antiquity have survived in much better condition and in larger quantity than paintings

---

7. See Hugh Trevor-Roper, *The Plunder of the Arts in the Seventeenth Century* (London: Thames and Hudson, 1970), and Cecil Gould, *Trophy of Conquest: The Musée Napoleon and the Creation of the Louvre* (London: Faber and Faber, 1965), pp. 30–102.

have. The sculptures of antiquity were made of more durable materials than paintings. Nonetheless most of the surviving pieces arc fragments. The sculptures of the Middle Ages, made for the adornment of ecclesiastical buildings, seem to have survived much better in countries which remained Roman Catholic after the Reformation, not only because these sculptures were created more recently than the sculptures of antiquity but also because the buildings to which they were attached or in which they were kept were sacred buildings and the sculptures also frequently portrayed sacred persons.

The history of works of art is a history of the unceasing warfare of nature, the military, thieves, and fanatics against them and of the unending defensive struggle, increasingly sophisticated in its aims and procedures, to undo the damage done and to avert future injury. The storage of sculpture and paintings inside buildings, unattached to their structures except for suspension on their walls, under the care of assiduous curators or collectors has been the most favorable arrangement for their survival. This presupposes of course that there are persons who care for them sufficiently to devote themselves to them in person or through their patronage and administration.

Without the humanistic outlook and the antiquarianism which went hand in hand with it the vestiges of classical art would never have been sought out, collected, and protected. The appreciation of the exemplary beauty of classical art did not find a fully articulate expression until Winckelmann's writings, but the collection of ancient works of art began more or less concurrently with the humanistic study of ancient literary and philosophical works and the efforts to discover the manuscripts of ancient written works and to reconstitute their texts in their presumably pristine form. Antiquity itself became intrinsically valued, not only because it was in the remote past but because it was thought that it represented a charismatic moment in the history of mankind, as it was then known.

Works of art, more than works of literature, science, and philosophy, are connected in various ways with majesty and sacredness. Works of literature, science, and philosophy were sometimes produced under royal or noble patronage. But royalty and the nobility did not usually constitute their subject matter; it was frequently otherwise with paintings and sculptures which could be kept to give long-lasting fame to their patrons. The ownership and presence of works of art testified to the majesty of their possessors and that provided a motive for their preservation. Palaces and churches are among the best preserved of buildings and, since many great works of art were used to embellish them, those in whose care these structures remained had a vested interest in keeping them safe from destruction. Antiquity as well as beauty, quite apart from subject matter, attest to majesty and sacredness. Rarity was another merit of works of art; rarity was associated with age, and once works of art began to be collected and watched over, old works in which so many values converged received especial care.

In more recent years, speculative investment in works of art, especially in paintings, has become very common, but by and large this is not one of the important factors in the preservation of works of art. Indeed the extraordinarily high prices now paid for works of art endanger their well-being because their costliness arouses the cupidity of thieves and the destructive passions of lunatics. Speculative private investment in works of art proceeds on the postulate that the paintings are valuable because others can be counted upon to value them for their aesthetic value and their age.

Works of art have a special property which affects their preservation. Only "originals" are appreciated. "Genuineness" is proportionate to proximity to the creator. This is true of paintings above all. A genuine painting is the painting made by the painter to whom it is attributed; a copy by another painter, however skillfully executed, is far less valuable; a painting, however meritorious, which is attributed wrongly to a famous painter loses much of the esteem in which it is held when it is reattributed to a less famous painter. A mechanical reproduction of a painting, however excellent the process, is not taken seriously as a work of art. No one who respected himself as a collector would acquire one; no museum would hang or even possess it for any other than pedagogical purposes. This insistence on the "original" intensifies the concern to keep the deposit from the past in the form given to it when it came finished from the hand of its creator. Paintings are "restored." Bronze sculptures are never "originals," but the castings made with the authorization of the sculptor are regarded as more valuable than those made subsequently.

Documents and Records

The re-presentation and differentiation of classical antiquity through the discovery of manuscripts, editing, printing, and study and instruction coincided roughly with the beginning of the search for a national past. The search for the manuscript records and monuments of the Middle Ages had an objective very similar to that of the search for the tradition of antiquity in literature and philosophy. Both were intended to discover the sources from which images and texts of the past could be correctly established in the present or at some time in the future. They were both concerned with documents which were works of the past from which truthful pictures of the past and of the past of present institutions could be constructed.[8]

8. F. Smith Fussner, *The Historical Revolution: English Historical Writing and Thought, 1580–1640* (London: Routledge and Kegan Paul, 1962), pp. 26–

Administrative archives, legal and judicial records, had been pre-served in the past because they had been needed to verify and legiti-mate claims to office, property, and privilege. The documents attest-ing to agreements and enactments had been preserved because past decisions and agreements legitimated present claims and decisively rejected contending claims to legitimacy. Actions in the past were the *loci* of legitimacy, and the documents which lay in archives were regarded as evidence of that legitimacy. An event which occurred in the past was regarded as the model or norm on the basis of which present conflicts could be resolved. That was why evidence of what had occurred in the past was vital. In the course of time, the practical, morally mandatory character of the past began to lose some of its grip; the cognitive curiosity about the past has become more active.

A gradual displacement of significance has occurred as the past has become more interesting cognitively. Documents of legal significance are still preserved as evidence of a past action which still possesses practical normative bearing. But the documents are also regarded as valuable because they disclose the intrinsically cognitive interesting past. Unlike literary manuscripts in which the content has an aesthetic and direct charismatic value—even though that value is accessible through reading a printed reproduction—the archival documents have primarily a heuristic value. But it is also their sheer pastness which confers value on them; a person who holds them has brought the past into his presence. They embody some quality which is inherent in their pastness—both in their own physical identity with what they were in the past and because they carry a record of a past event.

The Transcendence of the Transience of Physical Artifacts

The Two Strata of Tradition

Stones, bricks, wood, mortar, metal, canvas, paint, parchment, papyrus, paper, ink are all material things, dead matter formed by human action into buildings, roads, machines, statues, paintings, and books. They are dead matter infused with spirit by being formed or arranged under the guidance of the mind. This is true of wholly physi-cal artifacts which are used as shelter, tools, coins and pathways; spirit or mind presides over them. They would not have been con-

---

116; David Douglas, *English Scholars* (London: Jonathan Cape, 1943), pp. 70–123; J. G. A. Pocock, *The Ancient Constitution and the Feudal Law: A Study of English Historical Law in the Seventeenth Century* (Cambridge: Cambridge University Press, 1957), pp. 70–123; David Knowles, *Great His-torical Enterprises and Problems in Monastic History* (London: Thomas Nel-son, 1963), pp. 33–62.

structed in the first place had there not been some sort of an image of their shape and of the ways in which they would be subjected to human intention whatever its end and culmination.

Statues, paintings, medals, and books, having as such no significant practical uses, are even more obviously constituted by the spirit or mind which resides in them. The relationship to them of their audiences of readers and contemplators is not one of use, it is entirely a relationship of interpretation. They are created with the intention that they be interpreted, that their audiences apprehend the symbolic constellations by which they have been constituted.

The tradition of physical artifacts is thus a dual tradition. It is a tradition of the physical substratum and a tradition of the images and beliefs and the ideas of procedure, technique, or skill which have gone into them. The stratum of interpreted symbols could not endure and could not be handed down as traditions without that transient substratum at each stage of transmission and reception and it could not be stored without the intellectual activities of human brains resident in human bodies.

The Identity of Physical Artifacts through Time. The particular stones of a given building may crumble, and, bit by bit, a building may be replaced so that some hundreds of years later much of the particular materials which make up a building might not be the same as those it began with. We have no hesitation in pronouncing the Sheldonian Theatre, Oxford, to be the Sheldonian Theatre building as it was when it was first completed. The original beams and supporting stones are the same, but much of the surface and the outer statuary have been restored, which entailed much replacement. If there had been a gradual but complete replacement of all the original wood, mortar, and stone, it might still be said that the building was the same building. Each replacement followed the preexistent pattern. There are other cases of complete replacement such as was done in the Old Market Square in Warsaw after the Second World War. Regardless of whether the replacements were minor or whether they involved the construction of buildings entirely made up of new stones, new wood, and new mortar, the builders who built anew the destroyed buildings had a clearly defined pattern to which they had to conform. The pattern of the re-created Old Market Square was contained either in the drawings of the original architect of the buildings or in measurements, drawings, and pictures, made subsequently, of the parts which were destroyed during the Second World War.

The image of the style of a building could provide a general pattern for a particular building as a whole, the distribution, shapes, and proportions of windows and doorways, the lines distinguishing the different stories from each other, the forms of cornices, window frames, or door frames, the amount and kind of ornamentation on the outer surface of the building—all these together, without being identical with any existing or known past building, contain the particular patterns of other buildings. It is the pattern which becomes tradition, detached from any particular building. The particular building is fixed to a particular place; the pattern may be moved over great distances.

The traditions of patterns or styles have lives of their own. They flourish or become attenuated in a very loose relationship with the tradition of particular physical artifacts such as buildings or works of sculpture or painting or urban landscape. The reception and enactment of the tradition of designing and constructing Gothic buildings has receded practically to the point of nonexistence, but many particular Gothic buildings not only persist but are solicitously cared for; there is much study of and reflection on the Gothic style but it has ceased to be a normative tradition. The Palladian style too is scarcely ever reenacted any longer. Architects refuse to design according to that tradition nowadays although the tradition of the pattern goes on as an object of study and reflection. But despite the attrition of the Palladian tradition as a style which commands the creation of new buildings, the tradition of existing Palladian buildings is greatly cherished.

A particular building as a *traditum* is almost as plastic and flexible as a style. A building in the Tudor style might, in the eighteenth century, have been refaced with a neoclassical facade; in the nineteenth century a Palladian building might have been refaced in the style of the Gothic revival. A building might have additional wings built onto it and internal walls constructed or removed. The "modernized" building retains many of its old features.

Substantial traces of generally attenuated stylistic traditions may be found in the internal and external ornamentation of buildings which in other respects follow a different tradition. Cornices, transoms, wall panels, and moldings at the intersections of walls and ceilings may continue, in a blurred form, in the setting of a very different style. The skyscraper which seemed to be such a departure from previous styles of building moved slowly and gradually into the allegedly unadorned glass and metal blocks of recent construction. Sullivan, White, and the other pioneers retained very visible features of Romanesque and Renaissance adornment. The desire to be guided only by the "imperative" of technology left gaps which had to be filled in by bits of the past, randomly chosen. Stationary murals and statuary in courts are typical of the revival of fragments of past stylistic traditions which are themselves now widely refused. The external ornamentation of houses built by and for the working or lower middle classes in American cities early in the present century shows an extraordinary persistence of classical and Renaissance styles of ornamentation. There would appear to be more flexibility in styles than in particular artifacts when they move through a process of tradition.

Transience of Objects, and the Endurance of Traditions of Patterns in Empirical Technology. Few technological artifacts of three or four centuries ago such as ploughs, millstones, carts, chisels, scythes, saws, and hammers survive, and they are not in use, unlike buildings of the same time. Most of those which still exist have been recovered from the rubbish heaps of discarded things. Since they were regarded in their own times as expendable, they were treated accordingly. Their rarity is not to be explained wholly by their inferior efficacy in comparison with tools and machines of more recent conception and manufacture.

It is frequently asserted that technology belongs to the realm of the material, together with the natural "resources" on which it operates. It is part of the "material foundation" of society, it is the "substructure" *(Unterbau)*. There is a little truth in this assertion of the materiality of technology. It is very far from the whole truth. Every piece of technology is instrumental in the performance of a task of affecting material things. It takes an act of imagination to conceive of the task and it takes acts of knowledge and imagination to use a technological artifact to perform it. It takes an act of knowledge to reproduce the technological artifact—the tool or the machine; a model of the tool or the machine must be present in the mind in reproducing it. A model formed from the use and observation of the artifact performing its function and in its prime condition is an indispensable link between the ruined, worn-out tool or machine and the reproduction which is to replace it.

The reproduction of a type of artifact carries the past into the present by reembodying in each newly made incarnation the image which guided earlier generations in its production and use. In each generation, each particular instance of an artifact carries forward the embodiment of an image of the object—whether it be a chest of drawers or a house or a gun—an image which guides its reproduction. This image reassumes material form from hitherto unformed material of wood, stone, and metal.

The image leads a dual existence. It lives on in any particular existing material form from which it is taken as a model for the production of the next generation of artifacts of the same particular kind, or of some more general class of which the particular kind is a variant. It also lives on in its simultaneous existence in the memory of the craftsman or silversmith or engineer who uses it or makes it or who arranges the machines and the human actions which make it. It lives on in the drawings and in the minds of its makers from one generation of makers to the next. The knowledge of patterns, the knowledge of the properties of the substances which are to be formed in accordance with, and into, patterns, the knowledge of the tools and machines, and the knowledge of the movements of the mind and body, also move forward from generation to generation in simultaneous changedness and unchangedness. Without the tradition of knowledge and skill, the generations of worn out and ruined artifacts could not be replaced by generations of successors. Where a demand for the artifacts ceases or is greatly diminished, the flow of relevant knowledge for their production and use falls away also.[9]

The artifacts of stagnant empirical technology must be reproduced since they become dulled or broken by use and must be replaced. There too the mind—the model in the memory and in the imagination—is at work. The transmission of a stagnant tradition also is an interlacement of two strata; the model of the tool or machine and of the way of making it are transmitted by words of instruction and by graphic means, and it is also transmitted in the artifact itself. The model in empirical technology always remains concrete; it is not abstractly described; it is not placed in a theoretical context. A craftsman learns how to use it by seeing it used and using it under guidance; one learns to make it by seeing it made and making it under guidance. But the tradition of empirical technology is not necessarily a stagnant reiteration. Innovations and improvements, contrived by makers and users, can enter into the tradition of empirical technology. So they did before the appearance of scientific technology.

Rational Scientific Technology

Empirical technology differs from rational scientific technology in that in the former the image of how the tool or machine works arises from the experience of using the given tool or machine; in the latter, a generalized image of the process is borne along on a more generalized tradition of images and beliefs, which is the tradition of scientific knowledge. Rational scientific technology is one in which there is a deliberate and continuous search for improvement and replacement of particular models of tools, machines, and processes through the cultivation of the relevant traditions of scientific knowledge. The replacements are made on grounds of the rationally calculated greater efficiency and economy of the new models. As a result, the tools, machinery, and processes of a half-century or even a quarter of a century are replaced by the rather different and better kinds of tools, machines, or processes of the ensuing period. The replacement is not just of particular tools and machines but of the kinds of tools and machines. Furthermore, these very large, disjunctive replacements

9. In the midst of the recent concern about the increasing costs of the materials from which energy is generated, it was recommended that more windmills be constructed. On examination it turned out that the project was hampered because there were no longer enough craftsmen who understood how windmills work and how to construct them.

are realized through systematic and concentrated attention to the relevant tradition of scientific knowledge and to a more general conviction that what has been given in the tradition of the particular tool or machine can be improved. The models are learned by the ordered study of principles attained through a tradition of systematic investigation.

Modern technology, in its wide utilization, has brought about so many changes in the organization of labor, in the distribution of the population, and in the standard of living, so many new pleasures and new problems, that it seems utterly alien to anything traditional. The appearance of the new machines and the new products is vastly different from what was used and produced a century earlier. There is little in common between the workshop of an old-fashioned carriage builder and a modern automobile plant. There was nothing at all like a contemporary aircraft factory or a contemporary oil refinery or a plant for the generation of electricity. The scale of the application of this new technology is also unprecedented.

Yet none of the elements of contemporary technology came into existence without a long tradition behind it which has made it possible. Much of the tradition which sustains contemporary technology has grown out of traditions which were not themselves integral to the technology. Computers draw on traditions from Pascal and Boole as well as the tradition which immediately preceded Bardeen's and Shockley's work. The technology of communication depended on the tradition of the discoveries of Hertz.

Certain of the most imposing innovations still retain in themselves traditional patterns of tools. Earth-digging and earth-moving machinery are still constructed around the pattern of spades and shovels, although they are far more powerful in the energy behind them and in the amount of earth which they can move in a given time and with a given number of workers. Contemporary lathes and planing machines and screw-cutting machines, however new they are in their particular versions, however more powerful in the energy they can draw upon, however sharper and harder their parts, are also refinements and extensions of traditional techniques in a larger and more complex context. The great progress of modern technology has not turned completely away from the tradition of the wheel, the gear, the screw, the hammer, the shovel, the pulley, the capstan, the saw, the chisel, or the lathe.[10] The new machines have incorporated them. A rotating

10. A. P. Usher, *A History of Mechanical Invention* (Cambridge, Mass.: Harvard University Press, 1929); Charles Singer, E. J. Holmyard, A. R. Hall, and T. I. Williams, eds., *A History of Technology* (Oxford: Oxford University Press, 1954–79), vols. 1–6; Lynn White, Jr., *Medieval Religion and Technology: Collected Essays* (Berkeley: University of California Press, 1978), pp. 1–22, 75–92.

saw is still a saw, a pile driver or trip-hammer is still a hammer. These traditional tools have been fitted into machines of immensely greater complexity, precision, and power. The substances of which the tools are made have been made stronger and more resistant to abrasion and concussion, but the fundamental model still persists as a crucial element in the new machine.

The internal combustion engine had in its early years much in common with the steam engine in the use of the expansion of vapor in cylinders. Much else was different. Aviation, which was unprecedented, except mythologically, for human beings, began with the internal combustion engine. Nonetheless the traditions of rational scientific technology are not unilinear and continuous as the traditions of empirical technology are. The former are constituted by the fusion of empirical technological traditions with the tradition which has grown relatively autonomously in the course of scientific research and theory. With the entry of scientific research and theory, new technological traditions came upon the scene. Scientific chemistry, theoretical physics, and mathematics entered into technology and modified it profoundly and far-reachingly.[11] Nonetheless, the new rational scientific technology is far from traditionless and it has by no means superseded the older tradition of empirical technology.

The Tradition of Skill. Around the deepening mounds of the detritus of ruined and discarded tools and machines and of no longer active models and into a steadily thickening tradition of newly discovered physical and chemical knowledge, another general stream of tradition has made its way over centuries and even millennia. This has been the tradition of empirical knowledge, repeatedly converted into technological artifacts which depart to some extent from what has been received and the existence and use of which have, over and over, confirmed the validity of the tradition. The tradition of empirical knowledge embraced both the knowledge of how to adapt an inherited model of a tool or a machine so that it would be appropriate to the better performance of recurrently given tasks and the knowledge of how to use the tool effectively. Sometimes this empirical knowledge was written down into books and pamphlets.

Before the outburst of systematically designed technological innovation in the nineteenth century, it was from this empirical knowledge, mainly orally and exemplarily transmitted through numerous generations, that many new inventions came forth. The craftsman's practical knowledge of tools and machines was the substance of the

11. A. Rupert Hall, "Scientific Method and the Progress of Techniques," in E. E. Rich and C. H. Wilson, eds., *The Cambridge Economic History of Europe* (Cambridge: Cambridge University Press, 1967), vol. 4, esp. pp. 125–34.

tradition from which these important new inventions took their point of departure. Craftsmen and inventors had learned about the refinement of ores and the properties of metals and the problems of raising water from mines from the tradition of practically acquired and orally received knowledge passed down to them by artisans of the preceding centuries.[12] Their innovations were guided by the imagination and sensitivity which arose in the course of their own experience of long-performed operations, itself first acquired by seeing and being orally guided by their elders. This mastery of traditional empirical knowledge is not only capable, through persistent reproduction, of transmitting to others what was done before but, to some extent, of becoming detached from the tradition through efforts to see how work could be done more effectively.

Using a tool or operating a machine is a neural-muscular process which the user develops from his own experiences of its use and from instruction by others, which includes observation of how they use the instrument. Having a tool in one's hand no more enables one to use it than having a book open before one's eyes imposes an understanding of the text. The "use" of the tool, like the understanding of the book, requires possession of knowledge for the "user" to interpret what he sees in front of him, and he can only do this if he can draw on his perception of what others have done before him and what he himself has done in similar situations. Patterns of physical movement of his own body must be established as well as the patterns of perception of the situation to which the tool or machine is "appropriate" and of the immediate consequences which follow from its use. In principle, a human being faced with a task and given a simple enough tool, could discover what the tool was for and how to use it. For simple tools and machines, a user could establish, by trial and error, an effective pattern; if Köhler's chimpanzee could do this, human beings could do it too. If such a thing happened, the individual's own experience would compensate for the absence of tradition. In fact his imagination takes its point of departure in tradition. The trials and errors of experience have always played a part in the invention of a more effective or less costly way of doing things. The exploration into the unknown through trial and error and by the generation of insight always occurs from the platform of what has been attained previously. This exploration, which is cognitive and muscular, is made possible by the acceptance of much of the knowledge which has already been acquired by earlier users and the confirming and correcting experience of the user himself.

12. See John U. Nef, "Mining and Metallurgy in European Civilization," in M. Postan and E. E. Rich, eds., *The Cambridge Economic History of Europe* (Cambridge: Cambridge University Press, 1952), vol. 2, esp. pp. 458–69; A. Rupert Hall, "Scientific Method."

In the recent aspiration for the improvement of the economic condition of the more impoverished parts of the human race through the "transfer of technology" into their agricultural and industrial production, much has been made of the importance of "know-how." The industrial success of the richer countries is attributed in part to "know-how." "Know-how" is practical knowledge of how to do something rather than the knowledge of the theoretical principles which can account for the process set in motion by the user's action. It is almost subliminal; it is a nearly physical sensitivity to what will work effectively and what will not work effectively. "Know-how" was supremely important in the past, when technology was more empirical. It remains important now, when the component of exact, scientific knowledge is far greater than it was and when particular tools and machines are more complex in structure and yet seem to be operable by procedures whch can be described in a schematic way.

The operation and maintenance of these immense machines, if they have not been fully automated, requires a combination of empirical skill and articulated knowledge. These are not to be obtained exclusively by study, however careful, of the manual of instructions which the manufacturer of the machine provides and by what is learned in classes and from textbooks; nor is it learned only by experience, although that is indispensable for the intimacy—and even empathy—with tools and machines necessary for their mastery. The possession of the tradition of exact, scientific-technological knowledge must be supplemented by the tradition of empirical knowledge. It requires the clinical sense which a competent physician acquires and which cannot be formulated in or learned from books. Just as a medical student must, in addition to learning the constantly growing principles and facts of the biomedical sciences, have clinical instruction by an experienced teacher-cum-physician and thus acquire for himself types of knowledge accumulated over generations, so, *mutatis mutandis*, must the operator of a new and unprecedentedly complex machine draw upon the intimate understanding of machines acquired through successive generations of skilled machinists.

"Know-how" is the *traditum* of general, unarticulated categories and expectations, it is the tradition of a code, of a set of signals which only experienced eyes and ears refined by tradition can discern and interpret. It is the tradition which permits the discernment of the opening to invention, but it also imposes persistence along certain lines of the established path. A worker without a master cannot always make up by experience what he has lost from initial orientation. Systematic scientific study, which also requires a master is as indispensable as experience but it too needs the initial orientation which flows from a master, a presenter of the tradition of skill. The "transfer of know-how" is subtler than the "transfer of technology" in the sense of patents and licenses and even of the physical apparatus itself. It requires a tradition to carry onward; without it the physical artifact is dead matter.

The Tradition of Invention. Historical works tend to deal primarily with "change." The history of technology is a history of innovations; it is not about the persistence of the technological past in the productive and military activities of the human race.[13] The progressivistic outlook of the historians of technology and to some extent of economic historians causes the part of tradition in technological invention to be diminished. It does not quite do justice, therefore, to the tradition of the inventive outlook and to the traditionality of the technology which constitutes the matrix around new inventions and their adoption in practice.

The attempt to improve or invent a new tool or a new machine or process depends as much on tradition as it does on the use, without any alteration, of the tool, machine, or process which one has been using and which one's ancestors used. Both kinds of tradition represent different but intimately connected pasts.

When a philosopher like Professor Jürgen Habermas writes as if "technology" has become autonomous and has "got out of control,"[14] he would do better to say that the tradition of technological innovation has found such widespread and intense propagation and reception that it is difficult to make it occur less frequently. The tradition of the belief that invention is possible and desirable existed in antiquity in the West and in the European Middle Ages and in China, India, and Islamic civilization as well. This tradition however never became a widespread possession. It found little sympathy in the societies in which opinion was unfriendly to innovations. The persons with the resources to put the inventions into operation did not hasten to assimilate and adopt them, partly because they did not share the tradition of appreciation of innovation and partly because they did not anticipate any pecuniary or other advantage from giving their patronage to it. It is not that most of the users of a tool, machine, or process actively resisted technological innovation; rather they did not inherit a belief in the goodness of invention. Here and there an invention which departed from the traditional model was actually fought against be-

13. See, for example, John Beckmann, *The History of Inventions* (London: George Bell, 1883); Singer et al., *A History of Technology;* Usher, *Mechanical Invention;* John U. Nef, *War and Human Progress* (Cambridge: Harvard University Press, 1950), *The Rise of the British Coal Industry* (London: Routledge and Kegan Paul, 1932), and "The Progress of Technology and the Growth of Large-Scale Industry in Great Britain, 1540–1640," *Economic History Review* 5, no. 1 (October 1934): 3–24.

14. Jürgen Habermas, *Technik und Wissenschaft als Ideologie* (Frankfurt a.M.: Suhrkamp, 1968), pp. 104–19.

cause it was an affront to a particular tradition or to the general belief that established ways are the best or only conceivable ways or because its adoption would be economically injurious to some of the persons who might be affected by it. Instances of this kind of active opposition to innovation do not account for the relatively slow rate of the invention of new artifacts prior to the modern age. Uninterestedness in invention was more significant than resistance to inventions once made.[15]

The inherited technology was carried forward alongside the traditional belief that there was no alternative to hard labor and a scanty existence. The improvability of the conditions of life and of the ways of doing things in this life was not present in the imagination. Particular possibilities for improvements did not arise in the imagination because there was so little evidence of improvability apparent to the eye. Living in a culture in which traditions carry with them either a positive injunction of specific reenactment of received models or threats of damaging consequences from disregarding the injunction makes the imagination inert. The individual's powers are left dormant when he does not have the possibility of innovation suggested to him by the anonymous authority of what he sees about him.

Deference to ancestors and even fears of displeasing them—with injurious consequences—sustained the retention of ancestral ways of doing things. The common praise of ancestral ways—"old law is good law," "old ways are true ways"—obscured the novelty of those innovations which did occur and it had an inhibiting effect on any inclination to seek novelty. Questions of efficiency were practically never raised because, except among merchants and bankers, quantitative thinking about the benefits of any action was rare.

Such inventions as were made moved slowly and had little echo. The inventions which were made in different parts of China in the tenth century A.D. did not reinforce each other because the innovators were not aware of their fellow innovators elsewhere within the same loosely integrated society—the spread of innovations between civilizations was much slighter. The radius of an invention was small and the impulse to innovate was not sustained by the awareness of other innovations. There was little "demonstration effect" of innovations. The perception of invention arouses inventiveness; it stirs the im-

15. Scholars like William Ogburn, Bernhard Stern, and Richard Shryock have sometimes written as if the persistence of certain patterns of conduct is a result of "cultural lag" and of deliberate resistance to proposals for new ways. See William F. Ogburn, *Social Change* (New York: B. W. Huebsch, 1922); National Resources Committee, *Technological Trends and National Policy* (Washington, D.C.: Government Printing Office, 1937), pp. 24–66; Bernhard J. Stern, *Social Factors in Medical Progress* (New York: Columbia University Press, 1927); and Richard Shryock, *The Development of Modern Medicine,* 2d ed. (New York: Knopf, 1947).

agination into action by showing that it is possible to do things in a way which is different from the hitherto obtaining way. An improvement in the design of a ship would remain unknown to shipwrights in other yards for a long time. There was no way of communicating an invention except by the sight of it or the account of an itinerant merchant or craftsman. Since communication was slow, the cumulation of inventions such as would give rise to an image of invention as a normal and even imperative activity was not perceived.

The propensity to invent by deliberation is not an inevitable and irrepressible disposition of most human beings. It is probably a considerably rarer propensity than the propensity to receive, reiterate, and adapt tradition, and it is not, for most members of a society, self-sustaining. It needs the exemplary support of others in the same society. Traditionality is reinforced by the perception of traditionality, the tradition of inventiveness is reinforced by the perception of inventiveness in others. Inventiveness depends in part on the presentation of a tradition of inventiveness.

Yet, no society has ever been wholly traditional in its technology. Even the simplest technology for trapping or killing birds and animals or for catching fish was invented. The wide variety of agricultural practices, the use of harder substances for ploughs to penetrate more deeply into the earth, and the mining of new materials, improvements in the refinement of ores and in the hardening of metals, the development of boats with larger and more variable sails and with more oarsmen, all show that technological imagination was not absent from the human mind before the end of the European Middle Ages. Yet innovation in technology did not become a pervasive tradition until modern times.

The ideal of inventiveness in the modern age has become established as one of its major traditions. The responsiveness of the owners of capital was an incentive to inventors. The award of prizes by governments and private societies and academies had the same effect, and the possibility of creating an enterprise to exploit an invention stimulated the inventive propensity. The establishment of schools and academies of engineering, mining, agriculture, even without the performance of research, brought together traditions of knowledge and prospective "users" of the knowledge. All of this helped to precipitate changes in circumstances, threw up new tasks, and challenged imaginative minds which had acquired the traditions of knowledge in contexts wide enough to permit comparisons. In the nineteenth century, the growth of scientific research in universities and by private individuals placed original discovery, the discovery of things hitherto unknown, in a position of unprecedented esteem. The belief that the sciences and the arts were a single field of activity meant that the search for knowledge might legitimately include the search for new technological procedures and instruments. Traditionality took a new turn; it was felt that there was an antithesis between traditionality and technological innovation because the traditional aspect of the latter was not perceived.

The Presence of the Past in the Acquisition and Possession of Knowledge

Physical artifacts and intellectual things stand at diametrically opposed corners of a square. In artifacts it is the material object which is of interest; the tradition of patterns is significant because it is through that medium that artifacts can continuously be recreated, adapted, invented, and produced. The use of the artifact is the end, the pattern is the means to the end. Intellectual stocks and possessions—philosophical, theological, scientific, ethical ideas, interpretations of sacred books and historical knowledge—are symbolic constructions; they are "cultural objectivations."[16]

A "symbolic constellation," a "cultural objectivation," an idea, a proposition, an image is a phenomenon distinct from the material form in which it is embodied. A spoken idea is distinct from the sound waves on which it is carried; a printed or written idea is distinct from the ink marks imprinted on paper. It is not a psychological or neurophysiological phenomenon although it must have its counterpart in that realm as well as in the realm of paper and ink. No more can it be said to be a social relationship, although the communication of an idea is a social relationship. None of these realms is the realm of symbols. Symbols are realities with a realm of their own.

By the same token a scientific or a theological proposition or a historical statement is not a tradition. The formulation before us might have just been newly discovered or arrived at by observation and ratiocination and no one in all of human history might have ever attained it before this moment. It is in that case not something handed down as a tradition. But even a proposition handed down as a tradition is a proposition and not just a tradition. Its truth depends on rational and empirical evidence and its truth, as demonstrated by that evidence, is the ground for its acceptance. It is apprehended as a proposition offered in already existent form. This is perfectly compatible with its being a tradition.

16. They used to be called *geistige Objektivation* by some German writers; sometimes they were called *Ideengebilde* or *ideelle Gebilde*. Anthropologists used to call them "nonmaterial culture." More recently Karl Popper has recognized their existence under the name of "World 3." See Karl Popper, *Objective Knowledge: An Evolutionary Approach* (Oxford: Clarendon Press, 1972), pp. 153–90.

The embodiment of propositions in material form, in printed books, in written manuscripts, in visible equations and formulas, in enunciated ethical commandments and criticisms, in spoken and heard propositions is a means to the intellectual end. The physical embodiments help to maintain the life of these propositions in the stream of tradition. The end is a cognitive or evaluative pattern; the pattern is constituted by symbolic constellations representing specific perceptions and categorical or general statements referring to the external world of the cosmos and of man, including the interior life of man as an object external to the knower. These patterns have a discrete immaterial existence.

The material objects—printed in texts and manuscripts—are only the vehicles and instruments of intellectual activity and intellectual possession. The tradition consists, as in the case of artifacts, of several strata. There is the tradition of symbolic constellations of the intellectual ideas or propositions or beliefs achieved through intellectual activity; there is also the tradition of the artifacts, the books, the manuscripts, etc. There is another tradition closely allied to the tradition of books, except that it, on the surface, is even more instrumental to the creation of propositions in beliefs and is less vehicular. This is the tradition of instruments, of telescopes, microscopes, and other observational instruments, calculating and measuring instruments ranging from calendars, sundials, abacuses, chains, and meter rods to computers and electronic clocks. Like agricultural or industrial technology, all these instruments are derived from a tradition and they can be used only by those who possess the tradition of their use.

The propositions with their discrete existence as intelligible entities are enmeshed in tradition; most of them are handed down and are accepted in varying degrees from those who present them. Symbolic constellations are not traditions but they can be preserved only as traditions. An original proposition which breaks from tradition and which does not enter into a tradition is "lost." If it is not in the stock, and does not pass into the possession of others, it must be declared to be lost. Newly created propositions have their point of departure in the propositions handed down as traditions and they contain many elements received from tradition. Newly created propositions enter into traditions; they become traditions. This does not diminish their standing as symbolic constellations, because intellectual traditions are themselves symbolic constellations, transmitted, received, possessed, and transmitted. Each of these symbolic constellations, each of these particular artifacts, each of these patterns of skill in their use is enchained in a process of tradition; it begins from a tradition and it fosters the tradition.

The tradition of knowledge and the tradition of the vehicles and instruments of knowledge are very closely and variously connected with each other. The material vehicle and the intellectual substance which is recorded in it have different histories, each of which is, in certain respects but certainly not in all, the precondition and ground of the other. Elaborate philosophical ideas could not be elaborated over centuries and over widely dispersed territories without being placed in material vehicles. Could Aristotle's ideas have been taken up with such elaborations in the Islamic world, while he was disregarded in Europe, if there had been only an oral tradition for the transmission of his works and for their study? Could he have come back to Europe again with such force if there were no manuscripts? Could Jewish culture have persisted for so many centuries with such wide dispersion of the Jewish people and without any coherent Jewish political organization, if the Pentateuch and the Mishnah had been transmitted only orally? The relatively small radius of diffusion of the oral intellectual cultures of particular African societies may in part be a consequence of the absence of a written form in which words, images, and ideas could be precipitated and transported.

The line of movement of tradition in some fields of knowledge generally has a linear form. The striving for knowledge is a seeking for what is not yet known. Up to a certain point, it is also a striving to know what has already been learned by others. The intellectually ambitious student is, by definition, studying the works of others, taking their substance into his possession. This is an activity which can never be wholly left behind even by the mature scholar or scientist, who does what is generally regarded as original work. Originality lies not in rediscovering by one's own efforts what others have already known, but in the discovery of something validly believed not to have been known before. There is an inexpungible and minimal element of progression in the striving for knowledge. This is as true of the allegedly hidebound study of sacred texts and the study of Greek and Latin classics as it is of modern scientific research. It is in the nature of the active mind that it aspires to know what it does not already know; it postulates the prior existence of a pool of knowledge with ever-widening shores and a deepening floor. It looks towards an unattained destination of deeper and clearer, more valid understanding.

Oral Cognitive Traditions and Written Cognitive Traditions

In all the great cultural undertakings of the human race, the oral transmission of tradition plays a great role. In the production of material objects such as sculptures, paintings, and buildings, the instruction of the novice must to a large extent be oral, even though observation and empathy also provide guidance, as do written manuals, drawings, and models.[17] Among literary and other written works, some are intended for oral presentation to a wider public; such are dramatic works which have however been composed in written form. Other genres might have been at one time written with the intention that they should be read aloud; such was the case in Western antiquity with historical, philosophical, and literary works.[18] Some literary men like to read their writings aloud, either from unpublished manuscripts or from already published works; the public reading of poetry is still practiced, but the reading is often from printed works or from manuscripts which are intended for printed publication. In modern societies, the oral presentation of philosophical, scientific, and scholarly works as a definitive form is rare and of secondary significance. Nonetheless the oral transmission of tradition at the stage of the teaching of a novice is still very common in philosophy, science, and scholarship and in the communication at the meetings of learned societies of the most recent proposals for incorporation into the valid tradition. In universities, the spoken lecture, read from a written text or from notes is a major form of transmission of intellectual tradition. Oral transmission holds a preponderant position among the modes of transmission of intellectual tradition to children.

The oral presentation of tradition is not cultivated in modern societies because of the complexity and volume of the tradition to be transmitted, increased literacy, and greater skill in the technology and economy of printed reproduction. In preliterate societies, oral transmission alone obtain—by definition. In societies with restricted literacy, emphasis is laid upon oral transmission. This occurs even where there are written texts which contain what is orally presented. In no field of cognitive activity is this truer than in the religious sphere.

In all the great world-religions, except possibly in Christianity and Confucianism, great weight has been laid upon the oral tradition of sacred texts and commentaries or upon interpretations which are nearly as sacred. In the study of the Torah before the redaction of the Mishnah in ancient Judaism, there must have existed written texts of interpretation of the Pentateuch but these were regarded as auxiliary instruments to aid in the process of commitment to memory. Storage in memory of sacred texts was regarded as more appropriate, even mandatory. Without complete mnemonic storage, proper tradition was thought to be impossible. The medieval and the modern modes of oral tradition centered on a written text with the verbatim commitment to memory of crucial or exemplary passages and propositions,

17. See Rudolf Wittkower, *Sculpture: Processes and Principles* (New York: Harper and Row, 1977), esp. pp. 55–98.
18. A. D. Momigliano, "The Historians of the Classical World and Their Audiences," *The American Scholar* 47, no. 2 (1978): 193–204.

as was practiced in schools for a very long time and which is still necessary. This was apparently not regarded as an acceptable mode of transmitting and acquiring the understanding of sacred texts. Oral tradition had to be based on *verbatim* possession in memory.[19]

When it is technologically no longer necessary that the retention of a text occur through verbatim mnemonic storage, its continuation as an indispensable part of tradition and the high evaluation accorded to memorization as a guarantee of tradition must be explained on grounds other than technological necessity or the inertial force of prior existence. Oral transmission as an integral complement to written transmission is one thing—in that form oral transmission is probably inevitable and desirable for many good reasons. But its status as the only acceptable form of tradition for a text even when it had become technologically superfluous is perhaps to be accounted for by reference to a requirement of secrecy and for hermetic retention except in the presence of qualified persons. Only those could be regarded as truly instructed who had acquired their knowledge in seclusion and in isolation from the soiled routines of everyday life. Written texts were open to everyone who could read, who even in societies of restricted literacy might form a group larger than those who were to be initiated into sacred knowledge. The superiority of the mnemonic form of storage and of the oral mode of transmission was not derogated if the uninitiated read the sacred works; reading did not give them access to the right form of the sacred work under the right circumstances. It meant that their knowledge acquired through reading and only selectively stored in their memory was of inferior value.

Sacred writings were divinely inspired writings and their reiteration was a ritual activity. Specificity and particularity of reiteration are features of ritual. Summaries did not meet the requirements of ritual nor did paraphrases. The exact and complete pattern of words had to be reiterated. This requirement applied not only to the sacred text itself but to the nearly sacred commentaries.

The development of more secular intellectual activities meant that oral transmission of tradition could no longer enjoy a monopoly. There was another cause of the reduction of the primacy of verbatim memorization and oral transmission. This was the increase in the amount of material which had to be committed to memory. As the learned class increased and with it the output of learned works, whether they were more or less secular historical works or whether they were partly sacred commentaries and discourses having their acknowledged point of departure in sacred texts, the body of material

19. Birger Gerhardsson, *Memory and Manuscript: Oral Tradition and Written Transmission in Rabbinic Judaism and Early Christianity*, Acta Seminarii Neotestamentici Upsaliensis, vol. 22 (Upsala: Universiteit Nytestamentlige Seminar, 1961).

to be assimilated in its most minute form exceeded the mnemonic powers of individuals best endowed with the power of retention and recall. It was obviously more convenient and more effective to commit the substance of the text to memory but not the specific and particular patterns of words; the specific and particular details of content could be remembered without the ritually required verbatim form.

Of course, nothing can ever eliminate mnemonic storage and oral tradition entirely from human culture. Memory is an inexpungible part of the human mind and absolutely indispensable to human culture; oral tradition possesses powers which cannot be replaced by written or printed texts unless human beings become mute and deaf.

Religious Knowledge

Religious knowledge, the results of the study of the will and works of divine power, of the revealed, sacred texts in which these are recorded, and of the body of interpretation which has grown up around these texts from the effort to understand them and the divine will better has been regarded as the very epitome of all that reason refuses. Prejudice, dogmatism, superstition, taboos against rational thought, and plain error have been regarded as the marks of religious belief. The learned believers as well as the simple, unlettered believers have equally come under this charge. The transmitted unchanging religious dogma has been made into the prototype of traditionality and is one of the main constituents in the established rationalistic view of tradition. The rationalistic rejection of religious knowledge has given the word belief a bad name. This conception of belief is unjustified. Traditions of religious belief are different from other intellectual beliefs but they also have a great deal in common with them. The similarities are no less important than the differences.

The central object of religious life is the apprehension and experience of divinity, perception of and submission to the will of the deity or to the ultimate laws which govern human existence. These laws or the will of the deity in the great world-religions are to be mastered by the study of what has been revealed and what can be disclosed by the systematic study of the revealed. Revelation which is in principle all-sufficient is in fact never enough. It is not precise enough to answer all the questions which arise in the vicissitudes of existence or which are perceived by minds of great imaginative and ratiocinative powers.

The intellectual tradition of religious belief is two-sided. There is on the one side the tradition of the sacred text itself. The formation of that tradition, the amalgamation of sacred texts into a canon is a process of great complexity. It is not merely a matter of the transmission of manuscripts. It is a matter of determining which variants are best and which belong in the canon. Not wholly separate from this is the tradition of interpretation of the text. The meaning of the text is a creation of the interpretative tradition. The formation of the interpretative tradition is inevitable; its authoritativeness is variable. In the Hebrew religious culture, the Mishnah, which was admitted to be based on the Pentateuch, and to derive its validity from it, acquired an equal and in some respects paramount authority. It became autonomous. In Roman Catholic intellectual culture, tradition acquired an intrinsic authority, without which the sacred text could not be understood. The position of *hadith* in Islam is similar; it too acquires an intrinsic authority but it depends for its legitimacy on the Koran, just as in Judaism the Pentateuch and in Roman Catholicism the Bible is accepted, not so much as the superior authority but as the source of legitimation of the tradition of accumulated interpretation. The legitimacy of the increasingly self-contained, self-generating tradition lies in a sacred event which occurred in the past, in a revelation by a deity which is recorded in sacred texts. It is the sacredness of the past event, the endowment of a human figure with charismatic quality which lies at the beginning of the religion. The long endurance, accumulation, and refinement of a sequence of fundamental, affirmative interpretation adds to the authoritativeness of the tradition.

The authority of the interpretations is supported not only by the sacred character of the text which they interpret and the consensus of past authorities, it is reinforced by the rationality of the interpretations. The tradition is continuously subjected to rational criticism. Hitherto unsolved problems are discerned and resolved; critics who would reject the tradition of interpretation are confronted by reasoned argument—not always only by that—and refuted. The process of rationalization—clarifying, refining, and making logically consistent—itself modifies the tradition and therewith the meaning of the sacred text itself. The tradition of religious belief, particularly that current among the learned, has of course dogmatic elements but the tradition itself is not rigidly unchanging. If it were, there would be no history of, for example, Christian doctrine; there would only be an exposition of a doctrine which had remained completely constant from the beginning. Systematic theology purports to be this, but it is in fact only the precipitate of a tradition of interpretation at a given time.

The traditions of religious knowledge are received and affirmed in much vaguer, in less differentiated and more patchy forms among ordinary believers than they are among the learned. In both cases, however, the maintenance of the constant element in the tradition is supported by religious practice. Religious ritual, prayer, communion, the celebration of holy days, all reaffirm the cognitive beliefs of the religion. The collective character of religious practice helps to sustain the tradition by the recurrent reaffirmation of its postulates and of particular articles of faith.

The tradition of religious belief is also sustained by the tradition of artifacts such as relics which have had imputed to them or acquired sacred properties. Places where charismatic events are believed to have occurred, e.g., Sinai, Mecca, Jerusalem, and Galilee, buildings constructed for the performance of religious practices, graphic portrayals of sacred persons and events, altar and other paintings and sculptures in churches, religious instruments such as phylacteries, beads, rosaries, and prayer wheels, all help to sustain traditions of religious belief. Together with the supplementary traditions of religious music, tales of the lives of founders and saints and their wonders as well as edifying works—all these form a supporting system of traditions of physical artifacts, actions, and patterns of symbols which uphold and keep on the right track the presentation and reception of cognitive religious beliefs, popular and learned. For the learned, theological faculties and seminaries, monasteries and universities, by training and discipline and the presentation of the right version of the tradition, foster the continuity of the tradition. The opportunities to concentrate the mind under fortifying and disciplining circumstances keep the movement of tradition within the broad limits which define innovations as refinements and clarifications of the tradition and not as departures from it.

Orthodoxy

At every point in the transmission of a religious tradition there is a right way and a wrong way. Traditions encase the beliefs of human beings and are subject, in the process of transmission as well as when they are in possession, to reiteration or variation every time they are called into play. Persistent identity or variation joined with constancy are always present in one combination or another between the two extremes of perfect identity through time and random variation. Every orthodoxy in tradition is in incessant danger of breaking into heterodoxy. It may break at the point where the tradition passes from one generation to the other or it may break while in the possession of a single generation. Scrutiny and interpretation may go beyond the limits of what are generally regarded as defining the domain within which a tradition remains the tradition which it was and outside of which it ceases to be that tradition and becomes something else.

Every tradition is susceptible to modification by well-intentioned persons who wish to strengthen it by clarifying it and making it more systematic. There is no tradition, no transmitted and received symbolic pattern in any field of human creation which is wholly free from ambiguity, obscurity, uncertainty when viewed from within its own postulates, as well as from outside them. An honest effort to understand and affirm may end up by casting doubt, weakening confidence, and damaging faith.

The breaking out of the wide boundaries of tradition within which powerful and honorable minds can operate with a feeling of being at home can occur at almost any time.

There is a certain arbitrariness in the definition of the boundaries of a tradition of religious knowledge and in the decision as to what lies outside them. This problem would not exist if traditions were, as some of their detractors allege, entirely constant and incapable of any change other than complete rejection. The selection and training of the adepts of tradition and their incorporation into institutions which have the responsibility of maintaining the tradition, help to keep the interpretation of tradition within the boundaries which define it and which distinguish it from what it is not.

The belief of the adherents of a tradition that their beliefs lie within its boundaries is a datum to be taken into account in deciding whether the boundaries of a tradition have been exceeded. The custodians of orthodoxy might regard such adherents as heretics, yet to an external observer they might be very much inside certain major themes of tradition.

Confrontation with Alien Religious Traditions

Except for Hinduism, the great world-religions originate, according to their own self-interpretation, in a charismatic episode or an exemplary sequence of charismatic episodes in the life of the founder. Two of them, Christianity and Islam, acknowledge an annunciatory prehistory in the history of the Jews up to a certain time, although each of them regards itself as valid independently of its prehistory. Each major body of religious beliefs is regarded by its representative exponents as an internally consistent and distinctive pattern of knowledge, devotion, attachments, and norms; its adherents are usually at pains to distinguish themselves from rival claimants to the attachment of its devotees. The tradition is usually put forth by learned believers as homogeneous in composition and unilinear in interpretation. These self-interpretations are however incorrect. Every major tradition is a product of the confluence of contributory traditions, not only at its origin but in the course of its history. Ancient Judaism incorporated a considerable element of Canaanite religious belief; it assimilated into itself pagan beliefs and celebrations which it reinterpreted into the historical traditions of the Jews such as the flight from Egypt, the wandering in the desert, etc. Islam incorporated a considerable element of pre-Islamic Arabic paganism. Christianity certainly took into itself local religious traditions and reinterpreted them into parts of the specifically Christian tradition.

Christianity assimilated Platonic philosophy and later Aristotelian philosophy; it made peace with modern science, and now many Christians are attempting to incorporate a somewhat modified Marxism into Christianity. Protestant Christianity which covered such a wide range of possibilities assimilated into itself a good deal of liberalism—as well as contributing much to the tradition of secular liberalism. Many Protestants have attempted to incorporate a considerable quantity of secular tradition and many are now moving in the same way to assimilate Marxism.[20] All of these were alien to the Christian tradition of the earliest period of Christianity. Parallel adaptations occurred in Islam with the incorporation of Aristotelian and Platonic philosophy,[21] and in the nineteenth and twentieth centuries the varieties of Islamic modernism have attempted similar assimilations of alien traditions.[22]

The confrontation with an alien tradition is always a challenge to a tradition. By confrontation I mean being aware of the existence of alien traditions or being made into the object of attack by the proponents of alien traditions. In some situations, the alien tradition may be assimilated by adaptation, with the assertion that implicitly the alien tradition was always contained within the challenged tradition. The adherents of the challenged tradition might also struggle to refute the alien tradition by rational arguments or they might seek to destroy its proponents by discrediting them morally, by defeating them politically, or by annihilating them physically as occurred in India in the relations of Hindus and Muslims or in Roman Catholic countries in Europe through the Inquisition. A counteraction to a threat of revolution might make the challenged tradition more rigid than it had been previously. It might also incline the proponents of the challenged tradition of religious belief to lose confidence in the truth of their beliefs. This is what happened in the educated classes in Bengal in the early nineteenth century when Hinduism was challenged by a self-confident Protestant Christianity. In the twentieth century, Protestant

20. See for example, Edward Norman, *Church and Society in England: 1770–1970* (Oxford: Clarendon Press, 1976), and *Christianity and the World Order* (Oxford: Oxford University Press, 1979).
21. See Ernst Renan, *Averroes et l'Averroïsme: Essai historique* (1852), in *Oeuvres complètes,* ed. Henriette Psichari (Calman-Lévy, n.d.), vol. 3: 86–142; also Erwin I. J. Rosenthal, *Political Thought in Medieval Islam: An Introductory Outline* (Cambridge: Cambridge University Press, 1958), pp. 113–23.
22. See H. A. R. Gibb, *Modern Trends in Islam* (Chicago: University of Chicago Press, 1947); Albert Hourani, *Arabic Thought in the Liberal Age: 1798–1939* (London: Oxford University Press, 1962); and Elie Kedourie, *Afghani and Abduh: An Essay on Religious Unbelief and Political Activism in Modern Islam* (London: Cass, 1966). See also Zwi Werblowsky, *Beyond Tradition and Modernity: Changing Religions in a Changing World* (London: Athlone Press, 1976).

Christianity having already assimilated a number of alien traditions into itself was also troubled by its learned awareness of the other world-religions. From being the challenger of other religious traditions, Protestant Christianity became the challenged tradition. Among some of its adherents, the response was conciliatory renunciation of some elements of their own traditions.

The internal rationalization of a doctrinal tradition could, in the course of time, annihilate the charismatic legitimating source of the tradition, but that is not so likely. The entry of another tradition is more likely to have such an effect. It was the Christian analysis of biblical chronology which disturbed the intellectual authority of the Christian tradition. It was the presence of the alien traditions of astronomical, geological, and historical studies, the topics of which were within the Christian religious tradition, which reduced the intellectual authority of the Christian tradition.

None of these external traditions was impelled by hostility to the religious tradition; the higher criticism arose within the Christian tradition. The historical studies were intended to clarify the texts of the Old Testament in order better to establish the chronology of the history of the Jews. This involved the questioning of the pattern of the canon of received texts; the chronological reordering of their various parts from the sequence which had become a settled part of the interpretation had an unsettling effect on the confidence with which the religiously more important parts of the tradition were presented. Two paths of the rationalization of a primary tradition, i.e., of a sacred text, came into conflict with each other. The external tradition established its ascendancy. One consequence of this was that the religious tradition came to be regarded as having a narrower scope of reference than it had previously been granted or had claimed for it. The Christian religious tradition became one among a plurality of intellectual traditions, just as the Christian churches themselves became a plurality of sects and denominations in the pluralistic Western societies. In the Soviet Union, Orthodox Christianity, which had not responded to the challenges of the alien intellectual traditions, was deprived of adherence by a threatening countermissionary movement, by the hampering of the institutions in which the traditions of the Orthodox Church were enacted and transmitted, and by other coercive measures. The consequence was a burgeoning of divergent Christian traditions, some originating in Orthodox Christianity, others coming from other Christian traditions.[23] Orthodox Christianity retracted its claims and assimilated a certain measure of Marxist tradition.

23. See Chrystal Lane, *Christian Religion in Russia: A Sociological Study* (London: Allen and Unwin, 1978).

The Migration of Religious Traditions

Scientists claim that scientific knowledge is universal in its persuasiveness to all those who have acquired the requisite discipline of understanding. This is true. Western scientific traditions have repeatedly migrated to new territories where they were not previously accepted. From Italy they spread to central and then to northern and western Europe. Then they spread overseas to North America, to eastern Europe, and to Japan. Such migration did not occur in the case of Chinese science. Islamic science spread with the spread of Islam and a little of it came into the traditions of Western science. Indian science never spread beyond the boundaries of Hindu civilization. The migration of religious traditions has been much more extensive and the migrant traditions have penetrated much more deeply into the periphery of the societies which they have entered. The migrations of Christianity from Palestine to Rome and Byzantium and then to eastern, central, western and northern Europe and to North and South America and to a smaller extent to Asia and Africa is matched by the migration of the Islamic tradition of religious belief from Arabia to all of the Middle East, the Indian subcontinent, Southeast Asia and Indonesia on the one side, and to all of North Africa and to much of Africa below the Sahara, ranging as far west as the Atlantic Ocean and as far east as the Pacific. The implantation of a religious tradition in a territory in which it was not at home previously is a more transforming process than the migration of a scientific tradition. The implantation of a religious tradition involves not merely a set of theological beliefs being handed down from one generation, from one territory, to other generations in other territories but also to the implantation in a different territory of an image of the past which had been formed by those whose biological ancestors had lived in it and to whom it was endogenous. In the course of displacing the previously accepted religious traditions, the migrant tradition also changes. It assimilates some elements of the displaced tradition. Palestinian Christianity developed somewhat differently when it spread throughout the western and northern territories of the Roman Empire than it did in its course through the eastern territories.

The Presence of the Past in Works of Science and Scholarship

Science against Tradition

The past is in an ambiguous position in the field called *Wissenschaft*. For one part of *Wissenschaft,* namely, what in the English-speaking world is called "natural science" or just "science," the very existence of science which aims to discover what was previously unknown denies the validity of knowledge drawn from the past in whatever sphere science is conducted. Since the postulate of the search for knowledge defines the task of the scientist as the "falsification" of what has been received, only through the process of continuous falsification of prior beliefs does science progress.[24] This view is one source of the derogation of the past. Another source of the derogation of tradition is that the method of scientific inquiry means that nothing which is offered from the past is to be accepted unless it withstands the scrutiny of the skeptical, rational, and observational powers of qualified persons. Doubt being the beginning of scientific activity, only that which survives the test of contemporary doubt can be accepted as valid scientific knowledge. The skeptical attitude and the insistence on meticulous tests by systematic empirical procedures and rigorous logical analysis have been regarded as the solvents which would wash away tradition—understood as unfounded beliefs unthinkingly accepted.

The natural sciences made their way in a polemical mood. In the nineteenth century, they encountered the varying, sometimes bitter resistance of classical learning and idealistic philosophy within the universities; before that they had been in intermittent altercation with ecclesiastical authority which, out of a combination of theological considerations and others based on ancient science, disapproved of particular features of modern science in the seventeenth century. In the nineteenth century, they again came into other conflicts with ecclesiastical authority. Science was drawn into the battles of the main figures of the continental Enlightenment with the forces of darkness, and this too turned it against that loose cluster of things loosely called "tradition."

First, beliefs about the particular objects of scientific research and later about other matters fell before the scientist's fire. Beliefs which were inherited from ancestors and sustained by their mere availability and by their authoritative presentation in the works of ancient writers

24. The place of tradition in science is now more generally acknowledged by scientists and philosophers of science. The argument was first made in clear-cut form by Michael Polanyi in *Science, Faith, and Society,* Riddell Memorial Lectures, Eighteenth Series (London: Oxford University Press, 1946), and Karl Popper in "Towards a Rational Theory of Tradition," in *Rationalist Annual* (London: Watts, 1948), reprinted in Popper's *Conjectures and Refutations* (London: Routledge and Kegan Paul, 1962), pp. 120–35. More recently, Stephen Toulmin, in *Human Understanding* (Oxford: Clarendon Press, 1972), pp. 218 ff.; Werner Heisenberg, "Tradition in Science," in Owen Gingerich, ed., *The Nature of Scientific Discovery. A Symposium Commemorating the 500th Anniversary of the Birth of Nicolaus Copernicus* (Washington, D.C.: Smithsonian Institution Press, 1975), pp. 219–36; and John Ziman, in *Public Knowledge: An Essay Concerning the Social Dimension of Science* (Cambridge: Cambridge University Press, 1968), and *Reliable Knowledge* (Cambridge: Cambridge University Press, 1978), have stated the position more elaborately.

and their contemporary protagonists were regarded as part of the baggage which would be cleared away by the growth of science. Experimental and inductive methods freed the scientist from beliefs presented by authority and rendered him dependent only on his own observation, on his own senses, and on his own rational powers. Nothing was to be interposed between nature and the experimental-rational scientist. This doctrine was applied to the objects of natural science such as chemical substances, gases, fluids, physical bodies. It was extended to human institutions in eighteenth-century France, Italy, and England; Condorcet, Filangieri, Beccaria, Hume, Smith, Ferguson, Bentham, wished to create a science of man as scientific as the natural sciences and as free as they were from the domination of custom over the human mind. Science seemed to be inimical to tradition; tradition was held to be inimical to science.

This conception of the scientist unencumbered by the past was different in important respects from the conception of the artist and the literary man as it was taking form under the influence of romanticism and the idea of genius. The artist and writer rose though his imagination which was inside himself to the highest realm of being. The scientist, in contrast, disciplined his imagination and controlled his fantasy by discovering the world outside himself, heeding only the data of his senses and the requirements of logic. By these techniques he also rose to the highest realm of being. He reached it in the discovery and contemplation of the timelessly, universally valid laws of nature.

The timeless, universal laws were at first welcomed by poets.[25] With William Blake, however, the welcome was exhausted and for a long time thereafter the battle was joined. Science was charged with having denied to nature the sensuous qualities which the literary imagination could grasp. Through its steady progress, science, having gradually obliterated from human experience the apprehension and appreciation of those qualities, had left humanity alone in a cold and ultimately meaningless universe. The myths from the past, the memories of the past by which mankind had explained how it had come to be what it was were being obliterated by this scientific disclosure of the timeless, inhuman universe. The expulsion of directly experienced human sensations from the image of the universe also expelled images of the past, particularly images of the magical or supernatural events which marked the steps of the history of mankind. The devaluation of direct experience diminished the value of memories not directly experienced and implied the dissolution of the image of the past and of the value of the events of that incorrectly

25. Marjorie Hope Nicholson, *Newton Demands the Muse: Newton's Opticks and the Eighteenth-Century Poets* (Princeton: Princeton University Press, 1946).

imagined past. The poetic critics of the natural sciences did not clearly see this extension of the ravages of natural science to the past of mankind, but its implications were nonetheless apprehended. The milestones of the past of mankind—the great events of biblical history—were being torn out of the ground.

In the heroic age of science, some great scientists thought that their work had the same intentions as theology, that it sought to understand the universe through the discovery of the laws which God had created.[26] They insisted that their procedures offered a surer way to the comprehension of God's will than the method of verbal disputation used by theologians. Newton saw no contradiction between the traditional account of the history of mankind which was offered by the Bible and his views of the cosmic mechanism.[27] In the nineteenth century, the relationship of science to traditional Christian belief deteriorated. Geology, archaeology, and the higher criticism carried the battle directly into the camp of the Christian faith and Christian intellectuals defended their image of the past in a way which weakened their position.

Traditional governmental and economic institutions came under severe criticism from intellectuals who were the enemies of the errors of the past. The declining legitimacy of the powers of the traditional institutions of monarchy and aristocracy occurred also with respect to the position of the churches which were in such close affinity to them. The placing in question of the historical and cosmogenic beliefs of the church weakened the authority of other institutions and beliefs which were linked with it. It was not the intention of most of the great scientists of the sixteenth and seventeenth centuries to diminish the power of traditional institutions or to decry traditionality as such; although this inclination had been present in Bacon's mind, it was generally dormant until the nineteenth century.

Scientists did not press the battle against traditional institutions on a broad front.[28] Many scientists became agnostics in matters of reli-

26. Galileo looked upon nature as "God's second book"—the first was the Bible—and he thought that this "second book" had been written by God in alphabetical letters which had to be learned if the book was to be read. Kepler thought God created the universe in accordance with the pure archetypal forms which Plato called "ideas" and which can be understood as mathematical constructs. Heisenberg summarized this attitude in the proposition that "Physics is reflection on the divine ideas of creation: therefore physics is divine service" ("Tradition in Science," in Gingerich, *The Nature of Scientific Discovery*, p. 227).

27. Frank Manuel, *Isaac Newton, Historian* (Cambridge, Mass.: Belknap Press-Harvard University Press, 1963), and *The Religion of Isaac Newton* (Oxford: Clarendon Press, 1974).

28. Darwin's statement that he did not wish to be associated with Marx's views because he did not wish to give offense to believers in the traditional Christian view is illustrative of the conciliatory attitude of many great scientists. See Ralph Colp, "The Contacts between Karl Marx and Charles Darwin," *Journal of the History of Ideas* 35, no. 2 (April-June 1974): 329–38.

gion. They accommodated themselves to traditional political institutions; when the traditions of liberalism and democracy prospered in the nineteenth century they also accommodated themselves to these newly ascendant traditions. Most scientists were not themselves explicitly antitraditional; "scientism," which was antitraditional and hence critical of all beliefs and institutions which were not demonstrably true or valuable according to scientific criteria, was largely the work of nonscientists, publicists, philosophers, social scientists, and social reformers.

There was, however, one sphere of life in which scientists were avowedly distrustful of tradition, and that was in scientific work itself. There, the belief in the irrefragable foundation of scientific knowledge in the evidence of the senses, and the use of instruments which extended the powers of the senses, disciplined by hypotheses and experimental procedures and by mathematics, rendered unacceptable all claims to credibility which could not ultimately be reduced to empirical evidence. There was, thus, an inherent antithesis between scientific knowledge and traditional knowledge. It made little difference whether a scientist regarded himself as completely inductive in his procedures or whether he accepted the interpretation of scientific method as the inverse-hypothetical-deductive method. The decisive thing was that no belief accepted by a scientist could be accredited on any grounds other than its foundation in empirical observation and logical or mathematical analysis.

According to the severe inductivist scheme, the practicing scientist should accept nothing on faith. He should refer to no unverified facts or propositions; he should not use other scientists' theories for which he does not have experimental evidence. The responsibility of the scientist is to be skeptical of that which has been received from other scientists.[29] It is in the deficiencies of what has come down from the past of science that a scientist finds his tasks. A scientist who accepted unquestioningly what had been transmitted to him by his teachers would sink to the bottom of the hierarchy of scientists.

Scientific procedure is indeed very different from the traditional way of arriving at beliefs; the two modes of arriving at beliefs differ in their fundamental objective. Scientific effort is intended to achieve something new; traditional belief is content with what was believed before. The difference between the two is not merely that difference between systematically and empirically confirmed beliefs on the one side, and traditionally received beliefs on the other. The scientist justifies his existence by the discovery of something hitherto unknown; the confirmation of the tradition is either of secondary and incidental value or it is useless.

29. Professor Robert Merton has formulated this as "organized skepticism" (*The Sociology of Science: Theoretical Empirical Investigations* [Chicago: University of Chicago Press, 1973], pp. 277–78).

Not every scientist can discover important new things, but that is the aim and justification of science as an intellectual activity. It would not be a discovery if it reiterated the already known. Scientists who cannot do more than this are only handmaidens, helpers, fillers-in-of-gaps, no more than a supporting cast. These secondary figures too are committed to the same objective.

If the ordinary undistinguished scientist is antipathetic to tradition—as he sees it—so should be the great scientist, the genius in science. The accomplishment of the scientist of genius entails breaking fundamentally with the traditional stock of beliefs of his own discipline.

The image of science as a succession of discoveries, each subsequent discovery making the preceding one out of date, has ostensibly placed it in unremitting conflict with tradition. Thus, even when it was recognized that no scientist could begin solely from his own observations and that he had to begin with the consideration of the conclusions of his predecessors, his task was to render out of date what he had received. The responsibility of the discoverer was to destroy the tradition which he had received and to present a better one to the oncoming generation of scientists. And so it will go on—a tradition received, a tradition annulled, a tradition created and transmitted, a tradition annulled . . . .

The discoverer of genius goes far beyond his predecessor. The greater the scientist, the more he frees himself from the beliefs of his predecesssors and leaves behind a discovery, a theory, which may be more enduring than the results of other scientists but which in the course of time will itself be replaced by one which is more credible, according to standards which are themselves enduring.

Minds of the second order fill in the gaps of a theory in ways which leave the theory more or less intact. Minds of the first order create new theories. In "normal science," in Professor Kuhn's popular distinction, second-order scientists work within a framework given by an accepted general theory or "paradigm."[30] Paradigms are traditions of a limited life-span. The great scientist is in this respect like the founder of a great religion. Both are said to annul the tradition which has been presented to them. Both are aware of the inadequacy of what has been received and they aim to supplant the inadequate account by one which is fundamentally more adequate. In neither situation is the annulment of tradition complete.

Both have their point of departure in tradition, both change the tradition which is handed on to living disciples or colleagues and to subsequent generations. The prophet regards his message as endur-

30. Professor Kuhn emphasizes in places the discontinuity of the new paradigmatic science with respect to the science which has gone before (*The Structure of Scientific Revolutions* [Chicago: University of Chicago Press, 1962], pp. 92–110).

ingly true, the scientist knows that his proposition will be revised and in time apparently replaced. In fact, the prophet's teaching will be revised by the action of interpretation, the scientist's proposition will live on in a new and more adequate formulation.[31]

The disciples of the founder of a new religion attribute to him a more radical antagonism towards tradition than the adherents of the ideas of a scientific genius attribute to him. The tradition which the religious genius would supplant is as broad as all of existence. It offers a new outlook, a new way of life, a new promise of redemption. The scientific genius does not undertake to revise and replace all of science, all of ethics, all of politics. The tradition he would revise is not all of the tradition of science but only that of his special field; a great discovery, particularly in physics, will in the course of time disclose its implications for other fields such as geology or genetics, but for the time being the tradition which it confronts is not coterminous with all of science. The fruitfully productive scientist is thus not at war with tradition in general, insofar as he is attending to his business. In the field of his scientific work he is warily engaged in a complicated encounter with tradition. He cannot be oblivious to it, he cannot act without it, and he cannot just submit to it.

There is one thing in science which is not traditional and that is the newly discovered proposition or those elements of the proposition which were not known before with the same evidence and certainty. They might have been adumbrated before, they might have been hunches before, and in that sense and in that manner they are parts of tradition, but as propositions with the certainty of reinforced evidence they are not tradition. In science there is one feature which does stand as the barrier between tradition and what becomes tradition in the future and this is the experimental and observational procedure. This procedure is a declaration of partial independence from beliefs handed down from the past. The particular actions of observation and recording of experimental results are not traditions, although they are done in accordance with traditions and their results become part of future traditions.

As a matter of fact, natural scientists were not as hostile or indifferent to traditions as their detractors and the positivistic philosophy of science which was attributed to them declared and which some of them espoused. They by no means spurned the great accomplishments and heroic figures of their past. Newton has remained a great name of science. Even Auguste Comte, who was the chief propagandist of science of the nineteenth century and who regarded the

31. A. N. Whitehead said that when a religious belief is proved wrong, it is accepted as a defeat for religion; but when a scientific proposition is proved wrong, it is a triumph for science (*Science and the Modern World* [New York: Macmillan, 1929], p. 270).

theological and metaphysical knowledge inherited from the past and the society based on it as in need of replacement, wished to remind future generations of the great accomplishments of the past; his calendar of the "saints of humanity" was just such a tribute to the achievements of forerunners. Nor were scientists so blind to any kind of history as was alleged.[32] Some fields such as palaeontology and geology were in fact historically treated. Evolutionary theory was historical too. Certain branches of natural science certainly did deal with the past.

Nonetheless, natural scientists tended to be on the side of enlightenment and some were in fact aggressive progressivists. The latter thought that tradition was a "reactionary force" holding back the progress of the human mind. They shared the disparaging view of "tradition" as superstitious prejudice. Many natural scientists proud of their solid accomplishments and contemptuous of the uncertainty of the results of other intellectual activities, thought that their science was an intellectual undertaking utterly unlike and completely superior to all those others which were realms of arbitrariness, subjective fantasies, superstition, and uncritical reception of traditional belief.

Tradition in Religious Knowledge and Tradition in Scientific Knowledge. Tradition in natural science shares some of the properties of tradition in religious knowledge. The essential point in both, common to all human activities, is that no theologian or scientist begins *de novo.* A novice in science must master a body of established knowledge which is his tradition just as a novice in training for a religious profession has to do. The traditions are different in their subject matter and in their rhetoric; their procedures overlap in some respects and are also very different in others. The religious tradition focuses on the understanding of texts; the scientific tradition also focuses on the understanding of a textbook which is, as a work, not of intrinsic significance; its merits lie in its efficiency in the presentation of the best of the tradition, i.e., what has been accepted as true on the basis of strict criteria by the branch of the scientific profession in which the novice seeks instruction. The novice in religious studies also studies theological textbooks which themselves are also only instrumental and which are also regarded in the light of their efficiency for the purposes of conveying what is essential in the subject as judged by the best authorities.

There is also a major difference. The studies of the novice in religious studies center ultimately on a sacred text; the studies of the scientific novice treat no book as in itself sacred. But here again,

32. This was made clear by Heinrich Rickert in *Kulturwissenschaft und Naturwissenschaft,* 3d. ed. (Tübingen: J. C. B. Mohr [Paul Siebeck], 1916), pp. 55–66.

similarities are evident. The sacred text, although putatively the same text—once it has been established as canonical—undergoes revision through the interpretations which are made of it. The equivalent in science—the received body of knowledge, including fundamental theories—also undergoes revision. In the revision of their respective traditions, another, perhaps not so important difference appears which runs throughout these two fields of intellectual activity. In the field of religious knowledge, the revisions of the understanding of the sacred text are not understood as innovations; they are by-products of the quest for better understanding. The truth is already present in the sacred text and it is the task of the student to elicit it by interpretation. An innovation in interpretation does not imply an innovation in the sacred text; it is a better disclosure of what was there already. In the natural sciences and in other "scientific" or scholarly disciplines, innovation in the tradition is deliberately sought. Innovation is acknowledged as the means to better under-standing of a fundamentally unchanging reality. Not only is innovation sought in science but, the more fundamental the innovation, the more esteemed the innovator is once he has established its validity. But then so are great reformers like Luther and Calvin greatly esteemed for their "restorative" innovations. Fundamental innovation is re-garded as better than marginal innovation.

Thus, innovation occurs in both religious and scientific knowledge. In the former it occurs in the process of improving interpretation or the understanding of the sacred text or of the nearly sacred inter-pretations and it is not put forward as innovation; in the latter, in-novation is sought in the understanding of nature and it is acknowl-edged as such, once it meets the criteria of validity and is really a significant innovation.

The crucial tradition which is revered in religious knowledge is one which derives from an event far back in time; it carries an account of a divine revelation. The tradition to which a scientist submits is one of more recent formation although it too is continuous with the remoter past. The link with the remoter past in a scientific tradition is twofold: the most recently promulgated valid tradition has its point of de-parture in a tradition of more distant origin. The remoter phase of tradition is a causal precondition of the later stages of the tradition; it is also in varying degrees a logical or cognitive constituent of sub-sequent propositions which make up the later stage of the tradition.

In scientific knowledge as in religious knowledge there are two primary traditions—one written, the other oral. One is the substantive tradition, the body of substantive knowledge of problems and their solutions established by procedures meeting the criteria of validity appropriate to scientific procedures; this corresponds to the second primary tradition of religious knowledge, science having no written texts. Nature is the sacred text of science; it is always there but it is not disclosed by revelation. It is disclosed only by methodical observation and logical analysis and imagination. The second primary tradition of science is the unarticulated tradition of sensibility to significant problems and significant observations and of the ethos of cultivation of scientific truth; this is the oral tradition. The oral tradition is such because it cannot be codified; there are many hunches and rules which are not articulated, certainly not articulated in writing; there is no systematic body of rules for discovery and probity; what reaches formulation is never adequate to the effective transmission and reception of the tradition. The reality of the oral tradition in science is acknowledged by the "oral history" of science. It is an acknowledgment that the corpus of written works alone does not permit the reconstruction of the history of science as adequately as does the combination of written works and recollections of what occurred.[33]

Science and Its Tradition: Manuscripts and Books. The dependence of scientific research on the most recent form of its tradition results in a relegation of the earlier stages of the tradition. They are matters for contemplation brought into view by the animation of the sense of the past. They have no normative demands on present scientific activity in the way in which the prescriptions of an early church council had for subsequent Christian belief many centuries later or in the way in which Plato's and Aristotle's ideas about political life must be considered by political philosophers. Insofar as the scientific achievements of the ancient world still live on as traditions in modern scientific works, they do so in patterns of the utmost generality. Certain fundamental problems of ancient science such as the application of mathematics in the formulation of relationships in nature, the idea of an atom as a unit in the organization of material substances, the idea of gravity, and the idea of the process of generation of biological organisms continue to concern modern scientists but they do so with far greater differentiation and with very different substance.[34]

The physical tradition of the scientific works of antiquity and of early modern times, their rescue and preservation, have a significance somewhat different from the great undertaking of humanistic scholarship in the restitution of the corpus of ancient poetry, drama, philosophy, and historiography. Modern scientific knowledge is less

33. The new "oral historiography" of science is an effort to supplement the published scientific papers and monographs with unpublished written material, correspondence, drafts, sketches, and orally given recollections which fill in the interstices of the published material and even of the unpublished written material.

34. G. E. R. Lloyd, *Early Greek Science: Thales to Aristotle* (London: Chatto and Windus, 1970), pp. 145–46.

affected by the total loss of many works of ancient scientists and by the fragmentary and indirect survival of the works of others than is appreciative literary possession by the disappearance of the majority of the works of the greatest dramatists of antiquity.

The recovery and restoration of ancient scientific works were not thought to be much less urgent tasks by humanistic scholars than were the recovery and restoration of literary and philosophical works. Scientists did not constitute a definable class of persons in antiquity as they do in the twentieth century and their works were not separated from philosophical works into a separate category. Furthermore, the ideas of Galen, Hippocrates, and Ptolemy and certain medical writers continued to be of primary importance as the points of departure for the scientific works of the Renaissance. There is therefore little ground to believe that the tradition of scientific manuscripts before the age of print was neglected by humanistic scholars and that the proportion of recovered works is very much smaller in science than in literature and philosophy. It is of course possible that scientific works were more neglected than philosophical works because of the dislike of natural science by certain of the church fathers like Tertullian or the disparaging attitude of St. Augustine towards natural scientific curiosity. More of them might have been knowingly discarded or sacrificed to other uses. In any case, the loss of these manuscripts was not experienced by modern scientists as a handicap to their own work of discovery.

The survival of the corpus of modern science in manuscripts and printed form has had much better fortune—like that of modern literature, philosophy, and historiography. The existence of academies of sciences since the seventeenth century and of the Italian academies since the sixteenth century have provided places of security for manuscripts and books where a minimum of safekeeping was assured. The existence of royal libraries did the same. The ease of transforming a manuscript into a printed book, the better care taken of reproduction in print in comparison with the waywardness of copying of manuscripts by hand have assured the more comprehensive survival of the works of science as a whole for the great ages of science than has been the fate of works of literature and philosophy in their great ages in their remoter past. Much of this is to be attributed to print. Practically all that scientists conceive of as science has been done since the beginning of the printed book. Even though scientists do not much use older stages of their traditions, the works produced in those stages are the beneficiaries of the better custodianship which has been increasingly provided.

The older parts of the physical inheritance of scientific works are left unused; this contrasts with the intensity of use of the more recent parts. A novelist would not regard it as a dereliction if he had not read all the novels of the past five or ten years; a literary critic, unless he were trying to advance in an academic career, would seldom think it necessary to have read all of the works of the past decade about the poems or novels he was writing about. The scientist who failed to do so would be negligent. The scientist wishes to know exactly what has been discovered on the particular, precisely defined problem on which he is at work. He takes for granted that what he reads in a recent scientific journal has been carefully scrutinized by the editor and his advisers and that very little that has not been subjected to strict and rigorous methods of observation and analysis will have got through to print. He also takes for granted that the other authors have done what he is doing. If he receives preprints of papers which have been accepted for publication, he has the same confidence. If he receives a paper which has not yet been passed through the assessor's sieve, he will be confident—once he has seen that it comes from a laboratory which is known to live up to the traditional ethos of science, which goes much further back than any specified results—that the author of the paper has submitted to the most recent part of the tradition or has very persuasive reasons for not being willing to do so.

The scientist's dependence on the latest stage of the tradition of his subject confirms him in his belief that he has nothing to do with tradition except ceremonially, and that tradition and science are antithetical to each other.

It is not that the scientist disparages the achievements of his forerunners. They have a special pantheon to themselves. The deference which is given to them is not for the continued validity and pertinence of the propositions which they put forward. It is not thought that these propositions as they were promulgated are still essential to further work on the problems of current interest to scientists. It is accorded them because the propositions were important steps which led to the most recent phases of the tradition. The contemporary scientist no longer takes any scientific interest in their work.

It has often been argued, and increasingly in recent years, as the courses of study of scientific subjects have become so narrow, that the study of the history of the tradition of science would broaden the minds of young scientists and make them more aware of the larger cultural and moral significance of their investigation and studies. It is not argued that the study of the history of the scientific tradition in their own subjects or in the wider range of science would improve the scientific quality of their own research. The refined, and enriched tradition precipitated from the latest and best papers and monographs is thought to contain the substantive tradition which scientists need for the effective conduct of research.

For the same reason, the manuscripts and notebooks of scientists of the seventeenth and eighteenth centuries and the records of their observations are like the manuscripts of the ages before printing. They are a quite secondary sector of the scientific tradition. They have ceased to have a scientific interest, i.e., they are of no substantive value to scientists who are engaged in research and who are attempting to extend and modify the substantive stock of valid and important scientific knowledge. They are of interest to historians of science and they are of interest to persons who wish to be in contact with one of the sacred moments of the disclosure of scientific truth. A scientist might take great pride in possessing or having examined a manuscript of Kepler or Boerhaave because he appreciates being in the presence of a monument, old and sacred. Their manuscripts are not essential to his astronomical research, or to his chemical, botanical, or medical research.

The Traditional Element in Scientific Knowledge. The growth of scientific knowledge epitomizes the complexity of the pattern of a tradition which has developed through time. There is an overlay of strata of the tradition, each of which at one time was a new acquisition; each variation changes the other parts of the possessed tradition. If it were merely a matter of the juxtaposition of a number of discrete propositions, there would be no difficulty. Traditions are not like that however. The parts of a tradition which are represented in a single paper or book are connected with each other by subsumption and mutual implication. It is difficult to delineate the pattern in which a new increment or correction or rejection is brought into relationships with the preexistent body of scientific knowledge which constitutes, at any given time, the tradition. A scientific proposition which is narrow and without generality in scope may be discarded without changing the rest of the tradition. If it is broad in scope, its replacement or modification will affect much else in the tradition as it is passed on to the next generation of its recipients.

The overlay of elements in a tradition is like what Pinder discerned in the history of art, i.e., the presence of elements of works and of whole works recently created or being currently created. The elements are of different ages; some theories last a very long time in prominent and crucial positions in the actively possessed stock of knowledge in a particular field; others lose their prominence but continue to play a crucial role in the stock of knowledge in active possession; others fade away or are decisively repudiated. The rate of visible obsolescence is very high for many parts of the valid written tradition, although some of the theories are effective for a very long time, indeed for centuries, even though in forms adapted and modified in the light of new investigations and new theories.[35]

35. Professor Derek de Solla Price has asserted that a scientific paper has a short life. Older scientific papers are cited less frequently than recent ones. But

No scientist investigates and demonstrates every scientific proposition on which his own work depends. He accepts those propositions because they have been attested to by scientists whom he trusts, whether or not he knows them personally, and because those parts of his research which rest or touch on these traditional propositions do not disconfirm them. The rest of the large corpus of scientific propositions outside his own research, which he accepts because they are attested to by authoritative and trusted scientists and because when he studied them as a student they were patently true, plays a secondary part in his scientific work. Its function for him, like that of the oral tradition, is to sustain the scientific ethos; it confirms his confidence in the reliability of the scientific community and it thereby sustains his morale as a scientist and his confidence in the integrity of the scientific enterprise. It is a written tradition which he affirms but which he does not read; he is confident of it because he thinks that if he did read it and then set about testing it by scientific procedures it would not be disconfirmed. It is a tradition which makes a tremendous difference to every practicing scientist, however specialized he is in his own work.

The main intended function of the written tradition of science is to make new discoveries available for "public" scrutiny and assessment. The written tradition is the precondition of the sifting which determines which elements become inert and which are taken into the tradition. An immense social organization is required for the management of this tradition, for determining what may be added to it, and for determining what should be refused entry into it. The individuals and bodies which allocate funds for research depend on the interpretation of this tradition for their decisions; the first conception of an unsolved problem in the received tradition and the generation of an idea about its solution both depend on the availability of the tradition and its mastery. New knowledge would not be possible without old knowledge.

The Constitution of Scientific Originality. In discussing the relationship between the individual scientist and his contemporary fellow scientists in the heroic age of science, Professor Ziman accepts, in part, the view of the relative separateness of the great scientists of that age from each other. He is not unsympathetic with the view of "the man of science as a lonely, dedicated personality, grappling with

---

this would not prove that a paper has been discarded because it was incorrect. It might have been very sound and was therefore so fully assimilated into the subsequent generation of papers that the next generation ceased to cite it, citing mainly those which have been nourished by it. D. de Solla Price, *Little Science, Big Science* (New York: Columbia University Press, 1963), pp. 78–87.

problems that he has set himself, sensitive to the work of others, but not primarily governed by their demands on him."[36] But he then says: "the virtues of curiosity, intellectual freedom, the questioning of all accepted doctrines which were so essential in the heroic age of science (and which are, of course, still essential to good science now) are not sufficient to make a man into a successful research worker. Those virtues are to be found in many cranky, eccentric persons whose would-be contributions to science are worthless because they have not been subjected to the 'consensible' discipline."[37] No consensus can be attained about a problem where disagreement has existed unless there is a prior consensus about the conditions under which agreement can be established, about what is acceptable as evidence, about the rules for accepting evidence, and about many substantive propositions. This is exactly the point which Professor Ziman makes: "the scientific imagination is strongly constrained: scientific speculation is far from idle: it must act within a well-organized framework of ideas and facts, with rigid rules of argument and proof. Even the cosmologists do not spin their marvellous webs of space and time out of mere fantasy; they use the logic of the tensor calculus and astronomical observations to construct rational systems compelling by their elegance and simplicity. It is much more like extremely academic painting or poetry, in which the art is to say something new within the official stylistic conventions, than abstract expressionism or even blank verse. The typical scientific paper is akin to a sonnet, or a fugue, or a master's game of chess, in its respect for the regulations."[38]

The scientific genius does not create the "regulations." He accepts the "regulations" as given. A good rationale can be constructed for these regulations and most scientists would undoubtedly accept such a rationale once they examined it. The fact is however that they do not construct much of the rationale; they do not argue about the regulations. They accept them unquestioningly because they are the regulations which persons who are accepted as having been scientists have "always" accepted.

This "consensible discipline," as Professor Ziman calls it, is constituted by the demonstrated results of inquiry into a set of central problems and by the use of particular techniques. Most of these are accepted and insisted on by members of that branch of the profession of science who will criticize those who depart from them without acceptable grounds. Rational grounds can be given for the acceptance of the corpus of results, the central problems, and the techniques. but for any given scientists at any given time, they are given. They were, at an earlier stage, presented to him, and subsequently they are part of the intellectual equipment which he brings to any particular investiga-

36. Ziman, *Public Knowledge,* pp. 82–83.
37. Ibid.
38. Ibid., pp. 79–80.

tion. He raises questions about some of them which to him seem to be the most crucial and he conducts his research on them. Much of his research rests on the results achieved by others. Their acceptance in the past and in the present by his colleagues is the consensual framework within which he conducts his inquiry and presents its results to his colleagues. Nothing would be "consensible" about particular problems if there were not a prior consensus about other and closely related things. This consensus is the acknowledgment of the validity of a common tradition of concepts, observations, theories, techniques. The task of a scientist is to find a flaw in the tradition, breaking the consensus which the tradition presents, and persuading colleagues to reform the consensus by accepting his proffered improvement of the previously dominant consensus. He has to justify his breaking the previous consensus about old propositions and the new ones. There must be significant novelty in the results which he attains when he detects the deficiency in the scientific belief which made up the old consensus. The results are acceptable when they are compatible with what was and is essential in the consensually held tradition of accepted knowledge and procedure and because they affirm much of it, add to it, and modify it at the same time.

The Scientific Tradition. In science, tradition is foreshortened and condensed. The achievements of scientists up to the relatively recent moments of the past are concentrated and codified into textbooks, handbooks, tables of standards and constants. The brief lifespan of a scientific paper does not mean that its content is cast away and forgotten and that its life has been in vain. The name of its author and the particular achievement associated with his name might cease to be acknowledged, and its author and title might well be forgotten by the next generation of scientists. Later generations might never know those facts about it. Nonetheless, the results of the research which the paper contained, if they are true and important, are assimilated into the received body of valid knowledge. The observations reported go into the store of reliable observations which support or modify a given theory and they live on namelessly and without specific reference to themselves in the modified theory. And that theory, when it is in its turn modified, lives on still in its successor theories in the way in which parents live on in their children.

The value of past observations and theories is not exhausted only by their explicit employment by their successors. The physical similes of stepping-stones, points of departure, and so forth, are not quite adequate to describe the way in which the achievements of the past are handed on or live in a scientific discipline; the stepping-stones are not carried forward by the moving person as he advances. Nor is the simile of the carrying forward of a particular genetic constellation any more descriptive of a scientific tradition. Earlier works influenced the direction of later works so that the direction of interest and interpretation which any subsequent generation receives bears traces of the interests and interpretation of earlier, now forgotten, works.

The direction in which a tradition moves is partly a function of the centrality of certain problems. Part of the genius of a scientist lies in his discovery of problems which are important and for which the tradition provides no solution and which when solved will provide important problems for a long time to come. In somewhat different terms, Heisenberg laid similar stress on the tradition of problems: "Even within a fruitful period, a scientist has not much choice in selecting his problems.... One may say that a fruitful period is characterized by the fact that the problems are given, that we need not invent them.... In our century, the development of physics led Niels Bohr to the idea that Lord Rutherford's experiment on alpha-rays, Max Planck's theory of radiation and the facts of chemistry could be combined into a theory of the atom. And in the following years many young physicists went to Copenhagen in order to participate in the solution of this given problem. One cannot doubt that in the selection of problems, the tradition, the historical development, plays an essential role."[39]

Many of the categories and some of the observations and analyses contained in the report of an investigation, together with those of many others, live on in the subsequent investigations which have rendered them "out of date." A body of valid knowledge, as it is offered to elders, coevals, and to the oncoming generation at any given time, is a temporally stratified stock of propositions. Not all the propositions which make up a field of science at a given moment have been discovered simultaneously. But they are accepted as simultaneously valid by the community of scientists which is constituted by subscription to the validity of those scientific beliefs accepted as valid.

Michael Polanyi linked the present and the past by remarking that the recurrently reasserted "spontaneous coherence" of scientists in a particular discipline and even over the whole of science in certain issues, occurs despite conflicts and even profound divisions because they have a common tradition. They "are speaking with one voice because they are informed by the same tradition.... The whole system of scientific life [is] rooted in a scientific tradition.... The premises of science ... are embodied in a tradition, the tradition of science."[40]

The tradition of science is external to any particular scientists. It has the "exteriority" of a social fact, to use a term of Durkheim. It must be upheld by scientists, said Polanyi, "as an unconditional demand if it is to be upheld at all.... It is a spiritual reality which stands

39. Heisenberg, "Tradition in Science," pp. 221–22.
40. Polanyi, *Science, Faith, and Society,* p. 38.

over them and compels their allegiance."[41] This tradition is a product of the recurrent reaffirmations which have gone into its making. It is, of course, transmitted in the first and most tangible instance by the teacher in his relationship to his pupil, the teacher discriminatingly presenting an appropriate selection from the stock of knowledge which he possesses and, at the same time, inculcating into and arousing in his pupil a sensibility which permits him to apprehend the problematical elements in the tradition. There is a traditional content implicit in the very idea of a discipline since it is the outcome of the labor of generations of disciples who are not subservient "yes-men" but active continuators and modifiers of the inherited stock of knowledge which changes as it passes onward. Polanyi has spoken of the sequences of transmitters and revising and correcting recipients as an "apostolic succession."[42]

In Heisenberg's view it is not only in the relationship between teacher and student that tradition is maintained, transmitted, and developed. It is supported by the relationship of respect between approximate equals, some of them together in the same institution, some in other countries, all of them working towards the same goal.[43] He cites the intimate association of Einstein and Planck to illustrate the importance of mutual support and criticism and Einstein's correspondence with Arnold Sommerfeld about the theory of relativity and about quantum theory; Sommerfeld "was a dear friend of Max Born, although he could never agree with him on the statistical interpretation of quantum theory . . . . A large part of the scientific analysis of those extremely difficult problems, arising out of relativity and quantum theory, was actually carried out in conversations between those who took an active part in the research. Sommerfeld's school at Munich was a centre of research in the early 1920s. Wolfgang Pauli, Gregor Wentzel, Otto Laporte, W. Lenz, and many others belonged to this group, and we discussed almost daily the difficulties and paradoxes in the interpretation of recent experiments. When Sommerfeld had received a letter from Einstein or Bohr, he read the important parts of the letter in our seminar and started at once a discussion on the critical problems. Niels Bohr held a close association with Lord Rutherford, Otto Hahn, and Lise Meitner and he considered the continuous exchange of information between experiment and theory as a central task in the progress of physics."[44]

The selection of problems is affected by the availability of techniques which are not just a matter of technology but of their appropri-

41. Ibid.
42. Ibid., p. 40. See also Harriet Zuckermann, *Scientific Elite* (New York: The Free Press, 1977), pp. 98–143.
43. Heisenberg, "Tradition in Science," p. 222.
44. Ibid., pp. 222–23.

ateness to the problem and their conformity with the rules of scientific method. The rules of scientific method although often articulated are never exhaustively so. They are a stable element among changes in substance and technology. They are perhaps the most traditional part of science.[45]

The authority of the expressed and anticipated judgments rendered by contemporaries is strengthened by the peripheral perception of the additional authority of each scientist by virtue of his embodiment of the tradition and of his own prior contribution to the achieved state of the tradition. These overtones of ancestral voices say vague things about probity, about exertion, about the obligation to be imaginative and the obligation to be exigent towards what has been imagined, about the obligation to trust what the past has handed down and the obligation to be exigently demanding towards it and critical of it, to extend knowledge but to do so under very limiting conditions. These are the fundamental dispositions of the ethos of science; they supply the matrix of sensibility in which procedures and hypotheses are sought for and chosen. They remain remarkably stable through time, unlike the continuously changing and growing body of empirical observations and hypotheses or theories which form the substantive traditions. The extension and modification of the latter are the unchanging aims of science. The tradition which conveys the scientific ethos is, on the other hand, a reiteration of an identical set of beliefs, seldom articulated in explicit and systematic form, yet persisting unchangingly through time and imposing its authority by the self-evident rightness and by the consensus of submission and espousal by persons of great eminence in the past and present.

Genius and Tradition in Science. There can be no "untutored geniuses" in science. There can be no genius who refuses all tradition and who produces works of lasting value, or at least works which are capable of being incorporated into the pattern of knowledge at its most advanced points. Ramanujan was perhaps the closest to an untutored genius, but he, too, had already entered mathematics at a point already long surpassed when he studied it within the tradition of the nineteenth-century mathematics taught him in the Town High School and the Government College of Kumbakonum and at Pachaiyappa's College, Madras. He did not complete his undergraduate course. He gained his livelihood by menial clerical work and in his leisure time worked forward by himself from antiquated points of departure. He became connected with the latest developments of the

45. "The role of tradition in sciences is not restricted to the selection of problems. Tradition exerts its full influence in deeper layers of the scientific process where it is not so easily visible. Here we should first of all mention the 'scientific method'" (ibid., p. 225).

mathematical tradition only after he was brought to Cambridge before the First World War.[46]

Despite the antithesis between tradition and science which has been proclaimed by the unthinking adherents of scientism, scientific genius cannot live without tradition. It would be no more than an extremely vital, amorphously imaginative and ingenious curiosity. No wholly untutored genius could work out the rules of the scientific ethos, lay out its agenda of observations, design the apparatus needed to embody them, or develop the general ideas which, once established, would be extensions of the existing body of knowledge. It is out of the question that a wholly uneducated genius could make an important contribution to any science. It is just as impossible as it would be for a fully developed, rational, cultivated human being to emerge without any direct and indirect contact with persons older than himself. An autodidactic genius is possible in science—although less so nowadays than in earlier periods in the history of science—but a completely uneducated one is not.

Untutored genius in science is rendered utterly improbable because genius requires for its capacities to become effective that it be inserted into a tradition and even into a community—however dispersed— which embodies that tradition in its activities. Genius seeks tradition. It seeks out existing knowledge to which to attach itself and from which it can then work out towards a disciplined independence. A young person interested in scientific problems, in the processes with which a science deals, is drawn to them on early contact. He gains further instruction in school or from a tutor. Then once caught up in the institutions of science, even where they are rudimentary, as in the sixteenth and seventeenth centuries in Europe, they enfold him, infuse the tradition into him, and thus place him in a position in which he can move forward from them while remaining within them.

The instruction given by a master to his pupil, whether the master is a man of means and leisure or a monk or a court official or a university professor who dominates a department or the head of a team in a research institute, is the way in which the powerful intellectual dispositions of the superior mind are concentrated on particular sets of objects and are furnished with the tradition of valid knowledge about them. In the course of time, the balance shifts from submission to the tradition to independence of it; but both are always present. Even the greatest mind does not ever cut itself completely from tradition. Once it has submitted to tradition, it can never become wholly and totally independent of it. Whatever it does henceforward rests on tradition.

---

46. "Notice" by P. V. Seshu Aiyar and B. Ramachandra Rao, pp. xi–xix, and "Notice" by G. H. Hardy, pp. xxi–xxxvi, in Srinivasa Ramanujan, *Collected Papers*, ed. G. H. Hardy et al. (Cambridge: Cambridge University Press, 1927).

"Second-order minds," although they are less capable than geniuses of making major modifications of tradition, help to sustain it in each successive generation.[47] They reinforce the matrix within which genius works. They provide the secondary audience of published scientific works, and the success of a genius in establishing the new pattern of understanding which he has created lies in his persuasion of the wider reaches of the scientific community to accept his innovations.

Humanistic Studies

The differentiation and partial separation of traditions is manifest in the present separation of the natural sciences from the humanities. The antecedents of the natural sciences—insofar as they were not the rules of an empirical technology—were in Western antiquity not regarded as fundamentally outside the tradition from which the humanities emerged. The quadrivium and the trivium recognized different disciplines but they did not assert a fundamental difference between the two main classes.

Nonetheless, the paths of these two major branches of studious intellectual activity did become separated. They were not totally separated for all sorts of reasons, the main one being very simply that both depend on observation and reason, on memory and imagination. They were moreover—at least in the West—bound up with classical antiquity; they were both concerned with work produced in the ancient world. Although, as in modern times, some individuals concentrated wholly or primarily in what we now call science and others did what we now call humanistic research, a common education in some classical texts kept them from falling totally away from one another. The fact that the practitioners of the sciences and the practitioners of the humanities both wrote in Latin which had long since ceased to be a vernacular tongue even in Italy also forced them into a partial union. Nevertheless they did move off onto separate paths and they have never come together since that separation.

They separated because they had different subject matters and different tasks. The natural sciences dealt with things which were apprehensible by the senses, things which could be directly seen, heard, felt, smelt, or tasted or could be so apprehended with the aid of instruments which extended the power of the senses. The humanistic disciplines dealt with great symbolic constructions: works of literature, religious and philosophical works, and they attempted to construct images of past events of human actions. This means that they had to recover works from the past in order to analyze and con-

---

47. T. S. Eliot, "Introduction," *The Sacred Wood,* 3d. ed. (London: Methuen, 1932), pp. xiv–xv.

template them and to construct images of past actions; they also had to recover physical artifacts of the past and interpret them with respect to the intention of their production and their use in chains of human action in the past.

The attention which humanistic scholars gave to works produced in the remote past, given the prevalent modes of mechanical reproduction of texts, their physical location and state of preservation, meant necessarily that much of their activity was devoted to the retrieval of the physical precipitates of the works and the authentication of their texts. The humanistic disciplines took their name from their cultivation by persons who appreciated the outlook and style of classical writers and who regarded them as exemplary and worthy of emulation. (In Great Britain the study of classical literature was sometimes called the study of humanity.) The Middle Ages and the origins of the modern national vernacular cultures and states appeared much later as objects of scholarly study. Even the critical scholarly study of the origins of the dominant religion of Western civilization and of the source from which it partially derived came much later.

For the humanistic disciplines, concentrating as they did on the works of classical antiquity and beginning before the age of printing and being interested almost exclusively in works written before the age of printing and the production of numerous copies of written works, manuscripts constituted the primary "raw material" of scholarly research. So powerful has the normative tradition of work on manuscripts become that, even in investigations concerning works and events in periods when printed sources are plentiful, the study of manuscripts and other unpublished sources still retains a superior prestige among scholars. In any case, the critical study of manuscripts, the establishment of "genuine" texts and their exegesis became and remained for a long time among the highest responsibilities of humanistic scholars.

The scholarly interest from its beginnings in Italy was impelled by a variety of motives. The first was the desire to be in more genuine contact with the charismatic past of the contemporary European civilization of which the scholar felt himself a part. A second was undoubtedly the intellectual challenge, the desire for knowledge, and the desire to do better than one's contemporaries and antecedents in the task of retrieving and reconstituting the works of that charismatic past.

The study of the Christian past had already been taken well in hand by churchmen, and those who were later called humanists did not concern themselves primarily with the texts of old Christian writers. The border and antecedent civilizations—Egyptian, Jewish, Babylonian—also received attention from the humanists but were not in the forefront of their interests. The Italian humanists, like the Romans before them looked to Greece. They regarded the Greek past as an essential part of their past.

Educated persons in the West had continued to know Latin authors throughout the Middle Ages and they were not unaware of Greek authors, but it was only in about the fifteenth century that Greek authors became interesting to them.[48] Even then, Latin authors were the first to receive the editorial attention of the Italian humanists; the works of emendation began on Latin authors and moved on to Greek authors only later. The first efforts were to purify contemporary Latin to make it conform with classical usage.[49] By the second half of the fifteenth century the most important Greek prose writers were translated into Latin for "the common mass of educated men."[50]

The task was to restore the ancient authors' works. The comparison of several manuscripts of the same work showed discrepancies arising from copyists' errors in transcription and wanton "improvements." There were no manuscripts in the hand of any ancient authors; there were not even manuscripts made by copyists from the authors' own autograph manuscripts. It is quite possible that even in antiquity the proportion of autograph manuscripts written by the authors themselves was not high; the manuscripts might have been written from dictation in the first place. In any case, by the end of the first millennium of the Christian era, there were practically no complete manuscripts left from the first few centuries after the classical authors' own lifetime. Such manuscripts certainly must have existed but since they probably numbered only in the hundreds, or for some other reason, they have nearly all disappeared. What are left are copies made some centuries after the works were composed, sometimes more than ten centuries later; these copies were made from other copies which were often deformed by numerous inadvertent mistakes arising from misreadings, misunderstandings, and slips of the pen, sometimes by intended "improvements" of the text by the copyist.

The reestablishment of the classical tradition, i.e., the repossession of the intellectual culture of antiquity by Italian and later French, German, Dutch, and English men of learning, depended on the discovery and purification of the physical deposit of that tradition.[51] The manuscripts were scattered and their very existence was often unknown to living persons. Before comparison could be made and emendations proposed, the manuscripts themselves had to be located.

48. Roberto Weiss, *The Renaissance Discovery of Classical Antiquity* (Oxford: B. H. Blackwell, 1969).

49. Robert Bolgar, *The Classical Inheritance and Its Beneficiaries* (Cambridge: Cambridge University Press, 1954), p. 270.

50. Ibid., p. 277.

51. E. J. Kenney, *The Classical Text* (Berkeley: University of California Press, 1974), pp. 22, 59, 77.

Scholars like Poggio Bracciolini made extensive tours for this purpose early in the fifteenth century. By the first part of the sixteenth century most of the Latin literature now known had been rediscovered.[52] The task of the discovery of manuscripts was like the task of the anti-quarians who from the sixteenth century onward were preoccupied in the discovery of written records and other physical remains from which historical works could later be composed.[53] The editing of manuscripts and the publication of texts in printed form not only embraced works of intrinsic intellectual value of the highest quality but documents of value primarily because they had been produced in the past and would permit future scholars to reconstruct the course of events leading from the past to the present. Humanistic scholars set out to retrieve the highest stratum of the tradition they wished to assimilate; they went on to do the work preparatory for the re-construction of the phases through which the entire classical and then the national cultural traditions had moved. This activity of identifying, dating, describing, and cataloguing of documents, monuments, in-scriptions, and coins was first undertaken as part of this effort to become more intimate with past things and to conserve them; later it became instrumental to the writing of historical works which would bring a true image of the past into the present.

The task of biblical scholars was different than that of classical scholars. The Bible was officially a sacred book in a way which the writings of Latin and Greek pagan writers were not. There was an official interpretation; after the Reformation there were several offi-cial interpretations. Each of these interpretations was an established tradition. Scholars who studied the Bible in a scholarly way had to take these official interpretations into their reckoning in ways which the humanistic scholars of the fifteenth to the nineteenth centuries did not have to do with respect to their pagan authors. This constituted a constraint on the interpretation of the tradition beyond the traditional technique of interpretation. But at the same time, the existence of the canon, its official promulgation and espousal and the multiplicity of copies of the canonical texts rendered almost superfluous one of the main activities of humanistic scholarship, which was the search for manuscripts. The situation of the Bible was like that of books written after printed publication became the rule. There were many copies and they displayed a rather high degree of uniformity compared with the books of pagan authors studied by the earlier humanists. The Old

52. L. D. Reynolds, and N. G. Wilson, *Scribes and Scholars: A Guide to the Transmission of Greek and Latin Literature*, 2d. ed. (Oxford: Clarendon Press, 1974), pp. 120–24.

53. A. D. Momigliano, "Ancient History and the Antiquarian," *Contributo alla Storia degli Studi Classici* (Rome: Edizioni di Storia a Letteratura, 1955), pp. 67–106.

Testament had been attended to by Jewish scholars from antiquity and through the Middle Ages, and Christian church fathers like Origen and Jerome had collated and made translations of the Old Testament. Both Jews and Christians had been concerned to establish authentic texts.[54] The textual questions were grave but there was a greater volume of material from which to work in comparison with that available to classical scholars. The Jews reached a point which gave them satisfaction by the early tenth century when the Masoretic text became definitive after about five or six centuries of relative stability. Christians had a more difficult time. They were averse from using the text of the Jews and used instead a Latin translation made by St. Jerome from a Hebrew version supplemented by a Greek translation. Christian scholars were constrained by the rule that they must avoid any constructions or interpretations which conflicted with ecclesiastical doctrine.

The discipline of the collation of manuscripts of pagan authors, the establishment of the genealogical relationships of manuscripts, the emendation of manuscripts reinforced by the somewhat similar discipline of biblical scholarship were extended to other fields of the study of the past and its truthful portrayal. National literature and the origins of the vernacular language, the calendaring of the archival raw material of national, regional, and local history, the composition of historical works based on this preparatory scholarship moved into positions of some prominence behind classical and biblical studies within each of the major countries. Classical and biblical studies explored the past which numerous countries, far from the Mediterranean, had adopted as their own; consequently classical studies and biblical studies were conducted on an international level. In contrast, studies of national pasts in language, literature, and politics tended to be confined, each within its own distinctive territory.

The steady extension of "the historical method" brought hitherto uncultivated fields into its domain. The history of philosophy, the history of science, the history of historiography, the history of religious beliefs, the historical development of language and of particular languages, the history of art and literature became established by the production of numerous works of erudition. The ancient Middle Eastern civilizations came under disciplined study partly as a supplement to the higher criticism of the Bible and partly as subjects of independent dignity. The study of the great oriental civilizations, of their languages and their literary, philosophical, and religious works took a place alongside the study of the past of occidental civilization.

54. Martin Noth, *The Old Testament World* (London: A. and C. Black, 1966), pp. 301–48.

The eighteenth and nineteenth centuries, the epoch of the enlightenment, liberalism, and progressivism, were also at the same time the epoch of a prodigious unplanned but interconnected surge of disciplined reconstruction of the image of the past, the reconstitution and annotation of the intellectual works of the past, the recovery and appreciation of the artifacts of the past.

In all these extensions of the domain of humanistic scholarship, surviving works produced in the past, surviving artifacts of the past and the vanished actions of the past, reached and reconstituted through works and artifacts, were the sole objects of study. When in the latter part of the nineteenth century philosophers applied themselves to the task of classification of the sciences, they did so in a way which would vindicate and save the jurisdiction of those which dealt with the past and the inheritance from it. They wished to preserve the dignity of the study of the past and its intrinsic value and what was created in it. This was what, in their different ways, Dilthey, Rickert, and Windelband were attempting to do in their segregation of the *Geisteswissenschaften* or the *Kulturwissenschaften* from the *Naturwissenschaften*, of history from "natural science" and of the "idiographic" from the "nomothetic" disciplines; the distinction between *Verstehen* or understanding and *Erklären* or explanation appeared frequently in these discussions. What they were in fact groping towards was the proposition that tradition was the main subject matter of the humanistic disciplines, while there was nothing quite like tradition in the natural sciences.

They were for various reasons apprehensive about the implications of antitraditionality in the natural sciences, in the apparent annulment of the past by those sciences and their alleged rejection of the symbolic stratum of existence. The natural scientists themselves were not particularly interested in these problems but in general they did not go to pains to disavow the position attributed to them. There was in fact a significant difference between the humanistic disciplines and the natural sciences. The former dealt with the symbolic products of the human mind, the latter with events, phenomena, substances in which the human mind was not present. When the natural sciences did deal with the human mind, they tried to diminish the significance of the symbol-constructing function of the mind.

Nonetheless, the tradition of humanistic learning deserves the name of science because it too is a methodical, progressive penetration into an unknown reality, the unknown reality of the past and of the symbolic constructions in which it is perceived. The disciplines of humanistic scholarship have much in common with the natural sciences. Both live forward from their traditions. As with Newton, Galileo, Boyle and Harvey, in the natural sciences, so the great figures Valla, Politian, Bentley, and Scaliger are remembered with honor even after their work has been largely superseded. Their work has not been discarded but it has been superseded by revision and assimilation into the works of succeeding generations.

Humanistic scholarship, like any other serious enterprise of intellectual understanding which runs on for a long time, works in a tradition in which each generation has the work of the earlier generations as its point of departure from which it sets its problems and from which it draws its methods and lines of interpenetration. Humanistic scholarship is like the natural sciences in its possession of methods of observation and analysis. Its *Wissenschaftlichkeit* is constituted by its methodical procedures. Humanistic scholarship, seen in long perspective, is a continuously developing tradition, or rather a continuously developing family of traditions formed around different but related subject matters; the substance of each of these is itself borne forward by a tradition. Humanistic scholarship is a tradition of searching for the extension of a tradition of understanding; the objects of the understanding sought are traditions to be understood. It is in this last respect that the humanistic disciplines differ from the natural sciences.

Humanistic scholarship became differentiated into disciplines. The disciplines have diverse fortunes. The lines of tradition of some disciplines become flat; nothing important and new is added to them. The lines of tradition of other disciplines have periods of upward movement, of striking new discoveries of hitherto unknown materials and an influx of talents capable of seeing hitherto unseen features and patterns of previously known raw materials, and of new techniques for acquiring and interpreting newly discovered as well as long-known materials. The studies of Judaism received such an impulse from the discoveries of the Ras Shamra tablets, of the Cairo Geniza, and, again, of the Dead Sea Scrolls. The improvement of technique in archaeology, the multiplication of important excavations—perhaps because of the increased availability of financial resources—and the larger number of trained archaeologists have greatly added both to the stock of artifacts acquired and to the stock of knowledge by the illumination of documents and artifacts previously discovered.

Some lines of substantive inquiry become exhausted, partly because interest in them becomes exhausted, partly because the materials yield as much as can be obtained from them by existing theories and techniques, and arresting new materials cannot be discovered. The emendation of classical manuscripts might be near exhaustion; the critical editing of medieval manuscripts might be approaching the margin of profitability to scholars and to scholarship. The biographical studies of major modern authors has probably exceeded both the supply of authors worthy of such study and the supply of unused material. Because recent books are printed and proofread and are not copied by hand, errors in reproduction are not of sufficient importance to justify the labor of "variorum" editions. Thus it might come about that some parts of humanistic research in the philological sense, except in the hands of genius, fall on hard times. Those who can discern hitherto undiscerned features in documents previously known, who can assimilate so much knowledge of previously known things that they can add and give a new turn to the tradition by perceiving patterns hitherto unperceived are very rare.

The tradition of humanistic study might go into decline because the educational prerequisites for its effective practice are withheld by educational policies. Thus, classical studies are coming under strain because of the insufficient linguistic and literary training of the generation of potential scholars. The fewer the students of these subjects in secondary schools, the fewer will study them in universities and proportionately the fewer will become classical scholars.

A branch of humanistic study might go into decline because there is disapproval of it in consequence of a more general change in beliefs. Classical studies, which flourished as long as the past of Western civilization was thought of as a model for moral, philosophical, and literary excellence and as the source of what was worthwhile in modern civilization, have diminished in their interestingness to generations who think that there is little in what is presented in tradition and that it is even pernicious. A decline in respect for what is inherited from the remote past has led to a decline in the tradition of its cultivation, propagation, and investigation. A tradition of learning in one or a group of disciplines may go into attenuation because other disciplines have become more attractive to new generations. The social sciences for example have become more attractive. The social sciences which deal largely with contemporary things have, thanks to a great extension and ramification of interest in the present, contributed to weakening the tradition of the study of traditions. Yet it is possible that this new rival tradition contained in the social sciences which has helped to diminish the study of antiquity might also in time reanimate the diminished tradition. This reanimation might occur through the introduction of new categories and new problems and by opening the possibility of the discernment of patterns of interpretation which have become established in the traditions of sociologists and anthropologists. The invention of a new technique or its importation from other disciplines—for example, the introduction of mathematics into economics and the use of computers in archaeology—might add to and enrich an existing intellectual tradition. New themes and subject matters might make an old tradition more fertile and productive; the developments in social history under the influence of the school of Febvre and Bloch, of social anthropology and of a Marxist influence which has directed the interest of historians towards the lower classes illustrate the consequences of an assimilation of external intellectual traditions into one of the major traditions of the humanities.

The Migration of Scholarly and Scientific Traditions

The variations in the fortunes of particular disciplines of humanistic learning, the changing curves of important correction and discovery, and the changing adherence to their respective traditions do not always occur in identical patterns in different countries at the same time. The tradition of humanistic learning in one or several disciplines might flourish in one country within the civilization to which the tradition belongs, it might languish in others. It might soar ahead in one country; in others, it might haltingly follow the leading country. The spread of humanistic learning from Italy to France, Germany, the Netherlands, and England in early modern times was such a dispersion of a tradition from a center to peripheries which in consequence became centers which took their place alongside the original center. The centrality of German humanistic learning in certain fields in the nineteenth century and early twentieth century is to be understood as a propagation of the effects of the efflorescence of the tradition of learning in German schools and universities; the German traditions drew the traditions of the other countries in their wake. Scholars outside Germany read the literature produced by the Germans, they applied the techniques of the Germans, they studied problems like those studied by the Germans, they went to Germany to study under German masters. Where there were already distinct national traditions in topics, problems, and techniques, these persisted in partial fusion with the assimilated German traditions.

The traditions of humanistic learning, viewed from a universal standpoint, form a very complicated set of traditions of a variety of subject matters linked with each other at various points, at other points independent of each other, varying in the density of their cultivation over the earth's surface, sometimes linked across the boundaries of societies, sometimes developing independently within particular societies. Chinese historiography for example was completely independent of Jewish, Greek, Roman, and Islamic historiography until practically the twentieth century, when some of its practitioners attempted to assimilate certain modern Western historiographic traditions. But the parts of the traditions which they attempted to assimilate were traditions of techniques and interpretative themes. Their subject matter remained more or less what it was in the past, namely, Chinese events.

Traditions in the humanistic disciplines, like all traditions, have restricted adherence within their own societies and among societies. The traditions of humanistic disciplines tend to be restricted to pasts which have occurred, to works which have been produced, to artifacts which have been made within the boundaries of national territory, or within the more extended boundaries of the civilization of which the national territory is a part. In modern times the movement of the tradition of humanistic disciplines, when it has gone beyond the national and civilizational boundaries of Europe, has occurred largely within the confines of the former European empires as they existed from the sixteenth to the twentieth centuries.

Japan is the chief Asian recipient of some of the traditions of European humanistic scholarship but it has taken up the tradition of the techniques of research rather than the traditions of substantive problems and subject matters. A few parts of British humanistic studies were incorporated into the tradition of the modern educated class in India. The traditions of the study of English literature have become parts of the modern Indian tradition. Traditions of the British study of Indian history too were implanted into Indian historiography; they grew and underwent pronounced modification in the course of their assimilation; British traditions of linguistic study of Indian languages were also implanted. British tradition in the study of the classics of Western antiquity of European history, ancient and modern, of ancient Oriental civilizations other than India's and the traditions of study of modern European languages and literatures have found very little adherence in India. The traditions of Oriental humanistic, including theological, scholarship have not been assimilated into the Western tradition of humanistic scholarship in an approximately corresponding way. The pattern has been asymmetrical.

Traditions, in their wanderings, are very selective in their destinations and in their substance. The traditions of humanistic learning move much less than those of scientific knowledge or of religious knowledge. There is something relatively parochial about the traditions of humanistic learning as compared with scientific learning. The traditions of scientific learning are much more codified than are those of humanistic learning. The humanistic scholarly traditions are not as scientific in the way in which the natural sciences are scientific, i.e., they are not formulated in generalized and often mathematical form; they depend on the overtones of the oral tradition for their effective reception; too much lies in the interstices of their explicit references. These features limit the transmissibility of humanistic traditions to alien civilizations. Much to which the humanistic scholarly traditions refer is valued as part of the tradition of a national society or civilization. The humanistic scholarly traditions usually draw strength from attachment to the pastness of the national community or civilization and to the particular works which constitute part of its traditions and therefore do not pass easily to other national societies and civilizations.

The codified parts of scientific traditions are relatively easily transplanted beyond their particular areas of origin within a national society to other parts of the same civilization; the oral parts of the traditions on which the effective cultivation of the codified, written part of the tradition depends are more difficult to transplant. The subject matter of some of the natural sciences such as particular flora, fauna, and geological formations are parochial but even then they are analyzed in the light of categories of universal applicability and they must be explained by theories possessing universal validity. Other subject matters of the natural sciences such as physics, astronomy, mathematics, and chemistry have fewer or no parochial attachments; they are the most susceptible to implantation in alien territories—but many obstacles remain in their way even in such propitious disciplinary traditions. Scientific works written in the language of a major producer generally lose nothing of their meaning when translated and they often can also be read relatively effectively by scientists of another country. Literary works can be read with less precision of understanding by persons who are foreign to them, and translations of literary works are seldom as effective as the translations of scientific works. Scientists regard themselves as belonging to the same scientific community with the same scientific traditions as their specialized colleagues in other societies, particularly those in scientifically productive countries.

The traditions of the natural sciences are in principle more capable of living on in a society and culture alien to the one in which they were generated than most other intellectual traditions. In fact, however, there are many obstacles, and strenuous efforts to carry a tradition of scientific knowledge into an alien environment have often failed. The tradition of the natural sciences grew gradually in Europe with very little deliberate promotion on the part of persons who were not themselves scientists. The growth of the tradition took place in obscure ways; what was codified was transferred in writing and by teaching. What was not codified was acquired less knowingly. Where the latter took place, scientific work flourished. Where it was not yet in existence, the tradition did not find effective reception, despite costly efforts to provide the material equipment and persons to carry it forward.

Philosophical Knowledge

A philosophical truth is an intellectual construction in which reason has had the fullest sway. If there is an antithesis between tradition and reason, it should be most evident in philosophy, where the task is to raise and resolve by reason the most fundamental questions which the mind can conceive and to free the mind from the burden of error which was contained in past answers. Nevertheless in philosophy, it is tradition which brings forward past problems and past answers; this process of presenting problems constrains the answers given by philosophers. Tradition is ineluctable in philosophy. The cosmos, time, existence, the nature of thought and of the right ethical and logical rules are the object of philosophical analysis. These are in principle accessible by direct contemplation, unencumbered by what has been thought in the past. Nevertheless, the point of departure of much if not all philosophical thought is the study of books by other philosophers, recent and long past, and reflection on the ways in which they have thought about the fundamental problems. This gives great power to the philosophers who have gone before. They fix the most general terms in which the activity occurs.

Plato and Aristotle still remain no less than in antiquity philosophers whose problems and answers must be studied by all who take seriously the tasks of philosophy. Cicero and Seneca have fallen from their former prominence but Plato and Aristotle remain influential, not just by their influence on generations and generations of early philosophers but by the contemporary philosophers' obligation to know their works and to contend with their arguments. They are studied for their treatment of the proper problems of philosophy and not just as a stage in the unfolding of the tradition of philosophical ideas. Aristotle and Plato are like Homer, Virgil, and Dante; their writings, even if they have been assimilated into subsequent phases of the tradition, are not exhausted by that assimilation. Their works also demand direct study. In a sense they are more present than the works of contemporary philosophers. The ancient philosophers are doubly present; they are present in their own works and they are present in the works of many other philosophers whose problems and answers have assimilated those of Plato and Aristotle, even when diverging from them.

Whereas Isaac Newton or Laplace are studied by those who wish to see the development of a tradition through time rather than its most recent comprehensive and valid state, philosophical tradition seems to be a different thing. In the tradition of science, the great figures are revered monuments but their works cease to be read after what is vital in them has been extracted and assimilated. The works of the great philosophers retain their intellectual vitality and are a recurrently present point of departure for the philosophical reflections of new generations of philosophers.

Why do certain old works remain classics in philosophy in the way that scientific works do not? Is philosophy a subject without a tradition of self-correction and of achieved solutions? If it did have such a tradition of self-correction, the older classical writers would have yielded up to the tradition what was living in them, their solutions to problems would have been assimilated, the works themselves would have been discarded, together with their demonstratedly wrong ideas. There have been certain major changes in the philosophical tradition resembling the changes in the scientific tradition. The idea of a normative order inherent in the laws of nature has been discarded by most philosophers. This resembles the rejection of the idea of phlogiston, but the idea of phlogiston is nowadays of interest only to historians of science while the idea of a normative order embodied in the laws of nature is still a compelling presence. Its replacement by the ideas of Hume and Kant has brought little satisfaction, and the older solutions are put forward repeatedly albeit in different terminology. Logic has undergone steady progress; what was valid in Aristotelian logic has been assimilated and many subsequent innovations in logic have been assimilated. Logic is a branch of philosophy which is close to being a branch of science.

Some ideas have fallen to the side of the philosophical tradition; others have, through the centuries, become more widely adhered to, more closely studied, and more earnestly considered. Nonetheless, there are philosophers now who still espouse Aristotelian ideas about the organism, or about tragedy, or about justice. A great deal of thought and study has been given to these topics since Aristotle wrote and there are probably very few philosophers who would classify themselves unqualifiedly as Aristotelians, but a serious discussion of any one of those topics would be thought incomplete if it did not deal explicitly with Aristotle's ideas about it.

The long duration of philosophical traditions is affected by their degree of affinity and often explicitly perceived connection with religious traditions. The long endurance of many centuries of Aristotelian philosophy is partly a function of its value for the analysis of problems raised by Islamic theology and later by Christian theology. A philosophical tradition could in principle go on for a very long time even without association with an adjacent religious and moral tradition. Nonetheless, such solitary endurance is not likely. A philosophical tradition needs support.

Elaborate institutional settings such as universities, academies, and journals for instructing young persons in philosophy and for enabling mature philosophers to engage in discussion, oral and written, with each other, also contribute to the maintenance of the philosophical past in the present. These institutional provisions also help to maintain a self-contained elaboration and reproduction of a particular set of philosophical beliefs; they are a partial surrogate for an adjacent religious tradition but no more than partial. Indeed something like that has been the situation of philosophy in the past two centuries. The enduring strength of a philosophical tradition is much affected by the proximity of religious and moral traditions which touch on it at various points. When the religious tradition became attenuated for philosophers, they have turned to the adjacent traditions of natural and social science to sustain them and to provide them with substance on which to practice their philosophical techniques.

The high degree of traditionality of the substance of philosophical beliefs may also be attributed to the insolubility of philosophical problems by existing criteria and to the accompanying difficulty of achieving consensus among philosophers. The methods of philosophical demonstration, outside of these branches which approximate to mathematics, do not admit of the consensus which prevails regarding scientific knowledge. It is possible that the natural sciences have progressed by avoiding problems for which they did not have at hand the materials, instruments, and prior knowledge required for their solution. By reserving their powers for the treatment of the problems which are susceptible to solution at a particular time, natural scientists have been able to move on from the solved to the soluble. What was so insoluble that it did not even appear to be a problem to be seriously investigated was left alone. What was at one time thought to be insoluble, later becomes soluble and is solved. Science has been called "the art of the soluble";[55] perhaps philosophy is the "art of the insoluble." Agreed answers cannot be found because no agreed procedures and criteria can be found. In both science and philosophy, original ideas have their point of departure in the tradition which has been presented. In science something new is discovered which could not have been inferred from the previous state of tradition or, if it was inferred, was not demonstrated in a way which was persuasive to all qualified scientists. Progress consists in making the new idea persuasive by methodical, observational, and rational evidence; the solution remains persuasive until a better solution meeting the same criteria is agreed on. Solutions are also put forward in philosophy, but even if they are accepted, for a time, they lose their persuasiveness. The solutions which replace them have the same fate. The new solutions are usually connected with one of the major alternatives within the wider philosophical tradition. The difference between philosophy and science seems to lie mainly in the absence of a compelling consensus about what constitutes the demonstration of a solution to a problem. In consequence of this it is impossible to go beyond insolvent reflection on the problems.

Philosophers deal with problems which repeatedly appear to their successors to have been unsolved. Some treatments of these insoluble

55. Arthur Koestler, quoted by Peter Medawar, *The Art of the Soluble* (London: Methuen, 1967), p. 7.

problems have become more acceptable than others to ensuing generations. The differences in acceptability are differences in precision, consistency, confrontation with objections which can be raised from the standpoint of one of the irreconcilable treatments. Yet once these standards have been met, there is no intellectually persuasive reason for the dissentient interlocutor or successor to agree to the proposed solution.

It is probable that philosophy will never become a science, and for this reason the past in philosophy will remain more substantively present than it is in science. Writers of the logical positivist school tried to force philosophy in the direction of science by ruling out certain problems as meaningless and metaphysical, by which they meant insoluble. In the end, many of them renounced this position, acknowledging thereby the legitimacy of insoluble problems and consequently of works which would have been superseded had philosophy become a scientific discipline.

The tradition of philosophy embraces many traditions. Many are minor traditions which are variants of the major ones. These merge and fade because they cannot become sufficiently elaborated to become major traditions with a broad scope of reference. Some traditions subside for a time. They retain very little adherence; they might even cease to be in active possession of any but a few philosophers, remaining only in the stock of philosophical works stored in libraries, or they might recede into the possession of foreign cultures. They might then come into more active possession and to have more adherence; they might under these circumstances undergo elaboration and adaptation to competing traditions and new preoccupations. They might also be expressed in a different idiom.

Sometimes a topic which has moved within the overlapping circles of philosophical traditions moves off to become a part of science. This happened to certain problems that later fell into what came to be called psychology; thus, perception became the object of scientific study. Other topics of these philosophical traditions entered into the traditions of separate disciplines. Parts of the traditions of ethnology, sociology, and political science may be said to be such divergent parts of philosophical traditions. In their secession and independence they became in part like the sciences, in part like humanistic scholarship, and in many respects they brought with them some of the attributes of philosophical tradition. In some sections of their new form, they developed techniques for the establishment of rational consensus; they often did so by concentrating on particular subject matters of varying degrees of concreteness. Where the subject matters of philosophy were treated concretely, as in ethnology, the techniques of observation and description were improved; where they were treated more abstractly, as in sociological and political theory, they did not have a similar success, and they remained closer to philosophical traditions in which classics of the past are studied over and over again for their intrinsic intellectual relevance.

Institutionalization, the multiplication of numbers of practitioners, and the increase in resources for study, teaching, and research have not changed markedly the pattern of philosophical tradition. It is true that the increase in the number of persons writing doctoral dissertations on philosophical problems has increased the number of works produced and has fostered a larger number of minute studies of particular issues. The increase in the number of philosophical journals, together with the increase in the number of philosophers, has increased the published output of philosophical works. They have made more dense the supplementary traditions around the primary works. Some of these, like the traditions of commentaries on sacred texts, contribute to the modification of the traditions of interpretation of major philosophical works. The multiplication of works amplifies the meanings, opens the implications, and consolidates schools and circles. There being only a few major traditions within philosophy, the lines of the various traditions intersect more frequently. Many combinations occur. Neo-Thomism may mingle with evolutionary naturalism; traces of idealism pervade a mechanistic evolutionism. A few fundamental positions embodied in the main traditions remain; each of them presents a nearly self-contained tradition with regard to the basic philosophical problems of metaphysics, epistemology, and aesthetics.

Although the traditions of philosophy do not succeed in breaking away from the problems and solutions which they have inherited, except to overlap with other philosophical traditions, or lose a part of themselves to the specialized, more scientific disciplines, they also draw something from traditions external to themselves. But even then they move mainly within their own traditional paths. When the Aristotelian tradition of philosophizing was adopted by Islamic and then Christian philosophers, it acquired novel idioms but it still retained the distinctive character which it had before its entry into the Islamic and Christian traditions.

Like traditions of scientific, scholarly, technological, and religious knowledge, the traditions of philosophical knowledge also migrate from one part of the earth's surface to others, bringing to their new recipients a past which the ancestors of these recipients never experienced. A few philosophical traditions have been able to transcend their national or local areas of diffusion and to acquire adherence outside the territories in which they originated. Indeed the greatness of a philosopher is defined by the duration and territorial scale of the adherence to his ideas as well as by the pervasiveness of his problems and his proffered solutions. Ancient Greek philosophy moved far beyond the northern and eastern rim of the Mediterranean. But many of the subsidiary traditions of philosophy remain within the territory of their early formulation. When they do move they do tend to stay within the boundaries of their civilization; most of them indeed remain with their own national boundaries and, when they exceed them, they are often regarded as alien.

Movement of a philosophical tradition across national boundaries is usually dependent on its prior ascendancy in the country of its origin.[56] Philosophical traditions tend to be confined by the boundaries of their own civilization partly because of their connections with a complex of religious and linguistic traditions; their movements are therefore more or less bound to the movements of those traditions. Aristotle's and Plato's philosophies are perhaps the only ones which moved from the territory of one major religious tradition to that of another; the other philosophies of pagan antiquity remained mainly within their own territory until the establishment of the Christian tradition and its northward migration.

Marxism, although it is the heir of philosophical traditions,[57] is not quite a philosophical tradition in the sense employed here; it has not made its way as a philosophical tradition. It has been closely bound up with a tradition of ideological political beliefs about the reordering of economic activity; its intellectual persuasiveness is weaker than the obligation to accept it in consequence of the acceptance of the particular program or set of political beliefs and the experience of certain sentiments of hostility towards authority. Marxian philosophy does not constitute an autonomous philosophical tradition like the traditions associated with the works of Plato, Aristotle, Descartes, Kant, and Hegel.

Its migration is now more extensive territorially than that of any of the great philosophical traditions; it is comparable in scale to the migration of any of the major religious traditions and of the scientific tradition. It is a consequence of the spread of an ideological political tradition to which Marxian philosophy is subordinate. Such ostensible consensus about the main positions of Marxian philosophy which exists in countries in which it is the official philosophy is not a consensus arrived at by philosophical procedures. Its espousal by those

56. This is not invariably the case. The movement of Krausian philosophy from Germany to Spain is one mysterious exception.

57. Lenin went back only to German idealism, French materialism, and British political economy. See V. I. Lenin, "The Three Sources and Three Components of Marxism," *Selected Works* (New York: International Publishers, n.d.), 11:1–5. He could have found much older ideas in Marx's outlook. R. H. Tawney once said, "The true descendant of the doctrines of Aquinas is the labour theory of value. The last of the Schoolmen was Karl Marx" *(Religion and the Rise of Capitalism* [London: John Murray, 1926], p. 36).

who share in the consensus is a function of ideological and political considerations and the suppression of competing philosophical traditions.

The Study of Society

The social sciences are, at least in name, the latest major arrivals on the scene. Their institutional establishments came much later than the provision for the study, teaching, and investigation of religious, scientific, humanistic, and philosophical topics. Their practitioners, in seeking out their ancestors, go back only to the sixteenth, seventeenth, and eighteenth centuries for political science and economics and to the late eighteenth and the nineteenth centuries for sociology. Social scientists, however strong their aspirations to be scientific, are very aware of their ancestry. The ancestors whom they claim tended on the whole to belong to the progressivisitic camp; they proclaimed the desirability of critical attitudes towards authority, of reason as a criterion and procedure in legislation and in the conduct of institutions and of individual freedom. In the past half-century many of the proponents of the social sciences have recommended them as sources of information and general rules for making governments more "scientific," for improving the functioning of institutions, and for the reduction of social conflicts. The performance of these services depended on the social sciences becoming more scientific; that is the end to which many of the best social scientists have put their minds.

Long before they acquired their recent proximity to authority, many social scientists were social reformers and humanitarian critics of the social arrangements which were thought to generate poverty. In the last half-century, they have tended to favor what they call "social change," meaning mainly greater equality in the distribution of income and power, restraints on the accumulation and use of private property, and similar reforms. They have either been agnostics or liberal Protestants in their religious beliefs and have generally been critical of religious faith and doctrine. They have welcomed the emancipation of individuals from restraints imposed by traditional beliefs. In general, they have had a negative view of the traditional order of their society; they have generally been against tradition, which they have identified with primordial tradition.

Unsympathetic to traditionality, and nevertheless attached to the intellectual traditions of their own subject and even pious towards them, social scientists have usually given short shrift to tradition as an object of their studies, particular and general.

Humanistic scholars deal with the creative works of individuals, and they study these works as carriers and as formers of tradition; social scientists too have to deal with a subject matter in which tradition is a formative power.

Tradition is no less important in the subject matter of the social sciences than it is in the subject matter of the humanistic studies. This has occasionally been agreed to by social scientists. The older school of ethnography which flourished before the introduction of modern techniques of fieldwork did not develop theories of tradition but it was very aware of its ubiquitous presence. Likewise sociologists who wrote about society without the use of the methods of participant observation and systematic survey methods and who used historical and ethnographic monographs as their sources were very aware of the persistence of tradition from the past into the present.

One of the major changes in the development of the social sciences over the past century and a half has been a shift towards contemporaneity. It is not that contemporaneous subject matters did not interest social scientists in the past. They did; the early practitioners of empirical and quantitative social research certainly gave their minds to contemporaneous events. The techniques which they began to use early in the twentieth century were practicable only on living persons. The more recent developments in the use of sample surveys have also had that temporal limitation. Anthropological studies which were conducted through intensive observation and interviewing also tended to confine analysis to the living generations. Earlier epochs in the societies they studied fell into a very marginal position in the field of attention of social scientists, especially in the English-speaking countries. The decline of "historical economics" in Germany and of "institutional economics" in the United States were representative of the same trend. It is only recently that the historical dimension has been introduced or reintroduced into sociological and anthropological studies; this is not the same as an acknowledgment of the existence and effect of traditions.

The social sciences present a paradox. They live under the guidance of their own traditions and thus prolong the past into the present; they themselves both seek to escape from their past by making themselves scientific and they at the same time retain a self-conscious attachment to the ideas and great figures of their past—to which they sometimes add the new constituents of a past which has only recently been acquired by them. But as regards the traditional features of their own subject matter they have been rather obdurate.

All the fields of intellectual activity which we have summarily examined have been formed within the patterns of their own intellectual past. The human sciences, including the study of religion, bring into the present not only their own intellectual past but the past of their own society and civilization which is their subject matter. The social sciences are a partial exception to this. Having come into a more prolific existence in an epoch which has departed considerably from the past which preceded it and which has also belittled the value of the past as a guide in practical life and intellectual creation, the social sciences exist in a paradoxical state that seems integral to them in their present condition.

Yet, despite the desire to be as scientific as possible, most of the social sciences are more like philosophy and theology than they are like the natural sciences. Economics is something of an exception. For about a century economics seemed to move forward cumulatively, overcoming its past errors and assimilating diverse subsidiary traditions. Marshallian economics—neoclassicism—was modified by Keynesian economics and that seemed for a time to command nearly universal assent. The hegemony of Keynesianism was disrupted from a number of different sources. New concepts and hypotheses and new techniques of research appeared. Keynesian economics was made out to apply to special situations and it too has been assimilated and supplanted. Through all this, the idea of the market has continued to be the center of economic analyses.

The quantity theory of money, which has in recent years been one of the great achievements of economics, is traced back by its leading contemporary proponents to David Hume's essay "Of Money." Recent research and analysis have elaborated the quantity theory of money and made it the object of precise historical and statistical study but its old point of departure still stands out at its center. It is of course not piety alone which prompts such an acknowledgment or which underlies its espousal. Economics remains the most scientific of the social sciences notwithstanding the recrudescence of diverse and conflicting theories; at least the economists have been developing techniques of research which might permit the adjudication of the contending claims.

Anthropology and political science are least subject to contention when they are largely descriptive, but when they become more theoretical, contention and fashion prevail without any method of settling disagreements and without assimilation of past accomplishments. Sociology seemed to reach some measure of accumulative consensus over a long period of development but its main themes could not be adequately demonstrated by the techniques of investigation which had developed independently.

Thus, except in economics, the progressive character of the natural sciences has no close counterpart in the social sciences. Old problems and interpretations reappear, many remain what they were. In sociology for example, the fundamental concepts of social order and revolution, of *Gemeinschaft* and *Gesellschaft,* of status and contract, of achievement and hereditary status, of charisma, of exchange, and diffuse obligations, of power and inequality, of consensus and conflict, of equilibrium and change, were waiting for the social sciences when they first began to be taught in universities. The utilitarian conception of action, of the relations of means and ends, still dominates the thought of most social scientists. Their central conception of modern society, as a contrast with traditional societies, maintains in the present ideas which are at least two centuries in age. This stability of themes and interpretations corresponds to the enduring life of the classical works of social science outside of economics. The traditionality of sociology shows itself more in the identity of its themes over more than a century than by the progressive assimilation and revision of the accomplishments of past sociologists.

In all the social sciences, there is a vivid interest in their own past. Even the relatively scientific economists demand a sense of continuity of their own accomplishments with those of their predecessors; the sense of their own past is strong in them. The recent resurgence of interest in the history of economic thought is a product of such piety towards ancestors and a desire to keep them present in the minds of contemporary economists. The other social scientists show similar attitudes. Unlike the natural sciences and economics, in which textbooks synthesize the latest stage of the tradition to be presented to the novice, and writers like Smith, Ricardo, Say, and Quesnay are studied out of piety and the desire for a sense of continuity, in fields like sociology and political science the works of Machiavelli, Hobbes, Weber, Durkheim, Kant, and Hegel are studied in the same way that the works of great philosophers are studied. Their own past is still very much alive in the thought of contemporary social scientists and they do not hide it from themselves. Those social scientists who would have it otherwise and who would like their disciplines to become sciences like the natural sciences, take a somewhat different but not wholly different attitude towards their classics; considering themselves as scientists, they try to reformulate the ideas of the classical writers in the form of investigatible hypotheses. Others reject the classics of the "prescientific stage" and turn to another tradition, the tradition of technique, the tradition of Petty, Condorcet, Quetelet, and Engel.

The Presence of the Past in Literary Works

The Physical Tradition

The natural sciences are very differently placed from literature in their relationship to their past. In the natural sciences, it would not be a complete distortion of the truth to say that each generation assimilates into its work what was potentially fruitful in the work of the previous generation—allowing for the distortion which is imposed in speaking of generations as cohorts which succeed each other and which do not overlap. In works of literature, the assimilation of one work or an epoch of works by succeeding generations—immediately following or long after—does not reduce the merit of the works of earlier times. Alfred Marshall's *Principles of Economics* might have made it superfluous to study Mill's *Principles of Political Eonomy* or Ricardo's *On the Principles of Political Economy and Taxation* except for those who wish to understand the development of the tradition of economics. But however great any novelist of the twentieth century might be, his works do not render superfluous the reading of the works of Flaubert or Turgenev or any other great novelist of the nineteenth century.

It is not that there were more geniuses who wrote great novels in earlier centuries than in our own. Whatever the cause or reason, literary works of two millennia ago are not rendered obsolete by further literary production. They remain of continuing interest. The possession of them as symbolic constellations, as intellectual—or literary—works depends on their existence in physical form. The tradition of the physical vehicle of such works has therefore been a task confronting mankind at each point of its history. The task was more exacting before the development of printing which both produced more copies of particular works and produced them uniformly in any single printing. The invention and widespread use of printing made a tremendous difference in the physical tradition of literary works. The production of a larger number of copies has meant that the physical survival of at least a few copies of the work was likely. That survival was accompanied by genuineness of the text because it was possible, as a result of the printed reproduction of many copies from a single set of frames of type, to make sure not only that all the copies were uniform but that they were practically identical with what the author actually wrote.

Whereas a very weighty part of the tradition of literary works consists of works written in antiquity, by far the greatest proportion of scientific works were written after the invention of printing and even in the present century. When the author himself reads the proof of the printed version, there is a very high probability that practically all that appears in the printed text is as he wished it to be or he was content to have it when it passed from his hand.

The literary tradition was thus subjected to vicissitudes which the tradition of the natural sciences did not face to the same extent. Literary works of classical antiquity have had a much longer period to get through and they had to do so under much more unpropitious circumstances. They had to pass through periods of relative indifference to their literary value; these were also periods of indifference to their physical survival.

The Survival of Texts

Works of literature, like all intellectual works, have both a particular physical existence and a particular symbolic existence, which is conceptually distinct from their physical existence. Their physical survival is much like the survival of buildings and tools—they have in common the durability and the fragility of physical things which exist outside the memory of living human beings. In their physical form they can survive in their original exemplars or in subsequently reproduced copies. In their symbolic form, they might become inert but, as long as there is a physical exemplar, they are in readiness to be reanimated by entering into the active possession of a later generation of readers, actively in the possession of living persons, i.e., in memory. In the case of works of oral literature, only active possession in memory and in the act of recitation enables them to persist.

When "interest" in a literary work was suspended, its physical vehicle ceased to be cared for or reproduced and the small numbers of fragile copies of those works were exposed to obliteration without replacement by other copies. Some literary works ceased for a long time to be part of the actively possessed stock but they survived for reentry because their physical vehicles survived. Thus, much of ancient Greek poetry, apart from Homer, largely ceased to be read—or taught—for some centuries prior to the early tenth century, when it was revived.[58] Although some Greek and many Latin poets continued to be appreciated and transmitted in the early Middle Ages of Western Europe, the numbers and the volume of their works which was read diminished. The stream became narrower and shallower, and from the sixth to the tenth centuries it became a trickle. During this time of diminished interest, many copies must have been destroyed. Many remained in their physical form, although probably undergoing deterioration, but they were practically unknown to any readers. Centuries might go by in which a manuscript might remain wholly unread, although some of the author's words or ideas might appear in references or quotations in works by other authors or in a chrestomathy. The tenuous existence of *De rerum natura* in the twelfth century is characteristic of this situation; it appeared only as an echo or indirect quotations in other books.[59] Many works of antiquity and the Middle Ages ceased to exist in physical form and disappeared from literary

58. L. D. Reynolds and N. G. Wilson, *Scribes and Scholars,* p. 59.
59. R. W. Hunt, "The Deposit of Latin Classics in the Twelfth-Century Renaissance," in R. R. Bolgar, ed., *Classical Influences on European Culture: A.D. 500–1500* (Cambridge: Cambridge University Press, 1971), pp. 51–52.

tradition. Some survive only in a notice of their title or subject matter, in the name of their author, in a few passages quoted or summarized in later works which did survive. Others survive in larger fragments.

The huge number of works which have disappeared must have done so at a time when practically no one cared for them. Some were erased while the physical substance on which they were recorded was preserved, so that their readily available and costly materials—the parchment—could be used again for other purposes, just as dilapidated ancient buildings were ravaged in order to obtain already cut building-stone close to the site at which it was to be used. The manuscript copies might also have disintegrated from use but even more from neglect and rough handling, from careless storage which laid them open to destruction by animals, fires, storms, wars, etc.

The number of existing whole copies of manuscripts of particular works of even the greatest writers must have diminished drastically through most of the second half of the first millennium after Christ.[60] The rate of their reproduction by copying—with all the corruption attendant on that—was exceeded by the rate of destruction. Except for those destroyed by catastrophe, the disappearance must have occurred in times when the works were little read—or if they were manuscripts of plays, practically never enacted. The number of persons capable of and willing to read them diminished and the works themselves therefore led an intellectually exiguous existence. Yet as long as the works existed as manuscripts, however small their number, they still had a chance of being rediscovered and reproduced. This has happened even in the modern age when manuscripts and books have been better cared for than they were in the Middle Ages. The fortunes of the works of Thomas Traherne enable us to imagine the worst fates of the works of other authors before the age of printing and of professional men of letters. He had published books in his lifetime in the seventeenth century but his poetical writings and *Centuries of Meditation* were not published. They survived in manuscript form; if anyone read them in that form, they left no known record of it over two centuries. Discovered in a street barrow by W. T. Brooke, in 1896 or 1897, they came into the hands of Alexander Grosart, a man of letters, who attributed them to Henry Vaughan. Bertam Dobell, an uneducated but learned bookseller, came upon them, detected that they were written by Traherne and published them in the first decade

60. Of approximately 123 plays of Sophocles, only 7 survive in their entirety although about 100 are known through their titles or in fragments; of 92 plays of Euripides, 19 survive; of 44 plays of Aristophanes, 11 survive intact; of the approximately 90 plays of Aeschylus, there are 82 of which the titles are known, but only 7 have come down to modern times. No complete text of any of the approximately 100 comedies of Menander survives. (Oskar Seyffert, *A Dictionary of Classical Antiquities,* ed. H. Nettleship and J. E. Sandys [New York: Meridian Books, 1956], pp. 13, 229, 338, 598.)

of the present century. Thereupon Traherne was installed retro-
actively into active possession as one of the important poets of the
seventeenth century.[61]

The Authenticity of Texts

Physical survival of a literary work is one thing; the authenticity of its
text which survives is a different thing. In antiquity the handwritten
reproduction of texts in single copies and the institutional arrangements for transcription permitted wide variations in texts to occur.
The scrutiny and winnowing of texts, and the establishment of an
authoritative version which claims and obtains the preference of succeeding generations therefore became a major task of learned men. As
in "scientific critical historiography," which sought to establish an
authentic image of the past on the basis of documents and other artifacts, scholars worked on the manuscripts of literary works, restored them to authenticity. It was not sufficient to be in contact with
the past; it had to be the authentic past.

The editing of manuscripts as a task of humanistic learning could
never recover the tradition in the sense of reading a book as the author
wrote it. No copies of ancient works in the handwriting of the authors
could ever be found. There were no first editions which the author had
approved. The earliest manuscripts were far from the author's own
lifetime. The literary past as it "really was" could be reestablished
only indirectly.

The establishment of the authentic text of the work transmitted
became for a long time a major objective of scholars. It required an
intellectually exigent audience to require authentic texts and to develop the techniques for assessing and establishing authenticity. From
the latter part of the fifteenth century until the nineteenth century, this
was one of the chief tasks of classical philology.[62]

The purification of the tradition by the fixation of sound texts passes
imperceptibly into the interpretation of the author's meaning. The
interpretation of the meaning of the text entails the appreciation of the
work as literature and its place in the set of traditions of particular
literary works and broader currents of belief. This interpretation, appreciation, and placement also have the purification of the tradition
beyond the authenticity of text as an aim. Classical philology,
although often immersed in minutiae of little interest to the educated
laymen, was a reconstruction of the literary tradition, bringing more

61. See Thomas Traherne, *Centuries, Poems, and Thanksgivings,* ed. D. S.
Margoliouth (Oxford: Clarendon Press, 1958), 1:x–xiii. In the *Dictionary of
National Biography* published at the end of the nineteenth century, there was
no entry for Traherne; nor was there one in the *Supplement* published in 1901.
62. Rudolf Pfeiffer, *A History of Classical Scholarship from 1300 to 1850*
(Oxford: Clarendon Press, 1976). See also E. J. Kenney, *The Classical Text,*
pp. 21–104, and Mark Pattison, "Joseph Scaliger," in *Essays,* ed. H. Nettleship (Oxford: Clarendon Press, 1889), pp. 152–95, and also pp. 162–243.

clearly into the forefront the greatest surviving works; it was a construction of an image of the past and its re-presentation to living generations.

The reader of the important literary works of the past receives not only the tradition of the work but also a supplementary tradition of interpretation of the work. The tradition of interpretation of the work becomes imprinted into the work itself. The past does not present itself to the present, it has to be presented over and over again, at many levels of intellectual sophistication and in accordance with the traditions of philological scholarship and literary criticism which are the preconditions of bringing the works of the past into the present. There must be a tradition of the study, purification, and reconstruction of tradition.

Storage

It is evident that the physical tradition of early copies or of later copies of copies is not a guarantee that the physical tradition will bring the work into active possession as a work of literature. While the physical embodiment of a work may exist unread for hundreds of years in church or monastery or in a private collection unknown to scholars, it scarcely exists as an element in the tradition of the literary work. For a work to be a literary work contained in a literary tradition it must be read, and this means that the tradition must be focused through institutions which bring the work to a reader.

To pass from the stock to possession requires physical movement from author to repository and from repository to reader, whether the repository be a privately owned collection of manuscripts or books, a royal or public or ecclesiastical or monastic or school or university library, or a bookshop or the stock of a vendor of miscellaneous objects including books. To become part of the stock, a work must be written or dictated, becoming a manuscript or a typescript and then being duplicated in handwritten or typewritten or printed form. Once recorded or multiplied, it may remain an unknown part of the stock, no one else than its author or owner knowing of its existence; the owner might not even know that he owns it and no one else might know of it either. If it survives at all it does so primarily as a part of the inert stock. Even then it does not move unaided from the author into the repository of inert stock. It requires copyists, printers, publishers, wholesale and retail collectors, booksellers, librarians, archivists, cataloguers, and teachers in schools and universities. To be in a condition of active possession, it needs all these and publicity, by word of mouth, display, catalogues, critical periodicals, and other books to call it to the attention of potential readers.

Collections of books in the form of libraries have existed in all literate societies ever since books as scrolls or separate, joined sheets or leaves or tablets were created. After 400 B.C., private libraries in

Athens were not exceptional. The greatest library in occidental antiquity was the Alexandrian; it was said to contain all the books of Greek
literature.[63] Homer had pride of place in Alexandria as he had in other
libraries, but it was the greatness of his works rather than their antiquity which made the Alexandrian library collect so many copies.

The library and museum of Alexandria were the first instances of
the organized academic custodianship, establishment, and annotation
of the texts of great works of literature. The Alexandrian library was
probably not concerned with the earliest manuscripts, simply because
they were old, of the works which its librarians assembled. The scholars attached to the Mouseion studied Homer by collating manuscripts.[64] Their efforts were devoted largely to the more general task
of purifying and interpreting texts. It would be wrong to say that
Greek literature would not have survived had it not been for the
Alexandrian library and the scholars of the Alexandrian museum.
Nonetheless, the Alexandrian scholars and others who followed them
had a great role in the consolidation of the literary tradition. They
standardized the text of Homer and "did what was necessary to prepare a standard text of all authors commonly read by the educated
public."[65] Even though the great collection of the physical vehicles of
the tradition were destroyed in the great fire, copies of their copies
were in turn copied until some instance of the ensuing generations of
copies which were made around a thousand years later finally survived.

The beginning of humanism was the time of the revival of libraries
as depositories of books to be read and not just as depositories. The
renewed appreciation of Latin literature and the interest in a better
knowledge of what ancient authors had actually written impelled the
search for manuscripts and their deposit in libraries where scholars
could find them and read them. Humanistic scholars and their friends
searched whenever they could for manuscripts, and they found many
in cathedrals and monasteries where they had lain unstudied. They
brought them to Italy. Private collections in the course of time found
their way into public libraries. The momentous task of making classical antiquity an appreciated presence in their contemporary intellectual life engaged the attention of many scholars for about four
centuries.[66]

63. P. M. Fraser, *Ptolemaic Alexandria* (Oxford: Clarendon Press, 1972),
1:305–35; 447–79; Frederic C. Kenyon, *Books and Readers in Ancient Greece
and Rome*, 2d. ed. (Oxford: Clarendon Press, 1951), pp. 24–28; L. H. Pinner,
The World of Books in Classical Antiquity (Leiden: A. W. Sijthoff, 1948), pp.
50–59.
64. Rudolf Pfeiffer, *History of Classical Scholarship: From the Beginning to
the End of the Hellenistic Age* (Oxford: Clarendon Press, 1968), pp. 105 ff.
65. Reynolds and Wilson, *Scribes and Scholars*, p. 8.
66. Pfeiffer, *Classical Scholarship from 1300 to 1850*, pp. 47 ff.; J. E.
Sandys, *A History of Classical Scholarship* (Cambridge: Cambridge University Press, 1903–8).

Once books began to be printed, the probability of the survival of the written works of the past into the present was much increased. The increased number of copies with a uniform text increased the chance that at least a few copies would survive. The associated organization of the bookselling trade enabled these uniform copies to find resting places over a larger territory; this enhanced the likelihood of survival.[67] Abuse, neglect, and castastrophe were not uniformly spread over the wider territory over which the increased number of copies were deposited. The scholars constituted and created a large and stable audience for such books. Collections of such books began to be better cared for.[68]

The acquisition and accumulation of old books just because they were old, the collection of *editio princeps* and of *incunabula* came into the world only with the beginning of print. The act of collecting books as physical artifacts the distinctive value of which lay in their age attested to the value which is thought to be inherent in the age of the particular copy. It was in the nineteenth century that private bibliophiles and the administrators of libraries maintained by government, universities, and private foundations, even more than the private collectors, became interested in acquiring for their libraries not only works which were old and of acknowledged literary importance but which were old and little else.[69] This tendency has become more acute in the twentieth century. Librarians justify this, it is true, by reference of the value of these old works for scholarship. But there appears to be more to it than that. There is a desire to establish as large a gallery of works which were written in the relatively remote past as is possible. In the libraries which can afford it, the most advanced technology for the maintenance of the proper degrees of heating and moisture is employed. The care which is taken of old books in the libraries of the present century is at the other extreme from the negligence and destructiveness of the Middle Ages. Nonetheless, the printed and manuscript achievements of the past have not been safe in this century either. The destruction of important libraries through military action in the First and Second World Wars is evidence of the permanent insecurity of the physical traditions of intellectual achievement.

67. See Elizabeth Eisenstein, *The Printing Press as an Agent of Change* (Cambridge: Cambridge University Press, 1979).

68. On the history of medieval and Renaissance libraries see James Westfall Thompson, *The Medieval Library* (Chicago: University of Chicago Press, 1939).

69. Lord Clark tells of the ancestor of a friend who "had a prejudice against reading any classics except in the first editions, which meant that the Latin authors [in his library] were practically all in incunabula" (Kenneth Clark, *Another Part of the Wood* [London: John Murray, 1974], p. 185). Of course, these were very far from "first editions." They were not even the best editions of many of those works since the first printed versions of ancient literary works were frequently not of a high scholarly standard.

Tradition in the Composition of Literary Works

The tradition of scientific knowledge appears to the practicing scientist as the latest state of knowledge in his field of work. There are retrospective references in these recent works. If a scientist has a sense of affinity and seeks contact with his intellectual ancestry, he will make himself aware of the past in the present by studying the older classics of his field; not so many do this. In any case, there is an approximate consensus in his field as to what is true, what is plausible, what is interesting but unproven, and what is nonsensical. There is no officially established authority. In theology, the conscientious believer sees his tradition as comprising the sacred book and the authoritative interpretations on which he meditates and which he tries to understand. If he is studious, the believer can also see the intervening high points in the formation of the tradition which he has received. The theologian, being generally a conscientious member of his church or sect, has an authoritative interpretation of the tradition which he heeds.

The tradition which brings literary works into the present falls between these. Literary products are neither progressive like science, presenting the tradition in telescoped or synthesized form expounded by acknowledged authorities, nor are they based like religion on a crucial revelation, or an exemplary sacred life, represented in a sacred text produced at a remote point in time and subject to authoritative interpretation. There is no compellingly authoritative synthesis of literary tradition to which an author must submit; there is no single sacred text and no authoritative interpretation to which he must agree. There are rather many particular works and clusters of works and patterns embodied in these works.

The creation of a literary work seems to be a freer action than the creation of a work of theology or science or scholarship; it is not something learned through a supervised course of study. There are no degrees, diplomas, ordinations, or examinations needed to undertake the writing of literary works although degrees in "creative writing" are now being offered by some universities. The writing of literary works is nonetheless dependent on anterior texts and on all the social apparatus required to place an aspiring creator of a new literary work in contact with the works which are the points of departure from which he builds his own. The creation of a literary work depends on the existence of other literary works and hence on the social arrangements or institutions through which literary traditions come to the attention of the new generation of creators of such works.

There is no obligation on any author to have mastered any particular works or all of a particular cluster of those which have preceded him. There are neither textbooks nor compendia, neither sacred texts nor authoritative orthodox commentaries which he must have mastered before venturing to compose a work and to seek its diffusion. He will not be censured nor will publication be refused him because he has not read some important monograph or because he infringed on an authoritative declaration. The tradition of literature to which an author exposes himself by reading and to which he is exposed by education and the hierarchy of the literary world has less orthodoxy in it than theology, science, or scholarship. Nonetheless it is neither amorphous nor impotent.

The tradition of literature is a sequence of literary works each of which bears in its content and style an indication of the works and classes of works which have left a deposit in the imagination and style of the author. It is also the entire superior stock of literary works which are variously present at one time to the cultivated readers—and writers—of an age; "the whole of the literature of Europe from Homer and within it the whole of the literature of his own country has a simultaneous existence and composes a simultaneous order"[70]—this is the tradition of literary works from which an author takes his point of departure. No literary work has to be an adequate incorporation of all that is valid in the works produced in earlier times. The earlier works, even though they have had a profound influence on the later ones, retain their intrinsic value.

This is the tradition in which authors must develop and assert their individuality. Authors and their audience tend, as T. S. Eliot said, "to insist when [they] praise a poet, upon those aspects of his work in which he least resembles anyone else. In these aspects or parts of his work we pretend to find what is individual, what is the peculiar essence of the man. We dwell with satisfaction upon the poet's difference from his predecessors, especially his immediate predecessors; we endeavor to find something that can be isolated in order to be enjoyed."[71] But in doing so, what the author has drawn from the literary tradition is overlooked.

The oversight is a consequence of submission to the tradition of artistic originality which was given a pronounced accentuation by romanticism. It existed long before romanticism. It must have existed ever since authors came to regard literary works as their own, to be associated with their names, and since readers—and before that their auditors—did likewise. This is a continuous pressure to depart from what has been previously achieved in the works contained in the tradition and from what was contained in the author's previous works. Each new work must be different from what it was before.

Authors set out not only to tell a story or to compose a poem but also to do what has not been done before by others or themselves.

70. Eliot, "Tradition and Individual Talent," in *The Sacred Wood*, p. 49 (reprinted in *Selected Essays*, 2d. ed. [London: Faber and Faber, 1934], p. 14).
71. Ibid., p. 48 (*Selected Essays*, p. 14).

When they enter upon the role of authorship they also acquire a tradition which declares that each literary work must be the expression of an individuality which pervades all the author's works and that each of his works must be different from all his others. The great work is not only different from all other works but it is also far superior to most of them in quality. There is uniqueness in mediocrity and inferiority just as there is in superiority.

It is no wonder that so many novelists and poets have been repelled by the idea of tradition. Nothing seems less congenial to the aspiration for uniqueness and originality than to form one's works on the patterns of literary works written by other writers of the remote and more recent past.[72] The antitraditional animus of the tradition of literary creation as such has been accentuated by its confluence with the tradition of genius.[73]

Authorship and Fame

The image of the author also becomes an object of tradition. Oral literature has no authors who are reliably known as the authors of particular works. Once literature became written literature, the attribution of particular works to particular authors became the common practice. The oral presentation of written works by reciters such as minnesingers who were not the authors blurred this distinction; improvisation, error, and creation modified the work in the course of presentation and certain performers became associated with particular works. When the age of anonymous authorship ended, the possibility of literary fame began. The fame of an author is nothing else than the survival of his name and of the works grouped around his name in the esteem of his own and subsequent generations. "Genuine" fame, the fame sought, is enduring fame, fame which does not diminish through time. Of course, contemporary authors are much noticed, but even nowadays old established fame seems more authentic than contemporary fame. The latter is more like fashion and is not taken seriously.

72. T. S. Eliot was the first modern literary critic to point out the deficiency of the view that tradition and originality are mutually exclusive. He said, "if we approach a poet without this prejudice, we shall often find that not only the best but the most individual parts of his work may be those in which the dead poets, his ancestors, assert their immortality most vigorously" (ibid., p. 48 [*Selected Essays*, p. 14]).
73. Alexander Gerard, *An Essay on Genius* (1774), reprinted with an introduction by Bernhard Fabian (Munich: Wilhelm Fink, 1966), pp. xvii–xlviii. Edgar Zilsel, *Die Geniereligion: Ein kritischer Versuch über das moderne Persönlichkeitsideal mit einer historischen Begründung* (Vienna and Leipzig: Wilhelm Braunmüller, 1918), and *Die Entstehung des Geniebegriffs*. See also Robert Currie, *Genius: An Ideology in Literature* (London: Chatto and Windus, 1974), pp. 194–222, and Hans-Georg Gadamer, *Wahrheit und Methode*, 4th. ed. (Tübingen: J. C. B. Mohr [Paul Siebeck], 1975), pp. 50–55 and p. 127.

There was a tendency among academics ever since the beginning of the study of modern national literatures in universities to refuse to treat contemporary authors because their future status was as yet undetermined. Authors could not be regarded as established and worthy of study until their survival into the present demonstrated their merits. Contemporary and especially recent authors, not being part of the past, were not acceptable for serious study. Becoming incorporated into tradition was read as a sign of literary value. The selective process in the formation of tradition was thought to represent sound judgment. These restrictions have been relaxed in recent decades. The validation of being part of a tradition is not insisted on at present with the same tenacity as it was a half-century ago. But even now, there is an awareness that fashion is inferior to tradition.

The fame of an author is almost always formed from his works (Byron is a partial exception). The problem of connecting works with authors did not cease with the coming of the written and printed book, although it diminished. Part of the work of humanistic scholarship has been the attribution of works to known authors.[74] The problem is much less urgent since printing became the preponderant mode of reproduction of literary works. Anonymity or pseudonymity are now more deliberate and occasionally challenge scholars to perform feats of literary detection, but it is mainly around the margin of literature that such a problem exists.[75] There are no great works of literature the authorship of which is in doubt. The "Shakespeare-Bacon" controversy is something for cranks and not for scholars.

The author's name connotes an image of his literary character which can exist in detachment from any single work and which is attached to most of his works. One book is pulled through time by the other books of the same author. Literary traditions are ordered by the attribution of authorship. The multiplicity of works attributed to a

74. The task has still not been completed. Only recently the attribution of *Prometheus Bound* to Aeschylus has been questioned by a classical scholar (see Mark Griffith, *The Authenticity of Prometheus Bound* (Cambridge: Cambridge University Press, 1977). The "Homeric question" which was opened by F. A. Wolff in the latter part of the eighteenth century went much further. Homer was deprived of unitary existence; his works were said to have been composed by a number of different authors and the formation of the Homeric canon was interpreted as the culmination of a process of amalgamation of more or less separate works written by different authors. Despite the long debate, the *Iliad* and the *Odyssey* never became isolated from each other; they were coupled by presumed identity of authorship, even when it was disputed.

75. Large dictionaries and many elaborate investigations are devoted to this fixing of works to their authors. See, for example, Samuel Halkett and John Laing, *Dictionary of Anonymous and Pseudonymous Literature of Great Britain*, (1882–1888); and Antoine Barbier, *Dictionaire des ouvrages anonymes et pseudonymes*, (1872–1879), 4th ed. edited by P. G. Brunet. There are similar dictionaries for pseudonymous and anonymous writings in German, Swedish, Italian, and Dutch; such works have been produced ever since the seventeenth century.

single author increases his chance of being borne forward by tradition. There are not many one-book authors who are famous, i.e., well-known and appreciated. Many works by the same author increased the likelihood of a generalized and relatively enduring image. If each work were known only in its own right and without connection with the particular author, the process of tradition would be even more broken and disordered than it is when works are grouped and move more or less together through time.

Originality, Genius, and Tradition in Literature

"Originality" in its first usage in the English language did not describe the working of man's innate genius. It referred, rather, to the greatest of all burdens of the past, "original sin," which was the result of a historical event of the most overwhelming importance nearly at the beginning of time: the "fall" of man from his state of grace and his consequent expulsion from the Garden of Eden. "Originality," which in recent centuries has been a mine sapping the fortifications of tradition, was in its early history a reminder of the ineluctable dominion of the past over the present.

The word eventually became free of its historical and religious meaning and shed its association with the beginning of time. "Originality," when it began to acquire some of the connotations of "genius," retained a sense of a source located outside the individual. To be "original" in this new sense entailed "imitation" of nature, which was timeless. The writer who, untrammeled by convention, drew his materials from his own observation of nature, was an "original writer."[76] The greatness of a writer was measured by his success in the "imitation of nature." "Invention" was the finding of something in nature which had hitherto been unknown and which had not been previously copied or, if it had been copied, had not been copied in the same way. The concept of "invention" as the finding of something already existent in nature did not satisfy the new conception of the powers of men and their privileges with regard to what existed outside and before them. The word "create" took its place. According to Logan Pearsall Smith, Dryden was the first important writer "to employ in literary criticism the word *create* . . . with its solemn religious associations," when he said, regarding Caliban, "Shakespeare seems there to have created a person which was not in Nature, a boldness which, at first sight, would appear intolerable."[77]

"To create" meant being like the deity in making something which had no prior counterpart external to the act of creating it. Thus, the

76. Logan Pearsall Smith, *Words and Idioms: Studies in the English Language* (London: Constable, 1928), p. 88.
77. Ibid., p. 91. See also Irving Babbitt, *On Being Creative and Other Essays* (Boston: Houghton Mifflin, 1932).

main meaning of "originality" shifted from the world outside the acting human being to the world within him. The artist became a "creator" and thereby assumed god-like lineaments. By the latter part of the eighteenth century, the adjective "creative" to qualify "power" or "imagination" had become well established in the usage of literary criticism.

A "genius" had originally been a demon or a guardian spirit which possessed a human being and made him perform actions beyond the power of ordinary human beings. The person who possessed the highest order of "creative power" was the "genius." Genius, like originality, had once been conceived to be external to human beings. The term gradually came to refer to part of the subjective endowment or equipment of the individual and did not depend on external tradition. By the seventeenth century "genius" acquired the meaning of a capacity or ability which was inborn in the individual.[78] It referred to the existence of a special, unique, and fundamental propensity. "Talent" and "genius" became synonymous. Genius absorbed the religious word "inspiration," which had been associated with "enthusiasm" or "possession" by an external power. It became "secularized" as it was freed from association with deities or spirits. Like "originality," in the sense of the imitation of the model found in nature, "inspiration," too, had drawn on an external source to account for the production of intellectual works of high merit. A great poet was still said to be "inspired," but now the inspiration was within himself; it was not "breathed into" him from outside himself. It was not a product of the study of the works of classical writers. It did not require studious application as the precondition of its expression in a work of art or literature. It could dispense with the models taught in schools.[79]

English literary critics made a distinction between those writers whose accomplishments were based on study and imitation and those whose accomplishments were the result exclusively of their natural endowments. In the eyes of the literary critics of the seventeenth and eighteenth centuries who were discrediting the neoclassical theory of poetic production, Shakespeare was regarded as the supreme instance of the internally inspired author. For these critics, Shakespeare was

78. Logan Pearsall Smith cites Sidney's reference to the proverb, "Orator fit, Poeta nascitur" (*Words and Idioms,* p. 96). The distinction between the innate propensity and the learned art or skill is much older; it was known to the Italian humanists of the fourteenth century. "*Ingenium* was the innate talent that could not be learnt," while "*ars* was the skill or competence that was learnt by rule and imitation" (Michael Baxendall, *Giotto and the Orators: Humanist Observers of Painting in Italy and the Discovery of Pictorial Composition: 1330–1450* [Oxford: Clarendon Press, 1971], p. 15).

79. William Duff, *An Essay on Original Genius and Its Various Models of Exertion in Philosophy and the Fine Arts* (London, 1767; reprint edition, ed. J. L. Mahoney [Gainesville, Fla.: Scholar's Facsimiles and Reprints, 1964]).

the "natural" genius who by the power of his inborn gifts alone, quite unassisted by art or learning, reached the most sublime levels of artistic achievement.[80]

The idea of the genius, untutored in traditional learning, gained ascendancy. "Many a Genius, probably, there has been which could neither write nor read."[81] Submission to tradition actually impeded the manifestation of the creative power of genius. It was variously observed by literary critics that: "To the neglect of Learning, Genius sometimes owes its greater glory."[82] Other critics wrote: "Genius is from Heaven, Learning from man";[83] and "The less we copy the renowned Antients, we shall resemble them the more."[84] (This last sentence is an interesting combination of the new view of creative accomplishment and the older submission to the models of classical antiquity. It was only a way station towards the goal of complete emancipation.)

Sir William Temple also thought that learning might impede the working of genius.[85] Learning as the qualification of a poet, mastery of the traditional poetry, began to fall into disrepute; the untutored genius, the conception of the genius as one unburdened by the weight of learning, gained favor. Genius was hampered by rules; genius was spontaneous; learning was made or contrived. Less talented persons might not be able to dispense with studious imitation, but the real genius, who was becoming god-like in his attributes, had no need for tradition, which had to be assimilated by studious application of given models. Shakespeare, the greatest of all geniuses, being untutored, was a model for all others: he showed that great achievements were not founded on the cultivation of the lessons provided in the tradition of authorship. He was a model in his procedures, not in his substance. Those who aspired to discover their genius should, like Shakespeare, "disregard all rules and traditions and go direct to Nature."[86]

Geniuses, as the gods whom they succeeded, have their own laws.[87] The laws and conventions of society are not for them. Every-

80. Ibid., p. 99. *The Oxford English Dictionary* defines "genius" as follows: "Native intellectual power of an exalted type such as is attributed to those who are esteemed greatest in any department of art, speculation, or practice. Often contrasted to talent" (*The Oxford English Dictionary,* corrected reissue [Oxford: Clarendon Press, 1933], 4:113, col. 2⁵).
81. Edward Young, *Conjectures on Original Composition* (1759), quoted by Smith, *Words and Idioms,* p. 103.
82. Smith, *Words and Idioms,* p. 29.
83. Ibid., p. 36.
84. Ibid., p. 21.
85. See Spingarn, *Critical Essays of the Seventeenth Century,* 3:48 (cited by Smith, *Words and Idioms,* p. 99).
86. Smith, *Words and Idioms,* p. 105.
87. Dryden early acknowledged the freedom of genius from the obligation of submission: "Extraordinary Genius's have a sort of Prerogative, which may dispense them from Laws" (quoted in *The Oxford English Dictionary,* 4:113, col. 2⁶).

day life is constituted by beliefs and actions which are impelled either by practical interests or by the readiness to conform with rules and standards which have lost all traces of inspiration. It is the realm of the routine, the humdrum. The genius moves in the transcendent sphere. His genius consists in his capacity to transcend the routine of everyday life and to create works which belong to the stratum of sacred things.

The common element of the modern conception of genius and of the premodern conception is the belief that both are involved in a sacred, transcendent stratum of being. Whereas in antiquity genius acted under the impulsion of powers which were external to himself and which took possession of him, the modern genius acts under the impulsion of superior powers which are inherent in himself. The outcome is the same—a manifestation of charisma, which is antithetical to tradition.[88]

Such is the tradition of genius which developed first in England and France, and then in Germany in the eighteenth and nineteenth centuries. It was a conception which left little place for continuously maintained tradition. It found room for the remoter past, for a golden age at an earlier time long since past. Ancient Greece or the Middle Ages, when the artist was accepted as a priest or quasi-priest, was such a time. The praise of the medieval acceptance of the artist as a craftsman—as in the Pre-Raphaelites and William Morris—also postulated a belief that the artistic genius had to serve higher ends than those which were traditional in the society of the artist's lay contemporaries. These vanished epochs contained a mode of artistic existence which was contrasted with the recent times when the artist was not taken seriously. The antitraditional version of the tradition of artistic genius reached its extreme point in the *Futurist Manifesto*.[89] All of the past was condemned as a burden on the artist. All that had been inherited was to be annihilated. The artist was to go forward into the future free of the burden of artistic traditions and of the traditions of his society.

We know little about genius. We know that there are great works and that the persons who created them must have been extraordinary. The genius of an author is inferred from the works he produces. Because he is out of the ordinary, he cannot be as determined by tradition as more ordinary writers are. Ordinary writers, too, proceed on the postulate that they must produce a work which is not only distinctive but also superior in quality in the class which they accept for themselves. Many of them are content to follow a "formula" which enables them to produce works which can be easily sold. Even they have to try to find a distinctive turn in each work which is

88. Weber, *Wirtschaft und Gesellschaft*, 2:753–55.
89. See Renato Poggioli, *The Theory of the Avant-Garde*, pp. 52–55.

produced by formula. Hence tradition, however much it saturates the intellectual environment of a writer, cannot be adequate even for a mediocre author. If he followed tradition entirely, then he would foreswear the possibility of distinctiveness or individuality.

At the other pole, the genius cannot escape entirely from tradition. He must exercise his gifts of imagination and verbal expression within the elastic limits of the resources offered by the prevailing or the otherwise available traditions of his culture. These resources are, first, language, and then the genres represented by and the patterns embodied in the particular works with which he comes into contact.

The Literary Tradition as Interpretation of Past and Present

"The existing monuments form an ideal order among themselves, which is modified by the introduction of the new (really new) work of art among them. The existing order is complete before the new work of art arrives; for order to persist after the supervention of novelty, the *whole* existing order must be, if ever so slightly, altered; and so the relations, proportions, values of each work of art towards the whole are readjusted; and this is conformity between the old and the new. Whoever has approved this idea of order, of the form of European, of English literature, will not find it preposterous that the past should be altered by the present as much as the present is directed by the past."[90] Each time a new work of outstanding merit is added to the gallery of surviving works by which the tradition of literature is constituted, the tradition changes. It changes not by the addition alone but by the changes which occur in the understanding of the works which are already in the tradition. The generation subsequent to the addition to the tradition has before it a tradition which is different from that faced by its predecessors. The difference lies not merely in the addition of the works of the last generation but in the change in the reinterpreted totality.

There is a loose, partial, and changing consensus between the works of the present and the works of the past. They affect each other's appearance before the readers of every generation and the authors who come forth from among those readers. This ever-growing tradition which brings into a single cosmos ancient and modern works as well as a recent one is in many respects like the other traditions which bind the successive states of a society through time.

The young writer seeks a tradition rather than submitting to a particular tradition imposed on him in a course of instruction. The writing of novels and short stories is not and has not been taught in the way in which medicine, law, engineering, science, painting, and sculpture have been taught. At one time, it is true, incidentally to their

90. Eliot, "The Function of Criticism" (1923), in *Selected Essays,* p. 23.

study of Latin and Greek poetry at school, young persons learned how to write poetry. The mastery of metrical forms through the study of Latin and Greek verse has been renounced and the composition of Latin verse in schools is no longer required. These arrangements for contact with the tradition of poetic composition had not been intended primarily to provide future poets with models for composition. They were intended to provide a certain modicum of classical culture appropriate to a person of a particular station in life, within a particular national society with a particular cultural tradition. Nonetheless, many of those who wrote poetry had to learn to write in these forms which required systematic study. Readers expected writers to conform to these rules. The coming into predominance of modern poetry has dispensed with this body of rules. Poetic composition is now learned without prior instruction in prosody.

The writing of works of prose was subjected to a looser discipline. The instruction in grammar and composition which schoolchildren received was not intended to train them for the production of literary works. Nonetheless, writers of the past two centuries have not been as free from literary traditions as this would indicate. They have been subject to the opinions of an elaborate institutional system of publishing and publishers' readers; they have been subject to the opinions of booksellers and librarians for their distribution, and to the opinions of reviewers and scholars for their assessment. All of these receive traditions which are expressed in their judgments; the adaptations of traditions into fashions are also manifested in their judgments. They have been dependent on numerous other more or less intellectual institutions through which authors can earn their livelihood—and endanger their character—through authorship for films, television, journalism, etc. Traditions of style and substance prevail in each of these sets of institutions.

It has perhaps not been unreasonable for authors of literary works to think of themselves as writing under their own inspiration free of the authority of the past. They are after all not placed under authoritative tutelage as are aspirant scientists, scholars, theologians, physicians, lawyers, and artists; once they have learned to read and have had some elementary instruction of a general sort in school, where some literary models were presented to them for purposes other than training them for authorship, their training has been largely self-training. Through instruction of a very general sort, directed far more towards assimilation and appreciation than towards creation either at home or in schools or through the books made available to them in libraries or through the beneficence of older persons who have taken an interest in them, they gained first of all knowledge of the literary works which formed their ideas as to what a literary work is. They also began—at least in modern times—to form within themselves the idea of being a "writer." The idea of being a writer fixes their ambitions in a very vague way. To be a writer is to produce works such as writers in the past have produced. They find, by a combination of accident and an active, searching sense of affinity, other persons who also wish to be writers. The awareness that there have been other writers in the world, writers in their own society, and in their own immediate environment, encourages them in the belief in the possibility that they too can become writers of significant works.[9] Because an authoritative and persuasive tradition is not directly presented by institutions, aspirants attempt to find a tradition which can guide and justify their efforts in writing.

In the nineteenth century, many of the greatest writers had relatively little formal education, according to present-day standards. Charles Dickens had no schooling after the age of fourteen. George Eliot, who became very learned as well as a great novelist, had no formal education past her sixteenth year. Jane Austen attended no school after the age of sixteen. Even at the end of the century, Joseph Conrad, Thomas Hardy, Rudyard Kipling, and H. G. Wells had little more than a modest amount of secondary education. The leading poets of the nineteenth century—Shelley, Byron, Tennyson, and Browning—did attend university, although Keats did not. (Poetry still required at that time a mastery of prosody which was acquired in grammar and public schools.) But even those novelists who did not have prolonged education in classical literature knew something of the literary tradition available in British society. Dickens was given books to read as a child by the proprietress of a bookshop above which his uncle lived. Jane Austen, Charlotte Brontë, and George Eliot were brought up among books. They had enough knowledge to permit them to find the literary traditions to which they could attach themselves in the very beginning of their careers as writers.

The traditions of science are presented to novices with the coherence and authoritativeness of religious doctrine in a society with a single religion under a caesaropapist regime. There are no alternatives for the novice; later on he will be much freer and his originality—as

91. I cite here, from among many possible illustrations, the remarks of Mr. Dan Jacobson about the effect on his generation of young South Africans aspiring to literary accomplishment in the 1930s and 1940s of *The Story of an African Farm* by Olive Schreiner: "Nothing can take from her the honor of being the first to make usable the country and the people within it as a subject for fiction. Those who have followed her, no matter how different their perceptions, approaches or types of thinking and feeling, have had the encouragement of knowing the field not to be entirely barren; what is more they have seen in her work an example of how natural, how direct, how free from false consciousness, it is possible to be in presenting their country with its particular cultural atmosphere—or lack of atmosphere" (Introduction to Olive Schreiner, *The Story of an African Farm* [Harmondsworth, Middlesex: Penguin Books, 1971], p. 22).

ong as it respects considerable parts of the tradition—will be prized. The presentation of the traditions of literature and art is more like the presentation of religious traditions in a pluralistic society under a regime of separation of church and state, where parents are piously agnostic. The aspiring writer, like the seeker in the realm of faith, may turn where he will until he finds a "model which fits his needs" as a Harvard graduate in biochemistry once said in explaining his admiration for the works of Hermann Hesse.

One should not overestimate the completeness of the consensus of the scientific community and its numerous subdivisions about the right tradition. One should also not overestimate the freedom of the aspirant writer in the face of the plurality of traditions. At any one time, the plurality of literary traditions is also a hierarchy of traditions. But there is nonetheless a real difference.

Anatole France once wrote of "the adventures of his soul among the masterpieces."[92] This greatly exaggerates the freedom of movement of the soul in the world of books. Not all the masterpieces are equally accessible to the explorer, be he a lighthearted adventurer or a seeker in deadly earnest. The very category of "masterpieces" presupposes a long prior sifting and assessment of works of literature; it assumes an approximation to a canon.

The masterpieces and their derivatives have already been sorted and graded by numerous intermediaries through generations. No complete and wholly consensual hierarchy is the result of this sorting and grading; but Dickens has always been regarded as better than Charles Reade, Flaubert better than Champfleury. The explorer is thus not moving in an uncharted territory in which every possibility is open to him. Certain writers are famous; his attention fixes on their works first. The aspirant author can read freely and without strict tuition but his freedom is exercised in the light of what has been recommended to him by teachers and the critics of the journals which he has. When he finds a review to which he wishes to contribute, he is brought face to face with the traditions embodied in the judgment of the editors. When he seeks a publisher, by his own efforts or through a literary agent, he is brought into connection with the representatives of certain traditions, sometimes narrow and sometimes broad. When his first writings are published, he receives the assessment of reviewers; they too represent sets of traditions; and some of these traditions and those who represent them will be more congenial to him. Those dispositions within himself which have been formed in a particular direction by the traditions which he has found and by his own propensities are strengthened by these experiences and they are strengthened above all if his disposition and the traditions are both

92. Anatole France, *La Vie littéraire* (Paris: Calman-Lévy, 1888), 1:iii.

good enough to enable him to write things which please him, his critics, and his readers. In most cases the critics and readers are not as meticulous or as strict as the supervision and critical scrutiny which a young doctoral candidate receives in a university department of science, or even that an art student receives in a school of art, but the relations with tradition are not fundamentally different.

The beginning writer seeks a tradition until he finds one or several and then begins to develop his own style; but he must be a person of great courage and perseverance to disregard the traditions which are proffered to him and insisted upon by teachers, contemporaries, friends, critics, and publishers. If he has the financial means, from inheritance, patronage, or from his own occupation, and if he has the necessary obduracy of devotion to his own idea of the literary work which he wishes to produce, he can go his own way and take a chance on being published. James Joyce was one of the most extreme cases of such a writer in the present century. He had his own bent, his great pride, and his willingness to forgo many otherwise available satisfactions, so that his capacity for originality could work itself out. But he, too, began from the prevailing tradition of the second half of the nineteenth century, particularly from Flaubert. He moved far from this point and reached towards other traditions which were far from his starting point. He reached towards Homer and Sterne—and, possibly, before any literary man except Lawrence—towards Freud.

Any writer can take as his point of departure any other writer, any work, or any type of work of any period. If he is willing to be refused publication, he can persist in his attachment to any tradition which pleases him even though it is "out of date" or—what is really meant—"out of fashion." What he cannot do is become a writer without any tradition at all.

There is in the literary profession a tradition of antitraditionality, as well as a genuine striving for originality and occasionally some success in producing works of originality. For all these reasons persistent elements are sometimes difficult to discern. There are nonetheless elements which last for a long time. The naturalistic novel is often said to have ceased to be written any more; the modes of description of events, persons, and objects have indeed changed. But it was a distinctive achievement of the writers who could be grouped under this heading in the middle of the nineteenth century that they treated aspects of society and of individual conduct which were dominated by brutality, infidelity, selfishness, inhumanity, corruption, and animality. The portrayal of these vices has certainly not disappeared from the writing of novels; on the contrary, it has become a major feature in many novels. Emphasis on the incoherence of experience, on the self-defeating character of human activities, has certainly not diminished. It is one of the central features of what is called "modernism'' in literature. At one time the early proponents of modernism thought that they were breaking the veil which the traditions of bourgeois respectability cast over what the authors believed to be the ''realities'' of life. Modernism, because it has become so widely accepted among literary men and women, is now an enchainment stronger than the Victorian veil ever was. It might be called a ''fashion,'' but an outlook which lasts for more than a century is deeper than a fashion. It is a tradition.

In liberal countries, the traditions are not uniform and obligatory but they exist nonetheless and they affect the chances of success of an author's work and the mode which he chooses. In totalitarian societies, publishing is more centrally controlled and ''writers' unions'' or ''academies'' insist on an orthodoxy in literature which limits the freedom of authors to write under the tradition which is most congenial to them. The most notable instances of such restrictions are of authors whose political and religious views are uncongenial to the officials of the union or academy. These restrictions are not always successful where authors of strong character are involved. The unions or academies have not been wholly successful in preventing authors from writing what they wish although they have been able to prevent the publication of their works in their own country and the authors from gaining a livelihood from their writings. The traditions of literary composition are too strong and they are too widely cultivated internationally for great works to lose their power to attract and guide persons with a strong propensity for literary creation.

3   The Endurance of Past Practices

The Presence of the Past in Society

When we pass from traditions of cultural works and patterns and from the tradition of symbolic constructions such as works of science, theology, scholarship, and literature and their physical embodiments to social institutions and to society, we enter into a harsher sphere of reality; this is the realm of pressing biological necessity, the brutal struggle for power, the unswervingly pursued desire for wealth, the angry ambitions for survival and ascendancy and the exercise of coercion for all these ends. What place has tradition in this arena in which the state of nature is played out?

It would be surprising if traditions were not important in the symbolic realm. This is the realm of man's creative powers, relatively free from the constraints of power and scarcity. There are rivalries there; fame is not available to all, nor is talent equally distributed, patronage and appointments are scarcer than aspirants desire and the reading and buying publics could always be larger than they are. Ultimately however there is room in the ideal sphere for great works, however numerous. One great painting does not make another painting less great, although in their contact with society the attention and applause gained by one could conceivably reduce the amount available for the other. The situation is somewhat different in religion and science, especially in the former, since for many religions there is only one truth; for science, too, for particular problems there is one solution which is better or truer than others. But the problems are many and there is room therefore for many truths existing alongside each other. Nonetheless, the realm of symbols or of the spirit is free of many of the constraints of social action and social institutions, which constitute realms where what Max Scheler called *Realfaktoren* are at work.

Furthermore, despite this relatively unconstrained situation of the creative powers of imagination, ratiocination, and observation, traditions of one kind or another in any field of intellectual activity are always sought out, even when they are contemptuously rejected. The workings of the imagination and of reason are intensified by contact

162

with the imagination and reason of other persons, living and dead. The need for intellectual conviviality draws together minds with similar, strong propensities and they benefit from each other's constructions. The works of the mind from the past draw them as much as the works of their living contemporaries who are also formed on the anvil of past works. Such minds are drawn to the visible works of the past in their search for intellectual conviviality and communion. There they find prototypes of the kinds of actions they wish to perform and of the works they wish to create. Thus, even if cultural traditions were avoidable, they would still draw the minds of those who seek to dwell in the midst of symbolic constructions.

Piety or reverence towards the past is perhaps more pronounced among persons whose "natural environment" is made up of symbolic constructions, who are more sensitive to things remote in time as well as in space. Then, too, ineluctable educational processes conducted and even imposed by the adult generation in all spheres of life force the still unformed mind into contact with the symbolic constructions of the past of varying degrees of remoteness from the present.

With societies, the matter could well appear to be different. Life in society imposes exigencies, harsher, more pressing, more coercive, than the realm of symbolic construction. "Interests," the striving for power over others, and the sheer unthinking desire to remain alive place practical considerations in the forefront of attention. The struggle for power and the struggle against the powerful are oriented towards insistent realities, not towards ghosts lingering behind from the past. This is the hardheaded view of the matter. This is the view of those who distinguish between the "material basis" and the "super-structure," between *Realfaktoren* and *Idealfaktoren*, between "interests" and "ideas." Traditions are almost entirely symbolic, so what do they have to do with hard, cold reality? We shall see.

The Identity of Societies through Time

No society remains still. Each one is in unceasing change. Yet each society remains the same society. Its members do not wake up one morning and discover they are no longer living in, let us say, British society. Whether they approve or disapprove of the identities or changes which they discover on waking, they believe themselves still to be living in British society. It would be wrong to assert that the society in which those now seventy-five years old lived as children has persisted unchanged. It would be illusory to believe this. There have been many important changes; the peerage of great landowners no longer has great political influence, the unemployed are no longer short of food, children continue longer at school, deference has diminished and so, for the moment at least, has civility; many persons spend much of their leisure time looking at their television sets, and so on. These are among the changes which have occurred since the beginning of the century. Why still call it Great Britain? Is there any reason to call it British society other than the fact that at successive moments in time a series of events has occurred in a particular bounded space which has retained the same name? Are British society of 1930 and British society of 1980 the same society only because persons living in the society of 1930 and those in the society of 1980 refer to themselves by the same name and because both societies occupied and still occupy the same territory? Or perhaps the territorial designation itself is only a symbol of primordial membership in a society possessing identity over time? If so, what does the identity consist in? Partly, it is a society made up of biologically continuous lineages: it is generally granted that the lineage is a reality of enduring existence. But lineages lose old members through death and gain new members by birth and marriage so that over fifty years most of the members of a lineage are new. A lineage is furthermore a filiation of individuals with the same name—in various forms—and a biological, genetic connection, directly and indirectly, so that individuals living in the present are linked with each other by their common connection with an event in the past. But this does not amount to institutional identity. It is only nominal and biological identity.

The name of their society is important to most members of a society in their self-designation, especially when they are in contact with members of "other societies," i.e., persons from other territories. By means of the name, they classify themselves as possessing an undefined but significant quality in common with others who live within those boundaries. By means of the name, they also declare that they share an unexpressed and significant quality with others who, having lived within those boundaries in the past, were members of the same society as themselves. They have a very vague sense of affinity with those who lived there in the past.

Perhaps if asked why they regard themselves as being in a state of affinity with others who lived in the same territory in the past, they would say, "We are descended from them." This would be true as far as their own biological filiation running down to the present from their parents, grandparents, great-grandparents, great-great-grandparents. If one goes back about fifteen generations, one would have more than 32,000 ancestors and these would have been enough to settle a large town in 1450 in Great Britain. The number of collateral relatives runs into the millions. But the sense of cousinhood among those linked through five or six generations of common ancestors evaporates long before it reaches the boundaries of those linked by ancestors that far back. For any American alive today, except for a person of Red Indian descent, none of his more than 30,000 ancestors of five centuries ago lived in North America. They were scattered among a number of different societies. A sense of affinity with predecessors in such a society could not be accounted for by the reality of, or by images and sentiments about, biological kinship. The sense of identity with other members of the society, past and present, refers to nothing other than a sense of membership in the society as such, even though primordial images are adduced to refer to it.

But does this common name, this sense of affinity with members of a society which lived there in the past, this sense of belief in the existence of some qualities possessed equally by themselves and those others of the past mean anything important in comparison with much more "real" realities such as working for a livelihood at present, struggling to gain or retain power at present or in the near future, looking after one's family and after one's own "interests" at present and in the future? Are they not epiphenomenal or illusory and is this link with the past in society not equally epiphenomenal or illusory? What after all does the sense of affinity amount to? Is not the belief that one is similar to these persons, in ways that one cannot define, an intellectual moonbeam, a fantasy which makes no difference in real life? And even if this sense of affinity and identity with persons no longer living were acute and persistent, what difference would it make to the issue, which is whether there are grounds for speaking of a society as having duration? Is it reasonable to speak of a society existing in time when the state of the alleged society at one point in time is very different from the state of the allegedly same society at a time fifty years later?

The identity of name, the reference to identity of territory through time, and the belief in some sort of identity of the living generation with past generations living in the same territory are sometimes called myths. This is meant to disparage belief in these identities by intimating that they have no counterpart in reality, least of all in modern societies in which conduct seems to be dominated by considerations of gaining or retaining advantages of wealth and power and the rational pursuit thereof. W. I. Thomas once wrote that, "if men define situations as real, they are real in their consequences."[1]

It is evident enough that these identities are taken seriously by many persons. Mr. Enoch Powell in Great Britain is apprehensive about a damaging discontinuity which might occur in British society if the recent policies regarding immigration are not extensively modified. Of course, he might be deluded in thinking that until the Pakistanis, Indians, West Indians, and West Africans appeared in large numbers after the war, British society had been significantly the same for a long time. Those who take the opposite side from him in

1. W. I. Thomas, *The Child in America, Behavioral Problems and Programs* (New York: Alfred A. Knopf, 1928), p. 572.

politics demand "fundamental social changes" and in that sense they share his views about the identity of British society over a long period up to the present. They think that the changes they would institute would endure for a long time. They presuppose that the society so much in need of "fundamental social change" has been what it is for a very long time. They suggest that such changes as have occurred are of little consequence, since the basic social structure remained intact throughout all of these changes.

The identities are surely taken seriously by those who think that societies ought to change markedly. If each society fluctuated randomly in time, there would be no long-standing iniquities to be abolished, just as it would not be worth the strenuous effort to change a briefly existing iniquity into a transient virtue. Revolutionaries as well as conservatives think that societies endure, that they remain through time. Did not Karl Marx argue that "capitalism" replaced "feudalism" which replaced "ancient slave society," the three of them together covering about two and a half millennia? Heraclitus, so much admired by Marx, said, however, that one could never put one's foot twice into the same river. Geologists and physiographers would not agree, while admitting that the water in the river had not been standing still. Marx certainly accepted a view very different from Heraclitus's, where society was concerned.

It is not just hunger after stability which makes those who fear its disappearance imagine a nonexistent identity subsisting through change. It is not just zeal for change that makes some persons imagine a nonexistent persistence or identity in the pattern of society which they wish to change "fundamentally."

A human society, made of human actions, has as it is at any moment the same evanescence of physical movements, sequences of words, social actions. They cease when they have been performed. Spoken words are dissipated into nothingness, they cease to generate sound waves; actions cease when they are enacted. Unlike a written manuscript or a printed book or a piece of sculpture or a painting, spoken sentences and performed actions have to be commenced "anew" when desired or demanded or required. A society to exist at all must be incessantly reenacted, its communications must repeatedly be resaid. The reenactments and the resayings are guided by what the individual members remember about what they themselves said and did before, what they perceive and remember of what other persons expect and require of them; they are guided too by what they remember is expected and required of them, what they remember to be claims which they are entitled to exercise by virtue of particular qualifications such as skill, title, appointment, ownership which are engrained in their own memory traces, recorded in writing and in the correspondingly recorded qualifications of others. These particular qualifications change and the responses to the changes are guided by recollections of the rightful claims and rights of the possessors of these qualifications.

Of course, not only memories and records guide the performance of actions; anticipations of advantages to be gained and of losses to be averted by particular actions do so as well. But these anticipations are themselves guided by memories and records. The act of remembering is so much taken for granted that the perception of the immediately perceived actions and words is thought to be determinative. This is to be misled. The immediately perceived is perceived in categories set by remembered patterns, remembered expectations, and remembered rights and rules in relation to remembered qualifications. Coercion, which is in its nature so alien to guiding recollection, achieves most of its effects through the remembered anticipations of coercive actions and their remembered consequences. There is of course the irreducible fact of coercion; physical grasping, physical confinement, physical wounding and incapacitation, and killing are not at all acts of memory, but the efficacy of threats or the estimated probability of such coercive action is dependent on memory. Rational calculation and action based on it in the marketplace is not an act of memory but it depends on memory and traditional rules for the interpretation of the information provided by prices. Claims to the goods held by others and to their services are exercised in the setting of memory and records of the qualifications to assert the claim—in this case the memory of the meaning of money and the meaning of ownership.

Memory is more than the act of recollection by recollecting persons. Memory leaves an objective deposit in tradition. The past does not have to be remembered by all who reenact it; the deposit is carried forward by a continuing chain of transmissions and receptions. But to become a tradition, and to remain a tradition, a pattern of assertion or action must have entered into memory.

It is this chain of memory and of the tradition which assimilates it that enables societies to go on reproducing themselves while also changing. If we say that a society is a process of self-reproduction of a large, an infinitely large number of differentiated actions and assertions and imaginings, articulated with each other and in conflict with each other, within individuals and between individuals both as distinctive individuals with individuality and as instances of categories, we are in fact saying that a society is more than an instantaneous synchronic phenomenon. It would not be a society if it did not have duration; the mechanisms of reproduction give it the duration which permits it to be defined as a society.

Duration as a society entails identities but it certainly does not entail completely unchanging identity. It does so no more than the synchronic existence of a society entails complete integration—

although some integration is indispensable simply to its being a society.[2]

It is true that every institution in society is constantly changing its membership and that particular institutions like business firms cease to exist. But these cessations are not simultaneous. There is an unceasing falling away of particular and concrete entities and their replacement by others which are similar and different. A society is in continuous existence. Continuity is one feature of the oneness over time; it depends on the partial stability of identities. The constituent identities, those identities in the various spheres of social life, some longer than others and interconnected with each other, preserve the society by keeping some of its past in the present and by sustaining the sense of identity through time. These identities rest on the consensus of the present with the past.

As it has hitherto been used, the term "consensus" has referred to the state of a society only at a given moment in time or in periods of short duration. I wish to emphasize the existence of consensus through time. It has to be recognized that the consensus at one moment in time is not the same as the consensus at another moment in time in the same society. The variability of the degrees of consensus in a society over a sequence of points in time is evidence that consensus is certainly never complete in a large society—and in a small one as well. A similar observation is in place regarding the consensus of a society through time. The occurrence of change does not gainsay the existence of identity any more than the existence of conflict and competition excludes the coexistent consensus.

The identity of a society through time to its members and to external observers is a consensus between living generations and generations of the dead. The living forward into the present of beliefs and patterns of institutions which existed in an earlier time is a consensus between the dead and the living in which the latter accept what the former have presented to them. The content of the consensus changes through interpretation; the consensus is maintained through the reinterpretation of what the earlier generations believed.

The persistence of the past into the present, through the maintenance of the partial identity of a society between its past and its present may legitimately be described as consensus. Consensus is not the explanation of that persistence. The explanation lies in the grounds of the acceptance of and the searching for tradition; it is not too different in fundamental respects from the existence of consensus in society at a point in time.

2. See Edward Shils, *Center and Periphery* (Chicago: University of Chicago Press, 1975), pp. 164–81.

Families. The first link in the chain which binds past and present and future into the structure of a society is reforged every time an infant is born and survives. The survival of a child as a biological organism is simultaneously its formation as a carrier of beliefs and patterns which obtained in the past into the present and from there into the future.

The sequence of families in a lineage is a synchronized set of cycles. The child is being prepared to carry into its own future both general and specific patterns which are presented to it at each stage of its growth. Much that is specific becomes an enduring self-generalizing acquisition. Such is the learning of vocabulary. The acquisition of images of the character of authority and similar fundamentals begins specifically with parents, and is then generalized to other persons with power. The acquisition of the image of their powers is also an acquisition of the patterns of belief and action which they present. These are added to, generalized, differentiated, modified and refused, in various combinations. There is much refusal; some of the refusal endures, some of the refusal is transient and gives way to modified acceptance. Still, although there is much refusal, there is much that is accepted. Even psychopathic criminals and those who are revolutionaries out of doctrinaire principles assimilate a great deal of what has been presented to them in their families.

Biologically, through his genes, the human being carries parts of his self-producing past within himself; that past has no symbolic content. The other past, the past of beliefs, of symbolic patterns embodied in words and movements, is more variably received and repeated. It is a past which is presented to its prospective recipients in various orders of generality. The first extended contact the newborn infant has with the past of experience, and with the past of the cultural creations of human beings, occurs within the family. The first past he encounters is that presented in and by his parents. For most of human history the mother had her own mother's and grandmother's experience to guide her in the care of the infant; nowadays she also draws upon the teachings of psychologists. Regardless of the immediate sources of the mother's knowledge of the propensities of infants, the things the child learns from her and from both parents are specific rules regarding a child's behavior in the family at a particular stage of life and more general rules to govern behavior in a variety of situations outside the family both in the near and in the more remote future. The child's acquisition of what the past offers begins with the acquisition of language, vocabulary, and grammar. It learns the names of visible things and then of things material and immaterial, outside its own perception. As the child grows older, it acquires knowledge of existing children's games which are themselves traditions transmitted from one cohort of children to the slightly younger cohort over a long series of acts of transmission and reception. Grandparents appear on the horizon; in some societies the grandmother looks to the care of the young child and, through her, contact is made with the experience, knowledge, and benefit of about a half-century earlier. The child becomes human through assimilating traditions; Karl Popper once said that "if everybody were to start where Adam started, he would not get further than Adam did."[3] One does not know how much Adam knew as a result of his divine creation. Whatever it was, it was lost by expulsion from the Garden of Eden, and ensuing generations came into the world only with their genetically determined bodies and capacities. To fill those capacities required the assimilation of tradition.[4] To say that they had to assimilate culture is true but insufficient. The term "culture" does not underscore the pastness in the present of what is offered for assimilation. "Culture" contains beliefs and patterns discovered in the past; it is not just shared with contemporaries, it is shared with ancestors and other predecessors. The instruction given to the child looks towards the future; some of it is intended to serve the immediate present and proximate future but much of it looks towards the remoter future of youth and adulthood. It is a provision for the future from the past.

The child acquires his initial vocabulary and his most general moral standards from his parents. Much of what he first learns about the world beyond his immediate radius of experience comes from his parents, but their role as transmitters of tradition is soon supplemented and overshadowed by other authorities, particularly by schoolteachers, clergymen, and then by his own reading from a much wider range of sources. Friends, subjected to similar influences, convey similar beliefs. (He also acquires some of their anti-traditional traditions.) As he grows into late adolescence and early adulthood, he acquires additional provision from the past from persons with whom he associates daily whether in a workshop, in an office, on a farm, in a club, in the armed forces, or in any other setting. Even when he associates with coevals, his acquisitions are not limited to what his associates have learned simply from their own experiences. He acquires some of their acquisitions from the past. Much, if not all, of what he acquires later is set into the matrix of what he acquired from his family; it becomes more differentiated and it is applied in a more specific way to situations and objects not anticipated in detail when he first acquired them. Although his possessions change over the years,

3. Karl Popper, *Objective Knowledge: An Evolutionary Approach* (Oxford: Clarendon Press, 1972), pp. 106–90.
4. See P. B. Medawar, "Tradition: The Evidence of Biology," in *The Uniqueness of the Individual* (London: Methuen, 1957), pp. 134–42.

they do so gradually and what they were at first sets very generally the direction of what is acquired later.

Much of what his parents provided did not come from their own experience or from their own families. Much of it came from outside the family from a pool of beliefs more widely shared in the society. Religious beliefs were among these. No families have a religion of their own; their religious beliefs are the beliefs of a wider community. Where the family had domestic religious observances, the beliefs were drawn from outside and from the past. The congruity of domestic circle and religious observances reinforces attachments to these symbols formed in and transmitted from the past and attach the individual to the wider community through that common symbolic possession.

Families vary in the extent to which they cherish their pasts and in the volume of what they receive from them. Modern Western cultures have no religions of ancestor worship, and in the Asian and African societies in which the worship of ancestors once flourished, it no longer does so to the same degree. The transmission of familial heirlooms and familial houses probably was never great in the poorer classes, simply because they owned so little and most of what they owned was usually worn out in their own lifetime. The wills of the poor of the seventeenth century included a few shirts and undershirts which would not be regarded as worthy of testamentary transfer nowadays. Changes in styles and tastes, the weakness of materials and faults of construction and the cumbersomeness of transportation are not conducive to the transfer of domestic artifacts between the generations of a single family. In large towns, successive adult generations very seldom continue residence in the same building. In Western societies, the very wealthy and the rural population used to live in buildings which their ancestors had dwelt in but it is much less common now. The great expansion of the urban population has meant also much displacement. Economic necessity and opportunity and new standards of pleasure dispose towards changes in places of residence. Where families do live in older buildings, they have no sense of affinity with them and they know and care little about what went on in them in earlier generations of residents who were not biologically continuous with their own. There remain in the countryside houses where several generations of the same family have lived or where the present occupants know about who lived in them previously. As agriculture becomes a sector of economic life with very elaborate and expensive technology, and as it has become more of a commercial proposition, the countryside as the scene of domestic continuity in the ownership and occupancy of residential buildings and in the possession of domestic utensils and furniture declines. The discontinuity of residence and ownership weakens the awareness of ancestors. The visibility of artifacts of known previous usership reimprints in the memory the image of the past existence of those users.[5] It heightens the sense of continuity with the past and adds to its power.

The density and the dominance of specific traditions transmitted in the course of life within a family have decreased with the increase in the proportion of time spent outside the family and in the distance between place of residence and place of work, with the increased spatial separation of generations, with the increase in universal compulsory education, and with the progress of belief in the rights of children to self-determination. The authority of parents over their children has probably declined as a result of deliberate and unwritten renunciation on the part of parents and also in consequence of the greater frequency of the absence of one parent because of separation or divorce.

A family which incorporates into itself little of the past, and, of that which it does incorporate, little of high quality—not all of the past was of equal quality—deadens its offspring; it leaves them with a scanty set of categories and beliefs which are not easily extended or elaborated. To some extent subsequent education can arouse the powers and strengthen some of the enfeebled traditions acquired or fostered in the family but its power is limited. Ambition, imagination, and exceptional intelligence and the opportunity to exercise them enable their possessors to fill in some of the empty spaces left by parental inanition and to undo and replace some of the attenuated traditions which they have acquired in the setting of their families and to offset the antitraditional fashions which they have acquired from their coevals. The proportion of the culture of a typical adult of a particular class in the present time made up of specific traditions acquired through his family is probably less now than it used to be one hundred and two hundred years ago. Much more of the culture which the individual receives is made up of tradition which reaches him through other institutions and much of that culture at any particular time is of rather recent origin. This does not mean that the more general orientations, the general judgments of rightness and fairness so acquired are entirely inoperative. This is only a marginal possibility. Short of this extreme the family as a tradition-transmitting institution can recede and has receded. The deliberate disbelief of parents in the rightfulness of imposing their own beliefs on their offspring, the deliberate refusal to impose their beliefs on their offspring, the deliberate imposition of beliefs hostile towards authority, neglect by parents of the transmission of tradition to their offspring because of other preoccupations and because of their ignorance and the incapacity of parents—

5. Maurice Halbwachs, *Les Cadres sociaux de la mémoire* (Paris: Felix Alcan, 1935), pp. 199–368, 391–401, and *La Mémoire collective* (Paris: Presses universitaires de France, 1950), pp. 131–46.

especially where there are not two parents who reinforce each other's authority—make the stream of tradition narrower and shallower. The offspring are left to define their own standards; this means the acceptance of the norms of their most imposing coevals. This is a common phenomenon in the aftermath of a lost war and a civil war when parents become separated from each other and from their children.

For a variety of reasons, the family has been an object of severe criticism, attempted reforms, and deliberate neglect. Much of the war against tradition has placed the family at the center of the target. The bohemian outlook, the movements for the emancipation of the individual, for sexual freedom, for individual happiness, and for civil solidarity have all aimed their fire at the family. And in fact the family has changed, although not as much as was believed only a few decades ago. The increased powers of wives, the diminished powers of husbands, the greater rights of children, the decline of family firms and family farms have been involved in the changes in the structure of the family and its transmission of tradition in Western societies.

The inherent constitution of the family in the relations of parents and children is partly self-sustaining but its strength is variable; it has internal weaknesses which are intensified by inimical circumstances. Central though it is in the transmission of tradition, it is also dependent on institutions exterior to it. In societies which have become sufficiently differentiated to have a church or at least a cult outside the family and to have educational institutions outside the family, the success of the family in the transmission of substantive traditions is much affected by the strength of church and school in such transmission. Church and school transmit more specific substance to fill in the disposing, generalized traditions transmitted in the family. They also reinforce the legitimacy of the familial authority necessary for effective transmission. If they fail to do so, the effectiveness of the family is impaired. The same is true of the function of the family in the legitimation of authority in school and church.

The critics of the family are by no means wrong in their grasp of the centrality of the family in the maintenance of traditions in society and they are not wrong either in their belief that the family, especially the family as a structure of biologically related elders and children, is a bulwark against progress in an emancipationist sense.

In a society of a relatively high degree of differentiation of institutions, the family is only one of many institutions rather than the all-inclusive one. Yet in some respects the family retains one essential element of the inclusive functions of the lineage in a small, approximately self-contained agricultural community. The family is very seldom any longer an institution of economic production; nor is it the institution of territorial authority or of justice within and between units; nor is it the institution of the worship and cult of sacred entities.[6] The one function which the family does not lose is that of its self-reproduction, generation after generation. Every particular family of particular parents and particular children passes through a cycle of formation, growth, and dissolution, ceasing to be a family within a half-century in most cases. But each of the offspring usually then joins in the formation of a family and so on and on, each new family carrying forward the pattern of the institution, modifying it slightly. The family might be much reduced in the range of its activities in modern urban differentiated societies but its reproduction is still not confined to self-reproduction. In its self-reproduction and maintenance it is also reproducing and maintaining the performance of the functions which have been removed from it. The family is the root from which many separate and powerful trunks grow. The family does not perform the separate functions but it does provide the "orientations," the fundamental original attitudes which enable them to function.[7] These attitudes, normative and cognitive, contain in generalized and interpretable form attitudes which come into play in institutions outside the family, in economic institutions, in educational institutions, in military institutions, and in ecclesiastical institutions. They are often no more than "orientations" towards the authority and the conformity with expectations which are exercised in the specialized institutions of work, learning, and worship. Each of these types of institutions has its own traditions which are inculcated, maintained, and modified within it. Each of these more specialized institutions presents and adapts its traditions to persons who have already acquired the more generalized traditions into which these more specific traditions are set. Within each of these specialized types of institutions the incoming and incumbent members vary in the success with which they incorporate the more differentiated patterns of belief and action. Both the successful and the unsuccessful assimilators and reenactors of the specific institutional traditions are guided by traditions which they acquired in their families and on which the more specific traditions are overlaid. To the extent that the family has not inculcated the dispositional tradition, the more specialized institutions are disordered.

6. All this transfer and institutional specialization of functions has been well described by protosociologists and sociologists from W. H. Riehl to W. F. Ogburn. See W. H. Riehl, *Die Familie (Die Naturgeschichte des deutschen Volkes,* vol. 3) (Stuttgart and Ausgburg: Cotta'scher Verlag, 1855), and W. F. Ogburn and E. Groves, *American Marriage and Family Relationships* (New York: Henry Holt, 1928). See also P. A. Sorokin, C. C. Zimmermann, and C. Galpin, *A Systematic Source-Book in Rural Sociology* (Minneapolis: University of Minnesota Press, 1930–32), 3 vols.

7. See Talcott Parsons, "Age and Sex in the Social Structure of the United States" and "The Kinship System of the Contemporary United States," in *Essays in Sociological Theory, Pure and Applied,* rev. ed. (Glencoe, Ill.: The Free Press, 1954), pp. 89–103, 177–96.

Families are the points of departure for the entry into any community of belief, even though the family itself is the most primordial of institutions.[8] In the larger pattern of traditions which have generally prevailed in a society, the family has been the central panel of a triptych; another panel has usually been the church—or synagogue or temple or mosque, as the case may be. The third panel has been the school. The three institutions taken together have been the chief maintainers of tradition in any differentiated society. It is not that other institutions have not had traditions or that they have not striven and to some extent succeeded in maintaining their own traditions. Armies have traditions, business firms have traditions, political institutions have traditions, and they all usually attend in varying degrees to the maintenance of those traditions. Their traditions have been specific traditions; they have often been applications to their own fields of activity of the more general traditions presented in family, church, and school. These specific traditions worked within a matrix of dispositions congenial to the acceptance of tradition in general and of certain more specific moral and civil traditions. The specific traditions of institutions like armies, business firms, and the like have been under particular strain if the substantive generalized traditions have been poorly possessed by their members. Having the burden of adaptation to frequently changing external circumstances, they have become disordered if not sustained by an internal traditionality.

These three institutions of family, church, and school have inclined those who participate in them towards the conservation of beliefs and institutions which have existed continuously from the past into the present. But in each of the spheres of life over which these institutions have held jurisdiction, these substantive traditions have not had a monopoly. There have been alternative paths of interpretation of tradition, sometimes with affirmative intention but with modifying consequences and sometimes with deliberately negative intentions. There is no such thing as survival intact.

Churches and Sects. A church is an established institution into which human beings are born as members.[9] Membership entails re-

8. On primordial institutions, see Shils, "Personal, Primordial, Sacred and Civil Ties," in *Center and Periphery,* pp. 111–26.

9. Max Weber, *Wirtschaft und Gesellschaft,* 2d. ed. (Tübingen: J. C. B. Mohr [Paul Siebeck], 1925), 2:812–15; Ernst Troeltsch, *The Social Teachings of the Christian Churches* (London: Allen and Unwin, 1931), 1:331–43. Both Weber and Troeltsch, when they thought of churches, were thinking of state churches, which had a monopoly of official approval by the state. A person by virtue of his birth in the territory of the state was automatically a member of such a church. In a liberal type of Caesaropapistic regime, an individual could withdraw from the church and become a nonbeliever or a member of a religious body tolerated but not officially recognized by the state.

ceiving, affirming, and reenacting preexistent ritual acts of worship and beliefs. The sect has been regarded, even since Weber and Troeltsch made the distinction, as an institution of voluntary adherence. Sects proclaim their departure from the established institution; they deny the validity of its claim to be the authoritative tradition and purport to strike out on a new path. Membership in a sect is freely chosen by converts who wish to divest themselves of the tradition which their church of origin presented to them.

The distinction between churches and sects is a helpful one but is insufficient. It does not do justice to the features which are common to churches and sects and it does not refer to the tendency of sects to become churches in their own right. Sects begin with the allegation that they are opposed to tradition; they claim to reject the cumulative tradition of the church but they insist on the original charismatic tradition to which they attribute exclusive significance. Both churches and sects look back to a sacred book, a sacred person, a moment of revelation, all occurring or originating in the past; both construct a body of authoritative beliefs the acceptance of which is obligatory for their members.

The sect alleges that its immediate predecessor has falsified through its tradition of interpretation the original revelation to which the sect would return. The sect legitimates itself by claiming that it alone is correct in its interpretation of the original event and sacred text which represents it. Its relationship to the right tradition is disjunctive; it rejects the recently transmitted and accepted tradition. It purports to go back to the nucleus of tradition around which all else is illegitimate incrustation. The difference between church and sect in their relations to tradition is the difference between tradition regarded as continuous from the original event and text, and tradition regarded only as the original text and the events represented in the text.

Sects often castigate with great vehemence all other believers of the tradition from which they come. The countless sects of Hinduism and Christianity, the main branches of Islam and Buddhism are all nonetheless identifiable as respectively Hindu and Christian, Islamic and Buddhist. The doctrinal innovations of sects are always, in fact, smaller than what they conserve from the tradition which they purport to reject; indeed their distinctiveness in their own eyes is the purity of their contact with their own tradition. After a time, they cease to be sects in any way other than not receiving the status of official establishment by the state. They too accumulate traditions just like their rivals whom they revile.

The Roman Catholic church is an institution which conceives of itself as having a continuous history which runs back to St. Peter and a legitimacy which derives from Peter's designation as the vicar of Jesus Christ in his capacity of God's son sent to earth for the redemption of mankind. By apostolic succcession and ordination and through the Eucharist, the charisma of the founder has been transmitted to the entire church throughout its history. The great holidays like Easter and Christmas are evocations in the present of crucial moments in the sacred past. Doctrine is the accumulation of interpretation; it is the authoritative tradition which, in varying degrees of elaboration, is presented for acceptance to the various strata of believers.

The Christian community began in an intense state of charismatic possession. It was a charismatic sect to begin with but the charismatic sect became "routinized," it became part of "everyday" life—as Max Weber called it. It gave birth to an elaborate organization both traditional and rational in the service of the charismatic idea. The state of intense and concentrated charismatic possession was succeeded by the attenuation and dispersion of the charismatic into the institution of the church.[10] The laity is less continuous, less intense, less concentrated in its possession, reaffirmation, and reenactment of the charismatic tradition than the clergy. It knows less theology, it knows less about the details of the tradition, but it accepts their general tendency and comes into more precise possession and awareness only intermittently in acts of worship and in hearing sermons.

Ritual and worship too are tradition-formed activities through which the charismatic is experienced. They are fixed in accordance with tradition, their revisions are justified on the grounds that they represent a truer interpretation of the founding events of the tradition and of its subsequent interpretations. Mysticism would break through the dead incrustation of ritual and worship and enter into direct and vital contact with the deity, without the mediation of priests. The experience of the mystic is not a tradition but the idiom in which it is described and the way in which it is sought are traditions. Indeed the propensities to seek the experience of immediate contact with the divine are also traditional in many respects. The mystics seek a state of communion with the divine power which tradition has disclosed to them. They do not discover for themselves a hitherto wholly unknown god. They only enter directly into contact with the god disclosed by tradition instead of through priestly mediation. Enthusiasts would break out of the pattern of worship imposed from tradition and would experience holiness directly through the attainment of intense states of possession, but in doing so they also move within a pattern derived from traditional teaching including the teaching of enthusiasm. Enthusiasts live within the tradition of divinity to which they are seeking

10. See Weber, *Wirtschaft und Gesellschaft,* 2:753–78; and Rudolf Sohm, *Kirchenrecht* (Berlin: Duncker and Humblot, 1892), 1:16–66; also Shils, "The Concentration and Dispersion of Charisma" and "Charisma," in *Center and Periphery,* pp. 127–34 and 405–21.

a better path; the technique they use is also a traditional one, albeit somewhat divergent from that traditional technique which they reject.[11]

Churches are enduring institutions; they live in the kingdom of the temporal and they have a task which will not cease as long as the temporal realm exists. They intend to go on existing and part of their preparation for continued existence in the future is incessant contemplation of their past. Churches know that they live from a tradition and they secure their members to themselves by instructing them in that tradition. Sects are not at all different in this regard. Sects as well as churches are aware, in concrete terms, that without tradition, they would be nothing; they insist that their members acquire their tradition, the purified, restored tradition which discloses and brings them into contact with their "true" past. This is one of the reasons why education and religion are so intimately bound up with each other. It is also the reason why, when anticlericals and tyrants wish to break the attachment to religious institutions, they prohibit religious schools and theological seminaries.[12] It is through these that the traditions are maintained in active possession and carried forward.

Families, being primordial and small, do not generate a theory of the family, although there are family histories written by family members. Families are practically never seen by their members as constituted by beliefs or doctrines, although particular families possess a culture more or less shared by their members and parents have often been insistent that their offspring should share that culture especially when it is intertwined with social status. But few families have doctrinal prepossessions and doctrines about themselves. In contrast with families, churches and sects are formed around beliefs which are promulgated into doctrines, based on sacred writings and having written interpretations. Young persons and converts have to be inducted into the community of believers by being placed in possession of the body of beliefs. They have to be given the tradition, otherwise they could not be believers. Uneducated though believers might be in the light of a high standard of cultivation, they are required to accept an intellectual construction, a symbolic constellation about the deity, the cosmos, and human life. Religions are bodies of already attained intellectual belief and they are therefore inevitably bound to a certain measure of intellectual traditionality.

11. See R. A. Knox, *Enthusiasm: A Chapter in the History of Religion with Special Reference to the Seventeenth and Eighteenth Centuries* (Oxford: Clarendon Press, 1950).
12. See Georges Weill, *Histoire de l'idée laïque en France au XIXme siècle* (Paris: Felix Alcan, 1929); Nyazi Berkes, *The Development of Secularism in Turkey* (Montreal: McGill University Press, 1964).

The laymen's religious belief is not the same as systematic theology, and a church—or a sect— is more than a body of belief. A church and a sect are institutions with staffs, with members, rules of procedure, and of course bodies of doctrine. A doctrine as an intellectual construction could survive as an intellectual tradition without an institution and without believers. Institutions and societies too can survive without doctrine; so can families and tribes, political parties interested in offices and spoils, and business firms. Churches and sects however are institutions formed about a doctrine which derives from and rests on a tradition.

A church or a sect can cease to exist. Certainly particular sects have disappeared; sometimes they have been persecuted to death. Churches of the great world religions have managed to avoid disappearance despite persecution. Religious institutions last longer than states, they are older than any particular lineage or tribe, any economic enterprise, even any economic institution. All of the great world religions are older than any existing university. They last so long only because they embody a tradition.

Educational Institutions. Education is conservative of the past. To educate is to teach and to teach means to transmit something already possessed. To think that the education of children should be anything else at its heart is disruptive of the continuity of society and culture and hence disordering to those educated. Of course other things must be added to the tradition transmitted by education, things appropriate to the age, capacity, and vitality of the pupils. It must also be selective in what it transmits. It cannot transmit all the traditions of its society and its civilization; no human mind could absorb all that.

Education conserves, but its transmitted tradition leaves open the possibility of modification, addition, and improvement in the works, interpretations, and achievements which make up its substance. Until the present century, educational institutions for children were largely conservative. Until the last century, higher education was also conservative. A great change occurred in the nineteenth century when universities added discovery as a task to the previously accepted task of the transmission and interpretation of past accomplishments.

Universities as the highest section of the third panel of the triptych of the conserving institutions acquired their dual role through the acquisition of responsibility for *Wissenschaft,* i.e., methodical investigation which aims to discover what was not known before. The change first took place within the universities through the acquisition of responsibility for humanistic scholarship. In this field the task was the rediscovery of the lost past. In their acquisition of the task of teaching and research in the natural sciences, there was no rediscovery required. Only discovery was on this part of the agenda. In the study of nature and the attempt to attain to its eternal laws, there was no past to recover.

Thus to the task of transmitting at the most advanced level previously attained the achievements of Western culture in philosophy, logic, mathematics, theology, astronomy, and rhetoric, a new task of advancing the level of knowledge was added.

In every differentiated literate culture, the tradition of normative and cognitive beliefs have acquired special custodians who take them as far as they can. The provision for acquiring this advanced knowledge which requires long study, the mastery of preceding stages, and elaborate intellectual operations has been achieved through apprenticeship and individual initiative. Institutional provision for such acquisition was as fragmentary as provision for the intense cultivation of what was acquired. Much of it was done incidentally to employment for particular intellectual-practical tasks; it was done by annalists, court historians, court astrologers, and court physicians. It was done by priests and monks and civil servants who were sometimes educated persons recruited for governmental service as royal advisers and tutors and by other individuals whose interests, capacities, and opportunities enabled them to devote their minds to such activities.

Schools of advanced studies existed in certain fields. Dharamsalas like the "University of Nalanda," madrasas and theological seminaries like Al Azhar were such institutions. The Greek philosophical academies instructed aspirants to philosophical wisdom; the Roman law schools trained persons for the profession from which jurisconsults came forth; the rabbinical schools of the high and late Middle Ages which provided training at the furthest reaches of Talmudic studies were like "faculties" of particular fields but they were not universities covering the whole range of learning.

The maintenance of intellectual traditions at their most advanced levels was thus not left to the wholly uncoordinated activities of scattered individuals. It was however after the formation of the European universities first in Italy, then in France and England, and later in Germany and Scotland that advanced learning became the responsibility of special institutions covering the whole range of subject matters. Of course, they did not monopolize it. Learning continued to be attended to in monasteries, at courts, and in military camps, by tutors in rich families, by magistrates and landowners, but the universities became the central institutions in which young persons were inducted into the most fundamental principles and the highest stratum of the accumulated stock of knowledge. Universities at the same time became the institutions where there was relatively dense concentration of the individuals who were cultivating the traditions of learning at the most advanced level.

Alongside of the traditions of learning, the universities themselves gave birth to complex bodies of traditions regarding their own structure and procedures. Their long existence endowed them with many secondary traditions aside from the traditions of learning which were their primary responsibility. The only institution in Western civilization which is older than the University of Bologna or the University of Paris is the Roman Catholic church. No state in Europe has had a history as long and continuous, free of revolutionary interludes or violent disruption, as the universities of Oxford and Cambridge. Lloyd's of London is perhaps the only business organization which can trace its history as far back as the last years of the seventeenth century. By that time the University of Leiden was a famous center of learning for more than a century. No newspapers have traceable histories longer than those of the *Berlingske Tidning* and *The Times* (London) but Harvard University is older than these by a century. The Evangelical church in Germany is the oldest continuously functioning ecclesiastical institution after the Roman Catholic church but it is younger than about ten German universities. There are many colleges and universities in the United States which are one or two centuries old; each is a particular institution that has kept the same name, with a sense of awareness among many of its present members regarding the length and continuity of that history. Some universities are still housed in part in buildings which are among the oldest in their respective towns and countries. Only cathedrals and other ecclesiastical buildings, royal palaces, and a small number of residences which are infrequently used for their original purpose are older than the oldest buildings of many European universities; this is true in the United States as well.

There are many significant identities between the universities of Western civilization of two, three, or more centuries ago and their present state. In Europe there are numerous chairs which are more than three hundred years old and which have been made famous by the great achievements of their incumbents. In the United States, there are many departments which are more than a century old. The portraits and busts of famous teachers and investigators are features of many universities. There is an oral tradition about many of the professors. The traditions include too the records and the reputations of the achievements of individual scholars and scientists and of whole departments and faculties; some of these traditions of particular universities are shared by other universities as parts of a commonly shared tradition. The connections between Newton and Cambridge or between Kant and Königsberg are not just parts of the traditions of Cambridge and Königsberg; other universities view such connections as part of the tradition which they hold in common. Being as old as they are and being members of a species, individual universities are each acutely aware of the age of their own institution and of the class of which they are parts. This historical knowledge is an important part of the traditions about universities, and about particular universities, which are possessed by their respective members and in some cases by persons who have studied or taught at other universities. The images of these persons and achievements are legitimations of universities; they also constitute, in concrete form, the normative traditions which are in effect in many universities and in their parts. The "idea" of the university, the idea of what universities are "by their nature," the conception of what they should be, is the central theme of the academic ethos. The "idea" of the university is the normative tradition of the academic profession. All these factual details of names of eminent persons, famous discoverers, old buildings, apocryphal tales serve to exemplify this fundamental normative tradition in the minds of those who receive them. The main theme of the traditional "idea" and of its concrete exemplification is that universities are, ideally, autonomous centers of learning where well-established truths are taught, where critical powers are trained and exercised on the established truths, where new truths are discovered and established, and where young persons are trained for the practice of the "learned professions," which require the kind of learning which universities are qualified to offer.

These traditions of the idea of the university in general, of particular universities in many fields of study and research and of the peripheral features of particular universities are complementary to the specific substantive traditions of particular bodies of knowledge, such as are contained in disciplines or specialized fields of teaching and research. The substantive traditions of the disciplines are the consolidated stocks of valid knowledge about their respective subject matters and the technique of discovery appropriate to these subject matters. These substantive, mainly disciplinary traditions are cultivated in the matrix of the normative tradition—the academic ethos—which requires respect for the received tradition and the unspoken oath to press forward to add to the tradition and to improve it by thought, investigation, and discovery.

The universities are governed by a tradition which enjoins both conservation of what has been inherited from the past and novelty. The balance of the two is not easy to maintain; it is, above all, difficult to conserve what has at any particular moment to be conserved and to modify or transform that which is in need of such change. There have been times in the history of particular universities when conservation enjoyed the ascendancy and extended to sectors of academic life where it was intellectually damaging; this was especially true in some universities, famous before and later for their great merits, in the seventeenth and eighteenth centuries. There have been times, quite recently, when novelty, the normative tradition of novelty, has gained the upper hand; it has done so to the point where novelty has been sought as the be-all and end-all of higher education. Some novelties are easy to accomplish in universities; they can occur in subjects of relatively low intellectual standing, where there is little tradition of intellectual stringency, or in institutions of a similar position. Such novelties as "black studies," "women's studies," "consumer's education," "student-taught courses" have become relatively common in colleges and universities without a reputation for intellectual achievement to maintain, or they occur in those parts of superior universities which the more demanding parts of the university have never taken seriously. Important novelty, the novelties of new discovery, of the differentiation and joining of established disciplines made necessary by the growth of knowledge and of their corresponding courses of study, the emergence of new practical professions which genuinely require the intellectual discipline and substantive tradition of learning—these novelties have been continuously made in universities throughout the centuries and particularly since the beginning of the nineteenth century.

If universities did not adhere strictly to the main traditions of the academic ethos in the critical assessment of candidates for incorporation into their substantive traditions, they would not have lasted as long as they have. Their long duration is partly a function of their adherence to their central traditions. They have gained the respect of the society around them by their adherence to their central traditions in ethos, substance, and procedure and they have succeeded in inculcating these traditions into enough young persons to enable them to go on themselves and to demonstrate to the environing society that wider benefits accrue from the observance of these traditions.

The universities are institutions for which the respect of their members and the wider public for their central traditions is especially crucial because there is no exact way of assessing their achievements. They can be kept on the right paths only by the acceptance of the traditions which they have developed to control conduct in teaching and research.

The universities are not susceptible to being fruitfully controlled by any external authorities other than those who place themselves within the stream of the universities' own traditions.[13] They can, of course,

13. Friedrich Althoff, C. H. Becker, and Louis Liard were such external authorities who were steeped in the traditions of the universities. Althoff had an uncommon sensitivity to academic merit, although according to Max Weber, he intruded too much. See Max Weber, "On Universities: The Dignity of the Academic Calling and the Power of the State," *Minerva* 11, no. 4 (October 1973): 571–632; see also Arnold Sachse, *Friedrich Althoff und sein Werk* (Berlin: E. S. Mittler, 1928). Becker was an eminent Islamic scholar. See C. H. Becker, *Gedanken zur Hochschulreform* (Leipzig: Quelle and Meyer,

be seduced or coerced by the financial resources which are made available to them, they can be coerced into the exclusion or dismissal or appointment of members—teachers and students—on primordial or political criteria. They cannot be operated by the police or by the army or by the civil service, although they can be coerced, constricted, or suspended by them. The universities can work only if their traditions are effectively observed and this cannot be achieved except by persons who have assimilated the traditions and are at ease in them.

In this regard, the working of tradition in the universities is a microcosm of the working of tradition in the life of the society. The traditions of universities are not the products of legislation or of executive decrees. They are the result of the spontaneous collaboration of multitudes of persons who do not know each other and who are not members of a single unitary corporate body, controlled by a central authority. The collaboration in the cultivation of academic traditions takes place between living generations of many countries and with generations no longer living and also with many religious communities. The diversity of the traditions of universities—they differ somewhat from country to country, from university to university, from discipline and department to discipline and department, and among many fields of narrow specialization—coexists with much consensus among these separated divisions of the academic world. It is within the context of this consensus about the tradition that intellectual and administrative authority can be effective. And it is on this site that the substantive traditions of the universities continue and grow.

Family, Church, and School Together. Churches and schools, in contrast with economic enterprises, workshops, tribes, and villages, have an irreducible intellectuality. Schools teach traditions of skill in particular physical and intellectual operations, they also teach intellectual skills and intellectual substance such as mathematics, grammar and composition, history, geography, science. Some of these things are skills sometimes needed for the individual to gain his livelihood; others are also or exclusively beliefs thought to be "necessary," but not for any clearly stated practical end. They are what an educated person ought to know; they are intellectual beliefs referring to situations beyond immediate personal experience and practical necessity, remote in time and far-flung in space. Churches and sects

---

1920), and Erich Wende, *C. H. Becker: Mensch und Politiker: Ein biographischer Beitrag zur Kulturgeschichte der Weimarer Republik* (Stuttgart: Deutsche Verlagsanstalt, 1959). Liard was an academic philosopher before becoming a high official of the Ministry of Education.

center on doctrine, on intellectual constructions of the cosmos, of the powers which rule the cosmos, and of man's nature and obligations within the cosmic order.

The family, by contrast with church and educational institutions, is not intellectual. The traditions which families inculcate are not primarily intellectual traditions although they are influenced by intellectual traditions. Some families also inculcate intellectual traditions; intellectual families do so directly; wealthy families once employed tutors to inculcate intellectual traditions. Nonetheless families usually do not inculcate intellectual traditions except of a very rudimentary and general sort. They inculcate moral beliefs and patterns and images that refer to the family and also to a limited extent to the rest of the society.

This combination of institutions inculcating moral and intellectual beliefs is the foundation of the trans-temporal and trans-local structure of society. These institutions provide the internal spine and the outer frame of the culture which maintains a society. Where they fail to do so, the society is in danger of losing its character as a society. It becomes disordered in its present organization through the loss of the constraints imposed on its present by its past. To the generation of the living who are attempting to correct abuses in institutions, each stage of correction seems legitimate. But if the internal spine and the outer frame of moral and intellectual traditions are so corrected that they lose their transmissive efficacy, parts of the society are in danger of becoming a horde, other parts are in danger of lapsing into the state of *bellum omnium contra omnes.*

The State, Political Parties, and the Legal Order. The state is the one institution in any territorially bounded society which is authoritative beyond the authority of any of the constituent institutions of that society. Human beings need to live under authority and that without regard to the particular services the state performs for them. It gives them a setting in which they have a place. This does not mean that they obey the law of the state or that they love it; it is part of the cosmos which they need to create and designate themselves. The experience of living in a large trans-local society requires the perception and experience of being a member of that society.

An individual grows into membership in his society; he acquires an image of it only to a very small extent through his direct experience of it. He is told about it. Much of what he is told refers to its past. Part of his image of it is an image of its past. His conception of it is a conception of an entity in which its past is present. His loyalty to it is a loyalty to an entity of long duration.

In the individualistic liberal view, the function of the state is to maintain the minimal order, through law, so that individuals, alone and in concert, can with security pursue their legitimate ends and retain the benefits achieved. This is however only the principle; liberals like Montesquieu, Burke, Smith, and Tocqueville knew that governments and their enacted laws could maintain the order of freedom only if the laws existed in a medium of certain virtues which imposed restraints on both governors and governed. This was understood by Durkheim too. It was also understood by Max Weber.

Weber devoted a large section of his study of legitimate authority to traditional legitimate authority; by this he meant a type of authority which claims legitimacy by reference to its connection with the past and which also justifies its actions by claiming that they conform with precedents.[14] It was reasonable that he should do so since traditional authority, which includes patrimonial, feudal, and monarchical-bureaucratic regimes, has filled a large part of human history and covered much of the earth's surface. The other types of authority were also bound by tradition. Weber gave much attention to the transformation of charismatic authority into traditional authority. The rational-legal type of authority—bureaucracy—was encased in the tradition of its own particular form of legitimacy. In a rational-legal order, as understood by Max Weber, rules are derived from and subsumed under other rules, in an ascending pyramid. At the pinnacle stand the most general laws, written constitutions, fundamental principles, unspoken postulates—the things which are unquestioned. These fundamental principles and postulates of any legitimate political order, even a rational-legal order, are ultimately charismatic, but they are transmitted and received as traditions compelling respect both for their sacred properties and for their traditional givenness.

As the national state—and its government—gained ascendancy over local and regional authorities, the legitimacy of the state—and its government—became more important for the citizens'—or subjects'—sense of the orderedness of things.

Just as the traditions which derive some of their efficacy from the traditions transmitted in family, school, and church, so the traditions within each of these three institutions are helped to maintain their internal efficacy by their acceptance of the traditions of legitimacy of the state and its government.

But traditionality is protean. It cannot only confine the powers of the state; it can also impel their expansion. Where the traditions which prevail among the governed, sustained through the familial, religious, and educational institutions, are enfeebled as a result of the enfeeblement of the powers of these institutions over their members and where the absorbent attachment to these institutions is correspondingly enfeebled, restraints on the powers of the state are re-

14. Weber, *Wirtschaft und Gesellschaft,* 1:130–37; 2:679–752.

laxed. Then the strength of the hold of the traditions of ruling becomes determinative of the actions of the state towards its subjects or citizens. All states have internal traditions referring to their own actions but these traditions have relatively seldom been ones of self-restraint.

Even regimes which refuse to accept their traditionality and which attempt to break the traditionality of the rest of society cannot dispense with it. Yet, there are very few regimes, even among those which allege to be revolutionary and which intend to break the traditions of family, school, and church, which do not claim and encourage belief in the legitimacy conferred by connection with the past of the societies they rule. The celebration of heroes and of great events of national history, the adornment of places which are sacred in that history, and the invocation of the names and events of national history as auspices of great national undertakings are parts of this traditional legitimation. In the communist regimes of the present century, which proclaimed themselves to be internationalist and hostile towards the traditions and nationality of the regimes which they supplanted, the national, precommunist past has been restored to a place of honor. In some measure, it is a concession to the patriotic traditionality of the populace but in some measure it is probably also a product of traditional attachments within the ruling communist elites.

Similar manifestations of the ineluctability of some measure of tradition may be seen in the educational systems of progressivistic, collectivistic-liberal states. Their schools have been subject to a tremendous amount of "modernization" in the present century. Scientific subjects have been promoted, classical subjects demoted. The "creative powers of the child" released by "spontaneity" have become favored objects of cultivation. Contemporary and practical subjects have to a considerable extent replaced subjects which explicitly brought the past into the present. Many legislators and civil servants are now devoted to progressive and progressivistic education in all the forms destructive of tradition, but in all the ploughing up of the once hardened syllabuses of primary and secondary schools, history remains as a subject of study. Politicians would regard it as sacrilegious to eliminate the history of great events and the great heroes of their country from the school syllabuses. Their devotion to history is a manifestation of their own attachment to the past, of their conviction that the future governability of the present generation of schoolchildren requires reverence for an image of, and a sense of identity with, their own national past.

There are arrangements inherent in any regime which require a minimal amount of traditionality. Mortality, and short of mortality, changes in desires among the ruled require that governments and their societies deal with the necessities of succession. Hereditary monarchies deal with the determination of succession in a simple way;

lineage and order of birth prescribe the heir to the throne. Hereditary monarchy is legitimated by the belief that sovereignty resides in a lineage. This purely traditional legitimation of succession has also in the past been supplemented by the hereditary-charismatic doctrine of the divine right of kings.

These legitimations have been largely replaced by the belief in popular sovereignty which makes the present will of individuals, adding up to a majority or the collective will, the *volonté générale,* the source of legitimacy. The popular will is alive at every moment; in principle, it is bound by its own past. Its substance is only as permanent as desires make it; when it changes, the incumbents of the highest parts of government must change with it. The doctrine of popular sovereignty is supplemented by the utilitarian doctrine that the greatest happiness of the greatest number should be the guiding light of substantive policies. The past has no role in the guidance of succession. In fact, however, the theory of popular sovereignty is very qualified. In liberal-democratic regimes it is mediated by representative institutions; in revolutionary regimes, it is honored by theoretical invocation and by factual suspension. In both kinds of regimes, internal traditions of the allocation of powers are strong.

States have constitutions which have been promulgated or otherwise precipitated in the past and which are expected to govern the current actions of governments. Some are written constitutions, whether the sovereign be king or parliament or people; others are the de facto constitutions which bind the rulers within precedents, established conventions, and expectations which they themselves ordinarily accept. Even tyrannical governments like to give a show of constitutional legality, i.e., of conformity with some past promulgation, however brutal their actions are. Rulers who are not tyrants ordinarily accept these precedents, established expectations, and rules both because they do not question their rightness and because they think that if they infringe on them in ways which become visible to others, they will suffer subsequent losses from the enmity of their opponents and the withdrawal of support by their adherents and allies. They are thereby "kept in line," which means that they are forced to follow to some extent an already laid out path.

Rulers have always had provided for them room for initiatory prerogative, a sphere of free action. Legislation has been the major occupant of this sphere. It has been this way in all regimes, in those which Max Weber called traditional and in those which he called rational-legal. In both, there have been stereotyped areas where things have been left as they were—that is why in governmental budgets such a large proportion is committed to long-established types of expenditure. In both there have been areas of relatively free action by the ruler, whether it be a king, an emperor, the executive committee of a party, an elected president or prime minister, or a legislature. The sphere of relatively free action embraces the sovereign prerogative and legislation. Legislation has become increasingly predominant in quantity, in scope, and in aspiration to penetrate into the depth of society. In the rational-legal mode of legitimate authority it has taken an uneasy place alongside bureaucratic administration. Like bureaucratic administration, it is rule-bound and it lays claim to rationality, i.e., logical consistency within itself and with other already existing laws.

Legislation was a great invention for the changing of society in accordance with procedural rules and within the framework of the written or unwritten constitution. Legislation is intended to institute changes which will change tradition but which become traditions once they have been made. Legislation is seldom definitive; it is often modified; sometimes it is rescinded. But much of it lasts for some long time and with modifications it lives forward into the future like any other tradition. It is interpreted by officials who also change it and these interpretations then become stereotyped. Laws remain on the statute books for many years. In some instances they are subtly and gradually abandoned or subtly and gradually modified; in others they are dead letters from the beginning because of the inertia of what preceded them.

Legislation in principle annuls that part of the past with which it deals. At one time it was thought by scholars that legislation did little more than give explicit formulation to already existing custom and opinion[15] and that it should not contravene them because it was pointless to attempt to do so. The liberal formulation asserted that law should enact only what already prevails in reasoned opinion, meaning thereby that legislation should follow in the path of the tradition of the enlightenment.[16] In fact legislation did both; it accepted limitation imposed by tradition and it followed a contrary tradition as well. When progressivistic legislation undertook to change certain fundamental and long-enduring features of society, such as the distribution of income or the power of the landowning classes, it was supported by a current of liberal opinion which had already established itself as a weighty tradition, and it also attempted to do so within constitutional traditions. Thus even that institutional device which has become one of the chief instruments of innovation is itself enmeshed in traditions; it is limited in its scope and efficacy by traditions.

15. William Graham Sumner, *Folkways: A Study of the Sociological Importance of Usages, Manners, Customs, Mores and Morals* (Boston: Ginn, 1906).

16. Albert Venn Dicey, *Lectures on the Relation between Law and Public Opinion in England during the Nineteenth Century*, 2d. ed. (London: Macmillan), 1914), pp. 1–16.

Legal codes are very old but codification as a reformative policy did not take place until modern liberalism advocated the practice as part of its program. Jeremy Bentham regarded codification as a central part of the science of legislation and he spent his last years "codifying like any dragon." Much of Europe came under the influence of the movement for codification. Societies are thought to be "modernizing" when they install a legal code in place of a tatterdemalion of old statutes and judicial precedents which have never been arranged into a logically unified system.

Yet the codification of a legal system is not such a wholly new thing; it is a codification of already existing laws, modifying them to the extent necessary to make them logically more consistent with each other. The rationalization of the law—one phase of that process of rationalization of the world which would expel the traditional and the charismatic elements from life and society—was in fact never so irreconcilable to traditions as the announcement proclaimed. The rationalization of the law created some new laws and new procedures to fill the gaps and to overcome the inconsistencies in what was inherited from the past.[17] The bulk of the corpus of hitherto prevailing law was left nearly intact. It was not out of a yearning for the past that this was done but because it was a reasonable thing to do. Many of the inherited laws were "reasonable"; they had enabled life to go on, and that was the criterion which past laws had shown themselves capable of meeting.

There are of course exceptions. These are the cases of the importation of a whole new code, intact, from one country such as Germany or Switzerland or France to another country like Turkey or Persia. This importation does not bring in a wholly new system of law; it brings in subsystems such as commercial law or a criminal code. These new subsystems of law deal with situations which are quite new in the importing country; there is no traditional law capable of dealing with them. Islamic law does not deal with the situations of modern commercial life so that it could not be drawn upon in a country where influential parts of the society wished to conduct or benefit from modern commercial life; there was simply no traditional body of law which could be extended to deal with the situations of modern commercial activity.[18] In those spheres of social life, where institutions were indigenous and of long standing—the family was by far the most important in this respect—the traditional law and the traditional courts were left in charge. There, codification was not an importation but rather a

17. Weber, *Wirtschaft und Gesellschaft*, 2:403 ff.
18. Joseph Schacht, *An Introduction to Islamic Law* (Oxford: Clarendon Press, 1964); J. N. D. Anderson, ed., *Changing Law in Developing Countries* (New York: Praeger, 1969), *Family Law in Asia and Africa* (London: Allen and Unwin, 1968), and *Law and Reform in the Muslim World* (London: Athlone Press, 1976).

rationalization of the traditional law[19] with all the obstacles and constraints which that implies.

The growth in the volume of legislation which is intended to change the substantive tradition has been accompanied by a parallel growth of innovatory judicial action. In the United States in particular the judiciary has come to regard itself as a "force for social change." But even this deliberate arrogation of initiative in setting aside received traditions is enmeshed in tradition. The courts, whether they proceed by the common law or work under statutory law, whether they accept their own prior decisions or those of their superior judicial instances as binding, or whether they regard them as guides and justifications for the interpretations which they render, clearly work within a framework set sometime in the past. Adjudication by lot or ordeal is not oriented towards substantive models from the past—although, as procedures, those practices are of course as traditional as is rational adjudication. In the past, courts conceived of their tasks as finding and setting forth the law which had been fixed by customary practice[20] or by legislation enacted in accordance with a procedural tradition and certain traditions current in public opinion. Nowadays, when it is said in progressivistic circles that the courts should be pathfinders of "social change," that they should act independently of the law enacted by legislators or drawn from custom, and when they are encouraged by theorists of jurisprudence to take the lead in the movement of progress,[21] they are only following a path laid out by the tradition of "the school of free law."[22]

The growth in the power of the civil service is one of the most striking developments of the modern state in the present century. More than half a century ago leading students of modern society warned against the increasing power of the civil service and the dangers of rigidity and inadaptiveness to the exigencies thrown up by the changing environment of society and new tasks within the society.[23] The situation has not changed since then. In a society in which the

19. See J. M. Derrett, *Introduction to Modern Hindu Law* (Bombay: Oxford University Press, 1963), and *Religion, Law and the State in India* (London: Faber and Faber, 1968).

20. Fritz Kern, *Kingship and Law in the Middle Ages* (Oxford: Blackwell, 1939), pp. 149–80.

21. See Thurman Arnold, *The Symbols of Government* (New Haven: Yale University Press, 1935); Jerome Frank, *Law and the Modern Mind* (New York: Coward, McCann, 1936).

22. On the "freie Rechtsschule," see Weber, *Wirtschaft und Gesellschaft*, 2:507–9. See also Max Weber, *On Law in Economy and Society* (Cambridge, Mass.: Harvard University Press, 1959), pp. 309 ff. (Valuable footnotes have been added by Max Rheinstein to this edition.)

23. See especially Max Weber, *Parliament und Regierung im neugeordneten Deutschland: Zur politischen Kritik des Beamtentums und Parteiwesens* (Berlin and Munich: Duncker and Humblot, 1918), pp. 13–80. This important booklet has been published in English translation as an appendix to Weber's *Economy and Society* 3:1381–1461. See especially pp. 1393–1430.

leaders of opinion have been committed to "change," they have entrusted the task of administering "change" to institutions renowned for red tape, for the "cult of files and precedents," and for the rule of rule books. It is not that changes are not imposed on the rest of society, but rather that the changes are imposed and supervised with a degree of rigidity which approximates the kind of religious ritual from which the theorists of progressive outlook wished to relieve mankind. The traditions which dominate the activities of civil servants are not traditions understood as the tradition of piety and domestic authority. They are departures from the ideal-typical, rational-legal type of authority; they are in some respects closer to patrimonial authority which combines rigidity with a zone of arbitrariness.[24]

In the allocation of the resources which are available to him, the ruler, whether a prime minister, a parliament, or the head of a department or an office of the budget, is compelled to reckon with "vested interests." A large part of the budget in any single year in any governmental body is assigned in accordance with the expectations established by allocations in previous years.[25] To give one department more would arouse the discontent of those in other departments who want more for themselves and who would have to have less than they have had or expect to have; to give the department less would antagonize its members and their supporters in the legislature and the beneficiaries in the electorate who foresee advantages for themselves from an allocation at least as large as they have had previously. Hence it is only in emergencies that the distribution of resources among the various parts of a government can be changed drastically in a short period. Ordinarily changes in budgets occur through increases in the total sum of expenditures which leave existing agencies with what they have had before while supporting new agencies with the newly added revenues. "Vested interests" are not only interests, they are also "vested" interests. Being vested means having at least in their own eyes and in the eyes of those who respect them, the legitimacy of past appropriations.

Governments have acquired great powers and resources but their power to change themselves is limited for the reasons just given. Their powers over their citizenry have been greatly increased in recent decades and they have at their disposal an institutional machine which Max Weber said stood above all others in efficiency. Nonetheless, no government, however powerful it has made itself and has been allowed to become, has been able to accomplish all the transformations at which it has aimed. Its failures are results of insufficient knowledge of the social processes set in motion by its measures. It

24. See Weber, *Wirtschaft und Gesellschaft,* 1:130.
25. See Ira Sharansky, *The Routine of Government* (New York: Van Nostrand Reinhold, 1970).

fails above all to estimate the degree of resistance to its measures which is likely to arise from traditional attachments and beliefs of those persons, including those on its own staff, whose conduct is to be changed. Many of its failures are attributable to this lack of appreciation of the extent to which many of those it wishes to change are determined to keep the past alive in the present.

Popular sovereignty in modern liberal democratic societies effects its will through political parties, and the attachments of the main parts of the electorate to the parties which they support has the effect of anchoring them to their own past. Many political parties used to make a point of seeking the support of the electorate on grounds of their descent from a distinguished line of political leaders with great accomplishments in the past, but they seem to do so less nowadays; they now appeal more to "interest." Many of their supporters, however, still cast their vote for them because they have "always" done so. The electors view the parties not only as devices likely to be effective in the satisfaction of their present interest; what confidence they have in them is also based on their reputation inherited from the past. Many of them support these parties because of the beliefs which are traditional in their families, in their occupational groups, in their local communities, and in their religious institutions. The stability of the political order is partly dependent on the persistence of the traditional ties to parties. When there are too many "floating" voters, stable governments become difficult to form.

In recent decades the tendency to vote on the basis of traditional loyalties to parties seems to have declined in most countries.[26] In the Netherlands, the tradition of *Verzuiling*, whereby voters supported the party traditionally linked with their religious confession, has diminished,[27] as it has also in Belgium. In most of the Western countries, "independent voters" have increased in proportion to a degree sufficient to make it difficult for any of the larger parties to govern without a coalition. Nonetheless, traditional attachments, formed around traditional beliefs about interests, in support of parties traditionally committed to certain general lines of policy, continue to be common. If they did not, political instability would be greater than it is at present. Without certain traditional patterns of consolidation of very diverse interests and beliefs, the task of succession could not be resolved. There would be parties representing every specific interest and belief; voters would demand that parties please them in every

26. Morris Janowitz, *Social Control in the Welfare State* (New York: Elsevier, 1976).
27. Hans Daalder, "The Netherlands: Opposition in a Segmented Society," in Robert A. Dahl, ed., *Political Opposition in Western Democracies* (New Haven: Yale University Press, 1966), pp. 188–256. See also Arend Lijpart, *The Politics of Accommodation: Pluralism and Democracy in the Netherlands* (Berkeley: University of California Press, 1968).

respect which, given the diversity of desires in any large society, would result in a very large number of small parties each with a single purpose.

When there is a traditional loyalty to a party, the specific urgency of desire is blurred. In Western countries with social-democratic parties which command the support of a large part of the working and lower middle classes and which have done so for a long time, governments have tended to be stable. The tradition of party discipline among members of the legislature is also important. In the United States, where party discipline has always been weak, the loosening of traditional party attachments makes governing more difficult. This has been accentuated in the United States in recent years by the greater traditionality of the mass of the white electorate in comparison with the greater progressiveness of the leadership of the Democratic party. "Independent" voters, out of antitraditionality, together with would-be traditional voters who have been left politically homeless by the progressiveness of the party leaders, make an inordinately large proportion of "floating" voters in the United States in recent elections. Some of the main weaknesses of contemporary governments in Western liberal societies can be attributed to this attenuation of traditional political attachments.

4 Stability and Change in Tradition

Why Does the Past Hold the Present in Its Grip?

The Givenness of the Past

There are two pasts. One is the sequence of occurred events, of actions which were performed and of the actions which they called forth, moving through a complex sequence of actions until the present is reached. This is the past of the institutions of family, school, church, parties, factions, armies, and administrations, all firmly emplaced as resultants of these sequences of zigzagging interactions, awaiting the individual person who enters them or encounters them. This past is a sequence of technological performances and the physical products which embody the patterns towards which the skilled performances were directed. It is the past of the diverse and interacting streams of action controlled by genetic properties. It is the past made up of sequences of the states of knowledge assembled in each of the then occurring presents in which individual persons found themselves. It is the stock of works of art, literature, and thought existing at the time which were created in the past into which the individual arrives to become a possessor and possibly a creator. This is the real past which has happened and left its residues behind. The residues are these hard facts of the human side of existence. Nothing can be done which will change these facts which are the scene of human action in the present. This is the noumenal past which historians attempt to discover and construct.[1]

There is another past. This is the perceived past. This is a much more plastic thing, more capable of being retrospectively reformed by human beings living in the present. It is the past which is recorded in memory and in writing, formed from encounters with "the hard facts," not just from inescapable but also from sought-for encounters.

The past is too vast for any human being ever to be in contact with all of it. Of course, most of the events of the past, having already occurred long before the birth of any particular individual, are utterly

1. Henri-Irenée Marrou spoke of noumenal and phenomenal pasts. See his *De la Connaissance historique*, p. 37.

and irretrievably out of reach. Of the institutional residues of past events, he can only be in contact with those which he has experienced or witnessed or which have impinged upon him from the beginning of his own lifetime. There are physical residues and records and accounts, some contemporaneous with the events and some made later, and these later ones are also parts of the past as well as images of it from which our own images are formed.

The past of hard facts is a past of unfathomable depths. We can never be finished with discovering what it was and what it is as a result of what it was. The past of hard facts is ineluctable and unchangeable in principle but we are constantly having to change our ideas about those ineluctable and unchangeable hard facts as new ones appear, take their place alongside the older ones, and, in doing so, change what we see of those we knew previously. T. S. Eliot once said that the literary tradition is changed by what every important work which has incorporated the tradition adds to it. "The existing order is complete before the new work arrives; in order to persist after the supervention of novelty, the *whole* existing order must be, if ever so slightly, altered; and so the relations, proportions, value of each work of art towards the whole are readjusted; and this is conformity between the old and the new."[2] Our past is changed not just for the future generations for whom our own additions will be part of their past; it is also changed for the generation which is adding to it. Its appearance before and in the mind of the living generation does change, even if the noumenal past is ineluctable. The phenomenal past too, the past which we know and experience, variable though it is through time, is ineluctable at any particular moment.

The settledness of the past is a property of the past which we experience, albeit very unevenly. Only those parts seem ineluctable which exist in our presence and are directly and knowingly experienced. Those which are indirectly brought to us through incorporation into those things with which we are in direct contact are not seen as inevitable; they are not seen by us at all or only very amorphously. What does a philistine lower civil servant or a relatively uneducated workingman or businessman have to do with these sectors of the past dealt with by classical studies? Very little, except in the attenuated and indirect form of its influence, much mediated, on certain themes in television drama, or in the unread Latin inscriptions on the coins which they handle daily. Other parts of the past are much more immediately effective in the environment in which they act. The relationship is analogous to that of a person living in a valley; it is the valley that is the setting of his activity, not the peaks, although as a noumenal reality the valley could not be what it is without the moun-

2. Eliot, "Tradition and Individual Talent," p. 50.

tains around it. The workingman in a factory producing paint is exposed and subject to the traditions of technology, skill, and image involved in the production of paint; he does not see that his activity is also dependent on traditions of the chemistry of colors of different kinds, etc. Thus much of the noumenal past is not directly visible in what is immediately present. That which is effective need not be visible. It is simply there even if he sees only a small part of it and sees it only imperfectly.

An animal cannot deliberately change his anatomy and physiology in order to become an eagle or a swordfish. He also has to accept his environment as it is. Human beings have a little more freedom than animals. They can change their physical environment somewhat; they can raise animals for food; they need not depend on what is made available by the cycles of nature running by themselves. They can refuse to believe some of the beliefs which are offered to them; they can varyingly choose other beliefs from these which are available. For the most part, most human beings accept their beliefs from the existing corpus; when they change beliefs, those to which they change only appear to them to be new. All beliefs in the existing corpus embody, in precipitation, a long anterior pattern; most of those who accept any of them do not see their beliefs as a precipitate of past beliefs. Changing one's beliefs is ordinarily an acceptance of beliefs already accepted by others, often in a form which has obtained for a long time. It also involves rejecting one's own hitherto held beliefs in accordance with criteria and beliefs already resident in the mind of the person who is changing. Ratiocinated changes of belief draw on previously existent and affirmed beliefs and such changes are the freest which the mind can make.

It was not an arbitrary opinion of the liberals of the nineteenth century to see traditions as limitations on human freedom and to believe therefore that the breaking of tradition was a condition of the extension of the freedom of the individual. Tradition hems an individual in; it sets the condition of his actions; it determines his resources; it even determines what he himself is. It is very difficult for the individual to change what he has been given. It takes great imagination and insight, persistence, rational powers to change and to overcome, at least to some extent, what has been given.

Modern culture is in some respects a titanic and deliberate effort to undo by technology, rationality, and governmental policy the givenness of what came down from the past. The "given" has certainly not been left intact and unchanged by the use of scientific technology, rationality, legislation, and administrative authority. Indeed, the changes instigated in consequence of these initiatives have produced new conditions to which previously existent beliefs have been adapted and often attenuated on behalf of others not previously salient.

Archimedes in the third century B.C. was not ready to accept the given position of the earth in the cosmos; he said, "Give me but one firm spot on which to stand, and I will move the earth."[3] No one ever provided that firm place or fulcrum to Archimedes and so he had to accept as given the position of the earth in the cosmos. Many of the activities undertaken by scientists and governmental officials, technologists, and psychologists are efforts to create the fulcrum so that they can undo, minimize, or annul the influence of what has been given by the past to the present.

To think of jettisoning the entire complex of patterns which they have effectively available to them is beyond what most persons in a society want. Even if some wanted this, and the idea gained power in that society, they could not remake the society. It simply could not be done; one of the reasons why it could not be done is that too many persons would find it unbearingly abhorrent. One of the main reasons why what is given by the past is so widely accepted is that it permits life to move along lines set and anticipated from past experience and thus subtly converts the anticipated into the inevitable and the inevitable into the acceptable.

Where could the totally new come from? If it came from nowhere else than the imagination set wholly free, no one would know how to live under it. In fact, however, no imagination is so free as to be able to contrive something wholly new, comprehensive, and detailed. Who could imagine anew all the probable situations with which he might be confronted and devise his own rules to meet them? And since this would entail the cooperation of great numbers of persons, who would be his partners in these situations? There would have to be an extraordinary undertaking to plan the situations and the proper responses. The very idea is ludicrous.

Yet one comes across time and time again in reading the literature of the progressivistic movement that "man makes his own history." It seems to be the most self-evident thing in the world for these writers that man makes his own history. This might and might not be true; it is certainly reasonable to think that particular events result from human intentions in conflict with other intentions, working with the available resources, including the support of other human beings, and in face of conditions which themselves are partly constituted by the actions and intentions of human beings. But it should also be pointed out that no situation is made by a single human being. It is certain in any case that no single generation of men can make its own history. Can a single

3. This has been translated differently by Sarton and Neuberger. See George Sarton, *A History of Science: Hellenistic Science and Culture in the Last Three Centuries B. C.* (Cambridge, Mass.: Harvard University Press, 1959), pp. 77, 78, and Albert Neuberger, *The Technical Arts and Sciences of the Ancients* (London: Methuen, 1930), p. 203.

generation or several adjacent generations undo the effects of the past and make their society and its future history entirely in accordance with their desires? Even a ruthless, powerful group like the central committee of the Soviet Communist party cannot fully remake its society in accordance with its ideals. Can they act independently of the capital stock, the skills, the attachments, and the knowledge existing in their own society? Can they transcend their own limited knowledge, limited in the best conditions by the state of knowledge attained by the efforts of previous generations? Can they create a new technology which will not be a development from the technology which they have received? Could they act for the attainment of ideals which are totally different from the ideals which they have received?

Although the past is "there," its consequences can to some extent be circumvented or negated. Departures from it are possible and are incessantly occurring. This is true both of the treatment of the physical environment and of the instruments through which human beings have done much by deliberate action to depart from what was "given" to them in their physical environment. It is less true of cultural traditions—apart from the natural sciences—and the traditions of social institutions in which the deliberations of human reason and the exertions of human will have been less clearly successful. The given must be propitious to efforts to change some parts of it. At a certain point in the history of a particular science, problems which later turned out to be soluble were insoluble because what was given in the tradition of scientific knowledge and of the technology of investigation at the moment did not offer the means of new understanding. Those who worked on such problems worked on them in vain until either they or someone else solved the anterior problems, or until they or someone else invented the requisite observational instruments. Thus even the most rational of human undertakings depends for its effectiveness on the "appropriateness" of the available tradition. The past must have reached a certain point in its "unfolding" before the reasoning mind can go forward from it.

A corpus of literary works and a certain state of literary opinion are given to potential, aspiring writers. The literary given is modifiable by discoveries of works previously unknown and by new interpretations of works already known to readers. It is also subject to revision or circumvention or conversion by a writer of strong, inventive, and imaginative character. Departures from the given are certainly possible and occur; new genres or modifications of older ones do occur. But the great artists have to work from the various possible starting points available in the existing stock of works. T. S. Eliot could not have written as he did without Laforgue and without the long series of works which criticized the religiously agnostic or indifferent individualism of modern society in the stock from which he chose what he read. Modigliani could probably not have painted as he did without Picasso's prior modification of the received way of representing the human head and body. Max Weber could not have analyzed modern society as he did had he not had as part of what was given to him the ideas contained in the works of Sohm, Mommsen, Meyer, Tönnies, Simmel, Bücher, and many others.[4]

Thus the past is ineluctable as a point of departure for the actions even of original minds. For those less endowed, the given becomes the received and retained; they stay with what they have received until more original minds discover or invent some new pattern which then becomes the given. The traditional patterns of belief and conduct, even more than the artifacts of human contrivance, are very insistent; they will not wholly release their grip on those who would suspend or abolish or modify them.

Attachment to the Given; Normativeness. There is more to it than the mere givenness of tradition. Human beings become attached to the given. It becomes to them the "natural way" to do things. Being "natural" is nearly the same as being normative and obligatory, once a pattern is accepted as "natural." Other ways might be rationally recommended or even coercively imposed on persons but attachment to the traditional patterns of acting and believing is not easily dissolved. The Eighteenth Amendment to the Constitution of the United States was intended to obliterate the tradition of the practice of consuming alcohol from American society; it was a notorious failure. The similar tradition was certainly not obliterated in eastern European countries or in India, where the rulers frown upon it on moral and economic grounds and have attempted to stop it. The extirpation of traditional religious beliefs which was undertaken in Turkey, the Soviet Union, and in Mexico after the First World War has likewise been a failure. Neither the given nor the attachment to it could be abolished by command and the threat of violent repression.

To any individual, the givenness of patterns of social practices and arrangements and of beliefs resides in the visible presence of the performances, attachments, and affirmations regarding those symbolic patterns in the words and actions of the persons he sees around him or hears about. It is often the case that, technologically, the power to change certain given conditions exists but human beings do not wish to change the patterns of action which they have hitherto

4. The writings of Sir Ernst Gombrich are filled with penetrating observations and formulations about the ways in which the available, i.e., given, modes of perception shape and direct the imagination of outstandingly original artists. See for example his *The Story of Art,* 12th ed. (London: Phaidon Press, 1972), *Norm and Form* (London: Phaidon Press, 1966), *Meditations on a Hobby Horse* (London: Phaidon Press, 1963), *Symbolic Images* (London: Phaidon Press, 1972).

possessed. It is often the case that changes in the practices within an institution are rationally proposed but the individuals who would have to change their patterns of action do not wish to change them. The practice within a university for the teachers to spend much time—or, as the case may be, no time—in conversation with students is assuredly one of those things which in principle could be changed. There would be advantages to the teachers in a reduction in the time spent on students but they are reluctant to make the change in their own conduct because their image of the right conduct of a teacher includes spending time with students. They found that pattern in the practice of teachers when they themselves first became students and they found it among the established teachers when they themselves first became teachers. To some extent they might enjoy it, to some extent they might regard it as obligatory. What they first perceived as given became the norm of the conduct of teachers in this relationship to students. From being externally given, the pattern becomes part of the individual's practice and part of his image of himself as a teacher—half descriptive, half normative. In this way past practices persist while appearing as if their connection with the past, if noticed at all, is entirely secondary to their "naturalness" and their "rightness."

The Convenience of Tradition

There is a tendency to think of tradition in physical terms. It is sometimes called a burden or a "weight." Sometimes it is spoken of as "inertia," at other times it is considered a "drag." There are aspects of tradition to which these metaphors are more applicable than they are to tradition as the "given." Certain kinds of tradition are deliberately carried into the present by exertions which evoke images of physical force. But tradition as the complex of the inherited, as that which is given to the present from the past, is in fact not realistically interpretable in the physical metaphor. Those traditions or parts of tradition which are accepted are, in very many cases, accepted because, in a situation in which action is thought to be required, they appear to be self-evidently the actions which are called for. Most human beings do not have enough imagination to think up an alternative to what is given; nor do they feel an urgent need to think up something new when there is already a pattern ready at hand. This is especially so when action in accordance with the given pattern has already shown itself to be serviceable.

Some human beings are inventive by disposition and they will attempt to think up different ways of doing things because they are gratified by the act of invention. Others are discontented with the ineffectiveness of the given way of proceeding. They would like a less tedious or a more productive way of doing things and they exert their imagination and intelligence to find one. Others are perverse and anti-nomian and they wish to discard the traditional way simply because others have accepted it in the past and at present. The majority of human beings are neither inventive nor perverse. If something can be carried out conveniently, according to the accepted standard of convenience, it is good enough. Convenience means not being too painful or otherwise costly for the attainment of sufficiently satisfactory results. Its givenness is acceptable because it produces results which are desirable or acceptable.

Tradition as an Accumulation of Experience, Rationally Reflected Upon

There was a time before the First World War when peoples without an old and visibly continuous tradition were looked upon with condescension and pity. They were thought to be "raw" and "unseasoned" by experience. The experience which they lacked was the accumulated experience of their ancestors over generations. Each generation would have had to start anew if it did not have what was left to it by its ancestors from what those ancestors themselves had received in turn from their ancestors, and if they did not have what each generation of ancestors had added and corrected from its own experience. There was nothing which the citizens of the inexperienced new society could do except to try to learn from the older society. This was not infrequently believed by some of the members of the old one.[5] The cultural relations between Great Britain and the United States were much affected by these beliefs in the advantages of accumulated experience and the disadvantages of the lack of it.[6] Traditions were thought to be the precipitate of long experience, accumulated, sifted, tried, and tested over many generations, and they gave the Old World its advantage over the New.[7] The superiority of Europe was exhibited by "Old World diplomacy," skeptical and

5. Henry James was often ready to believe that the superiority of European culture to American culture lay exactly in this fund of accumulated experience.

6. A story by Kipling illustrates this attitude. An American journalist had witnessed an event which was very contrary to what could be expected in the ordinary course of life and he wished to write about it in a sensational manner. He was discouraged by a British colleague from attempting to write in that way for a British public. When the American challenged the reluctance of the Englishman to try to publish such an incredible report, he was told, "Don't be an ass, Keller. Remember, I'm seven hundred years your senior, and what your grandchildren may learn five hundred years hence, I learned from my grandfathers about five hundred years ago" (Rudyard Kipling, "A Matter of Fact," in *The Phantom Rickshaw and Other Stories*, [New York: Charles Schribner's Sons, 1913], pp. 207–8).

7. A similar belief appeared in the debates about the respective merits of the ancients and the moderns in the seventeenth century. The forerunners of progressivism declared that the moderns were superior because they had so much more historical experience. See Richard F. Jones, *Ancients and Moderns* (Berkeley: University of California Press, 1961), pp. 44–45.

lacking in idealism; it was thought to be a slowly formed tradition of skill and outlook. It was contrasted with the gaucheness of a "youthful people." Just as experience in life gave older persons advantages over the inexperienced young, so generations of experience enriched the spiritual and social life of a society.

Edmund Burke believed that the superiority of a system of government based on long-accumulated tradition to one based on ratiocinated principles lay exactly in the accumulation and testing of experience over generations; he spoke of "the collected reason of ages, combining the principles of original justice with the infinite variety of human concerns."[8] Burke's conception of tradition bore some resemblance to current conceptions of tradition in science: present beliefs are the consequences of the ideas of previous scientists subjected to methodical scrutiny. Burke had no exact equivalent of methodical scrutiny, but as an approximation to it he offered the repeated trials and errors of many generations.

There is some truth in this belief. Experiences do instruct, and what is learned from experience leads both to confirmation and revision of what was previously believed. These revisions and confirmations are learned by ensuing generations as children come into families and as adults come into groups and institutions. "Learning how the system works" means learning how to live in it by observing and assimilating what others do and have done in it. Each generation thinks that it is doing what is reasonable and it pays little attention, usually, to the fact that it is reiterating patterns recurrently reenacted in the past. Something is reasonable because it is efficacious, it is an apparently efficient means to an end. But it was not contrived by the persons who use it. They come upon it when it is already in place and they go on using it because it "meets their needs."

No tradition could long be sustained if it brought about obvious and widespread misfortunes to those who practice it; a tradition has to "work" if it is to persist. A tradition which repeatedly brings disaster, or which repeatedly turns out to be obviously wrong, will not persist.

Adherence to a rule which does not produce results which are satisfactory, according to a prevailing standard of satisfactoriness, to many of those who practice it will not be sustained; it will be infringed

8. Edmund Burke, *Reflections on the Revolution in France,* in his *Works* (Boston: Little, Brown, 1901), 3:357. Cicero, invoking the authority of Cato, said that the Roman constitution was superior to those of the states founded by one man because it was "based upon the genius, not of one man, but of many; it was founded, not in one generation, but in a long period of several centuries and in many ages of men. For . . . there has never lived a man possessed of so great a genius that nothing could escape him, nor could the combined powers of all men living at any one time possibly make all the necessary provisions for the future without the aid of actual experience and the test of time" (*De republica,* Loeb Classical Library, ed. Clinton Walker Keyes [London: Heinemann, 1928], II. 1., p. 113).

on to such an extent that it will be discredited. A rule which is believed to have lasted a long time acquires thereby a certain presumptive evidence of validity. Just as the efficacy of a government helps to legitimate it, so a rule of conduct retains its validity when action in accordance with it is efficacious. If it can be adhered to with tolerable results and if many other persons are seen to adhere to it with tolerable results, it will be strengthened in its hold. The belief that many persons in the past have adhered to it with tolerable results strengthens belief in its validity.

Beliefs which have been known to work are generally not lightly discarded. This may be seen in the fate of scientific propositions under criticism. A scientific proposition once accepted because it appears to describe and account for certain widely and reliably observed events will not be lightly discarded, even where there are phenomena which escape its grasp. Scientists renounce established scientific beliefs which cannot meet the test of new and demonstrated observations and new and demonstrated theories. Even then scientists, who believe that they do not accept anything as given and who are proud that nothing escapes from their skepticism, have to be shown very undeniably that what they have hitherto believed should no longer be believed. Scientists have sufficient confidence in themselves as a community to believe that their elders would not espouse a theory lightheartedly and that, if the theory is ultimately to be rejected, the burden of proof lies on the scientist who recommends its rejection. If a theory has "worked" hitherto, it has presumptive evidence in its favor.

The status of normative traditions is not substantially different. Their satisfactoriness is evident from their having enjoyed continued acceptance. The long acceptance of the traditional rule of monogamous marriage in Western societies must, with all the complaints against it, with all the infringements on it, and with all the recent legal provision for the dissolution of marriages, have been relatively satisfactory in view of the available alternatives for most of those who participated in it. It is only in the past century, when conceptions of what is an acceptable level of satisfaction have changed and when more intensive demands were made for a higher level of gratification of the spouses than the older pattern offered, that the traditional rules of monogamous marriage came to be widely criticized as ineffective and in need of change. Even then, the traditional rules are still generally accepted by most married persons in most countries. The traditional pattern of monogamous marriage has proved to be very durable. More exceptions and alternatives are now accepted but the rule is still predominant for most persons and it is acknowledged as right by many of those who do not live up to it in their own actions.

The stability of normative traditions has been assimilated to the stability of species in the evolutionary process. The rules which survive as traditions are those which have made the most successful adaptations to changes in the environment; they have shown their efficacy. The competition of moral traditions results in some being selected and others being rejected. The ground for survival is the accumulation of and the steady presence of evidence of the efficacy of adherence to the rule of conduct.[9] When the wants of individuals change and more is demanded than was previously regarded as satisfactory, then adherence to the traditional rule might not be able to produce results at the higher level now desired.

The demands themselves, above a certain minimal level of biologically determined needs, are traditional and they too therefore are subject to the same criteria of satisfactoriness as the rules; if the traditional level of demands or wants is superseded, then new possibilities of gratification are perceived. The rules which permitted actions leading to the previous level of satisfaction will then be discredited.

Most of what exists at any moment and which is given from the past has not been arbitrarily accumulated. It is not the outcome of a long series of arbitrary or accidental acts of selection. By acts of judgment less explicit and deliberate than the decision as to whether to retain or demolish an old building which can still be used with less cost than would be required for the construction of a new one, human beings adopt and adapt the practices and beliefs of their predecessors. They do so first because these practices and beliefs are "there" before them—it requires little thought or effort to do what one has seen others do, in contrast with the thought and effort required to devise new ways of acting. They also reenact these already existent patterns because they "work," more or less. They do not do so out of any knowing appreciation of the "wisdom of the race" and they do not see themselves ordinarily as the beneficiaries of that wisdom. They seldom feel grateful to their ancestors—except on special ceremonial occasions—for having nurtured and developed those beliefs, practices, and institutions; they do not frequently think of the more remote pastness of any of these patterns. They very seldom hold to them on the ground that they were created and maintained by their ancestors or that, having lasted a long time, they have a special claim on their adherence. The fact that a certain pattern of action "works," that by and large it procures advantages to those who participate in it, is ground enough for them to accept it.

9. F. A. Hayek, "The Three Sources of Human Values," Hobhouse Memorial Lecture, reprinted in *Law, Legislation and Liberty: The Political Order of a Free People* (Chicago: University of Chicago Press, 1979) 3:153–76, esp. 168–69.

The Past as an Object of Attachment

Muteness of sentiment and unthinking acceptance of a model visible in the conduct of others, the recognition of convenience and the acceptance of results at an expected level of satisfactoriness, are sometimes infused with an element of piety towards the past. The pastness of a model of action or belief may be an object of reverence. Not givenness, and not convenience, but its sheer pastness may commend the performance of an action or the acceptance of a belief. Deference divested of reverence is contained in the principle of the jurisprudence of the common law which commands respect for precedent. The fact of pastness is acknowledged as normative. A decision under the common law ordinarily entails no attachment to a particular epoch or a particular deed or a particular generation in the past, it is the pastness of the precedent as such. Its normative necessity is self-evident: that is the way it was, that is the way it ought to be. There is no sentiment of reverence formed about the way it was. Attachment to a particular past epoch infused with charismatic quality by sacred revelation or a sacred person and sacred events which is characteristic of the Christian attitude towards the age of the Gospels is a different sort of thing in sentiment and in the scope of significance from the attitude towards the judicial precedent. Both attachments have in common however the normativeness of the past pattern.

A remote historical epoch is capable of becoming an object of affection and reverence and of exemplifying and declaring the patterns of conduct and of works of art and belief which should prevail in the present. The belief that mankind had once lived in a "golden age," simpler and purer than the one in which it now lives is a common theme in intellectual history. It has many variants, ranging from the praise of "primitive communism" and "the noble savage" to the appreciation of great, no longer existent civilizations.[10] This was the attitude of Italian humanists of the Renaissance towards ancient Greece;[11] it was the attitude of the German Hellenists of the late

10. See Harry Levin, *The Myth of the Golden Age in the Renaissance* (Bloomington: Indiana University Press, 1969); Lois Whitney, *Primitivism and the Idea of Progress* (Baltimore: The Johns Hopkins Press, 1934), chaps. 1 and 2; René Gonnard, *La Légende du bon sauvage* (Paris: Librairie de Medicis, 1946); Henri Baudet, *Paradise on Earth: Some Thoughts on European Images of Non-European Man* (New Haven: Yale University Press, 1965). See also Hyppolite Rigault, *Histoire de la querelle des anciens et modernes* (Paris: L. Hachette, 1856), pp. 35–45; and Jones, *Ancients and Moderns*.

11. Weiss, *The Discovery of Classical Antiquity;* Paul Kristeller, *The Classics and Renaissance Thought* (Cambridge, Mass.: Harvard University Press, 1955), chap. 1; Georg Voigt, *Die Wiederbelebung des classischen Alterthums,* 3d. ed. (Berlin: G. Reimer, 1893); Roberto Weiss, *The Spread of Italian Humanism* (London: Hutchinson, 1964).

eighteenth and early nineteenth centuries towards ancient Greece.[12] In a more confined range, it was the attitude of the cultivators of the neoclassical style in architecture, sculpture, painting, and ornamentation;[13] such too was the attachment to the Middle Ages which flourished among German, English, and French writers and architects of the early nineteenth century.[14] The Pre-Raphaelites in England and the Nazarenes and the George-Kreis in Germany represented the same kind of attitude towards a past epoch. The affection may be broad or narrow in its object. It might be an attachment to the ideal of a whole social order and culture; it might be an attachment to some particular idea or institution or to a particular pattern of relationships. The remoteness from a repugnant present is often one of the features of this attraction; there is also a conviction that a high point in human existence was attained not in the past as such, not in the past continuous with the present, but in a particular epoch, place, and sphere of human life. The attachment is an intellectual affection or love. To dwell amid the images and facsimiles of the past, the documents and discovered artifacts, and the portraits of that past made by later writers, is soothing to the mind and exalting to the sentiments. The past is a haven to the spirit which is not at ease in the present.

It is not uncommon for a particular epoch to be looked upon as one in which mankind as a whole or mankind as represented in one's own civilization reached an especially high point from which subsequent ages especially and the contemporary age degenerated.[15] The past times were golden ages, "good old times," when life was free of the hideousness of scarcity and from the self-seeking and ugliness which are features of most advanced civilizations. Sometimes these high evaluations of the remote past are more appreciative than actively normative; they serve as standards for the disparagement of the present but not as standards for the guidance of conduct in any specific way.

The high point might have occurred in the past of one's own country or in the past of another country. In the eastern part of the United States in the half-century between the Civil War and the First World

---

12. E. M. Butler, *The Tyranny of Greece over Germany* (Cambridge: Cambridge University Press, 1935).

13. *The Age of Neo-Classicism*, The Fourteenth Exhibition of the Council of Europe: The Royal Academy and the Victoria and Albert Museum, London, 9 September–19 November, 1972 (London: The Arts Council of Great Britain, 1972), esp. pp. xxi–xciv; Mario Praz, *On Neo-Classicism* (London: Thames and Hudson, 1969).

14. Kenneth Clark, *The Gothic Revival* (London: Constable, 1950), pp. 60–122; Gottfried Salomon, *Das Mittelalter als Ideal in der Romantik* (Munich: Drei Masken Verlag, 1922).

15. Alfred Doren, "Wunschträume und Wunschzeiten," *Vorträge der Bibliothek Warburg* (1924–1925) (Leipzig: B. G. Teubner, 1927), pp. 158–205.

War, the early years of the Republic were thought of as a golden age; it was a standard by which to censure the corruption and degradation of the present; Tacitus thought of the Roman Republic; Roman intellectuals of the first century thought of Greece of five centuries earlier; William Cobbett and G. K. Chesterton thought of "merrie England"; Italian humanists and the British amateurs of neoclassicism admired ancient Greece. American and German Anglophiles of the nineteenth and early twentieth centuries admired the English past and they admired the British present because so much of the past lived in it. They admired old buildings, old towns, and old institutions with tenderness and awe. England acquired for foreign visitors a sacred topography almost like that of the Holy Land, Westminster Abbey, St. Paul's Cathedral, the Tower of London, Wren's city churches, St. James's Palace, the colleges of Oxford and Cambridge, the Crescent at Bath: every visitor had to see them. Others dreamed of seeing them. It was not only the beauty but the age of these buildings that mattered.

The self-exile of the Americans who went to live in Italy, France, and Great Britain throughout the nineteenth century had numerous motives. Some went to be artists or writers in an environment they thought more congenial to "the life of art," partly because it was not as puritanical as American society and partly because it contained more of the past; they thought that past societies had been more appreciative of artists and writers and their works than modern societies which cared mostly for commerce and for material goods. The dislike of commercial concerns and the aversion for the callow and plebeian tone of American life and politics were coupled with dismay at the desolate pastlessness of the United States. The shallowness of the sentiment and thought from which they fled was not only a shallowness of sentiment and thought, it was also a temporal shallowness. Most of these older American expatriates were "tenderminded" patriots; they would not have been so wounded by their country's deficiencies if they had not with such sensitivity felt themselves to be Americans. But they needed "a past" to which to attach themselves, and the Puritans of New England and the Quakers and Pietists of Pennsylvania did not offer enough of a past to which to attach themselves; they thought their country stunted and deformed by not having a real past which went back far in time. Their yearning contemplation of the past could not be satisfied by scholarly historical study. They had to be in contact with artifacts from the past and with manners which were like the manners which had been observed in the past; they wanted monuments and places with overtones enriched by age; they wished to live in the midst of institutions which still retained the patterns which they had inherited from the past. Some of their compatriots who wanted a past stayed at home. Some of them pined for old Europe, others tried to find a "usable past" in the United States.[16]

Some of the expatriates' Anglophilia might be accounted for by their respect for the great power of the center of an empire which spread over so much of the surface of the earth. Great Britain was the center of the world for educated American Protestants. Its centrality rested in part on its past. It was not simply powerful and rich; it did not merely have political institutions exemplary for their reasonableness and probity, and a long run of writers of genius. It had a great and worthy past. Contemporary merits which were unaccompanied by the presence of pastness would not have been so meritorious. Great power and wealth alone are tenuous grounds for maintaining a society in its position as center of the world. Greatness requires that it be traced to a great past; pastness is part of the legitimation of greatness.

Reinstatement of the Past. The polemical, rhetorical praise of the past as means of dealing with the present is not restricted to criticism. The past might be viewed as a model for the active reconstruction of the present. Chernishevsky thought that the *mir,* the peasant community of old Russia, offered a realistic pattern for the rehabilitation of Russian society.[17] Traditionalistic movements which would recreate a golden age have never been successful either in gaining power in the state or in dominating the intellectual opinion of their time. They have however found fervent adherents for short periods.

The attachment to some past state or condition is pervasive in all nationalistic movements. The nationalistic movements are not usually predominantly revivalist; often, they are too infused with modern progressivistic beliefs, humanitarian, democratic, populistic, and socialistic to seek a complete restoration of the real or fictitious past.[18] But it is the golden past that draws their hearts. Mahatma Gandhi's movement for Indian independence was directed towards an Indian past which had never existed; the efforts to revive the *panchayats* by the government of India, Jayaprakash Narayan's scheme of indirect democracy, and Vinoba Bhave's *bhoodan* movement were all equally impelled by a conviction that the old Indian village community represented an ideal which should be brought back into present-day life. The creation of Pakistan was associated with a fictitious national past.

16. Van Wyck Brooks, Waldo Frank, Randolph Bourne, Vernon Louis Parrington, and J. A. Smith saw that locus of inspired virtue in the first quarter of a century of the American republic.
17. See Thomas G. Masaryk, *The Spirit of Russia: Studies in History, Literature and Philosophy* (London: Allen and Unwin, 1919) 2:33–35.
18. See Elie Kedourie, ed., *Nationalism in Asia and Africa* (New York: Meridian Books, 1970), especially the Introduction.

Nationalistic movements in territories without sovereignty, practically invariably invoke a past of great deeds and of a pristine communal integrity. Nationalism in Ireland, in the various peoples of the Hapsburg Empire, in Asia and in Africa were all much preoccupied with the greatness of the precolonial past. All of these movements referred to a time of national independence and cultural achievement long in the past. This heartened them for the struggle; it made them feel worthy of the status which they claimed for themselves. Their past legitimated their future.

The proposal to reinstate a past condition is usually an intellectuals' project. The reestablishment of a system of estates, the reorganization of an entire society around rural communities and peasant handicrafts—these are intellectuals' programs which have on the whole had little impact on the actual course of events. The program of the French traditionalists around the Action française to reestablish *l'ancienne France,* with all its violence in word and deed, never influenced French governmental policy,[19] except for a short time in the early 1930s and under Marshal Pétain. The traditionalistic elements in Italian fascism had more influence on rhetoric than on policy and practice.

The National Socialist movement in Germany, like all nationalist movements, bore within it elements of traditionalism; it entered successfully for twelve years into the theater of the world history and had a profoundly destructive impact. The German National Socialist movement, which with much else that was contradictory to it, sought among other things to reestablish features of the "original" German society in religion and in a *ständische* organization; it looked back to a time of presumed ethnic purity which it attempted to reinstate. Only the reestablishment of a racial purity went very far; it progressed to the point of extermination of most of the Jewish population and the Gypsies. The rest of the program collided with other aspirations and interests and yielded to them.

The long endurance of the Jewish people during the diaspora when they were scattered among many countries and between Islamic and Christian civilizations was supported by their recurrent recollection of great figures and events of the Jewish past—Abraham, the Exodus, Moses, Exile, and the destruction of the first and second Temples. Jewish learning in the period of the diaspora was an elaborate body of interpretations of the records of these events. The major Jewish cele-

19. Waldemar Gurian, *Der integrale Nationalismus in Frankreich: Charles Maurras und die Action Française* (Frankfurt a. M.: Vittorio Klostermann, 1931), pp. 37–41; 118–31; Brunetière formulated his appreciation of tradition less ambiguously than Maurras. See Ernst Robert Curtius, *Ferdinand Brunetière: Ein Beitrag zur Geschichte der französichen Kritik* (Strassburg: Karl J. Trübner, 1914), pp. 1–2.

brations are directed toward reenactments of the great historical events of Old Testament times. Passover and Purim both have historical events as their objects of reference. History was expected to culminate with the restoration by the Messiah of the Jews to the territory in which they had lived in the remote past.[20] The dissatisfied stirrings of the Arabs and of the Indian Muslims in the time of decay of the Ottoman Empire referred frequently to the Caliphate and to the life and teachings of the Prophet and his companions.[21]

The ideal of a great event or series of events or of a whole age in the past lies at the foundation of the deepest preoccupations of mankind through millennia. The exemplary lives of Buddha, Jesus, and Mohammed are moments of the past with which contact must be maintained and renewed. Christianity, Islam, and Judaism are historical religions in the sense that they require their adherents to contemplate the past and to guide their course by the pattern of events which are clearly set in the past. Confucianism does not have a corresponding moment of revelation but it too looks backwards to the wisdom of its founder and his disciples. Buddhism is not so explicitly historical as Judaism and the religion which grew out of it, but it too looks back to the events of the exemplary enlightened life. The rituals of the great religions are primarily arrangements of contact with the ultimate powers of existence, but they also reenact vital moments of the past, moments of the most vivid epiphanies which occurred in the past.[22]

National states are not so different from the great religions in these matters but, since they are busy in coping with the present, they do not do so much in the contemplation and celebration of great past events. They too however have their recurrent anniversaries and centenaries and in some cases millennial celebrations and they have their monuments and sacred places—battlefields and buildings where great founding events occurred. They also have rituals of procedure linking them with the past, rituals that rest on precedent and are more symbolic than is required by convenience and effectiveness.

Not all human beings are engaged with the past. Not all imaginarily dwell in it; not all by any means yearn for its reestablishment in part or as a whole. The concern to be in contact with the symbols of the past is probably greater in the educated classes than it is in the uneducated ones, because those classes have acquired a more differentiated, although not necessarily more correct, view of the matter. It is greater

20. See Gershom Scholem, *The Messianic Idea in Judaism* (New York: Schocken, 1971), pp. 49–77; 282–303.

21. Hans Kohn, *A History of Nationalism in the East* (New York: Harcourt Brace, 1929).

22. See Mircea Eliade, *The Myth of the Eternal Return* (London: Routledge and Kegan Paul, 1955), pp. 73–92.

among those of religious sensibility than it is among those who are less responsive to sacred things. Concern to be in contact with the past is a fluctuating state of mind, intermittent in its intensity in individuals and societies.

It is difficult to explain this gravitation towards the past which is a feature of all cultures. There are times and situations in which human beings seek contact with the center. They want to have a center for their societies, however often they rebel against it. They need to transcend themselves as individuals in collectivities which are arranged about a central repository of vital things. They desire an order around this center and a place within it. The center is not a momentary occurrence: a center has a depth in time, like the society around it. Every feature of society has a depth in time; it is understood to have that temporal depth by those who live in it—not by all but by some. And some of them become almost exclusively attached to the temporally remote phases of their own society or other societies.

There is a measure of participation in the past inherent in one's identification with one's own society or with some of its constituent institutions, strata, and sectors. "Living in the past" can be an intense form of that participation.

Why Traditions Change
Endogenous Factors

The existence of tradition is at least as much a consequence of limited power to escape from it as it is a consequence of a desire to continue and to maintain it. Human societies retain much of what they have inherited not because they love it but because they grasp that they could not survive without it. They have not imagined plausible replacements for it. They have neither the material resources, nor the intellectual nor the moral nor the visual powers to supply what they would need to find a home in the world if they were deprived of the furnishing of tradition. They accept what is given to them by the past but they do so gracelessly for the most part. The acquisition from the past furnishes their home but it is very seldom a home in which they are entirely at ease. They try to bend it to their own desires; they sometimes discard or replace some of the inherited furniture.

Traditions are indispensable; they are also very seldom entirely adequate. Their sheer existence disposes those who possess them to change them. The person who possesses a tradition and who depends on it is also impelled to modify it because it is not good enough for him, even though he could never have accomplished for himself what the tradition has enabled him to do. We could say that traditions change because they are never good enough for some of those who have received them. New possibilities previously hidden are perceivable when a tradition enters into a new state.

A tradition does not change itself. It contains the potentiality of being changed; it instigates human beings to change it. There are endogenous changes, changes which originate within the tradition and are carried out by persons who have accepted it. Such a change is not "forced on them" by external circumstances; it is an outgrowth of their own relationship to the tradition. Endogenous changes are usually held to be improvements by those who make them. These "improvements" are not always accepted as such by successors or by contemporaries.

Rationalization and Correction

The creative power of the human mind in confrontation with the potentialities resident in traditions produces changes. Imagination of events and relationships not previously perceived or experienced, the invention of a technique not previously known or used, the creation of a work of art or literature of exceptional beauty of form, language color, and substance are all steps beyond the reiteration of the given. These steps are guided by traditions, they are extensions of traditions beyond the state of the transmitted. They are enrichments of the stock; enrichments are changes in tradition. Imagining, reasoning, observing, expressing are the activities which go beyond the tradition as it has been presented; they might begin within the tradition, being carried by persons who have assimilated the tradition. They are the activities which lead to endogenous changes in traditions.

There is something in tradition which calls forth a desire to change it by making improvements in it. There is an unceasing striving in the strongest human minds for "better" truth, for greater clarity and coherence, and for adequacy of expression of the perceived and imagined. Far from all minds strive for greater clarity and coherence, for sharper and more penetrating perception and imagination, or for more complete adequacy of expression; many of those who do so do not succeed in their efforts and none succeeds wholly. Nonetheless, when confronted with a transmitted stock, the very best minds desire to come into possession of some part of it. The very acceptance, indeed, the attachment to it makes it possible to perceive some ambiguity and uncertainty here, some inconsistency there, some features not previously perceived and expressed. Even if the circumstances to which the received beliefs and images refer did not undergo changes necessitating interpretation or extension by analogy, generalization, and differentiation, the superior human mind, restlessly seeking an order in which it can come to rest, becomes aware of inadequacies which need to be overcome.

The universe is inexhaustible. However great and indispensable the stock of achieved understanding inherited by any generation, it will not be adequate to answer all the questions of its heirs.

The inexhaustibility of the universe and the limited powers of the human mind render impossible the achievement of perfection in our understanding of the universe. Exhaustion could occur only when the universe or some part of it ceased to be interesting. One mind working subsequently, will perceive a vagueness, a gap, a logical or empirical incompatibility, which the mind which went before could not discern. Every solution to a problem perceived at an earlier stage of the inheritance can be made problematic by those who confront it at a subsequent stage. Many, perhaps most, of these critical attempts to render received solutions problematic are unsuccessful in persuading others that they are justified.

It is not because of any necessary proneness to error in the human mind that an intellectual tradition offers to each new generation the possibility of correction. It is rather that the radius of even the greatest minds cannot reach to the external limit of what is to be known, or even what will be known by future generations. In each generation a further step forward from the point previously reached is possible; it is a step which could not be taken without the prior steps having been taken. Once these steps have been taken as corrections of what was previously perceived, they allow further steps to be taken. The steps are resolutions of problems which could not have been seen to be problems until solutions to earlier problems had been produced.

Thus, within a setting of determined devotion to the tradition and with the desire to uphold it and without any intent to be original or to refute anyone, except perhaps some minor commentator, an alert critical intelligence will first sense that all is not as it should be with the tradition which it possesses. Although the tradition seen as a whole may be regarded as self-evidently correct and capable of demonstration should the need arise, the critical intelligence will attempt to improve the tradition by refining it. This refinement consists in making ostensibly minor reformulations, clarifying definitions, differentiating categories or grouping them under more general categories, resolving apparent contradictions, and restoring the unity of the body of belief, which had been diminished by critical analysis.

Scientific traditions differ from the other intellectual traditions by the deliberateness of the intention to change the tradition. They differ from other intellectual traditions by the rigor of the tests which they apply to the empirical referents of the tradition. Logical consistency and clarity of concepts are criteria which are applied within all intellectual traditions, but scientific traditions apply explicitly the criteria of empirical adequacy. The changing of scientific traditions involves the making of new observations systematically as well as the rationalization of already established observations.

We can speak therefore of correction as well as of rationalization in the case of scientific traditions. Rationalization is a process of being made more rational, i.e., clearer, more consistent, and more comprehensive; being made more rationally adequate to the problem given or discerned. It is the movement towards the establishment of coherent unity of ever greater comprehensiveness. Every clarification and every step taken to increase rigorous consistency is a step in the process of rationalization.

The motives for repairing the imperfections of a tradition may be as intellectual as any motive can be within the framework of an accepted tradition. The "rationalization" and "correction" proceed from a state of satisfaction with much of the tradition. It is like the codification of laws which takes the laws as given and modifies particular laws in order to make them consistent with the other laws which are retained and with the "general principles" which are embodied in the prevailing laws.

Sometimes the "defects" in the tradition might be seen immediately on presentation; the perception of the defects might indeed be part of the tradition itself. Often they are perceived only after long study and painstaking research by a person who at first did not perceive them. Sometimes the perception of the shortcomings of the perceived tradition is aided by the presence of another competing tradition but this is not by any means invariably so, except insofar as the tradition of the criteria of rationality, coherence, precision, and empirical veracity may be regarded as distinct from the tradition of substantive beliefs.

The development of Talmudic thought up to early modern times represents a development of a tradition of belief which occurred mainly through this kind of rational criticism, clarification, and rationalization. Of course, the postulates of the tradition—the divine inspiration of the Pentateuch and the obligation of the Jewish people to live according to the Law contained there—remained unchallenged. The task of understanding the Law required that its consistent application to known and conceivable situations be worked out. This entailed a continuous process of differentiation and generalization, by analogy and deduction, through imagining instances hitherto undealt with and in responding to problems put by applicants for rabbinical guidance and constructing correct, i.e., analogously and logically consistent, solutions. It involved bringing together and ordering the diverse views of learned rabbis in the various centers throughout the Islamic and Christian worlds where rabbinical learning was cultivated.

Codifications occurred from time to time through the work of al Phasi, Maimonides, Jacob ben Asher, and Joseph Karo. These changed the tradition in the same comprehensive way which occurs in legal codification, i.e., readjustments in some of the elements occurred in consequence of their rationalization; in some cases their scope was widened, in others narrowed. In some cases they were subsumed under a rubric which they had not been placed under before. They were given a logical relationship with each other that they had not had before. New situations were taken into account by extension of the old rules through analogy and generalization.

The changing of literary and artistic traditions is not a matter of rationalization or correction of the existing stock of valid tradition within the framework which some features of that tradition impose. The innovative work may lie very much within the tradition. It is an innovation with the intention of attaining the adequate expression of a superior insight by imagination or observation, a superior sensitivity to color and form and in the depiction of subject matter, a superior mode of verbal or plastic expression.

The greatness of a literary or artistic work is not necessarily an innovation in tradition in the way in which a major scientific or philosophical or theological work is. It does not aim to correct the tradition; it does not aim to supplant it. It aims to produce a work which is intrinsically superior to other works by its execution. The execution might involve innovation in the tradition; most great works of literature or art are innovations in the sense that they are unique. They do not however correct or rationalize past works; they do not replace them. They join the stock of works.

Even though they do not replace or correct the previous existent tradition, they do change it by adding to it; they change it also by changing the understanding of the tradition of great works.

The addition of new great works also changes the adherence to the tradition; they might cause earlier works to be less frequently read and less appreciated. They change the gallery of available models and points of departure for subsequent writers.

Changes in the Content of Tradition

A tradition of belief contains constituent beliefs about many particular things. A tradition of political beliefs contains beliefs about things such as the range of activity of the state, the organization of the economic order, the relations between church and state, the prerogatives of the family and other private institutions, the rights and duties of the citizen or subject, and the proper sphere of the organs of public opinion, among many others. It includes beliefs about the economic benefits of an economy of private business enterprises competing with each other in a free market and about the obligation of adult individuals to accept the responsibility for acting in a way to protect and enhance the well-being of themselves and their families.

These particular beliefs have practically never been a logically seamless whole. They form together a set of compromises balanced among themselves but not necessarily and at all times harmonious with each other. The relations to each other of the constituent beliefs about particular things within a more general tradition of belief are susceptible to change. Some elements may become more salient, others recede in prominence in the minds of their adherents.

Traditions may change endogenously through development of the moral sensitivity which they call forth in their requirements and which their recipients re-infuse into them. Just as each new stage of a tradition is subject to change through the application of critical reason which detects logical potentialities among its constituent elements, so each stage opens to its recipients, if they possess the requisite moral imagination, the possibility of an extended or deepened appreciation.

This does not mean that there is a progressive unfolding of a richer moral consciousness in the course of human history. Nevertheless, moral sensitivity does grow in individuals and in the course of an epoch, and the formation of a modified extended sensitivity is one of the ways in which it takes place.

The growth in the belief in the value of freedom of the individual in society was one of these changes. The idea itself was not new; there were forerunners. The acceptance of the idea from the seventeenth to the nineteenth centuries was probably not just a result of the rational persuasion of the new recipients of a political tradition by their fore-runners, dead and contemporary. It certainly was not a result of interests—as if the very conception of interests did not presuppose an anterior freedom to pursue those interests. It was at least partly a product of a moral awareness aroused by imagination and reflection on the state of the tradition as it was received. The new object of moral awareness then took a prominent moral position in the outlook transmitted in the tradition.

Similarly, if the appreciation of the material well-being of individuals changes to the point where it becomes more salient in the constitution of a political outlook such as liberalism, the tradition will also take a new turn.[1] As has happened in the tradition of liberalism, this change in the salience of the value of material well-being has entailed a change in the conception of the range of activity of the state. The change has not been brought about primarily because a previously committed logical inconsistency was perceived or because an ambiguity of definition or an empirical mistake was detected or because a newly apprehended potentiality was perceived in the latest state of the tradition. It has arisen from a change in the appreciation of a single element in a system of thought. The changed appreciation could be a result of the new moral sensitivity; it could be a result of the increased cognitive awareness of certain types of events which arouse existing moral sensitivity. In any case, the change in the tradition occurs in consequence of the shifted focus of interest of the recipient of the tradition. It is transmitted from him to others—who naturally include coevals—who regarded themselves as liberals and who began by being insensate to what he discovered through his sensitivity; to others who came later onto the scene of political belief, the new moral sensitivity within the tradition is part of the given. Once the new evaluation was successful in finding adherence, then the tradition of liberalism changed. It thus became established as a further stage in the tradition of liberalism.

One of the important changes in the tradition of liberalism was a

1. See Edward Shils, "The Antinomies of Liberalism," in Zbigniew Brzezinski, ed., *The Relevance of Liberalism* (Boulder, Colorado: The Westview Press, 1978), pp. 135–200.

change in the evaluation of the individual's responsibility for his own well-being; it took place against the background of an already existing tradition of appreciation of the rightfulness of the individual's material well-being, regardless of whether it is attained by the individual's own efforts. The change in degree of salience might have been brought by a change in moral evaluation which occurred by reasoning and through a modification of moral sensibility within individuals, without assimilation from a separate tradition in which it was already contained. The idea of a state of material well-being to which every individual is entitled regardless of his own achievements on his own behalf has been an element of immanent potentiality in ethical traditions of Western civilization at least since the earliest Christian communities. It was an immanent potentiality in the Christian tradition which came intermittently and marginally to the surface. The change in the evaluation experienced by some liberals in the latter half of the nineteenth century might have been an awakening of this. The awakening might have been made more prominent by a process of communication with Christians like Lamennais, Maurice, and other "socially minded" Christians of the middle of the nineteenth century.

In Christianity the immanent humanitarian potentiality was for much of Christian history kept in the margin of the Christian tradition. It was enjoined as a supplementary activity, it became the specialized preoccupation of certain orders especially concentrated on *Nächstenliebe, caritas,* caring for the ill, the widowed, the orphaned, the aged, the mad, and others neglected by most Christians in their everyday life.[2]

This increased prominence of the "social message" of Christianity in the Christian tradition, in which it had resided for so long in a recessive position, was not a result of a perception of internal contradictions, insufficient precision, or empirical inadequacy. It was the result of a heightened awareness of this element of the Christian tradition; it might have been aroused perhaps by the sight of the misery in the large cities of Europe in the first half of the nineteenth century. It was a great awareness of misery, hitherto justified or left unjustified, which made some sensitive and observant Christians more aware of the implications of an element of their tradition which they had accepted but had not acted on. In consequence of this coincidence of perception of external events and greater attention to a certain element already resident in the tradition, they changed their interpretation of Christianity.

Among educated Protestants in Germany and later in the United States and perhaps still later in England, this change in salience of the

2. See Adolf von Harnack, *What is Christianity?* (London: Williams and Norgate, 1901), and Troeltsch, *The Social Teachings of the Christian Churches.*

humanitarian element coincided roughly with the acceptance of the tradition of the "higher criticism" of the Bible which had originated within Christianity. A partial renunciation of certain parts of the Christian tradition which had hitherto been regarded as central, namely, the divine inspiration and historical accuracy of the account of events given in the historical works of the Old Testament and the Gospels conferred on the "social gospel" a more crucial position. Those persons who were attached to the tradition as a whole and yet felt that they were compelled to yield some of their attachment to the more specifically theological and historical parts of the tradition were left with the "ethics of Jesus" as expressed in the Sermon on the Mount. They clung to it all the more tenaciously and espoused it all the more fervently because it permitted them to reaffirm the tradition of the Christian religion and its church without infringing on the tradition of empirical scientific knowledge to which they had also become attached.

The development of socialism in England in the early part of the nineteenth century is an illustration of a similar change of a tradition resulting from the interpretation of texts—especially Ricardo's *On the Principles of Political Economy*—and its application to newly perceived events in such a way as to extend their arguments to the point where the conclusion that the laborer was being unjustly dealt with was the only one which it appeared could be consistently drawn from Ricardian economics.[3] The correction, by generalization, of Ricardian economics to the point where socialism appeared to be the only rational solution to the problem presented by the injustice suffered by the laborer is only one part of this picture of the cause of one of the important changes in liberalism in the course of the nineteenth century. It was clearly not the rearrangement of the Ricardian system of thought to eliminate inconsistencies in it and to rationalize it which led to the emergence of English socialism in the early nineteenth century. The change in the composition of the body of liberal traditions associated with the increased adherence to the socialist tradition was a result of the moral sensitivity which was heightened by the sight of so much misery in the large towns. The changes in the balance of the various elements of the tradition and the consequent changes within the particular traditions such as liberalism and Christianity, were much affected by the greater frequency and therefore the greater visibility of certain events which themselves were changes in the spatial pattern of settlement and in the extension of a certain structure of industrial production made possible—but not caused by—certain technological innovations.

3. H. S. Foxwell, Introduction to Anton Menger, *The Right to the Whole Produce of Labour* (London: Macmillan, 1899), pp. v–cx.

A change in the balance of the elements of a tradition and an associated change in adherence to it may be seen in the recent changes in the place of death in the Christian tradition.

Death has always been a problem for human beings and it can never cease to be a problem. Death, at least on the conscious level, is not as salient nowadays in Western societies as it was several centuries ago. There is still much preoccupation with its avoidance through resistance to war and the cure of illness. Nonetheless it has become a less salient, a less continuously obtruding problem with the extension of the span of life and with the great diminution of the death rate of infants and children. The great improvements in preventive medicine and in surgery and the increased consumption of nutritive foods have fortified the hope of remaining alive, of postponing death so that the thought of it can be put aside. The problems which the Christian conceptions of death and immortality treated, being terrifyingly painful problems and difficult to face, have been illusorily averted and put out of mind by many persons in contemporary Western societies. As a result, the Christian traditions regarding mortality and immortality have been attenuated. There are of course other factors in this attenuation. The achievements of scientific analyses—historical, archaeological, palaeontological and textual—have weakened the claim to factual veracity of the sacred writings of Judaism and Christianity, particularly among members of the educated classes. This has reduced the legitimacy of the beliefs which are not concerned with factual veracity and in fact are independent of the empirical validity of the historical content of the Christian traditions and the Jewish traditions which are associated with them. The Christian traditions regarding immortality have lost much of their persuasive power because the problematic facts to which they were addressed have been pushed into positions of lesser prominence. It is not that the doctrines of life after death and final judgment have been demonstrated to be untrue or even that they have led to disastrous consequences. Perhaps if the problems of illness, incapacitation, and early death reasserted themselves with their old force, if the life-span were to become much briefer and if the mortality rates of infants and children were to increase greatly, the fact of death would once more be continuously obtrusive. The uneasy secularist tradition might then recede before a resurgent religious interpretation, which it has, at least for the time being, replaced.

The traditional Christian interpretation of death was of course a grander and graver tradition than the traditions of socialism and liberalism; it was more elaborate and deeper intellectually. It dealt with a phenomenon more universal in society and history than these two doctrines. The fact of death is, in a certain sense, a deeper fact than the fact of material well-being. Nonetheless, it has been relegated, very uneasily and unsatisfyingly, to a less prominent position. It has therefore changed the pattern of the Christian tradition for many of its adherents.

Liberalism lost some of its adherents and also was infused with new elements which in the long run changed it simply because the facts of poverty became more visible than they had been previously— although poverty had probably not increased. So, when death was made less visible, it changed the urgency of what had necessarily been a very central element in the Christian tradition. As a result the Christian tradition has become attenuated for many persons.

Change in Adherence to Tradition

Traditions of belief also undergo change as a result of being subjected to the test of the claims their proponents make for them. If they claim that their traditions will explain the workings of the world, they have, more or less, to do that. A religious tradition has a less rigorously attentive audience than a scientific tradition—its vocabulary refers to invisible things and its procedures are less specific and its audience is less expert; but its adequacy to the deepest demands of its adherents and initiates is an ever present test of the adequacy and hence acceptability of the tradition. As long as the problems to which a tradition is addressed are pressing, the demands on the tradition which "deals with" those problems are likely to be exigent. If a tradition deals with important problems—and most do—it will be continuously under what amounts to scrutiny by its recipients and possessors.

Liberalism and socialism have of course not dealt with trivial problems; they have dealt with justice in the allocation of earthly benefits, the relations between merit and reward, and the value of physical well-being and pleasure. The proponents of these two traditions have made great claims for them, for the rightness of the ends which they put forward and no less for the efficacy of the institutional arrangements by which these ends would be realized. Neither liberalism nor socialism has ever acquired in any society the adherence which Christianity had. Indeed it is plausible to say that Christianity in various forms and fragments still has more adherents in Western countries than either socialism or liberalism. In intellectual circles however these two more or less secular programs have come to rival if not actually to exceed Christianity.

They too have both been subjected to a test which is more in accordance with their own empirical principles. As long as liberalism criticized the defects of absolutism, it gained in adherence. Similarly, as long as socialism criticized the realization of liberalism in capitalistic economic institutions, it too gained adherence; its gains were at the cost of liberalism. Liberal principles, so clear about the rational action of individuals competing with each other in selling their products and in purchasing the products of others, were not as satisfactory when practiced as they were when theoretically expounded. The economically calculable output of societies did increase greatly, the average income of individuals and families also increased; there was generally an improvement for most of the members of society. But unforeseen consequences occurred. When they were perceived, they were explained away as minor imperfections of the working of a beneficent system. The latter response was not by any means unreasonable. The majority of the society was much better off than it had been under a mercantilistic absolutist regime. It is true that parliamentary institutions did not bring remedies to all the victims of the liberal system but it brought many other benefits, such as a wider participation in the electorate; it restrained governments from arbitrary acts of authority and from oppressing their subjects. Nonetheless, at a time when liberalism spoke of the sovereignty of the electorate through representative institutions, there was marked inequality of influence among electors, and some parts of the adult population of liberal-democratic societies lagged behind in gaining the franchise. But, by more than anything else, damage was done to liberalism by the visibility of the condition of the poor in the great industrial cities and by the intermittent aggravation of that condition through the recurrent cycles of economic activity which in one phase left many persons in the working classes unemployed. The penurious and helpless animated traditions of humanitarian compassion and egalitarian conceptions of justice. Sensitivity to injustice and misery became more acute. The extension of moral sensitivity was accentuated by the increased visibility of misery and injustice.

The tradition of liberalism was affected in two ways by this development. One side of it became established and accepted. The higher standard of living which the liberal conduct of economic activity had achieved became the traditional norm by which the actual level of economic well-being was assessed; the high productivity of economic enterprise was accepted as the norm. Similarly, the established political and civil rights of the adult male members of the society were accepted as "rational." As they found wide acceptance, their connection with liberalism was forgotten; they were not counted by their beneficiaries among the positive accomplishments of liberalism. Many members of the society who experienced the benefits brought by liberalism failed to perceive them as consequences of liberalism or as integral to it. Whereas Christianity was made stronger because its adherents wanted to retain their connection with it while they perceived events which had not been taken account of in the previous state of the tradition, liberalism lost adherents because there was diminished perception of its consequences and less desire to preserve the relationship to its name. Only in the United States did the name of liberalism retain and even gain a large adherence while its content was being changed. In Europe, much of the tradition of liberalism was accepted but its name became confined in the minds of many to the elements which were rejected. Many of those who called themselves liberals, as in the United States, disavowed significant parts of the tradition. Certain elements of liberalism, particularly the appreciation of the material well-being of individuals, entered into combination with the tradition which had been animated and developed as a negative response to the failure of liberalism to raise the remnant minority of the population out of poverty. The outcome was a change in the content of liberalism and an increase in its adherence in the United States while in Europe liberalism retained a substantial amount of its traditional content and lost much of its adherence. Some of the elements of classical liberalism migrated to an outlook which denounced liberalism, while accepting much of its achievement as "natural" or self-evident. The outlooks which received the migrant elements from classical liberalism were collectivistic liberalism and democratic socialism which then became the dominant traditions of political thought and activity in Western countries.

The tradition of European liberalism came under severe criticism in intellectual circles in the latter part of the nineteenth century because of the discrepancy between its predicted benefits and failures to produce those benefits. For the most part the ideals or ends of liberalism continued to be esteemed, but they were also taken over into the competing doctrine of social democracy and there additional elements were added to them. In the United States, where the social-democratic tradition did not become established, liberalism underwent a different treatment. Certain of its elements were discarded and others, not so different from the social democratic elements, were added to it. The name of liberalism was kept, while in Europe it was objurgated by persons believing the same things as the liberals in America.

Changes in Adherence and Modifications of the Content of Tradition

With all its dependence on traditionality and with all its proneness to traditionality, the human race is also demanding of its traditions of belief. Not only do their proponents scrutinize them to correct them, to fill in their gaps, and to make them more consistent internally, but their proponents are expected by those to whom they offer the traditions to "live up to" standards of conduct which are contained in those traditions. Traditions which are explicitly or implicitly normative impose, according to the judgments of their recipients, certain standards of conduct on their proponents. Priests are expected to live up to a certain standard corresponding to what they preach to their flocks. Politicians are expected to approximate in the civility of their conduct a standard resembling that which they propose to the citizenry. Parents are expected to live up to the standards of decorum and probity which they propose to their children. Teachers who propose standards of intellectual rigor and integrity to their pupils are expected to adhere to these themselves.

The expectations are by no means always fulfilled. The acceptance of a tradition of belief is partly a matter of intellectual plausibility, but it is also a matter of confidence in the authority who recommends it. The authority's embodiment of it attests to its validity. The unworthiness of the authority to be granted such confidence thus weakens the disposition to accept the beliefs.

The anticlericalism of Roman Catholic countries originated in the *ancien régime*. It was neither the attractiveness of the Voltairean tradition alone, nor the persuasiveness of Bayle's critical attitude towards the historical accounts contained in the Bible which led to anticlericalism. It was to a considerable extent a result of the belief that the humility and self-abnegation urged on the Christians were not observed by the princes of the church. They lived in luxury and associated with the mighty of the earth, whom many persons who thought about these matters believed to be proud, selfish, and undeserving of their privileges. These imputations and associations did harm to the reputation of priests and bishops and rendered the beliefs which they proffered less persuasive.

The particular variant of the tradition of Marxism represented by Soviet communism had a similar experience. Communism, which was the particular form of socialism which became established in the Russian Empire, attracted much support from many collectivistic liberals and socialists in other countries during the quarter of a century which followed the Russian revolution of 1914. Despite differences on particular points, they regarded themselves as sharing to a large extent the same traditions of humanitarianism, emancipationism, and democracy. With the passage of years, the Soviet Union came to be viewed by many proponents of these traditions as having failed in important respects. The appreciation of the political rights of individuals which had been assimilated from and then dissociated from classical liberalism was discarded in the Soviet Union in practice; the improvement of the material conditions of life for most of the population which was so prominent in the tradition of classical liberalism and which was made central in collectivistic liberalism and social-democracy was not achieved in the Soviet Union. The productivity of the communistic economy, despite the ostensible avoidance of unemployment, was found to be poorer than that of the liberal economy.

The grip of the socialistic tradition and attachment to the names of socialism and Marxism were however so strong that, despite reservations of many sorts, socialists have continued for a long time to regard the Soviet Union as the realization of their tradition. To some extent they have modified parts of their own tradition to make it "fit" Soviet circumstances; the suspension of political liberties which certainly had not been a part of the socialist tradition in the latter part of the nineteenth and the early twentieth centuries was reinterpreted as a temporary necessity until the socialist society became firmly established. The poor performance of the Soviet economy was either evaded or explained as a necessary precondition for greater productivity in the future. Nonetheless the socialistic and the collectivistic liberal traditions still retained enough of their determinant features to lead their adherents to perceive the discrepancy between what they praised and the actuality of Soviet society as it became increasingly known in the Western countries. Gradually the Soviet Union fell into an ambivalent discredit among collectivistic liberals and democratic socialists in the West. Some communists in Western countries also found the undeniable discrepancies unbearable after they were confirmed by Khrushchev's address to the Twenty-Second Congress of the Communist Party of the Soviet Union in February 1956.

The responses to this failure of their ideals when put into practice have been diverse. For some proponents of the socialist outlook, the dictatorial, repressive policies of the rulers of the Soviet Union had already been abhorrent in the 1920s; they kept to their socialist tradition by denying any affinity with the activities of the Soviet government despite its claim of also being Marxist. This had been made easier for European socialists by the conflict between Mensheviks and Bolsheviks in Tsarist Russia since the beginning of the present century. Towards the end of the 1920s, a handful of communists began to see the divergence between the tradition which they espoused and the society in which that tradition was purportedly embodied. The great "purge" of the 1930s accentuated this awareness of the gap between the tradition and its realization. Some sought to preserve the tradition by "going back" to Lenin and claiming that the "true tradition" of communism had been suppressed by Stalin. Others turned to democratic socialism and collectivistic liberalism; a very few took up the tradition of classical liberalism with an admixture of conservatism.

In the 1970s the tradition of socialism was in a state of decomposition in Western countries. Many of its adherents wish to call themselves socialists and to hold to the socialist tradition of beliefs, but the actuality of the Soviet Union, which they think is integral to that tradition, has made it very difficult for them. Various ways of dealing with the problem have appeared. The image of the Soviet Union has by some been relegated to a less prominent place in their tradition but it remains effective in their image and assessment of the world; others have expelled it as completely as they can and replaced it with some other ideal socialist society such as Yugoslavia. Some, who once espoused it, have renounced the element of a political system with a single party while retaining much of the rest of the tradition; this represents a considerable change.

Many social-democrats have diminished their demand for central management of an economy without private property; others who still adhere to this important element in the socialist tradition have shown a greater awareness of the dangers of bureaucratic oligarchy. Poor economic achievement and political tyranny as acknowledged facts of the daily life of the leading socialistic country in the world have rendered their own tradition suspect to them. Even when the attempt at separation from the Soviet Union by explicit disavowal is made, it is still difficult to preserve the tradition intact. Many concessions have been made to the tradition of classical liberalism, e.g., acknowledgment of the importance of the market and of "economic incentives"; some socialists admit that they were wrong to belittle the "formal freedoms" espoused by classical liberalism and previously denigrated by Marxian socialists.

As far as the Soviet Union is concerned, the situation is probably rather different. There, no acknowledged modifications in the Bolshevik variant of the Marxist tradition are permitted. In public, the traditional view, adjusted from time to time for tactical reasons, is unreflectively reasserted over and over again in a dogmatic manner. All "derivatives" are vehemently rejected. What goes on beneath the surface of publication is difficult to say. Many of those who are called dissidents accept much of the socialistic tradition; private business enterprise is inconceivable to them. They lay emphasis on those elements of liberalism which were assimilated into democratic socialism. A few reassert the traditions of Russian Orthodox Christianity, with all the distrust of liberalism which is common to that tradition and to the Bolshevik tradition.

The desertion from the communistic version of socialistic tradition was not only a result of the failure of the proponents of the tradition to realize its promises once it was given an opportunity to do so; it had its chance and it did not work.[4] The intellectual coherence of the tradition and even its ostensible ethical rightness were not enough to sustain the attachment to it of many persons who once were very firmly adherent; the knowledge that those who were to fulfill the ideal had failed to do so made many skeptical of the ideal and it made others modify it. Still others reaffirmed the ideal and rejected its pretended embodiment. The eclectic dispersion of the socialist tradition shows

4. When Lincoln Steffens said, "I have been over into the future and it works," he testified to the criterion of realizability; what he meant was that the radical tradition regarding the right organization of society had been realized. (Lincoln Steffens, *Autobiography* [New York: Harcourt Brace, 1931], p. 799.)

both the strength of the will to affirm a tradition and the damaging effect on that adherence of a practice which is so different from what the tradition predicts and recommends.

Imagination

All these various sources of modifications of tradition are connected with the exercise of imagination. Sometimes the imagination works in an unarticulated manner to add small increments to the received patterns of action and to make small subtractions and elisions; linguistic changes are of this sort. At other times, the imagination makes a large movement and, through the instruments and institutions available to the person who exercises it, engenders large changes in a short time in the circumstances to which multitudes of persons must adapt themselves. In the case of the charismatic figure in whom extraordinary properties are discerned or to whom they are attributed, it is through a grand exertion of the imagination that the charisma becomes manifest and through which it is perceived and attributed. Imagination is the genuinely charismatic gift possessed in very similar ways by religious founders and prophets, by great lawgivers, business enterprisers, inventors, scientists, scholars, and literary men. They must all have this charismatic gift of capacity and scope of imagination in envisaging what has not been done, thought, or seen before. Other qualities are necessary too. Courage, memory, assiduity, and ratiocinative aptitude are all necessary, but without imagination no significant modifications in the traditions which provide patterns of belief and which control the circumstances of action could be made. Alongside of piety, and convenience, tradition imposes itself because the human race in its large majority is unimaginative. It does however have among its unequally distributed powers the capacity for imagination. Imagination, directly or indirectly, is the great modifier of traditions.

The Charismatic Figure

Max Weber regarded the charismatic personality as the "specifically 'creative' revolutionary force in history";[5] he regarded him as the breaker of traditions. The characteristic expression of the charismatic prophet was, "It is written, but I say unto you." It is certainly justified and necessary to emphasize the persistence of the past in the teachings of charismatic persons and in the intellectual content and techniques of mystics and enthusiasts. It is certainly no less justified and necessary to recognize that a tradition into which a charismatic figure enters does indeed persist. As a result of the appearance of a charismatic person the tradition persists in a form and substance very

5. Weber, *Wirtschaft und Gesellschaft*, 2:750.

different from what they were previously. The direction of the tradition is greatly altered so that, as the new direction moves forward in
time, the innovations become more and more tangible. The need to
emphasize the difference from the antecedent, parental tradition also
accentuates the degree of change of direction. Christianity in the
lifetime of Jesus could still be considered by Jews and Gentiles and
even by the first Christians as a deviant Jewish sect. Within fifty years
of the death of Jesus, it was clear that it was much more than that. The
greatest Christian thinkers never ceased to be aware of the continuity
between the Old Testament and the New but they were also convinced of the profound and profoundly significant disjunction between
the two.

The charismatic breaking of tradition may be regarded as both an
exogenous and an endogenous change. It is exogenous in the sense
that it probably occurs under particular circumstances of disorder and
of the failure of institutions. But it is endogenous insofar as a personality and mind of originality of imagination perceives a profound gap
in the adequacy of the prevailing tradition and seeks to fill that gap,
while acknowledging his derivation from it.

The achievement of the charismatic person is an accomplishment of
an original imagination working within a tradition and modifying it in
important respects but not leaving it completely behind him. His
imagination is aroused by incompleteness in the tradition for what he
perceives as a task which must be reckoned with. The perception of a
task to be resolved, of an inadequacy of circumstances is not always
or necessarily the result of a change in circumstances. Circumstances
might not appear dangerous or injurious or unsatisfactory to the persons who participate in them any more than an intellectual tradition
need appear to be inadequate to those who accept it. In both cases,
minds of unusual imaginative and ratiocinative powers might see defects in that received tradition and they might imagine ways to "improve" it. They might unsettle the hitherto more or less satisfied
possessors of the tradition by their promulgation of their criticism of
its shortcomings. Palestine was in turmoil in the decades before the
appearance of Jesus but it was also in turmoil during the century of the
Asmoneans, as it had been in the time of the Alexandrian conquest of
the Persian empire. In fact Palestine, being at the point of encounter
of several expansive and mutually inimical empires and the place of
meeting of many cultures, had been in a condition of disorder for a
very long time. The appearance of the prophets during the period of
the two kingdoms and during the Babylonian exile is evidence that
there were persons with a sense of charismatic endowment in these
situations, but they did not preach the message which Jesus preached.
Perhaps they could not have done so because the idea of an individual
soul surviving after death and being subject to a last judgment had not

yet reached a sufficient state of development. The fact is that Jesus cannot be accounted for simply by reference to the state of development of the tradition nor by reference to the changed circumstances and the charismatic needs of certain strata of the Jewish society of Palestine in Jesus' own time. It was Jesus' prophetic or charismatic imagination which determined his accomplishment. He had the gift of arousing in others an acknowledgment or attribution of charismatic qualities. He did this by the originality of his message and his own belief in its originality. He had to have the tradition as his point of departure; he had to have an audience which had the same tradition as its point of departure. In that sense he was continuing and developing the tradition, but so for that matter were the rabbis. He developed it in a different and more original way and his message found a reception far beyond Palestine and the Jews. The receptiveness of this wider body of converts, who were won over from paganism and not just from Judaism, might have been a result of the changes in circumstances and of the relative weakness of the traditions of paganism in confrontation with a more highly developed body of religious thought.

Changes in the Charismatic Message

The charismatic message becomes rationalized, elaborated, clarified, fortified to withstand criticisms from rival traditions very akin to the charismatic message. The "routinization" of the charismatic, as Max Weber called it, is an inevitable process.[6] Nothing charismatic could survive without becoming a tradition, and becoming a tradition imposes changes. It is not just the difference between the received and the created; they could conceivably be identical. If the charismatic message was to retain its charismatic force, it had to become a tradition. Becoming a tradition, it changed. Furthermore, a charismatically promulgated message or belief is a symbolic construction; it is an intellectual statement and it is therefore capable of rational criticism and logical rationalization. The combination of these two possibilities drives a charismatically founded tradition towards systematic expansion.

Ritual, being magical, technological, even though symbolically interpreted, is forced to maintain a constancy of pattern. Departure from the pattern and a variation in identity can render the entire arrangement meaningless. Because ritual is not subject to rationalization, only indifference or antinomianism can change it. A belief is a different matter. Rationalization is a constant potentiality of belief although it is not always realized.

The process of rationalization of belief is not the only source of change in a charismatic tradition. If the adherence of the tradition

6. Weber, *Wirtschaft und Gesellschaft*, 2:758–72.

expands, it gains converts whose prior beliefs and current circumstances are different from those of the first proponents of the message. The circumstances of the organization of adherents to the tradition also change. If the adherents of the tradition are held together in an institution like a church or a monastery, that fact alone imposes necessities and compromises. The maintenance of an institution requires actions which are sometimes in conflict with a charismatic message, and compromises in practice and in belief are called for. The new adherents might not have the urgent sensitivity and perceptiveness of the first adherents and allowance must be made for this by lesser exigency in the demands made on them.

The routinization of charisma goes beyond stabilization of the substance of the message which has become a tradition. It entails changes in substance in consequence of the discovery of new possibilities as well as modifications in response to changed and ever changing circumstances of the adherence and of the situations to which the tradition refers.

Antinomianism, Nihilism, and Boredom

At the other extreme from the traditionalistic antagonists of the prevailing traditions have been the genuine antinomians, who have been against any normative regulations whatsoever. Antinomianism in an extreme form is rare in any society. In modern Western society, radical Protestant sects, political anarchists, and criminals approximate to antinomianism of this sort. Their proportions are small but the dispositions to which they give a fuller representation are much more widespread. The anarchists in particular have enjoyed a favor among intellectuals which extremist Protestant sectarians did not.[7] There is a widespread belief among the influential and educated persons—growing in numbers and influence for about two centuries—that what exists is unsatisfactory, that what has been inherited from the past is unsatisfactory. Partly a product of doctrine, partly a product of moral sensitivity, this belief has been encouraged by antinomianism and it also encourages antinomianism by conferring patronage on it.

Antinomianism has been incapable of a complete and comprehensive rejection of existing tradition and of its complete replacement by a condition of utter rulelessness. Antinomianism rests on a temperamental disposition the full gratification of which in its pure form is unrealizable. As a temperamental disposition it is, in varying degrees of strength, broadly diffused. Disarmed by these compromises, it appears to be more continuous with a more moderately critical attitude towards tradition and a more realistic demand for emancipation.

7. Conrad's *The Secret Agent* and James's *The Princess Cassamassima* both indicate this patronage of anarchism in circles which would not go so far in their own beliefs or actions.

The maxim *Stadtluft macht frei* was more than the enunciation of a legal fact; it was a commendation. In the city, a human being could live without the burden of expectations, implied or expressed, in ubiquitous traditions supported by the explicit demands of authorities of lineage, village, and manor.

The attraction of the city was negative, it was a realm of freedom from traditions which were so strong in provincial society. At least that is how it seemed to many who reached it and who later wrote about it. There was a sense of aggrieved repugnance towards the village and the small town in American literature in the first quarter of the twentieth century; Stendahl and Flaubert, who were certainly no admirers of French society as a whole in the nineteenth century, were even more disapproving of the mode of life in the provinces and especially in small towns.

It was not only in the provinces that freedom was suppressed by traditions imposed by an authority which penetrated everywhere; the lives of the urban propertied and respectable classes—upper middle and lower middle and working classes as well—were constricted by submission to repressive traditions of conduct. Their respectability was constituted by their submission to bourgeois traditions of religious observance, familial obligation, industriousness, and political authority; they accepted without challenge the tradition which asserted the high value of private property and the pursuit of wealth.

Throughout Europe in the latter part of the nineteenth century, literary works told of the victims of an oppressive, stereotyped moral code which permitted no self-expression to the individual. This attitude was not confined to literary works. The emancipation of women from the restraints exercised by father and husband was a common demand in the writings of social reformers; the emancipation of children from the traditional modes of instruction and from the traditional programs of study was a commonplace theme of the writings of educational reformers.

An anguished cry for "life," for "spontaneity," for "experience," understood as the experience of sensation, was the response to this sense of suffocation, of the desiccation of vitality under the burden of tradition.[8]

Civilization seemed to have gone too far. It had become heavy with elaborate codes of conduct which had no rationale other than the fact that they were "done"; it had become so drawn into the complex, rule-bound institutions which had grown up that a great simplification seemed called for. Already in the eighteenth century, there had been an appreciation of the noble savage who lived a "natural" life. The

8. *The Book of Souls* of Louis Couperus, Galsworthy's *Forsyte Saga*, and the plays of Ibsen present many instances of the painful cry of the sensitive human being against the boredom of a tradition-encrusted society.

sagacious Chinese and Persians, who were ruled by reason, unburdened by contention, and the simple lovers drawn to each other by pure sentiments and kept apart from each other by elaborate rules and spiritually suffocating institutions became heroes. The voyages of discovery and the expansion of European commerce and then sovereignty into territories inhabited by illiterate gatherers, hunters, and cultivators brought before European intellectuals visions of societies which they thought had not been subjected to the weight of long-accumulated, excessively elaborated traditions in culture and in institutions. (The "noble savage" had not yet been replaced by the savage trembling in superstitious fear, bound hand and foot by inflexible custom.) By contrast with European civilization, the "primitive" had none of the baseless yet compulsory artificiality of European civilization.

European civilization came under the criticism that it had reached a point where its traditions were suppressing the physical vitality necessary for its survival.[9] It was asserted that its traditions had become so exhausted that they could no longer sustain life. Tradition had crushed vitality to such an extent that society was threatened with extinction. The world was in decline; its traditions were too weak to nurture life, too strong to permit it to find the forms through which a latent vitality could be expressed. Under these conditions, life itself seemed not worth living. In literary circles, a flamboyant flouting of the traditions of bourgeois society was cultivated. Gautier's red vest, Baudelaire's green hair, Huysmans' *orgue à bouche,* and Oscar Wilde's lobster on a leash were part of this contempt for the traditions of bourgeois society. Alongside the buffoonery and "fatigue," active nihilism, vehement and gleeful or somber and murderous, proposed the complete demolition of traditional Christian and bourgeois beliefs. In some cases there was an expectation that once the task of clearance had been carried out, a new order and a new set of values could be installed.[10]

The criticisms came from many sides. Some said that European civilization had become too old; it needed spiritual renewal which they thought could come from oriental religions and philosophy; from anthroposophy both in the form recommended by Annie Besant and

---

9. See Ernst Robert Curtius, "Entstehung und Wandlung des Dekadenzproblems in Frankreich," *Internationale Monatsschrift für Wissenschaft, Kunst und Technik* 15 (1921) 147–66; Eckart von Sydow, *Die Kultur der Dekadenz* (Dresden: Sibyllen-Verlag, 1922), pp. 104–84.

10. Nietzsche was the greatest of these active nihilists. His influence has been deep and pervasive and may be observed in many intellectuals who do not share his beliefs about the new order which should succeed the still living one. In passing, I draw attention to the forgotten Polish writer Stanislaw Przybyszewski. See in general Helmut Kreutzer, *Die Boheme* (Stuttgart: J. B. Metzler, 1971).

in that of Rudolf Steiner; and from the recipes of the Russian gurus, Ouspensky and Gurdieff, for throwing off the dry husk of dead tradition to enable vital powers to come forth.

The "century of the child" was proclaimed by Ellen Key; Wordsworth had said much earlier in the century, "Heaven lies about us in our infancy! / Shades of the prisonhouse begin to close / Upon the growing Boy." By the turn of the century educational reformers laid their axes to the tree of traditional knowledge. Between the emerging psychoanalysis which declared that the superego deformed the soul of the child and "progressive education" which aimed to emancipate the creative powers of the child from the bonds of rote learning of established knowledge and morals, traditions found to be unbearable were placed under siege.

Socialists called for a transformation of the economic order; the most influential based their argument for such a transformation on the proposition that the existing economic order, in the state of maturity it had reached, was so bound by its own traditions of private property that, unless it broke them, the potentialities of a new life could not be realized. In art a rebellion against the traditions of neoclassicist and naturalistic representation of reality led first to impressionism, then to an apotheosis of the "primitive" as a path away from the deadening consequences of tradition[11] and to the disaggregation of the traditional visual images which had prevailed in Western art for two and a half millennia.

The "conventional lies of civilization," the traditional beliefs which the critics said were necessary for society, were exposed. Traditions of respectability and hypocrisy repressed "true individuality" and stood in the way of "life." "Life" was set against unthinkingly inherited conventions. It was not an attack aimed at a particular objective; it was rather an attempt to break the grip of the past. The proclaimed objectives embraced newly animated ideals of justice, as well as the intention to correct and bring them into consistency with standards of empirical evidence and rationality. These were joined by amorphous and angry boredom with the burden of traditions in every sphere of human activity. Some of the critics thought that human beings could become more responsive, more sensitive and appreciative, and even more intelligent, if life could be directly experienced and not mediated through tradition. The "cry for life" was not just a slogan of socialistic propagandists; it was deeper. It was a cry for an unknown object

11. Marx thought that the attractiveness of Greek art and literature was a result of its "youthfulness" (*Einleitung zur Kritik der politischen Ökonomie,* in Karl Marx, Friedrich Engels, *Werke* [Berlin: Dietz Verlag, 1961], 13:641–42). See also Gombrich's talks on primitivism in art: "The Primitive and Its Value in Art," *The Listener,* 101, no. 2598 (15 February 1979), pp. 242–45; no. 2599 (22 February 1979), pp. 278–81; no. 2600 (1 March 1979), pp. 311–14; no. 2601 (8 March 1979), pp. 347–50.

called "life" because life was held to be antithetical to custom and convention. Many intellectuals and many less cultivated persons, too, were bored by what they had received. Society seemed too cut and dried, too much the same thing, too much the wrong thing over and over again.

This powerful movement driven forward by many motives did not by any means obliterate tradition. It did however open the way to large modifications of tradition in nearly every sphere of life. So immense did its impact seem to be that it appeared as if nothing were left of the stock of traditions of European civilization.

The Temptation of Positive Antitraditional Traditions

Antinomianism, and nihilism, were negative traditions. There also have been affirmative traditions dedicated to the obliteration of traditions. Sometimes they concentrated on a particular field of activity. Sometimes they were against all traditions as such, wherever they recognized them, and they hoped to replace them by a traditionless order.

These positive traditions have been particularly conducive to change in the established traditions of Western societies; they have also spread beyond Western societies and in those new territories they have been addressed to the task of dismantling substantive traditions. These are the "antitraditions" of originality, scientism, and progressivism.

Some preoccupation with "origin" is found in almost all human societies; contact with origins through ritual and lineage has almost everywhere been a valued condition in human societies. Myths of origin are practically universal; so also is belief in the sacred significance of founding events and their celebration in anniversaries. What is distinctive about the modern tradition of originality is the prominence which is attributed to ideas, works, and activities originating in the individual and having no reference to a time in the past. This modern idea of originality held that an individual makes "his mark in life" by beginning something which lasts. It accepted the inevitability of tradition; the main end of a serious life was therefore to make an object or to think of an idea or to write a work which would take its place in the tradition passed to future generations by virtue of its originality in the generation in which it was produced. So it was thought until recently. Most recently, originality has not been praised for bringing forth lasting ideas or objects. The main thing is to be original; to do something which was not done before, to produce a work which was not produced before. Even if such actions were performed before and such works were produced before, they have been appreciated as long as they originated in the very essence of the individual.

Originality as an obligation was a very special variant of individualism, which prized the achievements of the individual through the disciplined use of his own skill and resources. The most recent form of originality seeks not originality of achievement but originality of being. This however is only one possibility.

There is genuine originality and there is originality which is only different. Originality comprehends individuality, novelty, and significant seriousness. A work which has never been written before may be entirely wrong, it may be poorly executed, it may be trivial. If it is a serious work, then it adds to the tradition and modifies it in so doing; if it is a serious work, it enriches tradition by extending and improving it.

It is one of the features of spurious originality that it regards tradition as its enemy. It is an expression of hostility against tradition more than it is of the striving to gain a deeper vision of reality, to create something which is worthy of existence and which has not existed before in that guise and on that level. The ineffectual striving for originality is antithetical to the affirmative assimilation of tradition. The person who strives for originality at all costs is sometimes the powerless victim of tradition; in his powerlessness, the victim comes to hate the tradition which he cannot extend or change. The agitation against tradition in modern art and literature is in part a function of this striving for originality and the awareness of how difficult it is to achieve. Enmity towards tradition is inextricably mixed with the futile striving for originality.

The idea of genius is a belief that great works are creations of great spirits, rare in human life and hence not to be restrained but rather to be allowed full and uninhibited expression.

Scientism is hostile to traditions since it admits only those rules which are thought to rest on scientific knowledge joined by scientific procedures and rational analysis. Substantive traditions which are not grounded scientifically are to be replaced. Of course, the policies which presumably rest on scientific knowledge and procedure are rarely so; they are almost always policies drawn from utilitarian hedonistic and humanitarian traditions and are not at all scientifically derived. Nonetheless, the scientific tradition expressed a skeptical attitude towards traditional institutions and beliefs and contributed to the readiness to depart from them in favor of procedures and modes of action which have the authority of "science" behind them.

The other positive antitraditional tradition, constitutive in modern Western culture and now increasingly spreading in contemporary societies outside the West, is the progressivistic tradition. It is a tradition of the redeemability of man from his earthly imperfections.[12] But whereas the kingdom of God was not to be realized on earth, the progress of society towards human perfection was. The idea of progress accepted a secularized version of the tradition of the idea of the fall from grace and redemption by grace; to the tradition was later added the idea of the evolution of the spirit towards an increasing self-realization. The evolution of the spirit gradually changed into the evolution of society towards the realization of the potentialities of the spirit in a more perfect human life in the world. Lessing's notion of history as "the education of man by God" expressed very fittingly the idea of progressive evolution of man and society.

The idea of progress was both descriptive and normative; the relations between these two features were left in obscurity. It asserted that progress had occurred; it also asserted that it should occur and that it would occur if the barriers which blocked it were removed. The barriers were the attachments of human beings to their defective past practices and beliefs. The promotion of progress became the object of public policy and the measure of the merit of a society. The guides of public opinion applied the criterion of progressiveness to every institution and belief, and, with the increasing prominence of government, to the main decisions of governments. Tradition became the chief foe, interposed between the proper and natural aspirations of human beings and their realization. This placed the defenders of traditions other than the tradition of progress in a weak position. They were put on the defensive; their numbers were diminished, their self-confidence was made faint. The self-evident truth of the idea of progress made it vain to argue for the retention of patterns from the past.

Changes in Antitraditional Traditions

Antitraditional traditions are subject to the same vicissitudes as charismatic messages. They too become traditionalized and, as they do, they acquire elements which are difficult to assimilate. Revolutionary beliefs are carried by organizations, just as are the charismatic beliefs of religious prophets which become the possession of a church. The necessities of maintaining the organization call for officials to whom the substance of the message is not their exclusive concern. Compromises are made in doctrine through shift in emphasis and with relegation of certain elements to less prominent positions in the doctrine.

Antitraditional traditions, such as revolutionary traditions, when they extend their adherence bring into the circle of their possessors persons whose prior beliefs and circumstances are different from

12. See R. Newton Flew, *The Idea of Perfection in Christian Theology* (London: Oxford University Press, 1943); John Passmore, *The Perfectibility of Man* (London: Duckworth, 1970), pp. 190–211.

those of the first generation of the revolutionaries. They tend to be more eclectic than the founders. Their prior beliefs do not undergo complete suppression; they appear in fusion with the antitraditional beliefs. So it is with nationalism in association with Marxism, although charismatic Marxism was very hostile towards nationalism; when it appeared in conjunction with it, the conjunction was a deliberate contrivance of adaptation to the "prejudices" of actual and desired adherents.

When the exponents of a revolutionary antitraditional tradition come to exercise power within a state, their traditions undergo similar changes. The need to compromise among the different groups of exponents who espouse divergent beliefs enforces changes, as do the exigencies of governing which require actions proscribed by the tradition. The tradition might, as in the Soviet Union, be forcibly prevented from undergoing criticism but this too entails problems. As the tradition becomes less and less fitting to the factual situations with which it nominally deals, it becomes less persuasive to its adherents. The stability of the substance of a traditional charismatic belief under changing circumstances is followed by an attrition of adherence.

Finally, antitraditional traditions which have a strong admixture of antinomianism in them have little power of persistence. They are bound to run down. They run down because there is a charismatic element in antiomianism and, since charismatic gifts are uncommon and charismatic persons are mortal, such an element becomes diffuse and attenuated like all intense and concentrated charismatic endowments. Enthusiastic states, states of being possessed, which have much in common with charismatic endowment, are exceptional states; they are not capable of being sustained for long and continuous periods even within the life-span of a single individual. Antinomianism has a long tradition, but each of its institutional bearers and transmitters tends to be very short-lived. The tradition passes from group to group because no particular group which is antinomian in its concentrated theme and major object can survive long. It therefore has a flickering, fluctuating existence, losing adherence and losing intensity of belief in the realizability of its demands and expectations. If we think of a tradition as having a particular name, a particular content, and a particular institutional adherence which persist over an extended time, particular antinomian beliefs do not become traditions. But as a set of beliefs, with some historical filiation but without continuous institutional embodiment, antinomianism is recurrent and discontinuous. There is a very active general tradition of antinomianism, in which successive renewals turn back to a common source. Such a common mode for resurgent antinomian impulses is the primitive Christian community; the German social democrats at the end of the last century turned back to the Anabaptists in Münster with whom they proclaimed a sense of very loose affinity.

In a more diffuse way, antinomianism enters into a tradition through its partial amalgamation with liberalism. It renounces its unqualifiedness, its urgency, its demandingness, and becomes a tradition generally distrustful of authority, particularly of the authority of the state. It is probably significant that British liberalism for a long time had an association with the free churches and that even now British radicals invoke the tradition of dissent. In that diffuse and amalgamated form, it is a very different thing from the radicalism of the English civil war. That modified form, however, is the only one through which the enthusiastic hostility to authority of that period could have gained a continuous existence which was not confined to the outermost periphery of society.

6   Why Traditions Change
Exogenous Factors

Traditions can change through responses of their bearers to features of the traditions themselves in accordance with standards of judgment which their bearers apply to them. These standards of judgment may derive from newly presented traditions, from traditions previously unknown in the society although well developed in alien societies. The confrontation of a tradition internal to a particular society and an alien tradition is usually a consequence of demographic, political, military, or economic changes in the relations between the societies. Traditions may change in response to changed circumstances of action, themselves products of changes recurring with the society in which they were previously practiced.

Change in Tradition through Syncretism:
The Pressure of an Alien Tradition

Traditions change when their adherents are brought or enter into the presence of other traditions. The economic, political, and military power of the proponents of the alien traditions, the apparent convenience and effectiveness of the alien traditions and their superior intellectual persuasiveness within the postulates of the established tradition, all make for change in established traditions.

The spread of societies from one part of the earth's surface to areas where they were previously unknown affords the opportunity for the traditions of the expanding society to come into contact with traditions with which they have no common ground except that they both deal with the situations to which all human existence is subject. Every society which becomes an empire or which sends its members as explorers, merchants, soldiers, missionaries, and administrators experiences this juxtaposition of its own tradition with the traditions of the indigenous societies upon which it comes. The members of the indigenous societies experience the same thing, from their own standpoints. The respective adherents of the several sets of traditions do take notice of the other traditions of belief, although they usually do not see them as traditions. As long as gods were local gods and each society had its own, the religious cultures could coexist without comparison and derogation. It was only with the appearance in the world of religions of beliefs which claimed universal validity in place of primordial religions that a rivalrous attitude appeared. As long as primordial religions prevailed, there was practically no question of a person changing his religious belief. The tradition which he received was the tradition with which he had to remain content. The appearance of religions of belief changed this. Membership in a religious community ceased to depend in the same way as it had on the acceptance of the religious beliefs of one's ancestors. The communicants of other beliefs were henceforth seen as challengers of the correctness of one's own beliefs or as the victims of error.

In Western antiquity, the Hellenistic empires spread Greek philosophical and literary culture to parts of the world to which it was new. The partial renunciation of indigenous traditions occurred in a situation in which the traditions were not bound to lineage. The Jews did not yield to the Hellenistic cultural tradition but they had no impact on it.[1] The societies of Egypt, Asia Minor, and parts of the former Persian Empire yielded to Hellenistic cultural traditions but they did not do so completely.

From that point onward, Greek intellectual traditions were increasingly assimilated by the expanding Roman society, and, as the Roman Empire expanded, it spread the Greek traditions which it had acquired. The Romans and Greeks did not attempt to coerce intellectually the persons into whose midst they settled as rulers or as colonists. The Romans imposed new systems of authority which broke through the margins of the traditional patterns of authority of the indigenous peoples whom they conquered; they enabled them to depart from their own traditional literary, artistic, and philosophical culture, if they wished to assimilate themselves to Graeco-Roman civilization and to gain advantages of Roman citizenship. The Romans did not attempt to win their new subjects to Roman religion. The indigenous subjects were won over from their own literary and philosophical traditions to acquire the Roman—and therewith mainly the Greek—cultural tradition. The indigenous Celtic, British, Germanic, Belgic, Iberian, Dacian, and other cultural traditions yielded to the Roman. The alien cultural tradition evidently seemed superior to the indigenous one; whatever might have been the other considerations which led to the assimilation of the alien traditions, some of the acquisition of the alien traditions must be attributed to the evident superiority of those traditions to the indigenous ones. Just as traditions may be changed endogenously in recognition of the improvability of what has been received, so a standard of assessment which permits discrimination among traditions dealing with the same subject

1. A. D. Momigliano, *Alien Wisdom: The Limits of Hellenization* (Cambridge: Cambridge University Press, 1975), pp. 97–122.

matter may emerge in application to the conflicting claims of the alien and indigenous traditions. The indigenous traditions survived with relatively little modification in the lower, less-educated strata, although there too, perhaps in consequence of the learning of the Latin language by those who entered into Roman military service and the lower levels of the provincial administration, new knowledge and beliefs were acquired.

Also in the lower classes, in the opposite direction, Persian religious traditions spread into Roman society. In the higher classes of society, the indigenous cultural traditions of the peoples conquered by the Romans, except for the Greeks, had little impact on the traditions of the conquerors. Christianity was a religion of the periphery which moved upward, downward, and outward, first in Palestine, then more widely in the eastern Mediteranean, and into the center of Roman society. From there it moved outward with reinforced power from its establishment as the state religion and the formation of the Roman Catholic church.

The result of the juxtaposition of the two sets of traditions which had hitherto been autonomous was that, except in the case of the Jews, who mainly rejected both Roman and Greek traditions, one of the sets came to be preponderant over the other, acquiring new adherents in societies in which it had previously been unknown. Where Hellenistic cultural traditions were juxtaposed with the cultural traditions of the eastern Mediterranean, they replaced them to a considerable extent. Where Roman cultural traditions came into juxtaposition with the cultural traditions of Europe to the north, northeast, and west of Italy, they too modified the indigenous traditions and to a large extent replaced them. The relationship of the Roman conquerors to the cultural traditions of Greece was different; there the traditions of the conquered people were assimilated into and became parts of the Roman literary, philosophical, and artistic traditions.

The movement of Islam beyond its original Arabian locality was the prelude to the most extended series of encounters of indigenous and alien traditions until the expansion of Western scientific and political beliefs in the nineteenth and twentieth centuries. In the Middle East and as far eastward as India, and as far westward as the Atlantic Ocean on the southern side of the Mediterranean, and into the southwestern and southeastern parts of the European continent, the spread of Muslim military power was followed by the infusion of Islamic traditions into most of the indigenous traditions. These Islamic traditions moved further eastward into the Indian archipelago and the Malay peninsula, northward into Central Asia and westward across sub-Saharan Africa with similar results. The Graeco-Roman traditions in the areas of former Hellenistic and Roman dominance were replaced by Islamic traditions, except in philosophy and science.[2] Literary, historiographic, artistic, and institutional traditions of the conquered society were reduced but probably not wholly extinguished. Arabic literature elaborated its own styles and attitudes, drawing on its own traditions and making itself impermeable to the literary traditions of the conquered societies.[3] Large parts of Indian society wholly withstood the pressure which the presence of Islamic traditions and Muslim political and military power generated elsewhere. There were many temptations for Hindus to be converted to Islam, and in the north, where the rewards of conversion were most apparent, many did in fact abjure their traditional beliefs and adopt the alien tradition. A certain amount of fusion of particular strands of the two traditions did occur,[4] but neither the numbers of converts nor the examples of fusion were sufficient to affect the religious traditions of most of Hindu society which were protected by the strength of adherence to the traditions of caste and lineage. In Indonesia, on the other hand, the result was more syncretistic.[5]

When European societies began their expansion into India with its written religious and philosophical traditions, their cultural traditions were assimilated by the coastal parts of the society which provided their economic and administrative collaborators. Christianity, propagated by missionaries, unevenly and with uneven success, found acceptance, and educational institutions in the European pattern, welcomed by certain strata of the indigenous society, infused certain parts of Western traditions into the indigenous ones, although they by no means wholly replaced them. Christianity was not widely accepted in India; the traditions of Hinduism were clung to by most Hindus.

In Africa, the pagan religious beliefs of the strata which came into close contact with the Europeans through commerce and education yielded and were replaced, while the pagan religious traditions of the lower strata remained as they were. Uganda was an exception, largely because of the persuasive powers of the indigenous rulers who had been attracted by the European cultural traditions and whose own political power was left largely intact by the change. In the lower strata of black African societies syncretistic Christianity is with Islam

2. C. H. Becker, *Islamstudien: Vom Werden und Wesen der islamischen Welt* (Leipzig: Quelle und Meyer, 1924), 1:33–39; E. I. J. Rosenthal, *Political Thought in Medieval Islam,* pp. 113–224.

3. Reynold A. Nicholson, *A Literary History of the Arabs* (London: T. Fisher Unwin, 1907), pp. 235–48; 283–364.

4. See Aziz Ahmad, *Studies in Islamic Culture in the Indian Environment* (Oxford: Clarendon Press, 1964), pp. 140–66.

5. See Clifford Geertz, *The Religion of Java* (Glencoe, Ill.: The Free Press, 1960); Marshall Hodgson, *The Venture of Islam* (Chicago: University of Chicago Press, 1974), 2:548–51, attempts to qualify Geertz's analysis of the syncretic developments in Indonesia.

now the most common form of religious belief. Even the Roman Catholic church now makes concessions to local African traditions; in the Protestant African churches in which authority has passed into the hands of the Africans, Christianity is being adapted to indigenous traditions. This is most marked in the "independent churches" in which pentecostal Christianity and local paganism are being amalgamated.[6]

Syncretism in the Movement of Tradition between Center and Periphery

Traditions undergo changes by the process of migration. The reception of an exogenous tradition inevitably modifies that tradition, particularly those traditions which cannot be put into codified form and divested of connotations. The traditional stock of engineering knowledge or of abstract, rigorously logical and rigorously empirical sciences may be transplanted without amalgamation with indigenous traditions. Literary, artistic, and religious traditions, which entail many assumptions which are not explicitly contained in the traditions, are more pliant in their encounter with indigenous traditions dealing with similar tasks. (The reception of a tradition in intact form is not a guarantee of an extension of that tradition in its immanent path of development. Reception of a tradition does not automatically produce creativity, extension, and elaboration.)

The reception of a tradition is affected by the receptive capacities or qualifications of the recipient. A recipient who has been born into the larger culture in which a particular tradition is indigenous and who has been brought up in the language through which the tradition is expressed will assimilate it differently from the ways in which it is assimilated by recipients to whom it is exogenous. This is true of migrations from one sector of a particular society to another sector of the same society, just as it is true of the migrations of a tradition from one territory of society to another.

Social strata have traditions which have become established within them; the movement of a tradition from one stratum to another not only changes the traditions of the recipient stratum, it also changes the tradition in the process of being transplanted. The movement of a tradition of a mode of speech or of a religious belief or of the understanding of literary works from one stratum with a long history of education in the culture of which the tradition has been a part to a stratum which has in the past been less educated in that culture and

6. See Bengt Sundkler, *Bantu Prophets in South Africa* (London: Lutterworth, 1948).

which has different traditions will produce changes in the moving tradition. Education, which is a transfer of tradition from the generation of possessors to a generation which is not yet in possession, is a process of implanting traditions which enable the recipients to receive further variations and elaborations of the tradition. Education disciplines a recipient by the inculcation of a tradition in the form and substance understood by the transmitter; it is also a process of selection of persons more capable of receiving the tradition as it has been presented. Yet despite discipline and selection, the transplantation cannot avoid the intervention of a change between the earlier and later states of the belief as it passes from transmitters to recipients. The changes might be syncretistic amalgamations; they might be immanent elaborations and adaptations. A certain amount of leakage is inevitable. Not all that is presented, even if with the deliberate intention that it should be reproduced in full, arrives at its destination. Much has to be offered to many for a tradition presented in an educational institution to continue. Much of what is presented fails to reach its target; even if it reaches the target, it fades from memory as schoolchildren grow up. Many of them retain only traces and dispositions from what was presented to them. Those who retain a large amount of what is presented to them, change the salience of the tradition in various ways and degrees. Part of the substance of the tradition is carried forward. The tradition is a stable one if it remains fairly constant in content and if it retains as many adherents of the various strata cf possessors as it had before. But in many generations, among those recipients who come into an ample and retentive possession, the diffuse matrix of beliefs, the "apperception mass," of the recipients changes the tradition in the course of its reception or while it is in possession.

The wider the discrepancy between the "apperception masses" of the transmitters and of the recipients, the greater the likelihood of modification of the tradition at the point of its reception and in the course of its possession. The transmission of traditions from one social stratum to another occurs in educational institutions and in preaching. Tradition is also transmitted from one generation to another in situations of personal intercourse and through perceptions, often distorted, across greater spatial distances. Yet, despite this leakage and modification in the course of transmission among strata, generations, regions, ethnic groups within a particular society, some of the tradition does reach its recipients. This movement of traditions is one of the sources of such cultural consensus as there is in societies. This very partial consensus is in its turn a support of the traditions received more or less as transmitted in those sections of the population which are more devoted to them and more preoccupied by them. Awareness that a traditional belief is affirmed and shared, even if only

in its most general outlines, by other sections of society fortifies thos
whose possession of the tradition is ampler and more differentiated

The consensus about traditions within a society is limited not onl
by restrictions as a result of unequal opportunities and incapacity bu
also by resistance. The resistance has many forms and motives. On
motive is the attachment to the traditions which are indigenous to th
particular sector of the society to which the alien tradition is pre
sented. Still another is the dislike of anything coming from the highe
strata and the refusal to grant the deference which is implied by ac
ceptance of the tradition from the upper strata. In some groups, espe
cially linguistic and ethnic groups, such resistance is accompanied by
an accentuation and reinterpretation of the indigenous tradition. Ir
purporting to revive or reinforce an indigenous tradition threatened by
a competing tradition, individuals transform the indigenous tradition
into a doctrine or into an ideology.

The resistance guarantees the heterogeneity of the cultural traditions. The heterogeneity increases the lability of traditions because it
presents alternatives and arouses implicit and sometimes explicit
criticisms of the traditions towards each other. Despite resistance, the
traditions of the various strata influence each other. Resistance does
not prevent syncretism; it is often a condition of syncretism. The
power of the "alien" traditions which are being resisted is too great to
be entirely blocked. Those who are resisting have already acquired
much of the traditions which they are resisting and the result is an
amalgamation of the remaining unobliterable "alien" tradition and the
reaffirmed, selectively reinterpreted indigenous tradition.

The same process of rejection, acceptance, and amalgamation occurs in the migration of traditions from one society to another.
Nationalistic reactionaries are often traditionalistic reactionaries.
They attempt to reconstitute the indigenous traditions as they were
before the appearance of the alien traditions. They reject the actually
existing syncretic traditions in favor of the traditions which are
alleged to have once existed in a pure form. The practiced beliefs of
the traditionalistic reactionaries are practically never identical with
those traditions they seek to reinstitute; the latter are very selectively
reconstructed. The revival of a tradition almost inevitably involves
changing the tradition.

Expansion of the Center within a Society

The center of a society can expand within that society. The center
may expand—or contract—in its influence over its own peripheries. It
does so by changes in its coercive power, by changes in its ecological
and economic domination, and by changes in the authority which it
exercises over them. These latter changes may be a function of

hanges in beliefs, desires, and possibilities originating in the center r they can be a result of demands emanating from the periphery.

One of the most striking changes in modern societies is the increase n the power and authority of the center over its own periphery and in he simultaneous increase in the power and authority of the periphery ver the center of its own society. This diminishes the distance between center and periphery.[7] One of the phenomena of this narrowing f the distance between center and periphery is the change in the ubstance of traditions. Some traditions, particular to a region, village, town, occupation, or ethnic or religious community are lost in his process as a common culture is formed. The parochial traditions o not wholly disappear but they become attenuated, surviving sometimes for reassertion on ceremonial occasions, sometimes by amalamation with the culture which emanates from or which is imposed y the center.

The great migrations from Europe to the United States in the nineteenth and early twentieth centuries brought into a society previously English and Protestant in its high culture very great numbers f persons from eastern, central, and southern Europe, many of them Roman Catholic, Orthodox, or Jewish in religion and nearly all utterly gnorant of the English language. The American variant of the English anguage which had previously been diverging from the British stream hereupon underwent further modification. The immigrants and their descendants in the course of two generations lost their mother ongues and much of the imagery associated with them and acquired a new language which was different in many respects from the English previously spoken in the United States. The process was a relatively slow one. The process of change in self-designation also took several generations and many descendants of immigrants lost their sense of connection with the nationality of their ancestors. With this went a oss of sense of affinity, a loss of culinary traditions, convivial customs, apothegmatic wisdom of life, and celebratory ceremonies. They ceased to follow to the same extent their traditional occupations, and some of their traditional attitudes towards work were also modified.[8]

In the United States the program of Americanization which was much talked about and recommended in the first quarter of the twentieth century was intended to incorporate this immigrant periphery and to bring it to share the tradition of the center in a manner appropriate to the immigrants' circumstances. Some of the immigrant groups went further than others in the renunciation of their au-

---

7. See Shils, *Center and Periphery*, pp. 3–16.
8. The linguistic concomitants of these changes in traditions are described in H. L. Mencken, *The American Language*, 4th ed. (New York: Knopf, 1936), *The American Language: Supplement I* (New York: Knopf, 1945), and *The American Language: Supplement II* (New York: Knopf, 1948).

tochthonous traditions when they left their native countries. Som
became "Americanized" more speedily than others.

Nonetheless, the attenuation of the traditions of the immigrants wa
not unilinear nor was it very evenly distributed. In most of the sub
sections of the periphery, there was dispute about the desirability o
"assimilation." Nonetheless, some degree of assimilation could no
be avoided, and those who resisted or were immune became isolated.

The establishment of compulsory, free public education did a grea
deal to enfeeble the adherence to parochial traditions. The changes i
communication in consequence of nearly universal literacy whic
allowed a national press or a nationally uniform press to be read
technology which supplied inexpensive radio and television receivers
and political changes which made the central government mor
significant as a source of commands and services and as a focus c
attention have also, in the course of displacing attention from paro
chial things onto national and international objects, lessened adher
ence to parochial and ancestral traditions of speech, styles of life an
belief.[9]

The changes in parochial or sectional traditions are not confined t
formerly and still peripheral sections of society. The traditions of th
center change too. The Western center pays less attention to its prio
cultural traditions. Populistic and egalitarian attitudes among politi
cians, a reduction in the pomp of office, a belief in the need to flatte
the prejudices of the electorate to whom the political elite is mor
visible than in the past contribute to the reduction of the distance
between center and periphery. In intellectual culture the increase i
the numbers of and proportions of persons receiving secondary an
higher education have diffused elements of high cultural traditions i
sectors of society where they were little possessed before—except fo
biblical knowledge—while the educated public which shared knowl
edge of the ancient classics and the main works of world litera
ture and their own national literature has become so attenuate
that the general culture of a university teacher is frequently littl
different from that of the ordinary intellectually unintereste
graduate. The eradication of the boundaries between high art an
illustration and decoration, a similar eradication of the boundarie
between literature, especially dramatic literature, and entertainmen
are also indications of the approximation of center and periphery an
the retraction of the adherence of the earlier traditions of the center.

The formation of a common culture entails renunciations and ac
quisitions of traditions. Each sector takes over something of the
others' traditions, each in consequence acquires a culture differen

9. See Shils, "The Theory of Mass Society," in *Center and Periphery*, pp
91–107; Eugen Weber, *Peasants into Citizens* (Palo Alto: Stanford Universit
Press, 1977); also Richard Hoggart, *The Uses of Literacy* (London: Chatto an
Windus, 1957), pp. 27 ff.

from what its predecessors had. It acquires an image of its own past which it did not have before.

The changes which each undergoes differ from endogenously instigated changes. They are not primarily products of logical reasoning, of moral and aesthetic judgment, although these factors are not entirely without weight. Traditions from a foreign environment are renounced because they are too difficult to reenact in circumstances to which the traditions have little immediately apparent reference. It is difficult in an urban industrial setting to produce and participate in festivities which refer to events in the annual agricultural cycle. It is difficult to maintain attitudes towards tools which have been used in crafts like blacksmithing when the craft is no longer practiced. Other traditions seem to be more fitting to the new situation. They are likely to be available already in the conduct and precepts of persons who are already established.

When the center expands in its powers, it dominates the situation of the periphery. It institutes new conditions to which those resident in the periphery must adapt themselves. Its greater power is evident in its actual enforcement of these new situations. Its beliefs are made more persuasive by the power of their adherents. The combination of the power of the expanding center and the incapacity of the leaders of the subcenters and peripheries to maintain their autonomy increases the persuasiveness of the tradition associated with the newly ascendant center. Immigrants to the city from the countryside and from foreign countries have very weak defenses; the traditions to which they adhered before have no authorities near at hand to uphold them; they are outside the society which affirmed them and which presented to the individual a consensus which was difficult to challenge.

The center when it is effectively expanding controls the institutions of communication: schools, churches, and, if the society is a literate one, many of the organs for the presentation of representations and interpretations of the world. These all speak in the language of the center and its behalf. Social advancement to positions of authority, eminence, and renumeration is gained through submission to the demands and standards of the center; these lead to the acceptance of its standards and then to the traditions and traditional images of the past which support those standards. The traditions of the periphery become fainter under these circumstances in which there are incentives for acquiring the traditions of the center and losses from refusal to accept them.

Expansion of the Center beyond Its Own Society

Traditions change when a center expands beyond the existing boundaries of its own society into other societies. (The difference between the internal expansion of the center and its external expansion is not a fundamental one; the two types of expansion have much in common.) When one society extends its power over another society by military conquest, it weakens the self-confidence of the subjugated society and weakens therewith its attachment to its own traditions. Exclusively economic expansion has a less damaging effect on the traditions which it encounters.

One of the most successful expansions of a center is the expansion of Islam from Mecca into the realms of other societies and cultures of Asia and Africa. Not too different are the Graeco-Roman expansion, the Christian expansion into northern, western, central, and Eastern Europe, and the Western European expansion. The expansion of Islam, militant, and intellectually and organizationally superior to the rest of the sparsely settled, intellectually and organizationally weak, Arabian peninsula, was a simple matter. The expansion into the realm of Hellenistic and Graeco-Roman traditions was more complex. The intellectual tradition of this area, pagan and Christian, was still very strong, while militarily the eastern Roman Empire and what remained of the western Empire were weak. The consequence was military triumph, and the diminution of adherence to the hitherto dominant traditions of the area to very small enclaves. The expansion of the Islamic center replaced those previously dominant traditions. The changes did not take place only at the periphery; Islamic traditions also changed in the course of their expansion. Greek philosophy and science entered into Islamic thought. Islamic theology had to adapt itself to these, undergoing the changes necessary to incorporate them. It was little different in the case of the triumphant Christianity in its European expansion.

Power exercises a charismatic force of its own and draws in the wake of its cultural traditions those who have been overcome by it. This is additional to whatever cultural institutions the conquering power establishes through the use of its coercive power. The fixation of the language of the conqueror as the language of governmental business in administration and adjudication compels a decision on the part of some of the conquered to follow their careers through the acquisition of the linguistic traditions of the conquerer. Administrators, judges, and advocates drawn from the conquered peoples—this happens almost invariably—become the instruments of foreign authority and also become agents of the alien traditions. Their proximity to authority and their awareness of the advantages of serving authority lead them further into the acquisition of intellectual traditions carried in the foreign rulers' language. The establishment of schools for children and for professional training extends the reign of the rulers' traditions beyond the mastery of language and beyond the stratum of indigenous "collaborators."

A rather similar process occurs through commercial contact between societies. "Factors" appear to serve as intermediaries between the penetrating and the penetrated societies. In Africa and in Asia, these were most often in coastal settlements which became trading forts and ports; they also occurred inland although in the less dense settlements the factors did not begin to acquire the alien traditions to the same extent which they did in more densely settled places. Nonetheless once the factors acquired the language of the foreign merchants they too gradually acquired some of the traditions made accessible through language. Missionaries from the dominating society urged the process forward. They appeared a short time after the soldiers and merchants.

The cultural expansion of the center contains its own entelechy. It is therefore capable of movement without being drawn after the military and economic constituents of the center. The periphery, which is untouched militarily and economically such as was the case of Japan, can reach out towards the cultural traditions of the center. The Japanese assimilation of the traditions of the world center of Western Europe was very selective, not only because Japan retained its sovereignty and could exercise some choice of models in its emulation. The traditions of some fields of activity were not sought at all or very slightly; others were sought and segregated; in still others there was a modest amalgamation. A form of syncretism was the result.

The patterns resulting from the syncretism in a peripheral society of its own traditions and those received or sought from the metropolitan center are unable to reach a point of total fusion. Acceptance is always very uneven; those particular traditions which are most completely accepted are also usually segregated. In matters of religion in India, for example, attraction to Christianity and even conversion did not entail complete disavowal of the indigenous religious traditions. Domestic conditions prohibited a complete break; women were less tempted by the alien religious and domestic traditions than were the men who had contact with them outside the home. In none of the countries of Asia or Africa where European traditions were received did those traditions ever replace the indigenous religions; they did not even replace the traditions of indigenous medicine, although it was in science and technology that they became most effectively implanted. In prose literature and publicistic writing, in new genres like the short story as it was developed by Mérimée, Maupassant, and Chekhov, in the naturalistic novel, the European tradition was overlaid on the indigenous tradition of tales and novels. In publicistic writing, which was a wholly new genre, the acceptance of the European traditions was most extensive. In black Africa, which had no written culture prior to the coming of the Europeans and Islam, the replacement of indigenous traditions occurred only in a very small part of the population. Those traditions which were accepted by the small minority underwent modification.

The scientific traditions which were accepted became largely sterilized and lost the fertility which they had possessed in Europe because the oral and the unspoken parts of the scientific tradition were less transferable than the written part. Thus far it has only been in Japan that the scientific tradition after its transplantation regained its fertility; in India this was less so. Although a good number of Indians abroad have risen to the very highest levels of their respective branches of scientific work, the efflorescence of the modern scientific tradition has not been as rich as the resources of talent.

When the center has expanded into societies which already possessed traditions linked to those of the center itself by remote common origins—the expansion of Austria-Hungary into the Balkans which were, except for some Islamic pockets, already Christian—the result was an acceptance of the central culture by the educated classes and the production of a creative culture which continued a fusion of the culture of the center and its own peripheral culture. Poland, Bohemia, Moravia, Slovakia produced a vigorous literature which was a combination of peripheral subject matters and central genres, guided by standards of assessment very much like those of the dominant Continental centers. The traditions of France, Germany, and Austria were relatively easily assimilated in these societies. Poland in its educated strata became a creative center more or less on the level of the Netherlands and Belgium. In philosophy, literature, scholarship, it produced works of the first order, Hungary and Bohemia likewise. There is nothing anomalous or disharmonious in the assimilation of the intellectual traditions of the center when the periphery is already so close to it in its fundamental religious traditions. The amalgamation which occurs entails little deflection of the immanent potentialities of the particular traditions taken over from the center. The preconditions for their future development lie in the already accepted cultural traditions.

Nevertheless once they become established in the peripheral country, they begin to radiate into the other spheres which had previously been resistant to the direct incorporation of alien traditions. The peripheral traditions retain much vitality, even resilience and adaptive capacities. They are capable of expansion back into the center. This was what happened in the early acquisition of knowledge of Japanese and Chinese religion by the Jesuits. The expansion of the traditions of the West was also an expansion of the traditions of the Orient in the opposite direction.

In the main, when the center of one country expands into another country it encounters an established society with its own traditions. The tenacity of tradition is exemplified very well by the high degree of impermeability of large parts of these indigenous cultures. Except in scientific knowledge, syncretism is the furthest point reached in the movement of traditions. It is only when the expansion takes place into a territory which is very sparsely settled by any society or by societies technologically and militarily very weak that there is no syncretism of indigenous and exogenous traditions. It is then that the traditions may be transferred and implanted with little change. This is what happened in North America and Australasia. But once implanted, the traditions, if they are implanted in a society of some creative power, tend to run off in their own direction. In the American colonies and the United States, the practical bent of the dissenters became the dominant tradition which flourished for several centuries and has still not run completely aground. The theological and literary traditions on the other hand became ossified and did not develop for about two centuries. The fissiparous traditions of Protestant sectarians became very effervescent but they did not become theologically fruitful. The literary tradition broke out of its imitativeness and moved off in a distinctive path in the period after the Civil War. The scientific tradition had a course much like that of the literary tradition. It was largely imitative in its new environment and it was also very parsimoniously cultivated. It was reanimated after the Civil War partly by indigenous stirrings of a new generation and partly by becoming a periphery of the great animation and expansion of the scientific tradition in Germany. It was from about the turn of the century that the scientific tradition became fertile, and thereafter it has grown continuously.

The indigenous occupants of the territory into which the expansion from the center occurs have only a limited number of alternatives. One is selective syncretism which entails modifying their own traditions and modifying the traditions of the center. Another is withdrawal and self-maintenance as some of the Indians in South America were able to do, at least for a long time. This they could do as long as there were physical barriers to the invasion from the center and as long as in their native habitat they possessed certain technological and military advantages over the invaders. Once they became overrun, the benefits of withdrawal into isolation were lost to them.

Demoralization was the alternative forced on the Red Indians of North America. They lost the ecological conditions for the cultivation of their own religious and political traditions which were connected with hunting and with warfare against approximate equals; when they were deprived of the vast, open territories they required for their hunting economy and were forced to fight against much better organized, more expert, and more powerfully armed enemies, they succumbed. Their traditions deteriorated in the sense that they observed them less and less; their grasp of their traditions became less vital and they could not be adapted to the new circumstances of a settled, territorially confined life. The inability to hunt and conduct warfare caused the attrition of the traditions connected with those activities.

They did not assimilate the traditions of the center. They lapsed into torpor.

Expansion of the Center: Resistance

No large society can be entirely homogeneous in its traditions. At best its different parts share certain fundamental traditions. Such a society is bound to have different parts. The distribution of natural resources imposes a spatial differentiation of occupations; a complex set of desires requires very different kinds of goods, each produced by a special occupational group; different talents and different tastes and not least the fact that many large societies have been created through conquest or federation and have attracted immigrants—all contribute to the variety of traditions in the society. Since traditions are often addressed to particular activities and localities and since their area of diffusion seldom extends to the entire society, there is bound to be much diversity alongside of some consensus in the traditions.

The center develops its own high culture and, as it expands in power, authority, and attention, it seeks to impose its own culture in varying degrees on the rest of the society. This has become especially marked—until the recent abdication of the center in the United States—in modern liberal democratic societies which have prided themselves on their pluralism. But even before the expansive, collectivistic state, rulers were concerned about an excessive heterogeneity of their population; heretics and rebels were always thought to merit extirpation. It is contrary to the nature of organized politics to tolerate its unconstitutional replacement. (There are few states which have gone so far in their deliberate toleration that they have willingly allowed this to happen.) It is not necessary to go as far as the maxim of the Peace of Augsburg which declared *cujus regio, ejus religio* in order to give expression to the expansive tendency of a center to further the consensus which 'legitimates' it. But it never succeeds completely. It fails partly because of deficient technological and institutional means. Poor communication, poor transportation, an impoverished and fragmentary educational system, illiteracy, all make difficult the universal diffusion within the society of the traditions which are necessary for the attainment of the legitimatory consensus.

There is however another cause of this failure of the center to obliterate the parochial traditions and to inculcate either its own tradition or a newly constructed doctrine which embodies some of the older tradition. This is active resistance to the intellectual center, not just indifference to what is offered, although this is important too. Efforts are sometimes made in the peripheries of society to resist the introduction of the traditions of the center; such initial resistance is more rare than resistance after some amount of the alien tradition of the center has been absorbed. In many cases it occurs long after the process of assimilation has gone a considerable distance.

Resistance to the Expansion of the Internal Center

Plurality of traditions is a characteristic feature of large societies. Their constitutions may make no provision for it and their political rulers might make untiring efforts to prevent the plurality of opinions, especially on political, social, and religious matters from being expressed, but all they can do is to repress their public expression and to prohibit or hamper the institutions through which such views could be propagated. The plurality of opinions in modern societies is a result of many causes and reasons but, whatever they are, the plurality exists and cannot be extirpated. One of the reasons for this unextirpability is that the opinions have become traditions. Once an opinion becomes given, it is difficult to crush. Human beings become attached to their traditions and suffer great pains rather than renounce them under external pressure. But even where they would renounce them they do not do so easily. The presence of other traditions offers temptations; it also arouses resistance.

The resistance to the traditions which the center of society offers and attempts to impose is manifold. It sometimes results from indifference bordering on hostility, not primarily to the substance of the tradition but to the authoritative mode and source of its presentation. Indifference may also be a result of incompetence and of sheer uninterestedness in the content of the tradition. Religiously insensate persons may be obdurate in rejecting the religious traditions of the center or accept only a smattering of the tradition which is presented to them in school or by their parents. The resistance to an offered or imposed alien central tradition might also be a result of attachment to the tradition already possessed. The traditions of consumption and conviviality in one social class might be deliberately maintained in the face of an alternative tradition which is held up as the "right thing to do." The arrangement of the parts of meals, the kinds of food eaten,[10] the hours of their consumption[11]—table manners are traditional matters and they have spread outward within Western societies over centuries.[12] They have not spread throughout their respective societies. There are sections of the population which persist in their

10. J. C. Drummond, and A. Wilbraham, *The Englishman's Food* (London: Jonathan Cape, 1939).
11. Arnold Palmer, *Movable Feasts* (London: Oxford University Press, 1952).
12. Norbert Elias, *Über den Prozess der Zivilization: Soziogenetische und psychogenetische Untersuchungen,* vol. 1, *Wandlungen des Verhaltens in den weltlichen Oberschichten des Abendlandes* (Basel: Haus zum Falken, 1939), pp. 110–74.

own traditional patterns of conviviality and consumption; in these sections the refusal of the recommended "superior" pattern is a product of an insistence on the dignity of one's own ethnic or class community and of a refusal to accept the derogation implicit in the assimilation of a pattern presented from the center.

Certain ethnic communities which lived according to their own traditions while more or less accepting incorporation into modern states, have reached a point where they have revolted against further association. The Basques and Catalans in Spain, the Bretons and Corsicans in France, the French-Canadians in Canada, the Welsh and Scots in the United Kingdom, some of the blacks in the United States, and the Flemings in Belgium have all in recent years undertaken to assert the dignity of their own traditions against growing power and pervasiveness of the center in societies to which they had in the past submitted. The expansion of the culture of the center has in the twentieth century been more engulfing in consequence of the ecological integration of societies, the ascendancy of national over local and regional markets, and the attraction of the content of mass communication. The result has been the reaffirmation of traditions which had been receding. Some demand separation and the formation of an independent sovereign state; others demand legal and constitutional acknowledgment of cultural autonomy. Most of them demand the right to maintain their own cultural and linguistic traditions. Many do not go so far, but under vigorous leadership testify to their attachment to some of their weakening traditions.

Resistance against an External Center

Resistance to military conquest is a common occurrence; it is a resistance which has some connection with attachment to national or tribal traditions although there are other motives as well, such as the attachment to the exercise of authority and of ascendancy within one's own society, the protection of material goods from despoliation, and the desire to avoid the humiliation of submitting to a foreign power who has triumphed at arms. Traditions enter into each of these valued conditions and some of the resistance to conquest can therefore be said to have a motive in the protection of tradition.

If the conquest is successful, the subjugated people settles down to life under an authority which cannot be broken, and some assimilation of the alien tradition begins very soon. Apart from active resisters who engage in guerilla warfare against the conqueror, those who submit usually do so incompletely. Even where they accept the traditions which the conqueror offers or imposes on them through education and opportunities to enter into superior occupations, their own traditions remain in shrivelled and clandestine form. They persist for a long time in the privacy of the family and in syncretic combination with the traditions of the conqueror. Language and religion in such conditions of silent resistance may be taken over from the conqueror but they undergo changes in the course of assimilation. The sense of nationality which they acquire is not the same as the sense of nationality at the center. These important central traditions, where they are accepted at all, are warped by the persistence of the supplanted or suppressed traditions. Quiet rejections which are not as overt or extreme as armed rebellion or guerilla warfare occur on occasion. The propensity of the Welsh for Methodism and the special quality of Welsh English are modes of modifying an alien tradition. When alien traditions are rejected outright, as in the case of Great Russian traditions in the Baltic societies, the traditions of the center remain unchanged and those of the periphery also remain relatively unchanged, but the task of defense against supplantation or suppression forces certain changes in the endangered traditions. Elements once accepted and then allowed to pass into disuse may be revived in a form different from what they were before they yielded to the assimilation of the rulers' traditions. The emphasis placed upon ritual separation in Talmudic Judaism even prior to the redaction of the Mishnah was at least in part a response to the pressure from the successive Egyptian, Babylonian, Hellenistic, Graeco-Roman pagan, and Roman Christian centers which saturated most of the periphery around the mostly dispersed Jewish society. When Islam expanded, a similar challenge had to be met. The movement from biblical Judaism, much of which was constructed in the brief periods of Jewish sovereignty, to Talmudical Judaism was an immanent development from the canon of the Torah but the particular direction of the immanent development was to some extent a mode of resistance to the pressure of the alien centers.

It is alleged that the earth is becoming a single community. This may be accepted as an approximation—a very rough one; the truth of the statement is confined to the potentialities of the existing technology of transportation and communication. Beyond that, telluric humanity does not form a single community and never will. In the 1920s, a German, Müller-Freienfels, wrote a book on *Die Amerikanisierung des Geistes*. Since that time, the process has gone on apace and certain institutions and practices are now more common to the United States and other countries than was the case in the nineteenth century before the emergence in the previously colonial countries of Asia, Africa, and Latin America of the determination to "modernize" themselves, by which they mean to make themselves more like the United States, Western Europe, and in a few respects like the Soviet Union.

Despite all these technological potentialities of communication and transportation and the "transfer of technology," the societies of the earth are very heterogeneous among themselves. They are very heterogeneous in many respects and above all in their traditions. Even when they seek to become like some other country, which means adopting the traditions of that country, they cannot do so. They are prevented from doing so, in some cases, by their poverty, perhaps to an even greater extent they are prevented from doing so by their own traditions. There is an unmistakable tenacity in traditions; they can be modified, and they are continuously modified, by endogenously necessitated adaptations, by immanent critical scrutiny and revision, by changes in saliency of certain elements. They are also changed by their encounter with other hitherto alien traditions. Some traditions have been obliterated in this encounter; they have usually been the weaker ones, not having been subjected to intellectual rationalization and being adhered to by small populations which were weak technologically and militarily as well as intellectually. Those which were intellectually strong, that is rationalized and having a substantial intellectual embodiment in writing, have been very durable. Although the societies in which these traditions arose and flourished might have come upon very hard times and succumbed to militarily and techno- logically stronger and better organized societies, the traditions did not disappear. They have been relegated to more obscure parts of the societies but they have reappeared constantly in revivals and in amal- gamation and they still do so.

The prospects of a unitary and uniform mankind are not great in the foreseeable future.

Changes in Traditions and Changes in Circumstances

Traditions change because the circumstances to which they refer change. Traditions, to survive, must be fitting to the circumstances in which they operate and to which they are directed. If the technology of an occupation changes, the traditions which govern its use also change. Traditions may be adapted or discarded when their possess- ors move from countryside to town and, instead of living among plants, trees, birds, and animals, live in paved spaces where none of these are present as significant factors. The traditions surrounding these objects and activities leave only a few phrases behind. They might still survive in the countryside but there too they face altered conditions in consequence of changes in agricultural technology, the disappearance of horses and blacksmithing, the use of pesticides and herbicides, changes in the world and national markets, and the greater productivity of agriculture as a result of the use of artificial fertilizers, better strains of seeds, and the use of machines for sowing and reaping.

For the urban population, changes in methods of industrial production and in industrial organization and the emergence and expansion of tertiary occupations, some of them quite new, have also changed the economic environment in which much of life is lived. The increased productivity of industry and agriculture has increased the amount of leisure time, and technological innovations in transportation and communication have likewise brought with them new possibilities of recreation and entertainment. These changes in circumstances are the changes in the referents of traditions. The traditions as received do not deal with these new situations, and dealing with them "effectively" is a condition of the continued acceptance of traditions. Analogies with the circumstances prior to the change, emphasis on the common features of circumstances before and after the changes, and efforts to pass over the novel features were characteristic ways by which proponents of these traditions met the challenge. Other proponents sought to adapt their traditions to the new circumstances by amalgamating them with hitherto separate traditions which were about the new circumstances. This is what was done by many Protestant Christian churches in the nineteenth and twentieth centuries in the face of the new circumstances of the recently urbanized population drawn into industry.

Established traditions contain in varying ways potentialities for development. New circumstances sometimes, not invariably, arouse the imagination, and the logical powers working on existing traditions perceive hitherto unstressed applications fitting to the new circumstances. The stress placed on the Sermon on the Mount in Christian social thought in the nineteenth century is an immanent extension and adaptation of tradition to new circumstances without breaking outside it.

We may also speak of a change in tradition when a tradition loses its adherents—although the adherents who remain, in greatly reduced numbers, hold to it without modification. The adoption of a new tradition in replacement of the old is a change in tradition; the replacement is never complete and the outcome is more or less of a fusion or amalgamation. The increased adherence to secularism in the later decades of the nineteenth century was an acceptance of a tradition divergent from Christian tradition in essential respects. At the same time secularism contained traditional features of Christian belief in its piety of tone, its reverence for the saints and spiritual-intellectual heroes of humanity, its evolutionary perfectionist outlook, and its moderate humanitarianism. In these cases it is not the substance of the traditions which changes but rather the scale of their adherence.

The quantitative recession of a belief usually changes its content; similarly the expansion in the adherence of a belief brings with it changes in substance. The change in the circumstances of its adherents also modifies their attitude towards authority.

New circumstances and the heightened prominence of the new objects disclosed in those new circumstances change traditions. They do so not only because they first compel modifications in action, as in urban residence and industrial employment, and then engender adaptation of the traditions by reinterpretation or press for partial discard and partial replacement. The new circumstances bring before minds the existence of previously unforeseen possibilities and stir them to go on to imagine further possibilities still unrealized. Discoveries in a field of scientific activity may disclose possibilities to artists and writers which they had not seen before. Emile Zola's idea of writing a novel in the naturalistic style, describing accumulating changes in somber detail, was affected by the methods and results of the meticulous observation of naturalists and evolutionists. The breaking of the surface of consciousness by psychoanalysis and other doctrines laying bare the irrational character of many human activities and the illogical patterns of thought below the surface of everyday, matter-of-fact discourse modified the ideas of literary men and women like Marcel Proust, James Joyce, and Virginia Woolf about the proper mode and subject matter of artistic representation. The laying open of Africa to explorers and colonizers was followed by the bringing back to Europe of works of African art which were assimilated into and changed greatly the tradition of European painting and sculpture.

Prophets and charismatic figures change the tradition of their societies by ethical commandments and by their exemplary conduct. Their words and the images of their personalities enter into the world of symbolic constructions; therewith they act directly on the conduct of other persons in their own time and locality or indirectly through innumerable intermediaries over large spaces and at long distances in time. Their teaching and examples thicken, through the multitudinousness of these intermediaries, the dense circumstances to which those who have not yet been touched by the traditions must accommodate themselves. A pagan in fifth-century Roman society had a very different environment of belief from that of a pagan of the second century. Thus beliefs also become circumstances.

There are also other kinds of circumstances. They differ from these circumstances which are constituted by the profuse presence of certain beliefs. These other kinds of circumstances are striated and pervaded with beliefs but the beliefs are significant, not directly as beliefs, but insofar as they affect actions which offer opportunities to acquire those resources from others which are necessary to maintain life in a sufficient and appropriate style. These circumstances— sometimes called "material" or "social" circumstances—are the circumstances of the market with its special mode of allocating goods and services or they are the circumstances created by the exercise of legitimate authority and coercive power or both together. These circumstances are themselves a product of and embodiment of traditions and they could not exist without certain traditions of beliefs, but they themselves are not traditions of beliefs. They are the "hard facts of life"; nowadays they are thought to be more compelling than the environment of beliefs, although this is not true.

The circumstances of the allocation of opportunities and rewards also change. They are sometimes changed by coercive actions; they are sometimes changed by the decisions of legitimate authorities; they are also changed by the decisions of numerous participants as buyers and sellers in the market. In all of these types of changes in circumstances, traditions are being modified not only on the part of those who must live in the face of the circumstances but also on the part of those who are the circumstances. Coercive power, legitimate authority, and the market are actions of human beings, action performed under the guidance of tradition and reason and under the impulsion of desire in the pursuit of ends which are often given by tradition. Whatever their guiding or impelling forces, these actions make up the circumstances of action of multitudes of persons; hence, when these actions change, they compel modifications of patterns of belief and action, sometimes very long-lasting ones.

The actions of coercive power which compel modifications of action through threats of physical restraint and damage are sometimes permitted or even required within a framework set by tradition; sometimes they may be arbitrary in the sense that they are not restrained or prescribed by legal or unwritten traditions[13] but are permitted within limits set through tradition. These actions entailed in the exercise of coercive power are often stereotyped and traditional, sometimes they are modifications of tradition. For example a new tactic or strategy in warfare might be such a modification. They change the circumstances of action and compel departures from tradition by those who would survive or withstand. Legitimate authority too may be exercised in a mode prescribed by tradition, and the content of its exercise may also be prescribed by tradition. Legislation is a common form of the modification of action by legitimate authority; the legislative may enact ideas which have become tradition in parts of society, but, once enacted, it starts a process of changing the traditions of the rest of society through changing the circumstances of action. Likewise in the market, where for the most part myriads of individuals are making more or less rational decisions to realize their own objectives as economically as possible in the face of circumstances, departures from and modifications of traditions are constantly being made. New machines are being invented and they are being introduced into production; new methods of organization of labor in production are also often being made. These create new circumstances of action and require changes in traditions in techniques of work, in methods of marketing, and so on.

13. See Weber, *Wirtschaft und Gesellschaft*, 1:130.

7   Patterns of Change and Stability in Tradition

The Bearers of Traditions

The topography of beliefs of a society is constantly changing. And the beliefs themselves are constantly changing in substance. It is as if with the changing of the tides the water also changes in its chemical composition. If we speak about the traditions of religious belief or of scientific belief or of economic policy, we speak both of changes in adherence and of changes in substance. This is as it must be since traditions are both part of the realm of symbolic constructions or objectivations (called World 3 by Professor Popper) and they are integral to human action and hence to the arrangements of actions into social structures.

The adherence to a tradition is a fact of the structure of society. To put it differently, adherence is the social structure which possesses the tradition. It is the affirmative, receptive audiences of the tradition in its various changed and unchanged forms. The fortunes of traditions vary with the scale of that adherence. A tradition expands or contracts in its adherence; both of these changes could occur concurrently with unchanged and changed contents of the tradition. The same beliefs and practices could be adhered to by many persons or by few; traditions could in principle remain the same while their adherence increases or decreases. The changes in adherence are changes in scale and composition. Sometimes the increase is accompanied by the assumption by the new adherents that the belief which they are newly acquiring is the same as it had been in the past. Of course they are never in a position to know whether this is true; how could they know, if they are not scholars, what the belief was before they received it? It is common, when a tradition changes, for some of the adherence of that tradition in its relatively unchanged form to persist, often on a reduced scale.

The influence of a belief is a phenomenon of adherence. When one tradition loses adherence, other traditions gain adherence.

Human beings have to adhere to some beliefs; it is not in their nature to do otherwise, short of regression to idiocy or advancing to the highest state of the mind, in which it is emptied of most of its content.

They must believe something about the world in which they live, both about what they see and what they do not see. They renounce one tradition in order to accept a variant of that tradition or quite another tradition. They do not accept or reject at random. They have reasons—often poor ones—for their assimilation and divestiture of traditions. They swell the mob or they desert the dwindling band, and these acts of swelling and desertion are performed in accordance with reasons; they are acts of the mind; it is the nature of minds to know and have beliefs about the world in which their possessors live.

The Boundaries of a Tradition: Families of Traditions

Traditions are defined and recognized by their adherence as well as by their substantive content. They are also defined as sets of beliefs held or espoused over some generations having in common certain themes of interpretation, certain conceptions, certain assessments. A tradition can have a changing body of adherents, changing in size, changing in membership, and changing in their beliefs too. The boundaries of a tradition are in one respect the boundaries of adherence of collectivities defined by their community of beliefs; in another respect they are the boundaries of symbolic constructions. The boundaries of a community of believers or adherents are loosely related to the boundaries of sets of beliefs.

Adherents and observers give names to traditions which distinguish them from other traditions, with which they have affinities and contrasts. This is not simply a matter of analytical definition and of the convenience of defining a subject matter for rational discourse and academic study. The boundaries and overlapping of traditions are problems to those who espouse and oppose them. Collectivities define themselves partly in terms of their traditions of belief, which they regard as constitutive of themselves. Even collectivities which define themselves in terms of "objective" features such as pigmentation, or occupation, or income, or location, or biological filiation do so through the medium of beliefs, and the beliefs are matters of tradition.

The particular objects of beliefs may be clearly distinguishable but the beliefs about them are less easy to separate from each other. Not only are there different beliefs about the same objects but there are many objects to be judged, and much of each of these judgments might be a tradition or part of a tradition. These many judgments of different objects are grouped together by the individuals who render them and by other persons in their society. Individuals designate themselves not only by their primordial qualities but by their beliefs as well, and these designations and self-classifications refer to a more comprehensive outlook. These comprehensive outlooks subsume and guide many particular judgments of particular things and events. These particular judgments are sometimes logically consistent with each other but not always, by any means. There is a tendency in human beings to think that one judgment goes with another general disposition of belief which infuses their judgments of a set of objects which are of concern to them. More important, they acquire these similar combinations by education in similar schools, by membership in families with similar combinations, by living in a society in which such combinations are shared by many persons. These combinations acquire names; they are called liberal, conservative, socialist, progressivist, rationalist, Christian, Protestant, Catholic, Orthodox, Marxist, reformist, classical, avant-garde, and the like. In any society, the combinations designated by these names overlap with each other, even though in some cases the adherents try to distinguish themselves by sharply defined boundaries from the adherents of traditions which are very similar to their own.

Sometimes efforts are made to formulate one of these combinations in a way which will make it internally consistent and which will show it to be separate from all the others, but these efforts usually have no obligatory standing. The combinations which they construct are seldom made official and, even when they are officially promulgated, there are, within any collectivity officially so defined, numerous variations from the officially prescribed version. Earlier combinations show through the prevailing ones; individuals warp the prevailing combination into a form more congenial to themselves. Thus, in a given society, even a quite consensual one, there will be not only some widely divergent separate traditions about the same objects but there will be a number of traditions of combinations of judgments which have much in common among themselves but which also vary from each other in the emphasis which they lay on the different elements or judgments of the objects which make up the world of the members of the society.

Most traditions of belief in society are nearly always vague—the beliefs of the exact sciences and closely related intellectual activities are exceptional. In thought about society and morals, most of the constituent concepts are ambiguous. The combination of judgments formed from these concepts are also loosely integrated; there is furthermore rarely complete agreement except with regard to a few officially promulgated dogmas, and even these are subject to variant interpretations since they too are vague; notable individuals find some faults in them and try to repair them. That is why the protection of orthodoxy is such a difficult task for those spiritual custodians who think that uniformity of subscription to a dogmatically proclaimed orthodoxy is imperative. Such consensus as there is in a relatively consensual society is an overlay of overlapping combinations of beliefs. The fact that these combinations of beliefs have been formed as traditions renders the relationships among them even more complicated than it would be if each set of judgments were freshly worked out in each decade. The very suggestion of such a repromulgation of sets of beliefs in each decade shows how real such traditions are.

Within any society and any tradition, precision of reception diminishes from the center to the periphery. Most of the adherents of a tradition have a blurred apprehension of the tradition which they affirm. Who among Anglicans knows all the Thirty-nine Articles and understands the arguments for them? Who among ordinary Roman Catholics who are not theologians or church historians knows the theological arguments which support any of the dogmas of the church? Who among Marxists knows the intricacies of the argument regarding the "falling rate of profit" or the "increasing poverty of the working classes"? There is no one alive who knows all the numerous propositions, problems, and hypotheses which, together with its ethos, are the tradition of science.

Much of the substance of an intellectual tradition is known only in part or imperfectly by any one individual or even a group of individuals among its adherents, and yet it is among the intellectual transmitters and receivers and developers of tradition that a tradition can be seen most precisely. And it is in that stratum of transmitters and receivers that the disagreements and deliberate modifications are most likely to occur; varying emphases and idiosyncratic "slants" are the common fate of intellectual traditions in the course of their transmissions, receptions, and possessions.

If a tradition is not an intellectual one with a tendency towards amalgamation and rationalization, the boundaries of its constitution and adherence and the lines of transmission are inevitably vague. In the transmission of a body of fairy tales or children's games and doggerel and magical recipes and incantations, rationalization is improbable because of the nature of the subject matter—how would one rationalize children's games?—and because the custodians, transmitters, and recipients have no desire for rationalization; they probably have little capacity for it. Nonetheless various children's games and various pieces of doggerel might possess affinities or resemblances but the actual transmitters and recipients do not care about them. The children who play these games and who recall these rhymes do not know about the variants; they only know the specific rules and words of their own versions. But in matters of religion, politics, and morals, common themes and variant versions are frequently known to their possessors, and the intellectual custodians of the differing traditions are usually very aware of the differences and place stress upon them.

Once a game becomes stereotyped by officially promulgated rules, it becomes like a religious ritual each part of which is prescribed and fixed in place by written stipulations and regulated and supervised study and performance. Such a ritual can change, as can the officially promulgated rules of a game, but at any time it is fixed and precise. Its tradition may be spoken of without worry about what is inside its boundaries and what is outside them. The promulgation of ritual procedures and training in their execution are usually intended exactly to prevent their slipping away into something else; the rules of a game are officially promulgated and controlled by referees in order to prevent ad hoc innovations which would give one side an improper advantage, i.e., an advantage outside the rules. Where there are no precise rules and no custodianship which takes to itself, or has assigned to it and is acknowledged to possess, the powers of regulating and stipulating the tradition, as in the telling of fairy tales or legends, a great variety of possibilities of transmission of the tradition exists. Stories may become amalgamated with each other, they may acquire or be divested of elements, and they may slide into closer approximation to others from which they had in the past been clearly separate.

When we cease to speak of tradition in general and speak of particular traditions such as the tradition of the Free Churches or that of Marxism, we speak in the first instance of certain sets of beliefs and intellectual practices. The outer boundaries of the traditions are sometimes more or less clearly defined by a corporate body with an official doctrine; this was what the Roman Catholic church attempted to do through its councils and then, in the latter part of the nineteenth century and the early twentieth century, through the efforts of Pius IX, Leo XIII and Pius X. The Free Church of Scotland and its proceedings against W. Robertson Smith proceeded with a similar assumption of a defined body of beliefs incumbent on all members.

The Soviet, the western and central European, and the American Communist parties from the time of the formation of the Communist International until the 1930s likewise demanded a uniformity of belief of all their members and above all of their intellectuals and officeholders. But who now can say where present-day Marxism begins and ends? In the 1920s one could know more or less clearly, at least for each of the periods within the decade, what communist Marxism was because the Communist International promulgated the orthodox position and harassed, persecuted, and suppressed those like Trotsky, Lukàcs, Thalheimer, Korsch, and Nearing who deviated from the path. The declaration of the distinction between orthodoxy and heterodoxy is an attempt to deny the existence of families of traditions. However different from their own the beliefs of the heterodox appear to the orthodox, to the observer who looks at them from the exterior they can be seen to have many fundamental beliefs in common. The observer sees the orthodox as the member of a family of traditions, which the orthodox deny even more vehemently than the heterodox. The latter usually claim to be the continuators of the "original" tradition and regard the orthodox as aberrant but not wholly separated; the orthodox usually claim that the heterodox have misunderstood or falsified one of the fundamental articles or themes of the outlook.

The name by which an individual designates himself, for example, as "liberal" or as "Marxist" or as "socialist" or as Roman Catholic, is not at first glance an unreasonable criterion for his assignment to a particular tradition; it is certainly a more reasonable criterion than the denial by others of his self-identification. But in fact it is not adequate because there are identities which are often not perceived and which are in fact often denied. It is extremely difficult for an individual to know who shares the traditions in which he lives; it seems much easier for an observer of a later time to see the spread and variation of a tradition of an earlier period than it is for one who lives in that period, but it is difficult for the observers as well. The difficulties in the analysis of families of traditions arise from the very constitution of traditions as such.

The boundaries of traditions, considered either as a temporal chain of symbolic constructions, as a temporal sequence of sets of scientific or philosophical ideas, as styles of works of literature, as sets of moral beliefs, or as the beliefs of the members of a temporally extensive aggregate of individuals who possess particular beliefs, are always vague. Academic disciplines, as traditionally constituted at any given time, show the difficulty of specifying the boundaries of traditions. There are substantial differences between chemistry and physics and between sociology and economics. They also overlap with each other. There are clusters of beliefs or bodies of knowledge which clearly belong to a particular tradition and there are other clusters which are obviously alien to them, even though not completely alien.

Consensus, Orthodoxy, and Heterodoxy

It is improbable that in any large society there will be a complete consensus of the traditions of judgment about any particular object. The traditional character of judgments of particular objects complicates the establishment of consensus. The matter of consensus becomes much more complicated by virtue of the fact that traditions of judgments of particular objects are not simply judgments of particular objects, nor are they just the latest phase of traditions of judgment of particular objects. They are parts of interconnected sets of traditions of judgments of particular objects. They were heterogeneous in the past, and their diversified lines of development linking and separating them from each other over time makes the pattern of effectively accepted beliefs at any one time extraordinarily differentiated.

Individual human beings would be diverse enough because of the diversity of their experiences and roles, with temperaments adding to that diversity. Their diverse lineages make the position even more complicated. Yet with all that diversity, human beings are in many important ways quite uniform. So it is with the topography of traditions in society. They diverge from each other in ways which their respective possessors take quite to heart. Yet they do participate in an approximate, intermittent, partial, and shifting consensus of traditions of belief. Perhaps it would not be too much to say that this consensus is maintained by a traditional image of membership in the same society in which one's contemporaries and one's own and their ancestors have been living. Sometimes the consensus is an overlapping of general traditions, sometimes it is a congruence of judgments of particular objects, at others it is simply an outcome of the beliefs of many individuals in their common membership in their own society.

In these societies with a shifting, flexible net of traditions of beliefs, some traditions are dominant. These are the traditions which are espoused by the center of the society and which are either accepted or assented to or are left in unawareness by peripheral sectors of the society—usually all three simultaneously. There are always disagreements about their dominant tradition within the center and within the periphery and between the periphery and the center as well, but this does not alter the fact that there are dominant traditions.

Dominance is one thing, uniformity is another. It is not in the nature of human societies of any degree of complexity to produce a uniformity of opinion. There have been however, during long stretches of time, very outstanding societies in which the center—ecclesiastical and political—thought that it would be possible to impose uniformity of beliefs and to prevent the acceptance of beliefs which departed from the one, true, and right belief.

All societies have a tendency towards consensus of traditions and tendencies also towards dissensus. Before the age of liberalism in the West and after the age of the great ancient empires, which did not care especially about the beliefs of their subject peoples as long as they paid tribute, performed services, and did not revolt, there intervened an age when uniformity of opinion on the most important of all matters, namely, religious matters, was expected. Even then, when heretics from Christian orthodoxy were relentlessly pursued, Jews were fitfully tolerated for more than a millennium. Through the institution of the Inquisition the Roman Catholic church sought to impose orthodoxy of belief and with uneven persistence. The strain towards the requirement of orthodoxy and the uniformity which would accompany it is present in most societies but it is also moderated in them by contrary tendencies. These contrary tendencies are often beyond the reach of education, sermons, and coercion. Often they are tolerated out of indifference; sometimes they are tolerated out of principle.

Through families, schools, churches, and newspapers, a vague common focus, a vague common image of the past, a more or less uniform moral standard, and a more or less common conception of transcendent and earthly powers are maintained amid much diversity and conflict. Such uniformity as is achieved is not an aggregative uniformity, a uniformity of many similar separate judgments. It is a uniformity constituted by the dominance in a wide adherence to certain vague general traditions which are clusters of particular judgments.

Traditions as Clusters of Elements; The Rationalization of Traditions

The beliefs which are regarded as following within a tradition, i.e., which are regarded as belonging together, are analytically distinguishable into component elements. This is not the place to enter into the discussion about the possible existence of *Elementargedanken* or "unit-ideas."[1] Any outlook, moral, religious, political, or scientific, even if it is as thoroughly rationalized as a body of exact scientific knowledge, contains a multiplicity of judgments about a corresponding multiplicity of objects. The multiplicity of objects is given in the nature of the universe, even if the world is a unity and even if the One has been clearly apprehended. It still consists of many different things. The manifoldness of the Many is a primary experience, the oneness of the One has to be striven for. The respective judgments of the Many have their own traditions. These traditions are both independent of each other and connected with each other by ties of logical derivation, identity of moral and aesthetic tone, and traditionality of long association. They are however analytically separable.

Although a rationalization of an outlook by systematic thought or the tacit assent to preponderance of certain pervasive themes, gives to each judgment-cum-object a place in a coherent scheme, similar judgments-cum-objects may be found in other traditions of outlook or combinations of beliefs. A belief in the ultimate moral equality of all human beings for example, can be found in Christianity, in liberalism, and in socialism, which are all outlooks differing in many other very important respects. Moral "seriousness" or gravity may be found in

1. See Adolf Bastian, *Ethnische Elementargedanken in der Lehre vom Menschen* (Berlin: Weidmann'sche Buchhandlung, 1895); and Arthur O. Lovejoy, *The Great Chain of Being* (Cambridge, Mass.: Harvard University Press, 1954), pp. 3–7.

Christianity and in traditional conservatism, although the latter might deny the fundamental equality of human beings which much of Christianity espouses. The belief in the merit of a concentration of authority might be found in secular, hedonistic, antitraditional communistic Marxism and in Roman Catholicism. In the nineteenth and early twentieth centuries Marxists hated anarchists and did indeed differ from them in very important respects, such as the use of demonstrative violence or the desirability of participation in representative legislative assemblies. They agreed however in their conception of the future society which would be free of authority.[2]

There are numerous instances of this overlapping of traditions which are regarded by their proponents and enemies as fundamentally different from each other. It is sometimes a reason for embarrassment when such an overlapping is discovered; it is more often vehemently denied. The objects of the world are many, they might even be infinite in number, but certain major ones preoccupy the human mind, above all in a particular society and a particular epoch. The biological organism, external nature, the ultimate order and meaning of the universe, its intermittent catastrophes, the proper conduct of authority, the relationships between qualifications and rewards—these are some of the most common objects to which the human mind attends: each of them has many facets and about each a limited variety of judgments is possible in a given epoch and society.

The complex composition of particular traditions into more comprehensive ones is a necessity of the mind; the mind has a tendency toward the integration of particular traditions into comprehensive ones but the tendency is of very unequal power, varying with individuals and situations. The need for self-designation as adherent to or part of a transcendent entity is as present in the relationship to symbolic objectivations as it is in the collective life of mankind. The affinities of age, of kinship, locality and nationality, and of membership in ethnic groups, social class, and occupational groups are paralleled, for the same reasons, by the affinities which are created by self-designation as Lutheran or as Roman Catholic, or as social democrat or progressive, as conservative or scientist or secularist or fundamentalist. The tendency towards integration around a central theme or belief is a consequence of striving for a unitary and coherent order formed around a central power or principle. But it is also necessitated by the need for self-designation in a trans-individual entity. Only through such generalized and comprehensive integrations of traditions can enough easily apprehensible features held in common with

---

2. Marxists attempted to deny this affinity by avoiding as much as possible any reference to the "cookshops of the future." The "withering away of the state" was nevertheless one of the important themes of Marxism as it was of anarchism.

many other persons be found. Furthermore, these traditional clusters of particular judgments have come together over time because some individuals saw a logical connection between various judgments or because these various judgments seemed to "fit" with each other. For most human beings, presumably integrated and comprehensive clusters are given; they receive them in their childhood and youth or when they enter into the culture or a stratum of a profession or a society of which they were not previously members.

Traditions can be as narrow as the object or range of any judgment, and many who adhere to them are content to see each of the traditions they accept in that very narrowness. The craftsman who performs a particular operation in accordance with the traditions he has received does not necessarily regard the particular technological tradition which he observed as an integral part of a traditional handicraft economy, organized into guilds, each with its patron saint and its traditional rites affirming its mysteries. The microbiologist does not necessarily or always see himself as the recipient of a broad tradition of scientific procedure and ethos which applies to all of science, nor does he even see the broader "state of the art" one part of which was the point of departure of his own research. Such narrowness of interest is unusual but it exists.

Both the craftsman's performance and the scientist's experiment, neither of which is in itself a tradition and neither of which is absolutely identical with the anterior state of the tradition which they received, follow particular patterns received as traditions. Each is in fact part of a complex combination made up of other no less particular traditions and of more general, comprehensive traditions; it is usually designated by a name with which its adherents identify themselves and others. In the cases where the outlook formed in the tradition does not have a name, because intellectuals have not taken it up, its possessors have a vague and general conception of their outlook, of a mode of life, and of an ethos which are incumbent on them, whether they be farmers or soldiers or robbers or laborers or scientists or artists.

In these comprehensive, loosely ordered outlooks constituted by many distinguishable, more elementary beliefs or judgments, a few general beliefs tend to be pervasive. A general belief about the supreme value of bravery, with its concomitant virtues of manliness and hardness, of soldierly bearing in serious matters and in sports and convivial life, might enter into the secondary traditions of conduct and belief of a soldier regarding objects far from the battlefield and the camp. A socialist of the Marxist stamp regards private ownership of the institutions and technology of industrial production as the supreme abomination, and most of the rest of his beliefs are derived from or affected by this dominant article of faith. Artists have acquired in modern times a secondary tradition of the idea of the "art-ist" which is manifest in many spheres of life outside the production of works of art, a process which has its own primary traditions. Bohemianism as a mode of life, free from and disrespectful of the restrictions of philistine society, has become such a comprehensive outlook. The bohemian outlook, in which the appreciation of impulse, the high evaluation of originality, the belief in the prerogatives of "genius" are central, manifests itself in political attitudes, dress, sex-ual relations, and attitudes towards businessmen. Scientists also have a tradition which runs beyond the laboratory and their own traditional rules governing research and publication. This more comprehensive scientistic tradition comprises attitudes towards the deeper problems of existence, the ways of dealing with personal bonds, and the proper conduct of political authority. The scientistic outlook has no official promulgation and it is not incumbent on scientists to believe in all of it or even in any of it. The fact remains however that many do so.

These comprehensive clusters of particular traditions, covering a wide range of situations and objects and bound to each other some-times logically, sometimes by a pervasive tone, by harmony, and by long, adventitious association are capable of forming a variety of pat-terns. Despite their variety, these patterns possess affinities with each other. The affinities might be perceived as existing in a common his-torical origin; more significantly, the affinity may be seen by observ-ers as residing in substantive similarities, and even the common historical origin may be so represented by their possessors. The pro-ponents of these variant sets of traditions may be in conflict or in alliance. These families of traditions are separated from other families of traditions as well as being internally different to separate parts of "tradition" within the family.

Any world religion is such a family. Buddhism separated into Hina-yana and Mahayana Buddhism; Judaism into orthodoxy, Hasidism, and reform; Christianity into Roman Catholicism, Orthodoxy, and Protestantism, each with variants within itself; Islam into Sunnis, Shi'ites, and Wahabis; and so on. Political traditions are similarly constituted into families as are artistic traditions. Not only do the different branches within a single family, e.g., Lutherans, Cal-vinists, Methodists, Baptists, and Presbyterians within Protestant Christianity, share many elements in their outlooks with each other but they also reach other boundaries and share elements with other families within the same sphere. Some branches of the family are closer to the outer boundaries than are others in the sense that they share fewer important elements, fewer particular traditions.

Like biological and social families which intermarry with each other, families of tradition share elements of particular and even quite general traditions with others outside their boundaries. This is more true of families of political traditions than it is of families of religious traditions although there too, as with the case of the Brahmo-Samaj in Hinduism which assimilated elements from the Protestant Christian tradition, such extensions beyond the traditional boundaries do occur. Political traditions are usually less fixed in their doctrines, they live in a common situation with their rivals. They often share elements derived from a common descent; the traditional beliefs in the high value of material well-being, of individual gratification, and of secularism were incorporated into the moderate branch of social democracy from the tradition of liberalism. Elements of the tradition of humanitarian reform, fostered in the conservative family of tradition, were assimilated into the socialistic family, although in principle the value of such reform was denied by socialists.

Elements of a branch of tradition can, however, become detached from that branch and pass over into another family. For example the practice of written petition and demonstration as a mode of demonstration, at one time an integral element of the liberal family of traditions, has largely disappeared from that tradition and has passed into the collectivistic liberal and socialistic family of traditions.

Substantively different spheres of tradition—political, religious, and literary—likewise overlap; elements from one are incorporated into another while retaining their original affiliations. Traditions are not like scarce resources which cannot be acquired by others who did not possess them previously without their previous possessors having a smaller share of the available total. Traditions may increase their adherence in a particular society while their previous possessors retain no less of the tradition in question than they had before.

The Association of Traditions

The Imprint of a Dominant Tradition on Other Traditions

Particular elements in one family of tradition in one sphere of life may likewise be diffused into families and branches of traditions of another sphere, e.g., the diffusion of the "scientific attitude" into traditions of personal relationships and of the administration of corporate bodies. There have been periods in which traditions of religious belief have expanded within society so that they overlaid the traditions of other spheres. Thus in Italy in the fourteenth and fifteenth centuries a dominant religious tradition was accepted by adherents or practitioners of the traditions of the artistic sphere, providing from the Old and New Testaments and from the lives of the saints themes and subject matters of paintings and sculpture. In Germany in the nineteenth and early twentieth centuries, the tradition of nationality in the political sphere was such an expansive one that it entered into education and even into the outer regions of the scientific tradition. In the twentieth century, and not in the United States alone, the scientistic tradition—which had been at home mainly in the natural sciences—has expanded from science into many other spheres: economic activity, governmental and judicial activities, personal and familial relationships, and into a wide range of intellectual activities outside the natural sciences.

So, in any large society, there are major traditions coexisting alongside each other, in conflict with each other, and attracting elements from each other, incorporating mobile, expansible elements to themselves. In Italy in the sixteenth and seventeenth centuries, artists loosened the dominion of the central religious tradition and came under the dominion of parts of the scientific tradition and increasingly under the expansive tradition of the "artist."

It should be emphasized that, in the adherence to any family of traditions, complete consensus does not reign. Individuality, eccentricity, and attachments to other families of comprehensive traditions break the surface of adherence. The adherences as well as the traditions overlap. Sometimes a civil tradition or a tradition of nationality, although not continuously salient, serves to hold their adherents in check so that they act loyally to their societies when the conflicts between the adherences of the conflicting traditions would otherwise set them at each other's throats.

It is wrong to think of a *Zeitgeist* which pervades an entire society expressing itself in every work and action. Such a notion lays excessive stress on the uniqueness of the spirit of an age; it fails to see how much continues relatively unchanged from the past and how what is novel in the present is an extension and variant on what has preceded it. The idea of an all-pervasive *Zeitgeist* obscures the diversity of traditions in any complex society and their competition with each other about the same objects. Such a view also overstates the internal unity of the *Zeitgeist*.[3]

Nonetheless, there are many common elements in the major comprehensive traditions prevailing in complex societies. The common features begin from their contemplation of approximately the same set of objects: for example, work and works, merit, obligation, income, honor, rich and poor, authority, transcendent powers, and the past and the future. The traditions of judgments of particular objects often do not touch each other closely at the further reaches of specificity but they are bound together—although also separated—as parts of more comprehensive traditions.

A major family of traditions might be—it often is—dominant at one time in a given society. It has a wide adherence despite divisions within the adherence; the divided adherence is not broken up into parts which have no traditions in common. The major family of tradi-

3. See Gombrich, *In Search of Cultural History*, pp. 6–25.

tions is often so imposing that rival families assimilate elements from the major one. Thus, the result bears a resemblance to what the proponents of the notion of a *Zeitgeist* point to. Nevertheless, the alleged *Zeitgeist* is nothing else than a family of traditions of belief, elements of which become incorporated into rival families and into the traditions of spheres of life which are substantively far removed. In certain European societies after the Reformation, one Christian church was so dominant that other Christians, Jews, and unbelievers assimilated much from it; it extended into the traditions of arts and science, philosophy and literature. In the nineteenth and twentieth centuries elements of political traditions, especially of liberalism and socialism, and of the scientistic tradition of science were assimilated into the traditions of other spheres. It is not however useful to attribute these distant approximations to uniformity to a *Zeitgeist*. The approximations to uniformity are the results of a widely adhered to tradition which is never accepted equally by everyone. Under and alongside and contending with this dominant tradition are others, sometimes members of the same family, sometimes members of rival traditions. Furthermore, these are traditions which are special to particular spheres of life; these however have an existence of their own, although it is never a completely autonomous existence.

Addition

When once separate traditions come into contact with each other, several outcomes are possible. At one extreme, there is a possibility of a synthesis into a totally new tradition bearing none of the features of the parents. Another extreme would occur when one tradition extends its adherence so that it absorbs the other entirely without itself changing in any way; the other tradition disappears entirely. Neither complete fusion nor the combination of complete assimilation and complete renunciation is a common occurrence. With respect to the former possibility even individual genius cannot create a work which is entirely without a certain amount of traditionality in content and form, while collective genius works more slowly and more compromisingly. With respect to the latter possibility only physical extermination can utterly obliterate attachment to the traditions which a society or a section of a society previously possessed.

Short of these two impossible outcomes, the coming of several traditions into each other's presence does produce a variety of patterns of change. Addition is the most common; the recipient adds something new to himself while going on doing and believing more or less what he did before. When members of one society meet members of another society in more or less peaceful relationships, a very large part of the body of traditions in effect in each of the societies remains as it was. The traditions of domestic life are the most hidden and the most difficult to affect in both of the societies. Traditions about public things are more susceptible to influence. This happens frequently in political contention. Although polarization is one possibility, a certain amount of addition of new beliefs occurs, at least on the part of one of the contending parties. The addition often turns into absorption so that in course of time other parts of the tradition are affected by the added elements. Intellectual traditions are also relatively open to addition. Such additions are ordinarily only on the margin of their respective societies or adherences. The great sets of families of traditions continue in their own path, slowly inflecting in response to penetration from the affected sphere. The traditions even in affected spheres are unequally and not deeply affected. One of the parties to the relationship acquires some of the traditions at the point of contact; it acquires some of the language; in the course of time it acquires unequal amounts of the religion, literature, history, and science. Most of these new acquisitions are added marginally to the traditions already possessed while leaving the fundamental themes of those traditions intact. Combinations of elements of the two traditions become established within the patterns of belief and action of their possessors. The genre of the novel may be acquired; the forms of verse may remain what they have been. A painter may paint some pictures in the indigenous style, others in the alien style. Astrological and astronomical beliefs can coexist. New gods may be added to the old gods. The fundamental themes of belief and action in each of the mutually encountering traditions may remain as they were. What has happened is that there are some persons in the receiving culture who have acquired elements of the alien tradition while retaining the indigenous tradition in all other respects. The receiving culture has added to its own possessions a few practices or beliefs which are new to it.

When the relationship occurs over a great distance, through colonists, missionaries, or conquerors, the active transmitting traditions may remain unchanged; they might add words to their vocabulary and artifacts; a small number of the members of the society might learn the new language, gain new knowledge, but their use of their own language, their own traditions of arts, remain as they were and so do their religious beliefs.[4]

Amalgamation

Amalgamations occur by renunciation or modification of elements hitherto regarded as integral to one of the traditions and by replacement of those elements by corresponding elements, judging the same

4. Henry Yule and A. C. Burnell, *Hobson-Jobson: A Glossary of Colloquial Anglo-Indian Words and Phrases and of Kindred Terms, Etymological, Historical, Geographical and Discursive*, new edition ed. by William Crooke (London: John Murray, 1903), contains many good examples of such marginal additions to the English language as a result of British experience in India.

object, from another tradition. The acceptance of the rightness of the mechanism of the market for certain parts of the economy by many European socialists after the Second World War is an instance of this type of amalgamation.

The encounter of traditions within a society inevitably goes beyond addition. Where the contact is continuous and enduring the dominant set of traditions penetrates further into more spheres and more deeply. It is not always unilateral. When Islam replaced the Roman Empire in the Middle East, many Christians became converted to Islam. They acquired not only the religious beliefs, they also acquired the domestic traditions which were taking form in Islam. At the same time, the existing centers of philosophical study in the Middle East persisted and Islam assimilated from them the ancient Greek philosophy which in Islamic circles at least led to an amalgamation of Islamic theology and Greek political philosophy and metaphysics.

An amalgamation over a broad range of spheres of life but no less penetrating has occurred in India where a large amount of the intellectual traditions of the West, particularly of Great Britain and the United States and to a lesser extent of the Soviet Union, has been assimilated by the intellectual and professional classes. Traditional Indian patterns of thought and action persist in this. The lines separating the indigenous and Western traditions are no longer clear. Indian English has become a language with almost the distinctiveness of American English. Medicine in India after having run in the two streams of modern Western scientific medicine and Ayurvedic medicine is now in movement towards partial amalgamation. Political life in India has become an amalgamation of the Western tradition of representative institutions and traditions of loyalty to one's caste.

In the United States the amalgamation of British intellectual traditions and traditions of social conduct with the traditions of the farmers and urban lower-middle and working classes has gone much further. At one time it appeared that, in the process of "Americanization," the adapted traditions of British Episcopalianism, Presbyterianism, Methodism, the Baptists, and of representative institutions and political liberalism were dominant. They were so in the sense that they enjoyed great deference. Their bearers were self-confident, and the process of "Americanization" provided the prospect that the entire population of the lower classes would be assimilated to the tradition of the center and hence be assimilated into American society as it was then understood to be. The expectation has to some extent been belied. The lower classes held their own and the result is an amalgamation of the once dominant culture and the culture of the lower classes.

Amalgamations exist within particular families of traditions. Descent from a common ancestry is itself a sort of preestablished amalgamation. Newly formed amalgamations create a retroactive common ancestry of beliefs; the incorporation of an element of a tradition alien to one's own automatically brings with it the past history of that element. It does not equally automatically bring with it awareness or acknowledgment of that ancestry.

This is the process which has accompanied—sometimes with several centuries of delay—the formation of the national state in Europe and in most modern countries. Regional and tribal traditions reinforced by the traditions in the landowning, knightly class were slowly associated with the traditions of the royal court and the traditions of the military of the dominant principality.

It is difficult for several tenaciously observed traditions to exist in each other's presence without some degree of amalgamation. The amalgamation does not end in absorption or in fusion. Far from it! The antipathy felt by the proponents of each of these traditions for each other need not diminish while they become more alike. Conservatives, liberals, and socialists have each acquired some of each other's traditions but they persist in thinking that they are fundamentally and disjunctively different from each other.

Absorption

When the representatives of several traditions bearing on the same objects live within the same society, amalgamation is more likely to occur than when they belong to different societies. Beyond the point of amalgamation, there are the alternatives of absorption and fusion. The absorption by one collectivity of the traditions of another entails the renunciation of the traditions which it has hitherto possessed. Complete renunciation within one or several generations is improbable. Nevertheless the establishment of Graeco-Latin traditions in Gaul and Spain by the third century A.D. and the establishment of Christian traditions in Germany, Poland, the Scandinavian countries, the British Isles, and the Low Counties, to say nothing of France and Spain—after the explusion of the Moors—are instances of such processes of absorption and renunciation. The establishment of modern nationalities within the territories of the modern national state in France, Germany, Great Britain, and the United States has occurred through absorption by local and regional societies of traditions emanated from the centers of the respective national societies.

Absorption could never be complete because the center has too many particular traditions within its family of comprehensive traditions. Many of them connected to specialized occupations and particular localities are not subject to complete absorption by most persons who live far away from them. Still, a great deal of absorption has occurred. Countercurrents and resistance notwithstanding, a common culture of a sort has appeared in most Western societies. It is not the same as the common culture of the classes educated in the occidental and national classics and in the Bible which once prevailed in Western societies. The center has been somewhat relocated; its boundaries have been changed and it has become more differentiated. These changes have rendered complete absorption impossible because there are now too many, too specialized traditions.

Fusion

A new syncretic synthesis in which several traditions have contributed to the emergence of a unitary pattern with a new and distinctive central, pervasive theme is one of the major features in the formation and growth of traditions. In such a synthesis of traditions, the dominant new theme embraces elements from other traditions previously independent of each other. Roman Catholicism was a fusion of Judaism with a distinctive reinterpretation of Judaism by Jesus and then by St. Paul, to which was joined the tradition of Roman imperial authority. In the life of political societies, such fusions of traditions are not often attained.

In the traditions of the natural sciences, in contrast with the traditions of political societies, such fusions repeatedly occur. Fusions occur in the emergence of new fundamental theories and of new fields of specialized scientific work. The new fundamental theory makes possible the reinterpretation of the elements of traditions which were previously thought to be unrelated to each other. The new field of specialization is a fusion which arises from the opposite direction; it appears from the amalgamation of elements from several established disciplines and becomes a new science with fundamental explanatory principles. It might then spread its influence and acquire the pattern of a new fundamental theory.

Conflicts of Traditions

The encounters of traditions are also conflicts of traditions. The conflicts are not incompatible with simultaneous additions, amalgamations, absorptions, and fusions. The conflicting parties of adherents undergo these associations even while resisting them. And at the same time that some of the adherents of the hitherto separate traditions are in conflict with each other, other adherents are experiencing the associations. The conflict is often generated by the perception that combination is in fact going on; it is sustained by the desire on the one side to prevent further association and by the desire on the other to promote the new association.

The conflicts are also conflicts over traditions. The traditions are in conflict *qua* traditions; their adherents are in conflict to save or to promote their own ideals, power, status, and other benefits which are associations with the acceptance or rejection of the traditions which they espouse. In extreme cases, they might have little interest in the truth or validity of the tradition of beliefs about which they are contending. Sometimes the conflicts of traditions, whatever the motives of their adherents, result in additions, amalgamations, and fusions. The defeated tradition does not necessarily renounce any of its elements, but, in order to survive, some of its elements are accentuated so that it will be distinct and separate from the triumphant traditions.

The Dissociation of Traditions

Ramification

The movement of raindrops on a windowpane has already been adduced to illustrate the movements of traditions through time. A wavering stream of water slipping downward at an angle, comes into contact with another such stream moving at a different angle. They fuse into a single stream for a brief moment which then breaks into two streams, each of which might again break apart again, if the windowpane is large enough and the rain heavy enough. A stream of tradition may break up in several directions but each of the separated streams might be as full of a general tradition as the stream from which it broke away. It might have as complex and comprehensive a cluster of elements (where the hydraulic metaphor breaks down, the familial metaphor seems more adequate) as the parental tradition from which it came.

Traditions always develop through ramification. Unless all the adherents of a tradition move simultaneously at the same rate and in the same direction in the modification of the received, there are bound to be differences. There are differences between those who hold tenaciously and entirely to the details of what has been received and those who depart from them; there are also differences among those who depart, in the details they depart from. The possibilities of modification in any tradition are numerous, ranging from fundamentals to details. Whether the modifications result from corrections or from systematization through generalization and differentiation, they are inevitably ramifications from the trunk of the received or from earlier ramifications. Endogenous changes always take the form of ramifications. Associative patterns of change in a tradition such as amalgamation also result in ramification. Partial renunciations of tradition also take the form of ramification.

The ramification of a religious tradition into sectarian tendencies—it is called "splitting" in radical political circles, which are always undergoing such separations—leaves each of the branches claiming to be the true bearer of the tradition while denying the rightfulness of the claims of the other. Usually the branches are not of equal size or strength. The larger one, the one which retains control over whatever real property or governmental and coercive power belonged to the common previously unitary corporate group, usually regards itself as orthodox. The members who leave the main line as a result of expulsion or withdrawal are treated as deviants. It is likely that both are deviants in the sense that both have deviated from the tradition which they originally received.

The process of ramification need not be accompanied by a similar breaking apart of the social structure of the tradition's adherence. A purely intellectual movement which is not coterminous with the boundaries of a corporate body does not usually have such strict criteria for the determination of orthodoxy and heterodoxy. A "school" of philosophy or sociology or economics which becomes ramified usually does not split into mutually abusive groups in the way in which this occurs in religion and politics. For one thing, a "school" of intellectual activity seldom acquires an institution entirely concentrated on the propagation of a particular tradition within the larger tradition of that branch of learning. Individuals disagree and they sometimes add acrimony to their disagreement about the paths of the tradition on which they are moving. They possess a secondary tradition which asserts a difference between the rationality of secular science and learning on the one side and the dogmatic fixation of religious orthodoxy on the other; they are under obligation to continue to coexist within the same institution. Perhaps this is because it is more difficult to found a new university or independent research institute than it is to found a new religious political sect. Disagreement about intellectual traditions and the corresponding modifications of the tradition certainly can give rise to angry words. There was some harshness of sentiment aroused by the disagreement between the Keynesians and the determined adherents of neoclassical economics, but it was certainly negligible in comparison with the hostility between social democrats and communists or between Stalinist communists and Trotskyist communists. It is not that politics are taken more earnestly by political partisans than intellectual activities are taken by scientists and scholars. More important is the fact that the institutions in which scientific and scholarly activities go on are committed to the comprehensive tradition which prizes intellectually achieved results and are not committed to particular interpretations within that comprehensive tradition. Hence the boundaries of a particular intellectual scientific or scholarly tradition and the boundaries of a university are never coterminous.

The secondary intellectual tradition forbids—even though it does not always prevent—persecution, especially since the past century; the secondary traditions of politics are less stringent, and at their radical extremes they even regard persecution as one of the appropriate procedures for dealing with rivals.

Intellectual specialization and the division of intellectual labor are variant forms of ramification. The division of intellectual labor which occurs when a single science turns into several specialties does not give rise to recrimination. The exponents of the hitherto undivided discipline sometimes speak ruefully and disapprovingly of the special fields which have separated themselves from the single discipline but they do not persecute their practitioners. One of the reasons is that the practitioners of the newly specialized field do not deny the validity of the parental discipline; they are willing to acknowledge their own derivation from it. Where each of the branches which has ramified from a parental tradition comprehends all of the objects which the others comprehend, there are bound to be divergent interpretations of the same phenomenon. If the conflict between the branches is prolonged and if at least one of the branches has within it persons capable of intellectual rationalization, differences about fundamental as well as about more secondary, derivative matters will become issues of contention. The contention about differences, about secondary, derivative matters in religious and political traditions, is usually very disproportionate to the actual differences relative to points of agreement in fundamental matters. The tendency of sectarian disputes to extend their scope so as to cover the entire body of the comprehensive tradition produces bitter conflicts with the adherents of that tradition.

Disaggregation and Divestiture

A comprehensive tradition can become divested of particular elements which then become relatively independent traditions. Religion and art, religion and drama, religion and philosophy, and religion and science have historically passed through such a process of disaggregation. Each of the elements has then become a general tradition of its own with its own particular tradition. The divested traditions might retain many of the same objects of belief and activities as the parental religious tradition. For a long time, painting, even after it became a relatively separate and secular activity, with its own primary traditions of the art of painting, continued to depict religious subjects, persons, and events. Even now religion and painting have not become completely disaggregated from each other. Painting is no longer primarily the decoration of religious buildings or objects; it no longer has primarily religious subject matters. It has in some countries and for short periods become self-contained and in that state its possessors have even endeavored to make it into a surrogate for religion, namely, the "religion of art." Religion and drama are now almost entirely disaggregated from each other but again not completely.

Drama has acquired a tradition of its own, no longer derivative from ceremonial religious activities. Religion and philosophy, dealing to some extent with the same subject matters of metaphysics and ethics, have nearly reversed the old relationship but there has also been a very considerable degree of disaggregation. Science, which had one of its sources in astrology and which for a long time, in the West, was bound by the Aristotelian philosophy sponsored by the Roman Catholic church, was thought by some of its practitioners in the sixteenth and seventeenth centuries to be a better way of establishing the fundamental truths of religion and then became largely autonomous. For most of its practitioners it has become wholly independent of and distinct from religious traditions.

A similar process of divestiture has occurred in philosophy. Sociology in its dominant form in the nineteenth century was part of philosophy. Auguste Comte's sociology was the last part of his *Cours de philosophie positive;* Herbert Spencer's *Principles of Sociology* was the last part of his *Synthetic Philosophy.* In Germany, sociology, which was not an academic subject, was frequently practiced by philosophers. Georg Simmel and Max Scheler were among the philosophers who also regarded themselves for a time as sociologists and who left behind significant sociological works. L. T. Hobhouse and Morris Ginsberg in England were also philosophers who entered from there into sociology. Sociology also had a parent in political philosophy going back to Aristotle. It also grew out of economics; Max Weber's sociology emerged from the tradition of German historical economics. Pareto's sociology also emerged from his economic studies. Sociology is now a relatively autonomous academic discipline with its own traditions reaching into a number of disciplines which are now among its ancestors.

The Passing Away of Traditions

Attenuation

Traditions do not always change through the acquisition of new properties from other traditions or by rational thought or practically instigated adaptations. A tradition may become attenuated through defective transmission and through the indifference of those to whom it is presented. It might also become attenuated by the deliberate intention of authority in a given area or by the neglect of training in the skill necessary to sustain it.

Attenuation is the diminution of a belief, the loss of skill in the performance of activities, diminution in the degree of precision and detail of the knowledge of the pertinent subject matter, and the diminution of interest in particular objects. Attenuation is in one respect a change in the substance of a tradition, in another respect it is a diminution of adherence to it. The two usually go hand in hand, but not always. The diminution of adherence to the tradition of Latin and Greek literature has not necessarily lowered the level of mastery of the subject by the small number who still receive it. In fact, however, the reduction in the adherence to the classical tradition which has resulted from its near disappearance from the curriculum of secondary schools in the United States has meant that the study of these subjects has become almost confined to the universities. Learning the language later in life is also a restriction on the degree of easy mastery and hence in the refinement of understanding.

The restriction on the reading of the Bible in schools in consequence of a certain interpretation of the First Amendment to the Constitution of the United States has reduced the knowledge of the substance of the Bible in the American public. Biblical scholarship is still very advanced among professional scholars who specialize in it, but in the course of time this activity too might become attenuated in substance with the decrease in the size of the reservoir from which students of the Bible may be drawn.

Mastery of the skill of linguistic expression might also become attenuated as a consequence of educational policies which are directed to the ostensible "democratization of education." The tradition of linguistic expression still finds reception among young persons who have a natural propensity for it but even these talents are left undeveloped because of the reduction of opportunities to practice it. Those students who require an external, institutionally imposed discipline to train their weaker propensities do not come into possession of the tradition to the same extent. The former group might even be impeded in their acquisition of the tradition because it is not sustained in their environment by a general consensus of usage and vocabulary.

Attention may be withdrawn from the objects of a tradition so that the tradition, by becoming less interesting, fails to find the adherence necessary for its persistence. Elements of the tradition simply fade away from the consciousness of many of the adherents. Nonetheless, increased religious indifference has not led to total indifference. Adherence to religious beliefs has become more intermittent with longer stretches of indifference than was the case in most Western countries a century earlier. The religious indifference which is intermittently aroused into interest only at widely separated intervals results in an attenuation of possession of the specific religious tradition. Beliefs become simplified and blurred.

The empty space left by the attenuation of a tradition, in this case, the tradition of Christian belief, may be filled by other traditions or it might be left empty. The expansion of traditions of secularity is a concomitant of the attentuation of religious traditions. A secular attitude is given in the nature of the tasks of daily life, of the exigencies of routine existence. Even in societies in which religious traditions were more pervasive and more intensely possessed than they are at present in most Western societies, secular beliefs were widespread. They existed however in a framework set by religious traditions which hedged them in and dominated them. The diminution of these religious traditions which opened the way to the expansion of secularity into spheres in which religious traditions were strong was to a considerable extent a result of the vigorous propagation of traditions which were inimical to the religious tradition. The separation, constitutional and de facto, of church and state was a product of the deliberate effort to restrict the power of religious institutions which had as their main task the promotion of religious traditions, although they did other things as well. Thus the space once occupied by religious activities and institutions came to be occupied by secular activities; this increase in the scale of secular activities was supported although not in general caused by the promotion of traditions which were directly or indirectly intended to diminish the power of religious traditions.

Traditions become attenuated and even evaporated through the absorption of their adherents into other traditions. The assimilation of immigrants into their host societies is attended by a quite far-reaching renunciation of the traditions which they possessed in their societies of origin.

The Dissolution and Resurgence of Traditions

Changes in traditions are incessant. Particular traditions and general traditions lose adherence. Do the traditions which lose adherence ever die? They do die as well as undergo replacement by other traditions with generally similar objects. The practices of Greek and Roman religion, ancient Egyptian religion, Chaldean and Assyrian religion have been replaced by Christianity and Islam and by traditions of secularity. Astrological predictions have nearly dissolved in many countries; in others they still survive with a small number of practitioners. Some elements of these traditions might have been absorbed by their replacements in the course of the expansion of the Christian and Islamic centers; others have surely disappeared from religious belief and practice. They survive almost entirely in the works of scholars who have reconstructed them but do not "believe" them.

Traditions of certain technological skills lose adherence. Some of them live on in the skills which have replaced them. Others have practically disappeared; no one remains who knows how to practice them.

A tradition of skill or belief always has the chance of resurgence as long as there is a written record of it or attenuated memories in a small number of adherents. An American Indian or an African society can recover largely attenuated traditions of religious belief or ritual practice as long as there are still persons alive who know what they were in their past period of wide adherence; they might even be revived if they have been recorded in anthropological monographs written almost entirely by foreign students as long as a sense of identity with this vague, largely forgotten past still exists. A belief or practice could conceivably be reborn out of a resurgent desire for it and without any continuity with the tradition which once carried the belief or practice. In reality however this does not happen. Resurgences of attenuated traditions occur when there are still some adherents. The initiating agents of resurgences are often persons who themselves derive from ancestral possessors of the tradition and who themselves from childhood received some of the faded tradition. It is possible for persons who have had no ancestral connection with the tradition to become converted to it and to attempt to revive it. Just as great religious traditions have their origins at the peripheries of their societies, so it is also likely that revivals of once widely accepted, but now receded, traditions originate in the peripheries too.

The revival of a tradition can be effective without reconquering the center of society. The traditions which the prophets of Israel held before their audiences were the traditions which applied to the center of their society as standards which the center repeatedly disregarded.[5] The criticism of the center was made from the periphery. It was never wholly successful but it survived for more than two and a half millennia, recurrently reanimated. The prophetic tradition is indeed one of the oldest in human history. It owes its life however to its precipitation in the Old Testament and the Christian belief that the New Testament contained its fulfillment.

5. Max Weber, *Das antike Judentum. Gesammelte Aufsätze zur Religionssoziologie* (Tübingen: J. C. B. Mohr [Paul Siebeck], 1923) 3:328–39.

8 Tradition and the Rationalization of Societies

The ineluctability of traditions is very relative. In some societies they are more ineluctable than they are in others. Modern Western societies are generally regarded as being at one end of the scale which runs from societies where substantive traditions have been very attenuated to those where most action and belief are directly regulated by substantive traditions. That at least is the image of those who reflect about societies and who praise and recommend one line of development rather than another. This has been the view taken by nearly all the main thinkers who have contemplated modern societies and placed them on the scale of societies of all times and places. There is some truth in this view but it is really too simple.

One of the reasons why modern societies, especially in the West, have been damaging to substantive traditionality is that they have cultivated, in many forms, ideals which are, explicitly or implicitly, directly or indirectly, injurious to substantive tradition and which have become traditions in their turn. These ideals have been urged on rulers and in public opinion. Most of the ideals which have been held up as worthy of pursuit have been "dynamic" ideals. They are ideals which require active and deliberate movement away from substantive traditional patterns of belief and action. The dynamic ideals are not ideals of heroism; they are ideals which entail rationality in the application of abstract principles, and the thoroughgoing utilization of empirical knowledge for the attainment of ends still unrealized thus far in these societies. The "dynamic" ideal in Western societies requires departures from traditional ways of seeing and doing things. It is an expression of discontent with what has been received. The discontent focuses concretely on the insufficiency in the amount of material well-being enjoyed by individuals—so at least it is said in the doctrine prevailing among politicians, higher civil servants, and writers on social matters. In recent years government has become the favored instrument for overcoming this insufficiency. Before this recent assignment of all major tasks to government, the prevailing modern ideal was not less dynamic and no less antithetical to substantive traditionality but it left the initiative for the realization of the ideal mainly to private individuals and organizations. In the liberal version of the dynamic ideal, the individual was left free to rationalize his own action and the actions of those over whom he exercised authority; the rewards went to those who succeeded in doing so. In the newer version, government is favored overwhelmingly because it is thought that in the use of material resources and coercive powers on behalf of the ideal, only government will act rationally. Government alone in countries which are thought to be afflicted with excessive attachment to old ways is counted upon to act rationally, to disregard old ways, and to choose those means which will attain the desired ends with a minimum of waste. If the rational action of an individual is a good thing in itself but sometimes brings about injurious consequences to others, the government appears to be free of the dangers of individual rationalization while providing all of its benefits. If rationalization of action is the right mode of conduct, then rationalization by government is the best way of doing it since government is capable, so it is thought, of bringing everything into one, unified, rational scheme.

Of course, these doctrines are more honored in the breach than in the observance. No government lives up to the ideal of omnicompetent rationalization, but that is the ideal and that is what most politicians and most intellectuals who interest themselves in such matters nowadays think is the best instrument for attaining that ideal. The very name of the process of achieving the ideal of rationalization is significant: it is given the name of "modernization."

This is something which is novel in history. In the past, rulers attempted to strengthen their regimes vis-à-vis foreign and internal rivals; they also from time to time attempted to carry out policies intended to improve the conditions of their people or to regulate their conduct and beliefs. Generally the notion of modernity was alien to their beliefs. It was recognized that all societies were not identical and it was thought that some societies had attained a condition which was superior to that of others. Yet the acknowledgment of differences did not imply that one's own state should imitate those states by adopting their ideals and their arrangements. A foreign society might be admired but this admiration did not require that one's own society should be remade so that it became like the admired one. Nor was it thought that there was a natural, temporal order of development in accordance with which there was an obligation to conform with a norm derived from this temporal order. The idea of progress presents the latest form of society as better than earlier forms. There is merit in the "modernity" of a society, apart from any other virtues it may have. Being modern is being "advanced" and being advanced means being rich, free of the encumbrances of familial authority, religious authority, and deferentiality. It means being rational and being "rationalized."

This conception in itself is a rejection of the value of any patterns of action called traditional. This rejection is fortified by the norm by which the merit of a society is judged. Rationality is the criterion which distinguishes one stage of temporal succession from another. The disparagement of the past is directly expressed in the norm of rationality which requires the extension of rationality based on empirical observation into all spheres of life. A combination of the empirical, purposeful rationality of individual thought and action and the rationalization of the actions of all individuals taken together is the ideal. (The emancipated individual, gratifying his desires and impulses and aiming at experiencing the right sentiments, is an anomaly in this scheme of empirical, purposeful rationality and rationalization, but he is no less uncongenial to substantive tradition.) If the ideal is that of a maximally rational society, then government which has the resources, the powers, the competence, and the comprehensiveness of view for this task, is the most appropriate agent for it. No other institution has powers over the entire range of society; government alone can make the entire society rational. Otherwise society would be in a chaos arising from the rational self-seeking actions of individuals or it would be a slumbering thicket of irrational, traditional rules, or it would be both at the same time.[1]

The countries outside the Western liberal societies and the communist countries suffer from distinctive problems of their own. The demand for modernization—which means rationalization—is of concern predominantly to the centers of those societies; it is greatly hampered by the irrationality of seeking ends for which they lack the means, by the compromises they are forced to make among proponents of different demands, and by their own variety and corruption which divert resources from rational application to the ends which they ostensibly seek. The object of their rationalizing activity is the mass of the population which is set in its substantively traditional ways, and which, when it departs from them, does so with a practical rationality unacceptable to the officially announced ambitions to rationalize their society by governmental action. The Asian and African rulers and publicists mingle their desire to rationalize their societies with an incompatible insistence on conformity with Islamic law and with intermittent support for traditional religious and aesthetic culture, communal ceremonies, and therapeutic procedures. The ideal is rationalization, all qualifications and concessions to substantive traditionality notwithstanding.

1. This resembles what Karl Mannheim had in mind when he analyzed the crisis of modern society as a consequence of the transition from "laissez-faire" to "planning." He himself was an enthusiast for "planning," which he placed in the category of "substantial rationalization"; his usage was not significantly different from Max Weber's, which I am following here. See Karl Mannheim, *Man and Society in an Age of Transformation* (London: Kegan Paul, 1940), pp. 6–15, and Weber, *Wirtschaft und Gesellschaft* 2:468–82.

The leaders and official publicists of the communist countries are even more concerned to promote the rationalization of their societies, which they aspire to make much more thoroughgoing than the rationalization of the West. They, like the Western liberal societies, praise the rationalistic outlook on life which includes the individual rationality of belief and conduct. They praise the latter only in general terms and block opportunities for such thought and conduct whenever they can. They also make concessions to traditions of religious belief and nationality. They do so very grudgingly because it is their conviction that, unless their societies are subjected to complete rationalization by government under the leadership of the Communist party, chaos will result.

The ideal is rationalization. The reality is obviously different; it is because the reality falls so short of it that the ideal is so urgently demanded. Modern societies are very far from being entirely rationalized by rational rulers. There are many reasons for this failure to live up to the ideal. The first is the fact that the ideal is unrealizable by its nature. The ends of life are not construable by the rationality which is exercised for the adaptation of means to ends. Even that latter, purposeful kind of rationality is not realized, partly because those who are placed in the position in which it is expected that they will act rationally cannot do so. They cannot do so because they themselves are too irrational, they know too little, they understand too little of the situation in which they are to act; they also cannot act rationally to attain the ends which they espouse because the situations in which they must act are made up to a large extent by human beings who have ends of their own, ends which would be infringed upon by the ruler's rational pursuit of his own end of rationalization. The rulers are caught in a doctrine which although it praises rationalization is one of the obstacles to antitraditional policy. They are the victims of their own rationalistic, antitraditional tradition.

Many persons have ends or desired objects, many of them set by tradition, different from those who attempt to govern them and they do not wish to be prevented from seeking them. They do not want to live entirely in accordance with reason, even if they could imagine what it would be like to do so.

Despite all their frustration, the rulers and publicists of the Western liberal countries, those of the communist countries, and—unequally—those of the poor countries of Asia, Africa, and Latin America are generally committed to rationalization. If such rationalization were achieved, all traditions except the traditions of secularity, scientism, and hedonism would be overpowered. As it is, the traditions which have come together in the tradition of rationalization have already laid waste to much of the terrain of substantive traditionality.

The Rationalization of the World

Max Weber thought that he could make more sense out of the development of societies if he interpreted their cultures and their structures in terms of the extent to which they were rationalized. He saw modern Western society and culture as the most rationalized of any in world history and he thought that he would be able to understand why China and India and Islam and the ancient Hebrews had produced cultures and societies which were not as rationalized as those of the West. He meant by rationalization the coherent ordering of beliefs and actions in accordance with a unifying central criterion. The systematization of belief is the elimination of logical inconsistencies, the disarming of demons and local deities, the denial of magical technology, the increased comprehensiveness or generality of a theory, and the reduction of all individual instances, whatever their diversity, to the status of general classes. Rationalization of belief is the elimination of particular judgments which cannot be subsumed under a more general judgment. The rationalization of action is the elimination of decisions which cannot be justified in accordance with their anticipated consequences, themselves rationally assessed by more generally defined ends and rendered predictable by generally valid empirical laws. Rationalization is the organization of actions aimed at the attainment of an optimal combination of ends—whether the actions be those of a single individual planning his own course of action or whether they be those of a large number of individuals. Rationalization is the systematization of belief; it is the systematization of action.

Max Weber did not think that there had been a unilinear trend towards an ever increasing rationalization in the course of history. Nonetheless, he thought that rationalization had made such progress in the West that the world was being emptied not only of magic but of the meaning which great religions offer; he thought that this rationalization entailed the expulsion from the world of the power of divinity and of whatever powers are located beyond what is apprehensible by the senses, by the instruments constructed by human knowledge and skill to aid the senses, and by the ratiocinative analysis of the phenomena thus perceived. He thought that Western societies were moving forward steadily on the course of an increasing rationalization. He thought that the movement towards organizing human action in society into larger and larger units directed towards particular ends or sets of ends, testing and selecting actions in accordance with the criterion of their contribution to the end or ends, was an irreversible movement. Governments, legal systems, universities, armies, and of course economic enterprises were becoming increasingly rationalized or—as he called it—bureaucratized. Scientific inquiry was the most advanced mode of intellectual rationalization, pushing aside rationalized theology. Local markets were being absorbed into national and world markets; the division of labor was being extended to cover the earth's surface. Self-sufficient villages were being absorbed into the worldwide division of labor and into international markets. Status groups formed by similar styles of life, the sense of common identity, and common traditions were being replaced by classes formed by identical positions and acting rationally for their own advantage in the rationalized market. The allocation of occupations and statuses corresponding to occupations on the basis of expected performance and contribution to the attainment of the maximization of ends were supplanting the allocation of positions through a traditional order of privileges based on membership in families, in lineages, and in estates. He saw a single criterion of allocation emerging for roles and rewards through the spread of educational opportunity; society was becoming "diplomatized" as education became an increasingly important criterion of allocation of occupation and rewards.

This whole mighty torrent of rationalization grew originally from the rationalization of Jewish theology which emerged in Palestine in the eighth and seventh centuries B.C. and which had been intensified by the experience of the Babylonian Exile. The emergence of Christianity from Judaism extended the sphere of influence of a rationalized theology. Building on the rationalized Roman bureaucracy and the rationalized Roman law, the bureaucratic Roman Catholic church rationalized and routinized the charisma with which it had been endowed by Jesus and opened the way to its expansion over all of Europe. The Protestant Reformation and particularly its Calvinistic variant, elaborating the ideal of calling, placed those who acceded to it under the obligation to transform the surface of the earth by rationally disciplined labor for the glory of God. From this, modern capitalism emerged. The "secularization of the world" drove steadily ahead until the religious motivation too became secularized. The charismatic and the traditional modes of legitimation were obliterated in this process.

Max Weber saw only the reemergent charismatic individual as a bulwark against this apparently irresistible force of bureaucratization. Traditional modes of belief and conduct seemed to Max Weber to be doomed; he did not count on attachments to traditions to stand up against the solvent power of rationality and of the rationalization which it sustained.

The Rationalization of Traditional Societies

Max Weber was the one sociologist in the history of the discipline who saw beyond the boundaries of modern Western civilization. He knew ancient Western history as a specialist in Roman law and in the ancient economy. He knew medieval European society as a specialist.

He studied ancient and medieval India and China through translations and the best scholarly literature and he was informed of modern developments in those countries; he knew Russia up to the Russian revolution of 1917 as an expert who had written several monographs on the background and pattern of the revolution of 1905. He knew what Tönnies knew about *Gemeinschaft* and he knew it in a far broader and more differentiated perspective than Tönnies knew it. "Traditional societies" was not a residual category for Max Weber. His studies of feudalism and of bureaucratic empires are still unequalled. He did not live to see Asia and Africa emancipated from European colonial rule and he did not envisage the rapid adoption in those areas of the world of the Western model of rationalization. He did not speculate on the prospects of traditional patterns of belief and action in those parts of the human race but it may be presumed that he thought that their chances of survival were attributable to the absence from these societies of the drive towards rationalization.

The designation of a class of human societies as "traditional" has come about by indirection. "Traditional" has seemed to be a less pejorative term than words like "primitive," "heathen," "savage," "backward," "pagan," "barbarian," and "simple." The term "traditional" was no more than a last resort in the search for a designation which would not be derogatory. Yet it did refer to a significant feature of the smallest societies of Africa and the villages of India, albeit very unclearly. When African and Asian societies became sovereign, social scientists felt compelled to classify them. To refer to them as underdeveloped seemed condescending as well as implying a belief in the idea of progress. The most convenient and least embarrassing designation was "traditional." Although the adduction of "traditionality" was justified by an implicit contrast with "change," the traditionality in question was seldom described or explained. Beliefs, actions and arrangements were described to show them to be "functional" and reasonable within the context of prevailing beliefs and as rational and economical under the existing conditions of restricted resources and incentives. Nonetheless, the choice of the term "traditional" to describe these societies was not without fruit.

The characteristics of traditional societies have generally been said to comprise the following: preponderance of agriculture—and fishing—in the economy; relatively little occupational differentiation; absence of mechanical technology; a relatively low degree of orientation of production towards the market; high degree of illiteracy or very restricted literacy; pronounced dominance of communal opinion over the conduct of individuals; a widespread consensus of beliefs; rudimentary administrative machinery; widespread acceptance of authority; preponderantly ascriptive determination of status; saliency of biological descent as a criterion of identification of individuals; bureaucratic deferentiality; pervasiveness of magical and religious beliefs; little demand for modifications of distribution of resources and rewards; little active demand for enhanced income and status and no marked dissatisfaction with existing income and status; little deliberate initiation of change. In the analysis of such societies, there has generally been an assumption that they have not changed greatly over many years and that such changes as have occurred are primarily adaptations to changes in the external circumstances of the societies. When the societies are considered historically, emphasis has been laid on exogenously precipitated changes; stability has been thought to be the normal condition of these societies, barring the pressure of changes in their external circumstances. The societies which have been classified as traditional have on the whole been relatively small in population and territory and have been relatively isolated from other societies. The traditionality and stability of these societies have been postulated, not analyzed. "Socialization" has usually been regarded as the chief mechanism of their self-reproduction.

Max Weber did not interest himself primarily in this kind of society. He studied much larger societies, such as China, India, and ancient Jewish society. These were societies with differentiated intellectual strata. Chinese and Indian societies were not only large in population and territory but they had elaborate governmental systems which extended their authority over much of the large territories which the societies occupied. The ancient Judaic society was relatively small but its existence was in the midst of major empires, the expansive tendencies of which entered into the life and imagination of the Jewish people. Jewish society was not isolated and Max Weber did not treat it as such. The societies with which Max Weber dealt had furthermore a history which could be reconstructed and which, at least in the case of the ancient Jews, played a prominent part in their conception of themselves. These were histories of movement, of frequent changes in fortune, of conflict of beliefs, of the overthrow of rulers, scenes of perpetual turbulence.

Yet since they were not progressive, rationalized societies, were these societies to be placed in the category of traditional societies? This was not wholly unjustified because, beneath the turbulences of their centers, these societies were composed of many small local societies which were similar to those called "traditional." These traditional societies were enfolded within the larger sovereign or colonial societies, societies with more complex technology, a fair amount of occupational differentiation, relatively large urban settlements, elaborate systems of administration and coercion, a large stock of written philosophical, religious, and literary works, organized educational institutions, priesthoods and monastic orders, guilds of craftsmen.

Even during Max Weber's lifetime, which ended in 1920, these large Asian societies, which had not generated within themselves powerful forces driving them towards rationalization, had been drawn into the orbit of the rationalized societies of the West. They were becoming integrated into the world market and the international division of labor even though a rather sizable section of their economies remained outside of the world and even regional markets. They were being provided with an increasingly rationalized administration; modern industrial technology was becoming established in them, even though it was confined to a few major urban settlements. Modern educational and research institutions were being founded and they were producing graduates qualified to practice medicine, law, and engineering, and to follow—although in very small numbers—careers in science and scholarship. Parties and other political associations and organized revolutionary movements inspired by Western doctrines, civil reform associations, trade unions, and associations of business enterprises were also coming into existence. Modern economic theories were being discussed as well as nationalistic, socialistic, anarchistic, and liberal ideas. Newspapers in indigenous and foreign languages and a modern periodical press appeared. New literary genres, closer to those practiced in the West, were being used by writers, and European literary works were being translated or read in the European languages. A modern intellectual class was taking form, different from the traditional religious and quasi-religious intellectual class.

In the countryside and away from the urban centers society continued almost as it had been before. The indigenous religious centers retained their faithful adherents. Agriculture continued to be vastly preponderant and agricultural technology remained in a condition very akin to what it had been before. Family, clan, and caste were the objects of attachment which they had been in the past. The central government, indigenous or foreign, intruded only intermittently and superficially into the life of the ordinary cultivator and craftsmen. Substantive traditions about primordial ties, piety towards the gods, deference towards superiors persisted.

Modernization

Since the Second World War new governments have come to the forefront in these countries. In some instances, they have been indigenous governments of societies formerly ruled by colonial officials; in others, which had never lost their sovereignty to European powers and which had always had indigenous governments, the rulers had a different outlook and, in the case of China, North Korea, and North Vietnam, they were committed to a Marxist view of the ruling of society. In all these territories, the rulers alleged themselves to be devoted to the ideal of "modernization." Democratic and oligarchical elites, liberals and Marxists, civilians and military men were all determined to modernize their countries. By modernization, they meant making them like the European countries which were thought to represent "modernity." Regardless of whether they took the Soviet Union or the Western liberal democratic societies as their models, and in whatever mixture they combined them, their program was the rationalization of their countries. The aim was to "mobilize" resources, including the labor of their subjects or citizens, to bring them into a national economy which would produce for national and international markets, to increase productivity by rational technology in industry and agriculture, to arrange the educational system so that it would be rationally articulated with the economic system, inculcating the knowledge and skills necessary for the rationalized economy. The promotion of the sense of nationality was intended to foster attitudes of law-abidingness, respect for national authority, and other dispositions necessary for participation in the grand effort of the rationalization of society. Science was to be developed because it was central in the conception of rationalization; it was to be directed towards "use." In a few instances, the idiom of "planned science" was introduced. Regardless of whether the political elite was democratically elected or a self-selected elite of a regime of a single party, its instrument was to be primarily a rationalized and rationalizing bureaucracy which would saturate the society, control, plan, regulate, and initiate in a rational way the activities and organizational arrangements requisite for a modern society. The necessary "infrastructure" of roads, harbors, railways, airlines, and telephone communications needed to coordinate and articulate all these manifold activities into a single movement of modernization was taken in hand. Radio broadcasting and governmental information services were to guide the populace and make it compliant with the directives of rationalization.

By and large it cannot be said that the process of modernization has thus far been successful. Resources have invariably been inadequate to realize the proclaimed intentions. In the liberal, more or less democratic countries, opposition to incumbent political elites has usually been sufficiently widespread to challenge objectives and procedures of the rulers, forcing them to compromise and to depart from their rationalizing plans. Where opposition has been suppressed as a consequence of the seizure of power by the military or by the declaration of a state of emergency, the incumbent elite has almost always failed to gain the support of the populace on a scale sufficient to discourage challengers of its authority. It has often not been able to remain in power, to say nothing of rationalizing the society. Corruption and administrative ineptitude, regional and local interests, powerful groups of property-owners, insurrectionaries, trade unions, caste and ethnic associations, religious and linguistic communities have repeatedly broken through the surface of the effort to rationalize the entire society. Even in Communist China, the strong leadership of the Communist party, which suppressed all public opposition, failed in its "great leap forward"; it failed to control the bureaucracy and, in an effort to bring it under control, instigated a "cultural revolution" which soon produced countrywide disorder because it could not control the juvenile delinquents whom it had set loose. Progress in increased agricultural and industrial production was nevertheless incapable of realizing the goals set. Despite a system of unusual thoroughness for the control of behavior, down to the smallest agricultural communities and on the shop-floor of factories, discontent and vocal opposition have been recurrent.

The situation is little different in Black Africa and the Muslim Middle East. Murderous rivalries are endemic in Iraq. Lebanon, which had been a relatively prosperous and well-ordered country, pluralistic in character and dependent on a judicious self-restraint by the various religious communities in their demands on each other, was disintegrated by an ideological civil war aggravated by Syrian invasion and the intrusion of Palestinian immigrants. In Iran, a process of vigorous "modernization" aroused so much opposition from Islamic religious leaders that the government was overthrown after long and uncontrolled conflicts; now the country is the scene of much violence which has not yet been exhausted. None of these societies have much to show in the way of rationalization; the military as an internal political power and the security police seem to be the parts of the society in which rationalization has gone furthest.

The efforts of rationalization have aggravated disorder in nearly every country. The undertaking of an "educational revolution" to prepare the "high-level manpower required for development" has produced unemployed school-leavers, restless university students with the leisure and passion for violent and sometimes irresistible demonstrations. The increased prominence of the central government which is part of the program of modernization and an ostensible prerequisite of the rationalization aimed at has intensified demands and enlarged the range of participation in public conflicts over the distribution of benefits.

Rationalization, had it been successful, would have cut away the thicket of traditional attachments in these Asian and African societies. It has not done so, because the rationalizing programs have been beyond the means and powers of their rulers, and the intended subjects of the rationalization have been too bound to their own ways of doing things. Instead of rationalization, disorder has occurred. The proponents of rationalization have sought populistic legitimation; they have attempted to gain the support of the people partly because they are populistic (although undemocratic) and partly because they have tried to "mobilize the masses" for their policies. They have educated more persons than they could employ in the posts the graduates and school-leavers think they are entitled to; they have instigated a crowding of the towns with unemployed idlers, a highly inflammable material for public disorders.

Substantive traditions are more endangered by the disorder of urban idleness and the supplantation of local and tribal authorities than they are by the fragmentary and unsuccessful authority of a remote and spuriously rationalized bureaucracy. Had the program of rationalization been successful, had economic plans been well made and well carried out, had educational programs been correctly adapted to "economic and social needs," had the system of local government come effectively under the control of the national government or of the national council of the single party, had the various tribal and village arts and festivals and dancing been fused into a single national art and festivity, an axe would indeed have been laid to the root of the tree of substantive tradition. These things have not however happened. The substantive traditions of locality and tribe have not been destroyed but they have been attenuated in some parts of their societies and here and there they have become momentarily resurgent in response to that attenuation.

The Limits of Rationalization

The promethean aspirations of the scheme of deliberate rationalization have met with numerous frustrations. Much has been done in the way of the construction of physical plant and facilities—factories, roads, hydroelectric installations; new administrative institutions have been organized; a larger proportion of children attend school. The size of the national product has increased; otherwise, with increasing populations, the individual consumption of food would have decreased, which has not happened in most of the Asian and African states. Nevertheless, the program of rationalization as envisaged by its enthusiasts has not been successful. It is true that many of the governments are new to the tasks which they have taken upon themselves and it could be argued that, when they have acquired more experience, they will be more successful in their efforts to become "modern" by rationalizing their societies. It is indeed possible that they might be more successful than they have been. It is not likely that they will be very successful in the foreseeable future.

Rulers of countries with longer experience in planning and coercion have also not been successful in their efforts to rationalize their entire societies in the service of an apparently unitary ideal. The communist countries of eastern Europe and particularly the Soviet Union, with more than fifty years of experience in planning, are over and over again mistaken in their assessment of the potentialities of their resources, and in the articulation of the various parts of the societies they seek to keep under complete control. They will not reconcile themselves to the obduracy of the human beings whom they would treat as malleable materials. It is in the nature of the ideological belief in the necessity of rationalizing the whole of society on behalf of a single ideal that the shortcomings of human powers and the resistance of traditions are either overlooked or are erroneously regarded as subject to extirpation by rational arrangements and coercion. It is scarcely within the realm of the possible that the societies of Asia and Africa, less integral and more heterogeneous, will be susceptible to attempts at total rationalization.

The Western societies have been launched on a course of rationalization far beyond anything previously attempted in liberal democratic societies except in short periods of war. The proponents of rationalization in those societies have not aspired to such complete rationalization as has been attempted in communist countries. There are no equivalents in Western policies for the "new Soviet man." Although these efforts at rationalization are unprecedented for liberal societies, they are still partial in comparison with what they are urged to do. There is no need to dilate on the failures of Western rulers to attain success even in the limited rationalization which they have undertaken, other than to point to the high rate of inflation, the large number of unemployed persons in the face of policies of full employment, and the high rate of criminal activities. The language of social and economic planning appears from time to time in Western countries, but the closer the countries come to practical decisions the less influence such language has.

Why are these promethean efforts to rationalize society so unsatisfying to their proponents? Why despite evidence of successes do they not attain their goals? Why are these aspirations still relatively limited in Western countries?

Max Weber apparently thought that the main resistance to the steady growth of rationalization could come only from strong charismatic persons. He thought that only such persons could withstand the advance of rationalization which moved forward with the certain confidence that bureaucracy was by all odds the most efficient form of administration. Although he explicitly expressed reservations about this superiority of bureaucratization, in his remarks about the limits of "full socialization" without a system of prices,[2] his view in general was that bureaucratization was irresistible, primarily because of its superior efficiency, and also because it could establish a monopoly of the knowledge required for decisions.

2. Weber, *Wirtschaft und Gesellschaft*, 1:55–56.

Weber obviously thought that traditions had no resistive power. Rationalization was "dynamic," traditions could at best conduct a "holding operation," to use a military term. Putting Max Weber's views aside for a moment, let us look at the reality of the situation and ask why the logic of rationalization does not work out.

From within the circle of the rationalizers, the obstacles to success are numerous. Ignorance of the magnitudes to be rationalized and ignorance of the capacities and dispositions of the persons who will be charged with the execution of the scheme of rationalization are indicative of the besetting ignorance in which rulers must work. The complexity of that task of articulation of all the different actions to be rationalized would be beyond the real—not the fictitious or "simulated"—powers of human beings even if knowledge were ample and reliable, which it seldom is. There is also the sheer, irreducible irrationality of any single ruler; and when the rulers are multiple, as they are bound to be in many modern society, conflicts among their ideals and interests would tend to break apart the coherence of any unitary scheme of rationalization. Still, the rulers, with all their contradictions and shortcomings do not renounce efforts to impose their will on a comprehensive scale and in penetrating depth on their subject-citizenry.

Tyrannies in the past were usually limited and spotty, however cruel. Present-day tyrannies, nominally well-intentioned, are impelled by a dream of comprehensive rationalization of their societies. What is there to stand up to them? What is there outside the circle of all-rationalizing rulers to resist the complete rationalization of their societies? There is, in the first instance, the resistance of those whose chances for the attainment of what they desire are reduced by the scheme of rationalization. The subjection of all resources to the attainment of a single goal or to a single set of harmonized goals is bound to leave many of the goals pursued in any society in an unfulfilled condition; some of these unfulfilled goals will be left partly unsatisfied, others much more so. No scheme in the world of scarce resources, to say nothing of all-comprehensive ideals, could fulfill all the goals of all the members of a society. This is especially true for those goals guided by interests and ideals. The threats of noncooperation and of active resistance sometimes induce attempted compromises on the part of the planners or rationalizers. These compromises deform the scheme. In Indian economic planning, for example, the five-year plan, which usually aims at a set of nominally harmonized goals, as it passes through the hands of the council of chief ministers of the states, becomes a "share-out." Strikes, boycotts, ultimately armed insurrections are the recourses of resisters to rationalization, and the first of these is amply evident in countries where schemes to reduce the rate of inflation are undertaken by governments and where workingmen are legally free to strike.

Then there is the devotion to ideals and, in a less exalted form, to beliefs and, in a more humdrum form, to collectivities such as family, village, tribe, ethnic group, and nationality. There are habitual practices which cannot easily be suppressed. These ideals, beliefs, attachments, and habits are traditions. The interests depend on traditions for their definition and for the maintenance of the solidarities of class, occupation, and collectivity through which they are defended.

In the new states of Asia and Africa, traditional ideals, beliefs, attachments, and practices have not yet yielded to the rather feeble rationalizing exertions of their rulers. Nigeria, for example, broke down in the conflict of the interests and beliefs of several major ethnic and religious communities. The conflict was in part a conflict of interests in the anticipated advantages to be obtained through control of the federal government over appointments and the allocation of funds to regions. But the collectivities themselves were defined by traditions of belief and attachment. In India, the battle of the castes and regions over the allocation of appointments, opportunities to obtain the educational qualification for appointments, and the allocation of federal funds to regions is sustained, indeed, would be impossible without the prior definition of the contending collectivities by traditions of belief about the caste system and the theology from which it is derived, attachments to linguistic traditions and the regional communities thereby formed. The recurrent outbursts of violence between Tamils and Singhalese in Sri Lanka are of similar origin; the long-standing conflicts between the Christian South Sudanese and the Muslim government of the Sudan are likewise products of these intertwined interests and traditions of belief and attachment. In the communist countries, the unceasing resistance of the peasantry to the communist rationalization of agriculture is still another manifestation of the power of intertwined interest and traditions of belief and attachment to resist the unrelenting rationalizing schemes. The continued, usually silent resistance of the peasantry and working class to the efforts of the communist rulers to rationalize the Polish economy in accordance with its own communist tradition is a product of the combination of interest and the traditions of Roman Catholic belief, Polish nationalistic ideals, and the peasant's distrust of remote authorities. (Perhaps one should add here the firmness of the partly traditional practice, partly psychologically engrained habit, of drinking vodka, against which the communist regime has vainly contended in order to increase the efficiency of labor as well as to promote its own traditional puritanical ideal.) The courageous conduct of the ''dissidents'' in the communist countries is another manifestation of the tenacity of traditions in the face of coercive rationalization; they seek not just more freedom for themselves individually but also the realization of an ideal formed from various traditions of liberalism, aesthetic individualism, populism, Orthodox Christianity (in Russia), Hussite Protestantism (in Czechoslovakia), and Roman Catholicism (in Poland). It should be observed that in the Soviet Union, despite the unceasing campaign to propagate atheism by legal sanctions and "godless" propaganda, about one-third of the Russian people define themselves as Christians. These instances show that traditional beliefs and attachments are not easily cut down by rationalization, however coercive it is.

The Western liberal, democratic, capitalistic countries have been the most successfully rationalized. It was for these societies, above all, that Max Weber predicted the continuation of the process of dissolution of magical and supernatural powers, the extinction of the sacred and the extermination of all actions, institutions, and beliefs standing in the way of rationalization to its outermost boundaries. (His views on this subject were not entirely consistent or free from ambiguity.) Max Weber thought poorly of the resistive power of traditional authority and of the modes of belief and of the institutions in which it was embodied. Substantive traditions of piety towards authority, the respect for what already exists, religious beliefs, institutions of routinized charisma, the accumulated wisdom of practical experience, the sense of lineage and kinship, attachment to locality and nation appeared to him to be very weak in the face of the forces of modern society. Interests in pecuniary advantage and in the power to influence the distribution of pecuniary advantage, the interest in power as such, the driving pressure for rational calculation of efficiency and economy, and the pressing force of changing circumstances all promised an empty future for substantive traditionality.

Rational, empirical knowledge has indeed weakened confidence in the accumulated wisdom of practical experience. Tasks have been created and assumed which seem to be far too complex to be dealt with by practiced judgment and transmitted interpretations. The force of changing circumstances impelled by economic calculations, technological innovations, and the accompanying changes in the territorial division of labor have weakened attachments to occupations, localities, and regions. The multiplication of professions associated with rationalization and with science has reduced the attractiveness of ecclesiastical careers and reduced the prestige of the Christian clergy. Parental authority is certainly less respected now than it was a century ago; the inviolability of the marital bond has likewise been reduced. Administration in governmental and private bodies now appears to be much more rational; it certainly conforms with many of the criteria of bureaucratic, rational-legal authority as defined by Max Weber. The construction of policies seems to be rational; it attempts or claims to be based on rational—even scientific—assessments of consequences and costs. Arguments about policies are couched in terms of costs and benefits, rationally and scientifically calculated. Scientists and scientific technologists are called upon to replace traditional assessments and trial and error in the construction and execution of policies. In education, traditions of syllabuses and modes of instruction have certainly been ravaged by newer notions regarding the ends and techniques of education as well as its substance. In summary, traditional ways of conceiving of the world and of man's life in it, traditional ways of doing things, are thought to be in retreat along a very wide front.

Those who would halt the forward movement of rationalization very seldom invoke tradition as an alternative; when they do, it is in a particular domain such as education, but even there support for tradition is scattered and rather ineffective.

Not all of these changes are attributable to rationalization. Alongside of rationalization and the conquests of the "scientific outlook" there have been at work no less strong impulses coming from hedonism and individualism, and from a particular antinomian variant of individualism, namely, emancipationism. Emancipationism here means that every individual should be free to gratify his impulses, that he should attain happiness, defined by his own desires, and that he should associate only with persons who are akin to him in spirit. Yet with all of these profoundly influential movements, modern Western societies are still not fully rationalized and they are certainly very far from emancipation. Rationalization and emancipation are contradictory to each other, but their conflicts are not publicly appreciated because of their common enmity against a common foe.

The common foe is substantive tradition and the traditions of a more moderate individualism. The moderate individualism has itself aimed to rationalize the conduct of the individual, to discipline him from within in accordance with a code of ethics which had much traditionality in it. This moderate individualism was itself antithetical in its implications to many substantive traditions. In fact, however, puritanical individualism was sustained for some time by substantive traditionality. It was not aware of its implicit leaning towards its own acceptance of much of substantive traditionality, especially with regard to the family, in its commitment to traditions of pluralism, in considerations of individual and group interest and of civility and hierarchy. This common foe has not been conquered. The surface of events is different from their depth. On the surface, the proponents of rationalization and emancipation, especially the intellectual proponents and the political ones as well, have in varying measure dominated the public platforms of most Western countries for several decades. When we pass from the surface of discourse about events to events themselves, which consist partly of discourse and of actions compelled by it, the situation is somewhat different. The program of rationalization which is part of the larger program of the "party of progressivist outlook" has been steadily pushed forward over the past third of a century in most Western countries. Its proponents have not occupied the center of political authority during all of this time in any of the countries. Where nominally the conservative political parties, which contain "the party of traditional outlook," have gained political power at the center, they have shown themselves to be much influenced by the rationalizing and emancipating attitudes. Nevertheless, the processes of rationalization and emancipation have not reached fulfillment. Their failure to do so does not mean that they might not go much further than they have. It does mean however that the motive forces of their forward movement have not been strong enough to bring them further along the line. It also means that there is enough tenacity in the "party of traditional outlook" to inhibit the rationalizing and emancipating government from within and from outside it. The power of "interests" has partly coincided with the trend of opinion which has led in the direction of rationalization by governmental bureaucracy. But "interests" are not uniform and there is also opposition to this rationalizing trend arising from interest. There is also opposition rooted in substantive traditional attachments. Substantive traditional attachments are not usually well organized and they are not favored by the elites, intellectual and political, of the Western societies.

In the United States as in the United Kingdom a large part of the population is devoted to the beliefs of traditional Christianity; patriotism is still widespread although those who believe in it are dismayed. There is still much attachment to traditional beliefs about sexual activity and about the proper roles and spheres of men and women. There is still a strong desire for effective and trustworthy authority. There is still a belief that assiduous work is better than indolence and that supporting oneself by useful work is better than dependence on the government for unearned income. There is still much readiness to acknowledge the claims of superior achievement to higher rewards than are assigned to inferior achievement.

Substantive traditions are less prominent now than they used to be; those who staff the organs of publicity are unfriendly towards them and those who adhere to those traditions think that the tide is running against them. Substantive traditions continue, however, not because they are the exterior manifestation of still unbroken habits and superstitions but because most human beings constituted as they are cannot live without them. The great movement of rationalization and the closely connected movement of individual emancipation have made great progress; that is indisputable. They have made progress at the expense of patterns of conduct, organization, and belief which depended on substantive traditions. They also in the course of their triumphant advance dissolved many traditions which were not substantive but which were associated with substantive traditions. The prerogatives of absolutism, the privileges of established churches and the unqualified primacy of criteria of lineage, kinship, and personal connections in the allocation of appointments were not themselves substantive traditions but they were associated with them, drawing support from them and supporting them. When these derivative traditions were driven from the fields after the American and French revolutions, the fundamental substantive traditions were left exposed and without intellectual defenders. They did not lose them at once. Although intellectuals of the individualistic-rationalistic persuasion rejected the validity of substantive traditions, they did not persecute them. For one thing, they were liberals and they envisaged large areas of their societies free for determination by those who dwelt in them. They greatly desired that this freedom would secure the ascendancy of their own ideal of individualistic-rationalistic liberalism, but so convinced were they of the strength of the attachment to substantive traditions that the best they hoped for in the near future was toleration for the outlook which they themselves espoused. The penetration of education was neither very deep in society nor very prolonged for most of the population, and it was not inimical to substantive traditionality. The churches were still strong enough to assure that traditional Christian religious beliefs were taught or supported. Only in France and in the United States were secular liberal reformers successful in expelling religious instruction from educational institutions supported by the state.

Although the substantive traditions lost their ascendancy in the eye of public opinion in very large parts of the various Western societies, they did not cease to exist or to be effective. Their adherents lost their self-confidence because, in the course of the nineteenth century, they became sensitive to their intellectual vulnerability. As society became more rationalized with the growth of the national state and the extension of education, the secular bias of the movement of rationalization slowly and unsteadily began to reach into the culture of less educated classes. By the middle of the twentieth century, the pressure of changes in circumstances furthered the weakening of the self-confidence of the adherents of substantive tradition.

Governments were moving slowly to the view that their chief aim should be promotion of the economic well-being of the mass of the population. The accession to office of legislators who had been formed in the classrooms of collectivistic liberalism or its socialist variant accelerated the transformation. The change became more visible after the Second World War—it occurred with almost equal speed in both the victorious and the defeated countries.

The substantive traditions were deprived of the powerful allies which they had once had at the center of society. Churchmen became progressivistic, journalists and the new breed of television producers and their associates were contemptuous of the "archaic classes." Even those who mourned or claimed to regret the disappearance of "folk culture" and its replacement by "mass culture" were not interested in the revival of the former; they were almost to a man supporters of the rationalized and emancipated society of the future.[3] A large vested interest in rationalization appeared from the social sciences which experienced great prosperity in number and standing. Social scientists practically uniformly were devoted to the ideal of "social management," with themselves as advisers, and as research workers they hoped to be able to forward the ideal of a rationally ordered society in which "use and wont"[4] and "the ordering and forbidding technique"[5] would be replaced by scientific knowledge as the guide of rulers and their agents.

It has been said by some writers that the high culture of any age flourishes through its contact with the culture of the less educated classes. This is a plausible view although it applies more to certain fields of intellectual activity such as literature than it does to more scientific and abstract fields. It is no less true that the substantive traditions, which are more likely to be observed in the less educated classes than among the more highly educated, are affected, and increasingly so in societies of the present century, by the higher intellectual culture. It has taken a long time for the rationalistic culture to sink downwards from one stratum to the others in the hierarchy of deference, but it has now done so. Of course, the damage done to substantive traditions is not to be accounted for directly and exclusively by the rationalistic and emancipatory traditions. The force of changing circumstances has done its part in this too; yet the changes in circumstances are to some extent also results of the appreciation of the rationalizing outlook. This indeed was one of Max Weber's main themes.

Changing circumstances—changing places and modes of gaining a livelihood by work, changes in the character and conception of work,

3. I refer here only to Mr. Richard Hoggart *(The Uses of Literacy)* and Mr. Dwight Macdonald, "A Theory of Mass Culture," *Diogenes* 3 (Summer 1953): 1–17, reprinted in Peter Davison et al., eds., *Literary Taste, Culture, and Mass Communication* (Cambridge: Chadwyck-Healey, 1978), 1:167–83.
4. Thorstein Veblen, *The Theory of Business Enterprise* (New York: Scribner's, 1904), pp. 302–73.
5. W. I. Thomas, and Florian Znaniecki, *The Polish Peasant in Europe and America* (New York: Knopf, 1927), 1:3.

changes in the available supply of material goods—are not traditions, although they are the consequences of traditions. The exercise of the ratiocinative function, the issuance of a rationalizing command and an act of emancipatory expression are not traditions either. They are enacted mainly under the guidance of traditions; they are enacted within the patterns presented by traditions. They would not occur with their current frequency if they were not received as traditions. The human race is not more intelligent or more imaginative than it was in the past and very few of its members could either exercise their ratiocinative potentialities or organize and rationalize their own actions and those of others or act expressively if they had no preexistent patterns which they could reproduce. They are in other words living from and in the grip of the past no less, but differently, than those whose traditionality they disparage.

Traditions are not arbitrarily created; they are serious matters and they are about serious matters, even if their recipients are sometimes frivolous in the way in which they espouse them. The "party of progressivistic outlook" has its traditions; it lives from them. Its desire for innovation is traditional; all its beliefs are traditional; all its distinctive novelties are derivative from prior traditions.

Like all successful traditions, the progressivistic, rationalistic, emancipatory outlook is borne with strong conviction by a relatively small proportion of its proponents. These persons through depths of intellectual character, or through tenacious obstinacy and the unwillingness to allow themselves to appear to be in the wrong, are the crucial adherents of the tradition. It was no different in the time of the ascendancy of the "party of traditional outlook." Most of the adherents of any tradition are fairweather friends. They are sensitive to what prevails at the moment; they are not discriminating even when they appear to be enthusiastic. Their attachment to their own intellectual traditions, whether they are progressivistic or traditional intellectual traditions, has in it an element of the fashionable.

Traditions being about serious things, they do not vary randomly as do fashions; they also last longer. On the surface, intellectual fashions are as unstable as fashions in apparel, slang, and domestic decoration. But beneath the surface, the tossing of fashion passes and there is less agitation. Movements are slower and longer. Sentiment, sensitivity, and thought are more serious at the depths than they are on the surface of expression where they are distorted and exaggerated. This does not mean that at that depth, in the world of symbolic constructions and in the minds of individuals, these antitraditional traditions are not different from the dispositions which enter into substantive tradition. They are indeed different but they are not so alien and they are not so unqualified in their dominion as they are on the surface.

The dispositions which move towards the exercise of the faculty of rationality do not necessarily require the rationalization of all that man encounters. The motive to independent action, towards creation and towards the adaptation of the received does not prescribe antinomian emancipation. In the unformedness of the more extreme possibilities of these fundamental dispositions, they are less alien to the dispositions on which substantive traditionality is built. Man is not wholly harmonious in the deeper inclinations in his soul. Frank Knight once said that man is fundamentally a "rule-making, rule-breaking animal."[6] This is true. The desire to be free and the inclination to reason coexists with the respect for rules, with the need for continuity with what has gone before, with the sense of the past and attachment to locality and collectivity. They exist in a pendular equilibrium, inclining at one time more towards the one and at another time more towards the other of the two major dispositions. When they move towards the surface of articulation, they move into the grooves set by traditions, accentuated by interests and the acceptance of the prevailing dominant opinion of the time. When these dispositions come to the surface of public discourse, they also become susceptible to doctrinal intellectual promulgation. The doctrines never entirely lose contact with the fundamental dispositions but they also become partially autonomous. This occurs because they come into the hands of publicistic and academic intellectuals who are experts in the formation of doctrines but who are not so well versed in the deeper dispositions of the human race or of their own societies. When these fundamental dispositions are raised close to the surface and made articulate as the basic beliefs of a sect or denomination, they become more differentiated and more polemical; at the same time they attempt to separate themselves further from their rivals in the same family of traditions.

Thus the agitations on the surface lead to a distorted picture of the fundamental disposition from which they arose. The doctrinal formulations deform the pattern of the fundamental dispositional elements, paralyzing some of the latter, intensifying others. This does not make the doctrines any less real and effective. But in their acceptance of the account which publicists, intellectuals, and politicians give them of their traditions and their fundamental dispositions, the possessors of these traditions fail to perceive the balance and intertwinement of their own traditions and fundamental dispositions.

At present, on the surface, substantive traditions seem to be partly submerged.[7] They are relatively voiceless in the public debate except

6. Frank Knight, "Economic Theory and Nationalism," in *The Ethics of Competition and Other Essays* (London: Allen and Unwin, 1935), pp. 301–5.
7. They are like the church bells of the sunken city of Is described by Renan.

or occasional outbursts of doctrineless inclinations of the spirit fo-
used on a particular object, such as organized opposition to un-
estricted abortions. They have not ceased to exist. Many still adhere
o them. Many others would if the intellectual traditions which sup-
ort them were accessible to them. The future of substantive tradi-
ions is uncertain. The fundamental impulses which sustain them are
always in existence but they are at present weaker than those which
ustain the contrary traditions which support rationalization and
mancipation.

The opponents of substantive tradition have regarded themselves as
ree from the burden of tradition. While their crusade has been di-
ected against substantive tradition primarily, they have, by identify-
ng substantive tradition with all other kinds of tradition, believed that
hey themselves were emancipated from traditions of any sort. They
nclined towards regarding their own views as based exclusively on
eason; emancipationists and their romantic forerunners regarded
hemselves as the rational spokesmen for a spontaneity and "naturalness" which would be entirely free of tradition. The opponents and
esisters of rationalization and emancipation were treated as the rep-
esentatives of tradition. These rationalists failed to see that they
vere practically as much under the yoke of a tradition which belied
heir assertions of self-determination. In fact, they were closer than
hey would have liked to be to those who accepted substantive traditions and who were sometimes and even often aware that they were
following traditions.

To become aware that one is following a tradition and is dependent
on it can have a disturbing effect on persons who thought that they
were free from it. Intellectual and literary traditions have much in
common with substantive traditions. "Reason," "life," and
"naturalness" appear differently when their proponents become conscious that these too are borne by tradition. Just as the argument that
one's unquestioned beliefs were particular to one's own time and
culture unsettled those who espoused them as universally valid, so the
perception that the practice of reason and "naturalness" of conduct
are traditional has a similarly unsettling effect. As a result, the divid-
ing line between "wrong" traditions and "right" reason is being broken. The powerful force which put traditionality in the wrong and
which looked forward towards a traditionless future, guided by scientific knowledge and a standard of "naturalness," may well lose
some of the power which has propelled it forward.

There are genuine differences between the ideals of rationalization
and emancipation and those of substantive tradition. They are different ideals of life, but now they are beginning to be seen as having in
common the property of traditionality. To know this is not to discredit
the substantive ideals of secularity, hedonism, and individualism.

Nonetheless the confidence in these ideals which came from believing
that they were the products of rational independent thought marks
step towards acknowledgment of the right to existence of substantive
traditionality.

The movement of rationalization and emancipation still retain
great momentum, but it has begun to stumble at a few points. The
costs have begun to weigh with perceptible heaviness on parts of the
population which have to pay for it. The costs are not only financial
they are also more frequently seen in the intrusiveness of rationalizing
governments and their tendency to monopolize decisions. Argument
for regional autonomy and decentralization are increasingly heard
The inefficiency of the bureaucratic apparatus of rationalization be
come more visible as rationalization extends its scope and pene
tration.

There are also reactions against the emancipatory program, too
especially in the education of children. At the same time eman
cipationists are beginning to become aware of particular conflict
between their own ideal and the ideal of rationalization.

The Prospects of Tradition

The state of tradition in the future is as difficult to foresee as any other events which have not occurred. It is however worthwhile despite this difficulty to offer a few observations on the survival of tradition in the future. Many predictions are in fact made nowadays but they have little room for any tradition except the traditions of technological innovation and of continuing scientific work. These are not presented as traditions but as rational responses to changing circumstances of increased population and diminished supplies of energy from coal and oil. The idea of a totally rationalized society is never absent from these predictions. Scientific and technological research applied through the decisions of government on behalf of a society in need of such decisions and hence unquestioningly accepting them—this is the present-day notion of the rationalizers who think that it is self-evidently rational for the society of the future to accept such a form. This was an ideal first adumbrated by Francis Bacon in the seventeenth century and given trenchant expression in the nineteenth century by Henri de Saint-Simon and Auguste Comte. Those who are blind to tradition live in its grip, just when they think that they are really rational and really scientific.

The traditionality of the scientistic view of the future of society is an indication of the ineluctability of tradition and it provides a first step in my consideration of the future of tradition. Traditions will exist as long as science exists as a continuously developing body of understanding. If each generational cohort began its scientific discoveries wholly afresh, the whole pattern of scientific work would be annulled. Science would no longer exist, either as a body of knowledge or as a way of acquiring it. The anticipators of the wholly traditionless society never go so far as to delete this tradition from their catalogues of traits of that society; instead they speak of scientific training and pass over tradition in science.

The total rationalizers do not anticipate an instantaneously self-reconstituting government; they do not expect entirely new sets of legislative enactments every decade or every year or every day. Insofar as they reach the point of sophistication at which they envisage a constitution for their wholly rationalized societies, they apparently do not anticipate a constitution which is continuously replaced by a new one, no less rationally contrived.

What is said here about the survival of the scientific traditions and the traditions of technological adaptation applies to every other part of the ideal of the wholly rationalized society. What is true of science is no less true of scholarship. Those literary scholars who assert that every man makes his own classics and that there are no enduring classics[1] are bound to discover that the ingenuity of the human mind, including their own, will be insufficient to follow out the implications of their doctrine. Not only will most of the old classics remain, but the "new" classics will become stabilized and the idiosyncratic inter pretations which these scholars propose and declare inevitable, as well as right, will also show a certain measure of stability. Unserious frivolous things can live exclusively under the rule of fashion; serious ones will live under the rule of tradition, and significant innovations will become traditional.

Emancipation is also a tradition and the clamor for it falls within the framework of tradition. Rationalization is inimical to substantive tra dition because it would dissolve all that is derived from earlier phases of social and cultural life. The traditions of emancipation are real traditions but they are antithetical to the substantive traditions. In deed they were formed out of hostility to the substantive traditions. The conflict between them has in the present century appeared to be culminating in a victory for the emancipatory tradition, but conflict is not yet over.

The instigation to continue a program of rationalization lies in the force of external circumstances, given the level of "needs" which has now become traditional in Western societies. The movement towards the rationalization of society in early modern times was a product of a religiously impelled intention to rationalize the earth by diligent, ra tionally disciplined labor for the glory of God and of a traditional monarchical desire to establish and extend the sway of sovereignty throughout the bounded territory of the national state. The scientific rationalization of the understanding of the cosmos added further force to this movement. The result of this convergence of forces was a rise in the level of expectations regarding material well-being throughout the population and a tenacious insistence that this level be main- tained. There is therefore resident in the powers of rationalization, alongside the paradoxically distrustful attitude taught by rationality against substantive tradition, an antagonism toward whatever stands in the way of the process; this means antagonism towards substantive tradition. Rationalization also inevitably changes circumstances and

1. See Frank Kermode, *The Classic: Literary Images of Permanence and Change* (London: Faber and Faber, 1975).

that too breaks the hold of substantive traditions by enforcing changes in its objects and making observance less practicable and satisfying. Where substantive traditions are not infused with some intellectual reinforcement which permits reinterpretation and adaptation, rapid changes in circumstances shake the grip of these traditions.

Rationalization is not a fashion and its entrenchment is not likely to be undone. Emancipation is a different thing. It is not a fashion either but it is a movement of sentiment. There are clearly limits to the range of variation of sentiments; they move within an unclearly defined circle. Sentiments are incapable of progression in the way in which reason and cognition are; sentiments are moreover more subject to the agitation of fashion. Although the emancipatory movement is more rancorous against substantive tradition than are the proponents of the rationalizing movement, it is the latter who are fundamentally more injurious. The former contends with opinions and works through agitation and legislation, while the latter work through the changing of circumstances.

The Prospects of Rationalization

If we assume that the drive towards rationalization continues without reversal, what are the chances for survival of traditions other than the tradition of rationalization itself? Let us assume too that the level of demand for material well-being does not decline. It is likely that the scarcity of the raw materials necessary for maintaining the level of material well-being will become greater if there is no marked decline in population.

One likely consequence is that there will be an increased intensity of demand for efficiency. New arrangements in places of work will be pressed for, new technology in places of work will be sought. The cost of labor will not become a smaller proportion in the cost of production and there will consequently be a steady search for machinery which will reduce the cost of production. This will require the support of the institutions which inculcate and maintain the ethos of rationalization. So, the factors which lead to changes in circumstances are not going to lose their power.

The movement of rationalization by government has been promoted under the patronage of collectivistic liberalism and democratic socialism practically everywhere. Although dissatisfaction with the results is fairly widespread, many persons think that the way to deal with the unsatisfactory results is to increase the rationalizing efforts of government. This is to be done by an expansion of the powers of government and the activity of an immense bureaucracy. The costliness of this bureaucracy places a burden on the more productive parts of the society and it is difficult to dismantle. Its very existence calls forth more demands for rationalization. It wishes to rationalize the rest of society; its critics wish to rationalize it. Whatever they accomplish, they do not neglect to praise the ideal of rationalization and to denounce whatever stands in its way as "ignorance," "vested interest," "prejudice," and all else which stems from persistence in inherited ways of doing things.

Governmental bureaucracies, whatever the merits of their own actual accomplishments, are ceaseless in their recommendation of such rationalizations that are to be produced by "cost-benefit analysis," "organization and management," "policies, programs, budgets and systems." Econometric models have become the order of the day among economists who advise governments. "Social experiments" are repeatedly canvassed. None of these intellectual constructions is aimed at leaving anything as it was. Despite much discontent with previous and similar attempts to render the machinery of rationalization more satisfactory, there is an unceasing confidence and zeal for imposing throughout society an order thought to be rational and efficient. Hence it is not likely under these conditions that innovation will lose its favored place in the hierarchy of good things.

Scarcity plus indifference to productivity leads to the demand for governmental control of the use of resources and an undiminished demand for goods and services delivered through the agency of government, in a certain recipe for inflation. Inflation is one of the most unsettling circumstances since it brings with it a threat of diminution of the standard of living and hence stirs action to prevent that. Thus rationalization not only changes circumstances through economically introduced changes in technology, organization, and location; it also heightens the power of government, increases its illusion of omnicompetence in the pursuit of omniprovidence, and fortifies the conviction that government has inexhaustible powers of improving on everything.

Max Weber in his discussion of the propelling force behind the rationalization of the world referred to the earthly asceticism of Calvinistic Christianity and concluded that religious impulse had become exhausted. Yet the rationalization has continued, not simply by a purposeless mechanical reproduction of a pattern once established, but because there entered other motives. One of the main ones is the hedonistic outlook which desires the physical satisfaction that the rationalization of the economic order is thought to be best-suited to provide. It is also carried forward by the belief that rational choices are desirable and possible in every situation of action, regardless of whether the actions are taken by a collectivity or an individual and regardless of whether the object of the action is individual or collective. Rationality, which was once considered as a means of understanding the universe and of establishing the ends which should govern the life of individuals as rulers and citizens, has become the means of arranging actions for the attainment of politically, emotionally, or traditionally defined ends. (The traditionality of the ends is not acknowledged.) Nevertheless, although the tasks of rationality have changed, it is still cultivated because it is thought to be the right thing to do and the rationalization which it ostensibly guides adds a further justification for it. Weber intimated that the whole great movement had ended in an empty and meaningless exercise from which withdrawal and cessation were impossible. The movement is as a matter of fact more firmly founded than Max Weber said. It is founded on devotion to reason understood in a certain way, and devotion to an ideal of human well-being and both these devotions are established on the basis of a tradition which, once received, is terribly difficult to renounce. And on top of this, the devotions are reinforced by interest and an admixture of ideological zeal.

Under these besetting and compelling conditions, attachments to the past and to patterns of conduct received from the past have been repeatedly shaken and diminished. Tradition is like a plant which repeatedly puts down roots whenever it is left in one place for a short time, yet is frequently torn up and flung from one place to another, so that the nutriment of its branches and leaves is cut off and the plant becomes pale and enfeebled. Traditions may be unavoidable but they are not always very strong. Tendencies to seek and find traditions may be ubiquitous in human society and the tendencies to seek and find might always find a tradition to attach themselves to. The tendency to seek a religious tradition may be present in all societies but if they are unaided by the availability of traditions and proponents of tradition substantive traditions may become etiolated and very weak.

The combination of a rationalizing central government, of a strong desire for the services of government, of a strongly emancipationist opinion supported by government, and of universal public education which reduces the study of the history, geography, and literature of the local and national societies as well as of the high points of civilization, and of churches the ministers of which have lost confidence in their religious traditions can certainly leave the propensity to seek tradition rather ineffective. If the schools become separated from religion and family and work against them, traditions will not be transmitted; they will become very attenuated. The creative tradition-seeking capacities will be left without the framework which they need. They will be like vines unwatered and untrimmed and without a trellis on which to grow or without a wall to which to attach themselves. If the universities become very contemporaneously, very technologically, and very vocationally oriented, the traditions which bind a society to its past will become attenuated. They will not disappear but they will become the objects of specialized study. This is what has been happening in modern Western societies.

The tendencies which have been considered here are of course not likely to attain completion. The rationalizing capacity of central government can never be wholly successful in attaining its objectives. Even if it aspires to bring the entire society thoroughly under its control, it will not be successful. Not all of the society will be equally, constantly, and thoroughly under the pressure of changing circumstances. Some parts will be less vulnerable than others. The entire educational system will not be thoroughgoingly emancipatory, even if its superior authorities and its teachers wish it to be so. The family cannot be abolished; many parents will nourish in their children some of the tendencies which seek and hold on to substantive traditions. It is also not outside the limits of the conceivable that the rationalizing and emancipatory will overstep the limits of tolerability.

Rationalization has thus far been successful because it has not been completely successful. The more successful it becomes the more it endangers itself, the more it lays itself open to resistance. The emancipatory movement has also gained its successes against a retreating traditionality which has not and cannot lose all of its vitality. It has been as successful as it has been because the full consequences of a complete success have not yet been felt very widely. It too might become unbearable. Not everyone in society wishes to live according to the emancipatory ideal.

The Prospect of Tradition in the Discomfiture of Progressivism

Progressivists might think that no problems will remain unsolved as long as the program of progressivism is faithfully followed—the more faithfully, the more successfully. This however is not what they all believe, nor do those who believe it believe it wholeheartedly. Progressivism has come up against difficulties, and progressivists—some of them—have been courageous enough to admit their reverses. They have not jettisoned their convictions because of this but they do admit that something is amiss.

Radicals, despite the obvious failures of their favorite regimes, either to live up to their own alleged ideals or up to the standard of the Western societies which they denounce, are undismayed by what is glaringly evident. They are immune to contagion from experience or knowledge; inexperience has made them insensate, insensateness blinds them to the moral enormities of their favorite regimes. This is not so with the progressivists. The long incumbency of progressivistic governments in their own countries has made them aware that the problems which are acknowledged in their respective societies are not going to be resolved by the wave of a wand. Some progressivists have turned into radicals in the face of these difficulties, thinking that more drastic measures will resolve them and permit the attainment of their ideals. This is intellectually a relatively simple modification since the ideals of rationalization and emancipation are common to both— although in different proportions and intensities. Nevertheless many progressivists—collectivistic liberals and social-democrats—have not undergone that transformation. They have begun to acknowledge that the world is more complicated than they previously believed and that the past is not as unrelieved a record of crimes and errors as they have previously believed.

The first signs of this change have occurred in attitudes towards primary and secondary education. Dissatisfaction with the emancipationist ideal as applied in education has begun to appear. It has not yet made as much of a mark on educational practice as it has in the opinion of some intellectuals who had been in the forefront of the movement. There has been a resurgence of appreciation of such "basics" as learning to read correctly, learning the traditional educated versions of the national language, learning how to write grammatically, and learning arithmetic of a traditional sort. There is a somewhat less disparaging attitude towards "law and order" and less confidence in the fundamental innocence of criminals. The small but widespread shifts of electoral opinion in a number of countries away from communist and socialist parties towards liberal and conservative parties is an indication of the diminution of confidence in the progressivistic tradition and of a modern resurgence of belief in some dimly perceived alternatives; the alternatives are closer to substantive traditionality.

Behind the facade of power, glory, and publicity, the affirmation of rationalization and emancipation does not rest on an exclusive and unchallenged supremacy. Much of what appears to be affirmation is acquiescence. Some of it is little more than yielding to the idiom of the times while inclinations run in a different direction, in the direction of the substantive traditions. These inclinations could lead to acquiescent affirmation, perhaps even to a more positive affirmation of the substantive traditions which still have many devotees.

The rationalizers have not renounced their program. The slight movement towards conservatism represents a slighter shift than the names would indicate. Rationalization has become the dominant tradition and many of those who oppose it are permeated by it and cannot conceive of a society or culture markedly different from the one it has created. But by the same token, the rationalizers are also not unalloyed in their attachment to the program of the rationalization of society. It is true that, whenever they think about particular policies, they are faithful to the principle of rationalization; they mean their policies to dominate the objects they would deal with. They assume at the same time that the society will be there, that it has its own laws and necessities, not just the laws and the necessities of the rationalizers, legislators, and administrators. They assume the constancy of those institutions. Tax policies assume the existence of marriage and of children who are looked after by parents. The rationalizers assume the existence of civil spirit and religious belief and philanthropy and of the traditions of science and learning. They attempt to influence these things but they reckon with their continued existence. Intrusive though they are, their rationalizing actions are not in practice as comprehensive or as penetrating as they might be. There are undoubtedly proponents of programs of rationalization who would attempt to go much further than they do at present but they cannot do so because they are held in check by anticipation of resistance. Other rationalizers are held in check by inhibitions in themselves which are often unquestioned beliefs—traditions—which admit the rightfulness of those traditions which complete rationalization would obliterate.

As well as these scattered representations of traditionality, holding in check and containing the possibility of shifting the existing balance between rationalization and traditionality, the program of the rationalizers is running into great difficulties. To attain its objectives it is even putting nearly unbearable burdens on the market, which is the mechanism of the adjustment of interests. It is consuming or causing to be used for consumption the production which is a necessary condition for further production. It is in other words undoing itself. In pursuit of the program of rationalization which requires vast resources to remunerate the rationalizers and to distribute goods and services, it is consuming the production which should go into the maintenance, replacement, and expansion of the equipment which should produce the resources required for the program of rationalization. The program of rationalization is a self-frustrating program and is bound to fail.

The intended beneficiaries of the program of rationalization thus fall outside the pattern foreseen; discontent will alienate them from its promulgators. The victims of the program of rationalization, those who are frustrated or deprived by the direct or indirect execution of the program, are also bound to deny the validity of its claims. This does not mean that they will espouse the merits of adherence to substantive traditionality as an alternative to rationalization. Some of them cleave to the model of the market as an alternative tradition. Nonetheless, the discredit of the program of total rationalization restores the possibility of substantive traditionality in the setting of moderate individualism and a more limited rationalization.

The proponents and agents of the program of total rationalization themselves might cling to the rationalizing tradition in which they have vested so much intellectual effort, pride, and vanity. However loyal they are to their ideal, they too will lose self-confidence. In totalitarian countries they might hold with desperate tenacity to the program with which they are associated because to admit error or failure would endanger their livelihood and their lives. In liberal democratic countries, their disillusionment is bound to modify their attachment to their program and some of them will cease to be adherents to it. The ensuing generation, having invested less of its intellectual resources in the program, will be less drawn to it. It might of course, turn to the emancipatory tradition since this has been so closely coupled for a century with the rationalizing tradition. But this is not inevitable.

The tribulations of the program of rationalization have been aggravated by the increased cost of energy which has placed it in a weaker position. This might, as it has in the United States, lead one side of the party of progressivistic outlook to demand a more thoroughgoing rationalization but it is also deepening the discontent with the program of rationalization. Hostility against an ineptly rationalizing government is increasing and it is spreading in the range of its objects. A government ineptly intrusive in one sphere loses the legitimacy of its rationalizing intervention in other spheres as well.

Scarcity of energy from fossil fuels and obstruction of the use of nuclear energy might lead to an increase in procedures which use more human energy; this is bound to be a slow process and one which will be resisted. If it does nevertheless take place, it is likely to increase the amount of technological traditionality in the work place. Scarcity of resources for building materials might encourage great caution in the destruction of old buildings and restraint in allowing them to be declared obsolete.

The apprehension of impoverishment might simultaneously intensify the demand for innovation in methods of producing energy and it might also replace the demand for improving standards of living by a desire to avoid their deterioration. The central tradition of the rationalizing outlook is the belief in the superiority of the new to the old.

The increasing life-span and the increasing burden of the older section of the population on the younger section might reduce the demand for early retirement and might keep more older persons in paid employment. This might be an obstacle to continuous and intensive innovation because these older persons might be more resistant to circumstances which make it more difficult for them to practice the skills which they acquired many years before.

The failures of the great project of rationalization will not inevitably bring with them a reestablishment of traditionality. They might aggravate conflict in society, as indeed inflation, which is one of these failures, has done. Relative positions are endangered by inflation, and even in a relatively egalitarian society inflation which destroys savings cannot but increase the bitterness of savers against those who are supported by the proceeds of inflation. A general restlessness is engendered by inflation which is even more damaging to tradition than the unemployment of the Great Depression of the 1930s which had such disastrous effects on traditional ways of thinking and acting (e.g., on family life and sexual relations, on respect for authority) and which at the same time strengthened the demand that authority be empowered to take drastic action to relieve unemployment and its consequences. This was a decisive step in the formation of the belief that governments are omnicompetent. It was an epochal turning point in the formation of the program of rationalization, accepted by both its agents and its prospective beneficiaries.

It is not only that central governments would be incapable of the comprehensive and pervasive rationalization which they claim to be able to carry out; they are especially incapable of attaining this high degree of rationalization together with the level of benefits which they promise and which are expected by a large part of the population. Such success as they have had has kept them in office for long periods in Western countries. They are doomed to be discredited but their discredit does not mean that the desires which their promises fostered and the prospective gratification of which enabled them to hold office so long will be dissolved. The total demand at the present level of wants and the tradition of commitment to the future well-being of society as a whole are incompatible; the former cannot be fulfilled and the effort to fulfill it is standing in the way of the latter. The failure, necessary and inevitable, of central governments to achieve the former will leave the desires unsatisfied. Unsatisfied desires are not conducive to the renewal of traditions. Restlessness and discontent might settle down to acceptance of limits and to a recession of demands for goods and services which are ostensibly "free" but which must be paid for by production and by created money which does not correspond to production.

The acknowledged failure of rationalization is probably as uncongenial to tradition in institutions and beliefs as the continued belief that it will be successful. If it were successful its very success would be devastating to all tradition except its own. Its failures are likely to arouse reactions which would be no less devastating. One response to its failure would be to demand a more energetically pursued and more ambitious program. Another is random discontent, social conflict, wandering gullibility in the presence of unstable, apparently charismatic individuals.

Increased social conflict will spread into institutions with their own autonomous traditions, e.g., into the churches, universities, and local associations. The tendency towards the adoption of ideological traditions which is aroused by intensified conflict is hostile towards substantive traditions, centered as they are around familial and religious authority and attachment to locality and other primordial things. When nationality becomes their object, it is an ideological nationalism which is no less unsympathetic to substantive traditions which include nationality among their objects.

The Immediate and the Remote Prospects

Where will it all end? The answer is that it will never end. Not at least as long as mankind survives. Traditionality however has never had an easy way. Had its way been easier, it would not have undergone such immense developments. Traditions have grown and changed; they have become enriched; they have been attenuated. Changing circumstances, changing interests, changing outcomes of conflicts of interests, the unresting powers of reason and imagination have all put strains of all sorts upon traditions. They have not themselves escaped from traditions while they were straining traditions.

The particular traditions which have been cultivated with great resourcefulness in modern times have been antitraditional intellectual traditions. Long-standing traditions of religious belief have been attacked directly by the antitraditional traditions; they have been weakened from within by the penetration of these antitraditional traditions, particularly but not only, scientific traditions. Other traditions, less intellectual, have been brought down by tremendous changes in circumstances. Yet, although substantive traditions have been shaken, they have not been obliterated. They cannot ever be obliterated as long as human beings are born to human beings, as long as they retain their capacity for love and their sexual appetites, as long as parental care is necessary for the survival and growth of infants and children. As long as the universe remains mysterious, as long as human beings seek order in it, and as long as they are curious to know it, they will create and form and attach themselves to traditions. As long as they wish to be something more than what is fully enclosed by their skin and their apparel, they will seek and find traditions and they will create them. As long as human beings need rules and categories and institutions and as long as they cannot create these for themselves just when the occasion arises and for that occasion only, they will cling to traditions, even when they proudly think that they are not doing so. As long as the separate actions of separate individuals do not suffice to achieve all the ends which any human being can want, enduring arrangements of the actions of many human beings will be necessary, organizations will be necessary; where there is organization, there will be authority and authority will become enmeshed in traditions.

Human beings cannot survive without traditions even though they are so frequently dissatisfied with their traditions. This does not mean that traditions are always equally strong in all times and in all places or that the pressures against traditions are equal at all times and in all places. Sometimes the stability is greater; sometimes more actions escape from tradition, sometimes these actions escape from reason and from tradition at the same time. The ways of escape are numerous and they are not matters of indifference.

Although mankind cannot live without traditions and although it cannot live contentedly with the traditions which it receives, traditions are both persistent and disrupted. They survive, nonetheless, in some form. The particular configurations of persistence and disruption are not matters of indifference to the societies in which they occur. The patterns of traditionality make a genuine difference to all who experience them. They are not epiphenomena which always exist in the same proportion. If they were, they could not give ground for concern because they would have no effect and because nothing could be done about them. But this is not really so. Every one of our actions and every one of our beliefs affects the fortunes of one or another tradition. One person alone, unless he is a charismatic person on a grand scale, will not cause much of an inflection. The inflections of many persons do affect the course of traditions and the policies of institutions.

10 The Permanent Task

There is no permanent solution to any important problem in human life. Only transient and minor problems have solutions; they too often do not have them, but they pass and are replaced by other problems, or the solutions which are given to them generate new problems. The important problems are important because they touch on the lives of many persons in serious ways, they weigh on important institutions and on highly valued things. The solutions which are applied to these problems are no more than better or poorer stopgaps which do not resolve the problems permanently and which generate other problems, both important and lasting ones, and unimportant and transient ones. Reason and tradition are the two main means of struggling with these problems; neither alone is sufficient and both together are insufficient also. Nature is a problem-generating system; man is a problem-engendering animal. He finds problems, he creates problems. He is not satisfied by the solutions which he finds awaiting him. Those who are satisfied are often disturbed by those who are dissatisfied and by changing circumstances which are often not intended by everyone.

In what has been written here, I have more frequently than not seemed to express a preference for traditions. There are many traditions which I would like to see conserved; there are many traditions for which I wish a larger adherence. There are also many traditions which I would wish to see diminished in their adherence. I know however that the matter is not as simple as it is made to appear in the three last sentences. Even the best traditions are not perfect and even these have costs which have to be paid in terms of other valuable traditions.

There is much in human life which needs improvement and many of these activities and situations which need improvement are in fact capable of improvement. There are many which are not capable of being much improved, not because they are so close to the ideal—they are frequently quite far removed from the ideal—but because it does not lie within the powers possessed by human beings to do much about them.

323

The capacity to exercise the function of reason is one of best qualities with which human beings are endowed. The tradition which forms, praises, and encourages this capacity is among the best of the traditions of civilization. The exercise of the capacity to reason and observe, disciplined into scientific activity, is one of the greatest which we have cultivated in our civilization, above all in modern times. The intellectual results of this disciplined exercise of the mind are, with works of art, among the greatest accomplishments of the human race and it is iniquitous to derogate them and to hamstring the activities and the institutions through which they are achieved. But they have been cultivated and acquired at heavy costs, direct and indirect. Necessarily and unnecessarily, they have eroded other traditions which are no less precious and not less needed by human beings.

The tradition of emancipation from traditions is also among the precious achievements of our civilization. It has made citizens out of slaves and serfs. It has opened the imagination and the reason of human beings; it has opened to them the possibility of the good life. It too has been purchased, sometimes knowingly, sometimes ignorantly, at the expense of substantive traditions which are conducive to an ordered life—and an ordered life is a good which is part of the good life. These substantive traditions have been badly damaged or discarded by many human beings. This has resulted in the loss of much that is indispensable to the good order and happiness of individuals, and it has contributed to the creation of a widely ramifying disorder.

The Enlightenment of the seventeenth and eighteenth centuries in Europe and America was one of the noblest epochs in the history of the human race. Its instrument was reason and its end was emancipation. The instrument diffused into science and scholarship and into public life, and the end for which it strove with some considerable success transformed the condition of Western mankind; the transformation has by and large been very beneficial. Sympathies have been broadened, the worth of human beings has been acknowledged and improved. Societies have become more humane and more just than they were in earlier epochs and in other civilizations. Mankind, and not least the Western part of it, has by no means been made perfect. Some of the ideals of the Enlightenment have not been realized. Others have been realized and are contradictory, and as a result, evil potentialities have been brought into reality. The spokesman for these ideals did not anticipate this. The tradition of emancipation has developed very far and in some respects it has exceeded the limits within which it was an ideal worthy of the highest exertions. Other parts of the ideal have turned out to be not as good as they were thought to be. The emancipation of mankind from superstition and from belief in magic has been carried so far that it has destroyed for many persons the ideal of a morally ordered universe in which some things were sacred. The praise of progress towards greater material well-being was motivated by a great ideal and it is still worthy of pursuit, although not by the arrangements through which it is now pursued. But even when it was most effective, it was doing damage to other traditions of familial life, of religious beliefs, and of restraints on desire.

The Enlightenment was antithetical to tradition. At least its great spokesmen and its lesser interpreters thought it was. The success which the Enlightenment achieved was owed to its becoming a tradition. Its success was owed also to the fact that it was promulgated and pursued in a society in which substantive traditions were rather strong. It was successful against its enemies because the enemies were strong enough to resist its complete victory over them. Living on a soil of substantive traditionality, the ideas of the Enlightenment advanced without undoing themselves. As long as respect for authority on the one side and self-confidence in those exercising authority on the other persisted, the Enlightenment's ideal of emancipation through the exercise of reason went forward. It did not ravage society as it would have done had society lost all legitimacy. As long as individuals remained faithful to their churches, the political powers of the churches and the excessive privileges of the churches could be diminished without the destruction of fidelity.

Once religious beliefs were discredited and religious and neighborly communities shaken—which occurred to some extent through the successful prosecution of the ideals of the Enlightenment, the ideals of rationality and of rationalizing economic activity—societies became endangered. The rational consensus which was anticipated did not come about over as wide a radius as had been desired. Societies became endangered through the enlarged scope offered by the removal of communal restraints on egoistic aggressive impulse and action and through innovations which their sponsors introduced for their own immediate advantage and without thought for their disruptive consequences in drastically changing the circumstances of daily life. Class conflicts which became more openly acute in the course of the nineteenth century, not only in consequence of industrialization and urbanization of the working population and because of the new type of open politics, the new freedom of action, and the idea of the rightfulness of demands for greater material well-being in the lower classes did not endanger society. They did not endanger society because they were still very confined in scale and intensity; traditions of authority were still strong enough to contain them. Traditions still have this strength where they are not aggravated by special circumstances such as inflation, defeat in war, the ideological penetration of the public sphere, and a large "lumpen-intelligentsia."

The Unchartedness of the World

There is an order in the cosmos but it is not immediately apparent. It requires hard thought and prolonged study to discern it and to construct an image of it. There are many orders below this cosmic order and they too are difficult to discern. The orders of human society are not only difficult to discern; they are also difficult to maintain in the course of all the multifarious activities of practical life. The disorders of human societies are caused by the actions and beliefs of human beings.

Yet human beings, at least most of them, much of the time do not fare well in a disordered world. They need to live within the framework of a world of which they possess a chart. They need categories and rules; they need criteria of judgment. They cannot construct these for themselves. This is one of the limits to the ideal of total emancipation and total self-regulation. Authorities in family, church, community, educational institutions, army, and factory cannot construct all of this chart, and those rudiments of the chart which they can present are limited in their range and their acceptance depends on the legitimacy of their promulgators. Human beings need the help of their ancestors; they need the help which is provided by their own biological ancestors and they need the help of the ancestors of their communities and institutions, of the ancestors of their societies and their institutions.

The destruction or discrediting of these cognitive, moral, metaphysical, and technical charts is a step into chaos. Destructive criticism which is an extension of reasoned criticism, aggravated by hatred, annuls the benefits of reason and restrained emancipation.

The loss of contact with the accomplishments of ancestors is injurious because it deprives subsequent generations of the guiding chart which all human beings, even geniuses and prophets, need. They can not create these for themselves in a stable and satisfying way. They lose something more when they lose contact with their ancestors' accomplishments. Scarcely less of an impoverishment is it to be without an image of ancestry. They lose the sense of being members of a collectivity which transcends themselves and which transcends their contemporaries. The acknowledgment of the unity of the past and present states of society is faint in many of the members of contemporary Western societies.

There is a demoralization arising from the loss of contact with ancestors. There is always a crisis among immigrants to another society when they feel the loss of what their ancestors offered them and have not acquired what the host society has accomplished. Their offspring are in danger of lying in a trough between the lost accomplishments of their ancestral society and the unacquired accomplishments of the

society into which they have come as immigrants. It is not so bewildering to give up one's own linguistic and social ancestors if one is
acquiring new ancestors through assimilation into the new society. To
have experienced the disappearance of one's own biological and cultural ancestors in this sense without the compensating acquisition of
new ones confines a person in his own generation. This is not easily
borne although the sources of the unease are not perceived because
the vocabulary available to describe this experience is very poor. The
vocabulary to describe this phenomenon is poor because modern
societies in the West have been trying to make it appear that the
affirmation of dependence on the past is a defect. "Ancestor worship" is the derogatory polemical counterpart to the positive principle
that a human being should be estimated for what he can accomplish by
the exercise of his own efforts or that he should be rewarded the same
as anyone else regardless of his accomplishments and simply for the
property of being alive.

There was much that was morally reprehensible in the monopoly
of opportunity for the wellborn. A large society is not made up only of
families and the ranks or classes into which they are clustered. These
are parts of the civil society which has to have a past which is the past
of the whole society. The civil ancestry is a matter of gradual growth
and acquisition, not formal promulgation. There are many things
which stand in the way of its formation and there are many things
which disrupt it once it begins to form. It is very vulnerable, but
individual members of the society need it for their own lives and for
the lives of their descendants.

The Temporal Integration of Society

A society is a "trans-temporal" phenomenon. It is not constituted by
its existence at a single moment in time. It exists only through time. It
is temporally constituted. It has a temporal integration as well as spatial integration. To be cut off from the past of one's society is as
disordering to the individual and to the society as being cut off in the
present. *Anomie* has a temporal dimension.

Those who are constantly recommending innovation have never
thought about this aspect of things. They are as dangerous to society
as those who think that their "class" or "race" should dominate in
every sphere, that it should monopolize all that society has produced,
that it has no obligations to a society which includes but is not constituted by each of its "classes" or "races." "Civil amnesia" is as
dangerous to society as the argument that the government should
preempt the resources of society for the benefit of a particular "class"
or "race." It is as untenable as are the arguments of those who assert

that society should consist of wholly emancipated individuals whose sole concern should be the "fulfillment" of their own "individuality" and that governmental power should be increased in order to serve that end.

The connection which binds a society to its past can never die out completely; it is inherent in the nature of society, it cannot be created by governmental fiat or by a "movement" of citizens that aims at specific legislation. A society would not be a society if this bond were not there in some minimal degree. The strength or efficacy of the link can vary considerably, just as can the state of integration of a society at any point in time.

Our Western societies have taken too much to heart the command to innovate and emancipate. It is not that these commands should not have been taken seriously or that their execution has not brought notable benefits. The mistake lay in regarding them as the only goals to be pursued; it also lay in not giving thought to the consequences of the pursuit which caused the already accomplished to be neglected. One of the consequences has been the attenuation of the matrix of rules and standards of conduct in which individuals should live.

It would be a mistake to think that this matrix was always thick or strong enough to resist all the strains produced by impulse, interest, and reason. Nor would it be correct to think that where it was in effect, it was always benign. Not all traditions are benign; not all of them merit survival. Nonetheless, the fact that a practice or belief has persisted for an extended period is an argument for its retention. The mere fact of existence is generally an argument for continued existence. It should not be regarded as the sole argument to be taken into account. Other arguments might go against it and the case for its retention be thereby weakened or overcome. Not all traditions should be clung to although the heavens fall. But they should never have been dismissed as lightly as they have been.

Traditionality as an Intrinsic Value

The fact that certain beliefs, institutions, and practices existed indicates that they served those who lived in accordance with them. The human beings who lived in accordance with them in the past were not fundamentally different from those who lived in succeeding generations or who are alive now. They did not arrive arbitrarily at their beliefs; the institutions in which they lived were not forced upon them from the outside. These institutions had to make sense to them, if they took them seriously. These traditions were not so crippling that human beings could not live under them. Nor did they prevent the human race from accomplishing great things. Rather the opposite!

They enabled many great things to be accomplished by individuals in a dramatic form and by collectivities working much more gradually and silently. They should be dealt with more respectfully, perhaps even reverently. Gratitude for the human achievements which went before us and respect for the efforts of countless individuals, known and unknown, to carry out their various responsibilities in keeping their societies, their families, and their churches and kingdoms afloat around the miseries and catastrophes of existence calls for patience with the traditions which are offered to us. It is not only that the rightful place of piety in human life requires acknowledgment and that a life without piety, including piety to the past, courts grief and does damage to the life of the living individual. The respectful treatment of traditions is also enjoined on us by awareness that to refuse a tradition is not a guarantee that it will be well replaced. It might be replaced by a pattern of conduct or belief which is a poorer thing.

It should be remembered that, once a particular tradition of belief or conduct is jettisoned and has remained in relegation or suppression for an extended period, it might fade away entirely or nearly so, leaving an unfilled place, which will be felt as a gap and then replaced by a poorer belief or practice. Specific traditions may be lost forever or retained only in the record of physical artifacts. A tradition once it has receded from regular usage cannot be deliberately restored. The conditions and motives to say nothing of the memories of those of later times who would restore it are unsuited for the task. What will appear will be a fanatical distortion of the receded tradition, a distortion which cannot last if it is reimposed because those to whom it is offered or on whom it is imposed will not find it congenial to their circumstances and tastes. It will be an ideological reconstruction, and an ideological fervor does not last. Traditions cannot be dealt with experimentally; they cannot be suspended for a trial period during which something presumably better will be tried and after which the tradition will be restored if the replacement turns out to fall short of expectations.

Restorations are doomed to failure; traditionalistic movements are doomed to failure because long-existing traditions—traditions which are continuous into the present—cannot be wholly extirpated. This is one of the reasons for moderation in policy; all policy is ultimately, and often immediately, about traditions. Immediate advantages are often expected to follow the institution of a policy which puts aside a tradition. The advantages may be genuine and long-lasting, although just as often they are not. What will be renounced is generally not sufficiently considered, particularly with regard to its effects on substantive traditions.

The fact is that our knowledge of future events is very poor and very unreliable. All actions are oriented in some respect towards future events and towards the future consequences of present actions. This cannot be avoided. Actions have to be taken in conditions which are nearly always partly unprecedented. This cannot be avoided either. Practically all actions entail some deviation from or some independence of tradition. There is nothing intrinsically bad and nothing intrinsically good about this—although sometimes a new and great good results from an action of courageous innovation. What is important about these circumstances and these decisions is that tradition is always involved and is always affected by the actions attending them. What I would like to emphasize here is that great circumspection should be exercised and that traditions should be taken into account not just as obstacles or inevitable conditions. The renunciation of tradition should be considered as a cost of a new departure; the retention of traditions should be considered as a benefit of a new departure. Not that cost-benefit analysis could ever be applied except very vaguely. I wish to stress that traditions should be considered as constituents of the worthwhile life. A mistake of great historical significance has been made in modern times in the construction of a doctrine which treated traditions as the detritus of the forward movement of society. It was a distortion of the truth to assert this and to think that mankind could live without tradition and simply in the light of immediately perceived interest or immediately experienced impulse or immediately excogitated reason and the latest stage of scientific knowledge or some combination of them. It was wrong then, however admirable the motives for the mistake and whatever the benefits which the mistake helped to bring about. The Enlightenment was a very great accomplishment and it has become part of our tradition. It would be an exercise in the discriminating appreciation of traditions to discern what is living and what is dead in the tradition of the Enlightenment. Much of the overgrowth has lost its vitality and is an encumbrance. What is vital in it merits persistence. Substantive traditionality merits persistence, active cultivation, and solicitous care. To amalgamate some of the traditions of the Enlightenment and some of those which its heirs have attempted to discard is a task for patient watchfulness and tact of the utmost delicacy.

Index